Entrepreneurship, Innovation and Regional Development

D0222224

Entrepreneurship, Innovation and Regional Development is unique in that it addresses the central factors in economic development – new venture creation, product and process development, firm formation, institutional change and organizational learning – as regional phenomena.

This definitive text focuses on different types of organizations to illustrate the value of entrepreneurship and innovation both for businesses and for regional development. Establishing a firm link between entrepreneurship, innovation and economic regeneration, the book also examines the factors contributing to their success.

Replete with international case studies, empirical evidence of concepts and self-assessment questions, this is an ideal text to support postgraduate teaching and research related to entrepreneurship, innovation management and regional economic development.

Jay Mitra is Founding Professor of Business Enterprise and Innovation and Director of the Centre for Entrepreneurship Research and Head of the School of Entrepreneurship and Business at the University of Essex, UK. He is also Director of the Scientific Committee on Entrepreneurship for the Organization for Economic Co-operation and Development in France and Italy and a Visiting Research Fellow at the Beijing University of Foreign Studies in China.

Entrepreneurship, Innovation and Regional Development

An introduction

Jay Mitra

Routledge
Taylor & Francis Group

LONDON AND NEW YORK

First published 2012 by Routledge
2 Park Square, Milton Park, Abingdon, Oxon OX14 4RN

Simultaneously published in the USA and Canada
by Routledge
711 Third Ave, New York, NY 10017 (8th Floor)

Routledge is an imprint of the Taylor & Francis Group, an informa business

© 2012 Jay Mitra

The right of Jay Mitra to be identified as the author of this work has been
asserted by him in accordance with sections 77 and 78 of the
Copyright, Designs and Patents Act 1988.

All rights reserved. No part of this book may be reprinted or reproduced
or utilised in any form or by any electronic, mechanical, or other means,
now known or hereafter invented, including photocopying and recording,
or in any information storage or retrieval system, without permission in
writing from the publishers.

Trademark notice: Product or corporate names may be trademarks or
registered trademarks, and are used only for identification and
explanation without intent to infringe.

British Library Cataloguing in Publication Data
A catalogue record for this book is available from the British Library

Library of Congress Cataloguing in Publication Data
Mitra, Jay.
  Entrepreneurship, innovation and regional development : an introduction / Jay Mitra.
  p. cm.
  Includes bibliographical references and index.
  1. Entrepreneurship. 2. Technological innovations—Economic aspects.
  3. Regional economics. 4. Economic development. I. Title.
  HB615.M58 2011
  338—dc22
  2010050710

ISBN: 978–0–415–40515–7 (hbk)
ISBN: 978–0–415–40516–4 (pbk)
ISBN: 978–0–203–81378–2 (ebk)

Typeset in Times New Roman by Swales & Willis Ltd, Exeter, Devon

Printed and bound in the United States of America
By Edwards Brothers Malloy on sustainably sourced paper.

Contents

Foreword by Zoltan J. Acs

In a classic essay published exactly twenty years ago, Francis Fukuyama wrote that the triumph of the West was evident in the total exhaustion of viable systematic alternatives to Western liberalism. The end of the 20th century witnessed not just the passing of the Cold War, but indeed the end of history, a phrase Fukuyama intended to signify not the long-predicted convergence between capitalism and socialism, but rather the end point of mankind's ideological evolution and the universalization of Western liberal democracy as the final form of human government.

Now, however, the size and nature of the current economic crisis is causing some who have both understood and agreed to wonder whether the end of history has been replaced by the end of growth, the return of Malthus, or some other such phrase whose real meaning is plain: the replacement of liberalism's inevitable universalization with its more likely decline or even demise.

Whatever lines pundits may like to draw from the present back to the 1930s, from the standpoint of the human experience there is absolutely no comparison between the country that lay beyond the portico of FDR's White House and the county into which Barack Obama sends his YouTube videos today. To be sure, even in relative terms the magnitude of the Great Depression far exceeds anything experienced to date or, we dare to venture, anything that lies ahead. But what is certainly true is that the extent of societal advancement experienced over the past seventy years is so great that it has transformed America from what we would today refer to as an underdeveloped country into the most prosperous nation in human history.

The triumph of the Western idea – the end of history proclaimed by Fukuyama – has not, in fact, been called into question by the global financial crisis. Nor are future developments likely to reverse the judgment in favor of liberalism. Yet the institutional architecture of liberalism remains a work in progress. Continued institutional innovations will be required to ensure that democratic societies with market-based economies are as resilient in the future as they are prosperous.

The engine that propels global capitalism forward is entrepreneurship; the fuel is opportunity; the work of foundations recycles the energy of society, making progress and prosperity sustainable. This is the entrepreneurial society. Yet, just as a Tesla Roadster is no Model-T, 21st-century entrepreneurial society derives from a formula far more complex than the 1 percent inspiration and 99 percent perspiration once cited by Thomas Edison. Far-sighted government policies are an essential element. Political leadership must do more than celebrate the risk-takers, the doers, the makers of things who create opportunity and extend the reach of prosperity.

The emergence of the entrepreneurial society three decades ago was based on the discovery that small firms were the engine of job creation and innovation. First in the United States, then in Europe and finally around the world, policy makers promoted the idea of small is beautiful. However, by the 1990s the idea that it was a subset of firms that led innovation and growth started to take hold in the United States. New firms and especially high-impact firms were responsible for most of the job creation, innovation and economic growth. In Europe this message started to spread in the 2000s and it is now spreading to the rest of the world.

However, the policy conclusion that picking winners by government can lead to more of these billion-dollar corporations, the next Facebook or Google, is misguided. The intersection of liberal democracy and economic opportunity created the entrepreneurial society. It is the recognition that opportunities are available to the broad cross-section of society and that the entrepreneurial society represents an institutional and policy landscape that must be overarching in its scope and intent. This institutional structure is a work in progress. It is a global project that must be monitored, measured and tracked.

Jay Mitra's *Entrepreneurship, Innovation and Regional Development* takes an important step in this direction by moving us along the path of marrying liberal democracy and the entrepreneurial society. It does so by focusing on regional development and global change. For if the triumph of liberal democracy is universal then the future of entrepreneurship is surely a regional phenomenon.

Zoltan J. Acs
University Professor and Director
Center for Entrepreneurship and Public Policy
Editor: *Small Business Economics*
School of Public Policy
George Mason University
Arlington, VA 22201
703-993-1780
http://policy.gmu.edu/faculty/acs/index.html

Foreword by Dott. Sergio Arzeni

While the process of venture creation has long caught the attention of economists and management theorists, the growing importance of entrepreneurship in driving growth in economies increasingly based on knowledge and rapid change has undoubtedly increased the attention being paid to this subject by academics and policy makers. Various factors underlie this shift, many of which are closely analysed in this publication. Firstly, increased competition and new technologies have reduced the average lifetime of products, making product standardisation and large-scale production far less important than before. Secondly, the growing importance of knowledge as a factor of production means that innovation is ever more related to creativity, and the latter fits better the *modus operandi* of new and small firms. Thirdly, business innovation has become increasingly open and collaborative, as opposed to the 'more traditional closed' in-house innovation model of large-firm R&D labs. This 'distributed' model creates new opportunities for small firms, which can largely benefit from knowledge-based partnerships and networks. Fourthly, new non-technological forms of innovation (e.g. marketing strategies, organisational improvements) that do not require large investment in R&D enable small firms to participate more actively in the innovation process, enhancing their contribution to productivity. Finally, as we live longer and economic development engenders new social expectations, personal needs are emerging that cannot always be met by budget-constrained governments. New 'social' forms of entrepreneurship and innovation have also risen in importance to address these new needs.

In the entrepreneurial economy new firms support innovation in manifold ways. They upgrade the overall productivity of the economy by replacing inefficient units and by placing a competitive threat on incumbent firms. They exploit knowledge that would otherwise be left commercially 'unused' by universities and existing companies. They sometimes produce breakthroughs, especially in knowledge-intensive industries. And they actively participate, both as sources and users, in 'knowledge flows' occurring with customers, suppliers, universities and other 'third parties'.

However, the picture is not so idyllic and thinking that all new and small firms are equally innovative would be very misleading. The often high innovation performance of the small number of gazelles and high-impact firms is not matched by the large bulk of SMEs, which often hardly innovate at all. Significant barriers hinder their innovation, including access to finance, poor management and entrepreneurial skills, lack of qualified personnel, short-term perspective and limited awareness of innovation needs. Both innovative and traditional small firms need attention from policy makers, although specific policies and programmes will differ depending on the target.

The design and implementation of effective policies require a sound understanding of how new and small firms innovate, both the gazelles and the more typical SMEs. And what really makes such firms different from large corporations in their 'road to innovation' is their stronger emphasis on collaboration. Because of lower internal resources and limited search patterns, small businesses rely more often than large and established companies on cooperation with other organisations (suppliers, customers, universities, and public agencies), often geographically close, for their innovative activities. Knowledge spillovers, from both public research organisations and other firms, strongly contribute to the innovativeness of small-sized enterprises. Interestingly, cooperation does not replace direct investment in innovation, as shown by recent OECD analysis highlighting strong correlation between the two.

This specific approach to innovation has important policy implications for the extent to which policies for entrepreneurship and innovation will have both a national and a local dimension. At the national level, taxation, labour and product market regulations, and administrative rules are examples of areas where government intervention can help 'level the playing field' for all enterprises, regardless of age and size. At the sub-national level, local level policies can go a long way in promoting knowledge spillovers through, for instance, the establishment of a solid business support infrastructure and active business networks. This is precisely the approach of the Organisation for Economic Co-operation and Development (OECD) and, namely, of its Centre for Entrepreneurship, SMEs and Local Development. At the local level – the main focus of this book – the OECD experience suggests that entrepreneurial culture, workforce skills, knowledge networks, business infrastructures and access to finance are all critical domains where policy makers can intervene to make their regions and localities more innovative and entrepreneurial.

Entrepreneurship, Innovation and Regional Development is a must-read for anyone who first approaches the 'mystery' of entrepreneurship and innovation and how they impact on our economic and social welfare. It analyses entrepreneurship from both an economic and a social perspective, discussing the concepts of 'entrepreneurial opportunity' and 'entrepreneurial organisation', the factors underpinning an entrepreneurial environment, the process of learning associated with entrepreneurship, the role of higher education institutions in entrepreneurship promotion, entrepreneurship and internationalisation, and the wide spectrum of entrepreneurship policies.

This publication is authored by Professor Jay Mitra, a leading academic figure in the field of entrepreneurship. He is founding Chairman of the International Entrepreneurship Forum, with which the OECD has fruitfully collaborated for a number of years. He is also a longstanding consultant and partner to the OECD Centre for Entrepreneurship, SMEs and Local Development, where he acts as lead scientific advisor on entrepreneurship. The great contribution of Professor Mitra's approach to the study of entrepreneurship lies in its convinced multidisciplinarity and in its vision of the entrepreneurial process as one of both economic and social value creation.

I hope that this book will instil in some of its readers, at an earlier or later stage of life, the 'wild spirit' that Schumpeter recognised in the figure of the entrepreneur. But the book will already accomplish its mission by the extent to which it will enlighten the reader about the role and function of entrepreneurship and innovation in the knowledge-based and globalised economy, influencing his or her way of thinking and acting in no matter what job he or she will perform in the future.

Dott. Sergio Arzeni
Director
Centre for Entrepreneurship and Local Economic and Employment Development,
Organisation for Economic Co-operation and Development (OECD)
Paris, France

Acknowledgements

Nothing in this book could have been written had something else, perhaps something better, not been written first! For all who have generated new knowledge and a better understanding of this critical subject of our times, I have much respect and gratitude. I have derived much of this knowledge not only from the growing canon of literature on the subject but also from the direct interactions with and the experiential insights of numerous individuals and organizations around the world. I have been fortunate enough to meet and know some of them well, and I acknowledge readily my debt to them.

First, Brian Loasby, who taught me at the University of Stirling and from whom I learnt whatever there was to learn about the economics of entrepreneurship. Chapter 3 draws in good measure from the inspirational lectures that he gave but I take responsibility for my understanding of the topic and of the work of pioneers. Many of the ideas in the book have been stimulated by discussions with Sergio Arzeni at the OECD, and by the strength and robustness of his thoughts and extraordinary advocacy of entrepreneurship and innovation in economic policy making, institutional development and making productive use of lateral thinking in supporting my modest contribution to the work of the Centre of Entrepreneurship at the OECD under his leadership. I owe my appreciation of the proper intellectual distinction between entrepreneurship and small business development to Zoltan Acs at George Mason University. He is one of those rare economists who can tell a real story! Y. K. Bhushan, previously at Narsee Monjee Institute of Management Studies and now at ICFAI, Mumbai, in India, has shown me how to optimise real value in teaching and research, how to manage Centres of research and teaching in good and hard times, and also how to make an effective connection between entrepreneurship and management. Mathew Manimala at the Indian Institute of Management, Bangalore, India, has been a source of many good ideas stemming from his depth of understanding and insights during many years of joint project work, writing and teaching. I thank Chunlin Si at Fudan University, in Shanghai, China, for giving me the opportunity to obtain direct and real exposure to the unfolding of creativity, innovation and unique entrepreneurial activities in China, especially during my time as a Visiting Professor there.

A full list would cover too many pages for any publisher to allow such latitude of expression of thanks. There are others who, as individuals, have had sufficient faith and belief in me to support me in my entrepreneurial endeavours. Roger Jinkinson is one such individual who deserves special mention for his faith and encouragement for delivering on new ideas.

My students in the four universities in which I have taught, in the UK and in the other campuses around the world, have been the source of considerable value and intellectual delight. They have helped to shape the direction of my own learning, my teaching and my research. I owe special thanks to Ganomotse Ntshadi, a doctoral student at the University of Essex, for some of the data collection on universities, incubators and science parks referred to and discussed in Chapter 7, and to Yazid Abubakar, formerly a student and now a colleague, for our joint research work on different aspects of entrepreneurship and innovation to which I have made reference in Chapters 6, 7 and 11. A text is dedicated to students, and I hope the publication of this book will demonstrate my appreciation of their understanding of the subject beyond the use they may have of the contents.

Routledge and its editors have shown unusual patience and fortitude with me and my dilatoriness. In particular, I cannot thank Terry Clague and also Alex Krause (and their colleagues) enough for 'holding on' till the finish! The completion of this book would not have been possible without Wendy Toole's fine editing and correction of many mistakes of mine and Tamsin Ballard's support. Their ideas, suggestions and time have been invaluable to me all throughout the creation and production of the book.

I defer to custom to leave things personal till the end, even if the embrace of heart and mind comes first. To Gill, my wife and my kindred Prospero of the soul, all that I have in spirit, effort and determination in writing this book, I owe it to her. My son, Daniel, whose courage has taught me much about creativity, connectedness and innovative solutions to problems, allowed me much space for serendipitous moments and a productive outcome. They help to create my values and to both I dedicate this small contribution to the world of entrepreneurship and innovation.

1 Entrepreneurship, innovation and regional development

An introduction

You will know everything there is to know, about how entrepreneurship is born, nurtured and developed in this, the glorious 21st century of man.

(*The White Tiger*, Arvind Adiga, 2008)

A fantastic voyage

In 1966 the film *Fantastic Voyage* showed a miniaturized team of doctors travelling through human blood vessels and making life-saving repairs in the brain of a patient. Fantasy became comedy in 1987 when Hollywood remade the film with the title *Innerspace*. By this time engineers in the real world had absorbed the inspiration wholeheartedly, but instead of miniaturizing themselves they began building pill-size robot equivalents that could travel through a person's gastrointestinal tract. After another 13 years, in the year 2000, patients began swallowing the first commercially built pill cameras. Since that point in history, doctors have literally opened up new vistas of medical science using the capsules to obtain unprecedented sights of places in the human body, such as the inner folds of the small intestine, that are otherwise difficult to reach without surgery.

Overcoming the initial problem of a high rate of false or negative results because of the absence of human control, the engineers devised two-way high-speed wireless data transmission of images and instructions.[1] As for the product (the pill), it had to transform itself into a robot with the ability to respond quickly and effectively to the orders of a technician. The components needed to fit into a 2 cm^3 container and they needed sufficient power to complete tasks over up to 12 hours!

By 1999, the Israeli firm Given Imaging had introduced the first wireless camera pill, the M2A, with subsequent models confirming the usefulness of a wireless device to examine the gastrointestinal tract, establishing a practice called 'capsule endoscopy', used routinely in medicine now. The debut of the M2A was accompanied by the inauguration of separate ten-year project by the Intelligent Microsystem Centre (IMC) in Seoul, Korea, to develop a new generation of capsular endoscopes with the robotic pill containing on-board sensors, a light source for imaging, and mechanisms for delivering drug therapies and taking biopsies. Furthermore, the endoscopist's wireless remote control would have the ability to locomote.

Since 2000, 18 European business and research teams have formed a consortium with IMC to develop capsular robots for cancer detection and treatment. A group led by Paolo Dario and Arianna Menciassi at the Scuola Superiore Sant'Anna in Pisa, Italy, under the medical supervision and guidance of Marc O. Schurr of Novineon in Tubingen, Germany, handles the scientific and technical coordination of the project, called VECTOR (versatile endoscopic capsule for gastrointestinal tumour recognition and therapy). The industry and academic research teams have come up with a variety of innovative ideas offering a range of solutions to a major challenge – how to control the capsular devices inside the body. A fantasy became reality!

Fantasy, story-telling, imagination, visioning, creativity, science, technological application, research, testing, team effort, commercialization, and changing the lives we lead – of such stuff is entrepreneurship and innovation made!

Creating value

The extraordinary story of the robot pills is one of hope and the creation of real value. Fantasy is transformed into reality through the mediation of scientists, engineers and medics, and the productive economic activities of entrepreneurs. Between the fantasy and the medical journey that has led us from Israel and Korea to Italy and Germany, among other countries, there lay opportunities – for better non-invasive medical treatment, for generating new products using multiple technologies, for multidisciplinary and cross-sectoral teams working across borders to harness talent and competencies, and for business to provide the commercial organization base and resources with which to make the product widely available in the market.

It is in the creation of value that entrepreneurship and innovation find their meaning. Where innovation can be defined as the generation of new products, services and processes, entrepreneurship is associated with the identification of opportunity in society for such products and services, and in the realization or exploitation of that opportunity through the organization of resources with which to make the products available in the market. They enjoy a symbiotic connection and together they create value.

The value creation process takes the form of organizing resources with which to develop new products and services for the market and for society. There is *economic value* in:

- the assigning of a price to the product that enables it to be made, bought and sold in the market;
- the generation of a surplus value arising from the reward for actions taken in an environment of uncertainty and for the investment made to create such value;
- the effective manipulation of risk associated with taking up new opportunities even in a known or familiar environment where incumbents can thwart the realization of such opportunities;
- the identification and use of new technologies with which to develop a product that can be exchanged in the market;
- the creation of jobs for those who make, market, buy, sell and evaluate the product or service;
- the creation of wealth for both the entrepreneur who organizes the resources and the wider community of employees, medics, engineers (as in the 'robot pill' case), who work across the value chain, save money and provide a benefit to users by deploying key new technological developments.

Value creation has a social dimension, too, which is perhaps as important as the economic one. There is *social value* in

- the relationship and ties of, and the exchanges between, different talents (researchers, medics, engineers and entrepreneurs, for example) that are forged to design, create, make and benefit from the new product;

- the networks of organizations (as in the research laboratories and the business groups) that support one another through the representation of different capabilities and competencies in a particular time and in a defined space;
- the non-economic benefit that lies in the effective use of a product providing economic, psychological, physiological and social satisfaction of needs and wants at both individual and community level (as in the treatment of gastrointestinal problems of people);
- the replication of products and services across the global marketplace, making it possible for all communities and all people to derive appropriate benefits from their use once political and unproductive institutional or trade barriers are overcome.

The interplay of economic and social values in the act of entrepreneurship also helps to create personal value for both the maker and the user of a product or service. The interaction between all three value sets also generates cultural value as certain products or services, such as for example the Internet or the iPod, begin to work like symbols of a generation representing the values of a society. In the use of these symbolic artefacts and services people define their own personal and social values; they carve out their identities and become representatives of either their unique personal space or the collective arena of a group of people.

The aggregation of all these values (which could be referred to as 'entrepreneurial value') provides the basis for economic development in countries and their regions. The aggregation of these values is not simply an impersonal academic process; it follows from the actions of entrepreneurial people, in or with entrepreneurial organizations and in entrepreneurial environments. These people, the organizations and their environments come in many shapes and guises and it is in their differences rather than in their similarities (behaviour, actions, judgements, situations) that we are better able to examine how entrepreneurship, innovation and economic development occur. The fact that much of the value creation process occurs in local situations before they are adopted globally suggests that it is what happens in those local regions that captures the imagination of the curious researcher, the policy maker and even the entrepreneur. The fact that it is occurring across the world suggests that entrepreneurship and innovation are of significance the world over.

Interesting ideas and theories (some complex, others formulaic) now abound. They help us to make sense of the world of value creation. These ideas and theories and their currency will be discussed in the chapters that follow to give shape and purpose to the journey. For now and in introducing this book, there is some purchase to be obtained in exploring why the words 'entrepreneurship' and 'innovation' are falling off the tongues of almost every decision maker despite the limited real coverage they obtain in policy circles, in academia, in the media and in society at large.

The growing currency of entrepreneurship and innovation

In a special report on entrepreneurship in March 2009 in *The Economist*, Adrian Wooldridge argued that

> the entrepreneurial idea has gone mainstream, supported by political leaders on the left as well on the right, championed by powerful pressure groups, reinforced by a growing infrastructure of universities and venture capitalists, and embodied by wildly popular heroes such as Richard Branson and India's software kings.

Wooldridge used the term 'creative creation' to describe entrepreneurship in the attempt to rethink the idea of entrepreneurship as 'creative destruction' (Schumpeter, 1942) in modern times, and especially after the economically and socially ruinous effects of the current recession.

Entrepreneurship is exemplified in Wooldrige's story about aspiring Indian entrepreneurs wanting not just to become rich but to play their part in forging a new India in the aftermath of the terrorist attacks in Mumbai in December 2008, the government-sponsored economic policies of the Regan-Thatcher era of the 1980s, the adoption of entrepreneurship and innovation by the select institutions of the European Union, the World Bank and the United Nations, and the mushrooming of entrepreneurship education and training programmes in universities across the world.

As with many other flat or spiky world activities, entrepreneurship is being globalized. In previously command and now often rapaciously open economies in Central and Eastern Europe and Russia, or the hitherto closed economy of China, entrepreneurship and innovation have been 'let loose' with varying degrees of success and productivity through a minefield of policies, institutions and practices.

Entrepreneurship today acquires a special significance. The standard models of economic growth, the machinations of high finance coupled with relatively free flows of capital across borders, and the connected technological resource bases of countries have come under severe scrutiny with the recent and continuing economic crisis.[2]

Growth, entrepreneurship and development

The continued and almost unyielding focus on economic growth by policy makers and researchers has not generated any consensus on either the best form of growth or its value in terms of human and wider economic development. The growing levels of income disparity between the developing world, especially in sub-Saharan Africa, where the poor have been getting poorer, and the developed world, where the rich have been getting richer (while at the same time the poor in these same rich countries are getting poorer), have created an economic divide that does not square up with the vanities of growth advocates. Easterly's (2001) devastating critique of public policies for growth points to the failure of external aid, investments in machinery, the raising of education levels, the control of population growth and loan reparations to improve the living standards of people in poor countries.

One of the problems with growth theory is the poor correlation between investment and growth. Capital accumulation and increased labour inputs do not produce positive results because of diminishing marginal yields (Solow, 1956). Even new theories on increasing returns (Arthur, 1990) do not explain these anomalies, partly because of the failure to recognize the different conditions of growth that apply to specific economies at varying stages of economic development.

Across poorer or developing countries, for example, patterns of growth performance varied between 1970 and 2001, with individual rates showing up to 10.8 per cent in Botswana and −1.3 per cent in the Democratic Republic of Congo. Using the standard groupings in the World Economic Outlook and focusing on the 30 strongest and 30 weakest performers in terms of economic growth during the same period, Beaugrand (2004) concludes that it is difficult to establish common patterns. Strong performers (examples: Botswana, 10.8; Taiwan, 8.0, Oman 6.6) and weak performers (examples: Argentina 6.7, Azerbaijan, 0.8 and Congo −1.3) are to be found in all continents, among fuel exporters and non-fuel exporters and among countries that have experienced conflict. Both groups also included exporters of mineral products such as oil (strong performers: UAE, Oman; weak performers: Gabon, Trinidad) and diamonds (strong performers:

Botswana; weak performers: Sierra Leone, Congo). Per capita GDP figures at constant US $ prices point to an even more problematic picture with variations in the range of 7.6 per cent in the newly industrialized Asian countries to –6.0 per cent in the CIS and Mongolia. The ratio of per capita income in the major advanced countries relative to the least developed nations rose from 30 in 1970 to 39 in 1980, 68 in 1990 and a peak of 102 in 1995 (Beaugrand, 2004).

The evolutionary process of moving away from traditional industrial sectors, especially from primary products, to manufacturing also embraces structural change at the level of institutions and by way of adoption of new technologies and industries. While the rhetoric for change is easily promoted and while it is almost impossible to see miracles being performed, the relatively impressive progress made by countries such as Bangladesh, Bhutan, Cambodia, Laos PDR, the Maldives, Swaziland and Yemen are good examples of success stemming mostly from the creation of new ventures relying often on relatively low technologies (Beaugrand, 2004). In other words, where nations and regions have adopted entrepreneurship and innovation as vehicles for economic change, they have unleashed opportunities for wealth creation. Using innovative organizational tools and technologies such as micro finance and mobile technology, they have also been able to distribute some of this wealth among the population.

Entrepreneurship in terms of economic value creation, and especially local entrepreneurship, in less developed countries can be a spur for economic development, especially if it is supported by certain framework conditions such as governance, attitudes, access to resources, infrastructure and credible political systems. The nature of these framework conditions and the type of entrepreneurship that might emerge are a function of the stage of development, as Acs and Szerb (2009) have found. There are, however, a number of other, distinctive variables to consider that challenge the assumptions made by uniform framework conditions.

Rapid growth in China is associated with foreign direct investment. Huang and Khanna (2003) have called into question this approach to transferring large amounts of income from the rest of the world, especially when comparing it with India's support for private enterprise which they consider to be more beneficial in the long run. However, this argument does not necessarily consider local dynamics. Huang and Khanna's prognosis is questionable, particularly in the Indian context where successful entrepreneurship has so far been limited to the information technology (software) sector (although that is changing), where growth is evident, or micro enterprises, where scaling up is a problem.

State-owned enterprises are not the only examples of entrepreneurial success in China. As Huang (2008) notes, private Chinese entrepreneurship in the rural areas the 1980s was displaced by state-owned economic activity in the urban regions in the 1990s. However, he does not account for the phenomenal changes in the attitudes to the economic, social and cultural lives of the Chinese people as evinced in the transformation of the cinema, the theatre and other performance and visual arts, representing a real opening up of China's society and spawning a wide range of highly creative and economically successful ventures (Sinha, 2009), and in the innovative potential of networks of manufacturers engaged in the Shanzhai phenomenon[3] of imitative electronic products (Li and Mitra, 2010). The creative environment of a region or a nation has begun to emerge as an essential pre-requisite for attracting talent and technologies from across the world (Florida, 2007).

Growth, entrepreneurship and the developed nations

The importance of economic, social and cultural value creation is not restricted to the dynamics of less developed economies as they jostle for economic development. Moving along the 'S' curve that Acs and Szerb (2009) draw in their new study on the Global Entrepreneurship

Index, we can identify new business models emerging from new combinations of resources and also the forging of new coalitions of interest groups seeking critical social changes. The emergence of these phenomena is suggestive of levels of collaboration between firms, across regions and national boundaries that relies less on a zero-sum competitiveness agenda and rather on a shared platform of complementary skills. Such a platform does not indicate a fixed or permanent state of play for the firm, the region or the nation, but rather a continually changing position depending on specific economic and social conditions that are prevalent at any point in time. The dynamic environment in which firms, regions and nation states operate can mean an abandonment of previous leadership positions. It also means that there is not necessarily only one agency for entrepreneurial change. Small, medium and large firms all play a part. Thus IBM shifted from being an essential hardware producer to being a purveyor of advanced services when it sold its PC empire to Lenovo. Its eventual repositioning in the market place has enabled a return of IBM to a new position at the vanguard of the knowledge economy.

The change process at the organizational level could apply equally to nation states, as Bhide (2007) argues in his reference to America's greater commercialization of new ideas, technologies and services, set against protectionism and over reliance on high-end R&D activity. New R&D activity in China and India does not jeopardize the USA's leadership in creating economic value from R&D because of the latter's more advanced status in business activities compared to the other two countries. Thus China's advance in R&D does not pose a threat to American firms, which are better able to derive commercial value from research and development activity carried out anywhere. What it does show, however, is the need for greater connectedness across firms, regions and countries in a much more distributed environment for the development of new technology, business creation and growth. In this environment, there is an urgency to search for new business models where, for example, revenue is generated not from what is sold to the customer, but from what is built with the latter, the end-user.

Technological change today

The rapid emergence of entrepreneurship is being driven to a great extent by technology. The invention of the personal computer, the mobile telephone and the Internet are opening up possibilities which *The Economist* (March, 2009) terms the democratization of entrepreneurship. These technologies have applications and low-entry thresholds that are making it possible for individuals even with limited financial resources to launch new enterprises and reach wide markets. This is evident in, for example, the rise of internet bloggers or Twitter-users outsmarting well-established newspapers on breaking stories, while various automated news-collecting services such as RealClear Politics are using small amounts of capital to set themselves up as 'tools for news junkies'. eBay entrepreneurs flourish, as any international student in, for example, a British university will confirm! Sophisticated business services can now be provided by small outfits using cloud computing to small businesses at relatively low prices because of negligible or low investment costs. With around 3.3 billion people using mobile phones around the world, the technology is enabling unusual opportunities for entrepreneurs to break into one of the world's most regulated markets. Apple has allowed third parties (or 'app entrepreneurs') to post around 20,000 programs, or applications, on its App Store.

Crucially, mobile telephone technology is enabling developing economies to leapfrog their richer counterparts by almost dispensing with landlines and providing services to the poor and needy in ways that could not have been dreamt of before. The Grameen Bank's micro finance story of women being lent money to buy specially designed mobile phones that enable them to sell time on their phones to local villagers has produced 270,000 phone ladies. Grameen Bank has emerged as the largest telecoms producer in Bangladesh (*The Economist*, 2009). Kenya's story of people being able to remit money by selling phone credits for their mobile phones belongs to the same stable of creative thinking and social change using technology.

Mini case study 1.1: Technology today and creative entrepreneurial opportunity: Local Motors case study

Chris Anderson (2010) suggests that in an age of 'open-source, custom fabricated, DIY product design . . . atoms are the new bits'. He narrates the story of Local Motors, the first open-source car company to reach production in the USA. The company released the Rally Fighter a $50,000 off-road (but 'street-legal') racer whose design is 'crowd-sourced', as is the selection of its off-the-shelf components, with the final assembly being carried out by the customers in local assembly centres. Each design is released under what is termed a friendly 'Creative Commons' licence, with customers being supported in their endeavour to improve the designs and produce their own component parts which they can sell to their peers (see Figures 1.1 and 1.2). The company claims it can take a new car from design to market in 18 months – about the same time 'that it takes Detroit to change the specs on some door trim'!

Local Motors Case Study

June 2010 – Launch of Rally Fighter $ 50,000 off-road racer

Prototyped in workshop at back of Wareham office

Manufacturing from Factory Five Racing – a kit car company. Overcame problem of kit car design (lawsuits licence fees because they copy famous cars) by going for totally original design (re-imagine what a car may be?)

Crowd-sourced design

Community of volunteers – engineers, designers, car hobbyists equipped with 3D design software & photorealistic rendering technology, entering a competition)

Design released under share-friendly Creative Commons Licence

Customers encouraged to improve design & produce own components

Figure 1.1 Local Motors case study

The Local Motor Story-2

Motivated by refusal to design car for mass-market

Selection of off-shelf components; chassis, engine, transmission designed/selected by LM & relationships; With firms which helped to source dashboard dials, new BMW clean diesel engine; Final assembly by customers - "build experience"

Sketch to market in 18 months model

Figure 1.2 The Local Motor story 2

Anderson's technology-driven world of entrepreneurship offers a business model based on five principles – invent, design, prototype, manufacture and sell. He regards every garage as a 'potential micro factory and every as citizen a micro entrepreneur in the age of democratized industry'. The following table shows how a micro entrepreneur citizen can build a micro factory.

Table 1.1 Building the entrepreneurial dream

Steps	Actions
Invent	Dream up your own products. 'Pro tip': check patent office web sites to ensure no one else has had the idea first
Design	Use free tools like Blender or Google's Sketch Up to create a 3D digital model, or download someone else's design and incorporate your groundbreaking tweaks
Prototype	Make a prototype: desktop 3D printers such as MakerBot are available for under $650. Just upload a file and watch it render your vision in layered ABS plastic
Manufacture	The garage is fine for limited production, but if you want to go big, go global – outsource. Factories in China are standing by: sites such as Alibaba.com can help you find the right partner
Sell	Market your product directly to customers via an on line store such as SparkFun – or set up your own ecommerce outfit through a firm like Yahoo or Web Studio. Then become the poster child of the DIY industrial revolution.

Source: Anderson (2010).

We reflect on open innovation and aspects of technological change in more detail later in the book, but what it is important to stress here is the entrepreneurial context of technological change (the world of new venture creation).

Technological change and new venture creation

Technological change is associated with knowledge production and entrepreneurship. It provides the means for the appropriation of revenues accruing from investments in new knowledge. The production of such knowledge and its potential application in the real world can be regarded as innovation. In a perfectly rational world, where all economic agents have perfect information, any idea for producing something different from what is currently available is likely to be accepted by an incumbent because pursuing an innovation is going to have more value than taking it elsewhere. This holds because the incumbent will, in a perfectly rational world, have access to all the necessary information without incurring agency or transaction costs.

Despite rational economists, the real world does not generate perfect information. The valuation of an innovation by a new player will be different from that made by an incumbent when there is uncertainty about a new product. In this situation an employee with a new idea may not be able to obtain a reward for his or her innovation inside the organization. The employee may, therefore, exit (rather than, in Hirschman's (1970) words, have a 'voice') and start a new venture. Whether or not such new ventures will eventually grow will depend to some extent on the type of industry in which they are located. The issue of scale economies matter. New firms are inevitably challenged in their act of survival as they have limited resources at their disposal. Their ability to grow will depend on whether they are able to harness resources quickly, which may be difficult if they face direct competition from large firms benefiting from economies of scale and sometimes scope.

The nature of the industry and the market will therefore make a difference, as will the conditions of demand. As Acs and Audretsch (2005) state, in markets with only limited or negligible scale economies new firms are more likely to survive. This analysis accounts for the possibilities of growth of many new firms in the modern internet era, where many of the markets do not require scale economies at least when they start. However, if new firms do not grow in markets where scale economies are more evident, then not growing may have drastic consequences. A cognitive capability on the part of the entrepreneur to help distinguish between different types of market and demand would be necessary in order to make relevant decisions about growth because all firms will need to maintain a minimum efficient scale (MES), even if this scale might differ from one industry to another.

Even in the internet era not all markets and industries can opt out of considering the importance of scale economies. Empirical research evidence suggests that in the manufacturing industry 'there is a gap between the MES level of output and the size of the firm' (Acs and Audretsch, 2005). As the gap increases, the chances of a new firm surviving decreases. If the new firm offers a product that is viable in terms of demand and production efficiency then there is a greater likelihood of it surviving and growing while achieving scale economies.

The above argument suggests that both small and large firms can be entrepreneurial subject to their place in specific markets and industries and the level of demand for their products and services in those markets. As we shall see later, small, medium and large firms all have distinctive capabilities for innovation. Where new entrepreneurial firms provide real value is in their ability to tap new ideas and act as sources of experimentation that might otherwise remain in the shadows. In the end we come back to the question of opportunity and the means by which it is realized for productive gain in society.

To understand 'how, by whom and with what consequences opportunities to produce future goods and services are discovered, evaluated and exploited' (Shane and Venkataraman, 2000, p. 218) is to determine what entrepreneurship and innovation are about. However, as stated earlier, there is a distinction between the two in that while the term 'innovation' is well covered by Shane and Venkatraman (2000), 'entrepreneurship' finds its meaning in the creation of new ventures. 'Entrepreneurial behaviour involves the activities of individuals who are associated with creating new organisations, rather than activities of individuals who are involved with maintaining or changing the operations of on-going established organisations' (Gartner and Carter, 2003, p. 195).

The entrepreneurial organization context

If entrepreneurship finds its real meaning in its organizational context, then the immediate question that engages the mind concerns the type of organization that is most conducive to entrepreneurial activity. Gartner and Carter's (2003) definition refers only to discretely identifiable new ventures and excludes any activity carried out by larger firms. As we shall see later, this rather purist view limits the scope of entrepreneurial activity and excludes the new venture creation process (through spin-offs, the development of new structures to support innovation, and value creation through new products and services) in existing small and large firms. In other words, the scaling up of firms and the ability of medium-sized and large firms to create new value by way of the production of future goods and through the creation of new organizational structures fall well within the purview of entrepreneurship, as far as this book is concerned.

Small firms in particular have been able to challenge the orthodoxy of the past where larger firms were held to be the main engines of innovation. Schumpeter (1942) found in the monopolist firm the bastion of innovative competitive advantage. The monopolist market has market dominance, and this dominance is essential to bear the risks and uncertainties associated with the innovation process. Similarly, Galbraith (1956) and others recommended that because of the high costs of innovative activity including R&D, the critical mass necessary to attain power in or obtain a large share of the market power, scale economies, and the ability to reduce costs to generate larger relative profits, only a large firm could offer any reasonable prospect for an organizational basis for innovative activity.

Curiously, this faith in large firms, corporations, belies the suspicion of their power that dates back to the eighteenth century and Adam Smith, who condemned them because they evade the laws of the market by artificially inflating prices and controlling trade. Even though American colonists limited corporation charters to a specific number of years, the courts of America began to remove the restrictions and with the onset of the US Civil War corporations began to 'use their huge profits from the war along with the subsequent political confusion and corruption to buy legislation that gave them huge grants of land and money, much of which they used to build railroads' (Robbins, 2008, p. 95). Robbins goes on to quote no less a person than Abraham Lincoln who commented that the

> corporations have been enthroned . . . An era of corruption in high places will follow and the money power will endeavour to prolong its reign by working on the prejudices of the people . . . until wealth is aggregated in a few hands . . . and the Republic is destroyed. (cited Korten, 1995, p. 58)

There are uncanny echoes today of the uses and abuses of such power and the impact of this power buttressed by the egregiousness of the helpmeets of such corporations, and some of the players in the financial services! Theirs is the kingdom of consumption and the value of consumption based on the notions of self-interest, not the creation of economic value through opportunity creation and widespread innovation that could even reduce the harmful effects of concentrated growth through excessive consumption. So there are historical antecedents that question the value of large firms as they are driven down paths that exclude democratic participation in the creative and innovation process.

Small firms, large firms

It has required another form of empirical evidence to shatter the notion of innovation being the domain of large firms. This evidence is drawn first from the work of Birch, who suggested that job providers in the market were mainly smaller, younger firms (Birch, 1979, 1987). Once firms grow older, their ability to generate new jobs declines substantially. Birch found that in the US, about 60 per cent of all jobs were created by firms employing fewer than 20 people; and almost 50 per cent of the jobs were generated small by independent entrepreneurs. In contrast, large firms (employing more than 500 people) had less than 15 per cent of all net new jobs.

Not all small firms were job generators. Rather, it was the smaller, younger firms that created jobs – and job generation abilities of firms declined once they were up to four years old. Birch's work influenced a whole generation of researchers and had a big impact on public policies promoting small and medium enterprises (SMEs) in many countries (Storey, 1994; Landström, 1996; Acs *et al.*, 2008b). But job creation is not necessarily a product of innovation, and those small firms creating jobs were not necessarily new firms.

Where the smaller firm demonstrated innovative advantage was in their management structure (Rothwell, 1989). They are not bureaucratic, and decisions can be made by a few people. Acs and Audretsch (1991) also found that there is no evidence that the increasing returns to R&D expenditure produced by scale economies actually affect innovative output.

Some scholars of firm growth argue that most job creation by small firms occurs within a relatively small number of firms – called 'gazelles' (Birch and Medoff, 1994; Acs *et al.*, 2008b). However, gazelles are firms that 'move between small and large [size] quickly . . . and to classify them by their size is to miss their unique characteristics: great innovation and rapid job growth' (Birch and Medoff, 1994, p. 163). Since then, this perspective on gazelles has attracted attention from prominent writers on the subject.

Acs *et al.* (2008b) extended the work of Birch beyond firms with mainly employment growth, by adding the revenue growth variable to that of expanding employment. Firms showing both revenue and employment growth were referred to as 'high-impact firms' in order to distinguish them from gazelles (Acs *et al.*, 2008b). High-impact firms are relatively old and rare. They contribute to the majority of overall economic growth (Birch and Medoff, 1994; Acs *et al.*, 2008b). On average, they are 25 years old, they represent between 2 and 3 per cent of all firms, and they account for almost all the private sector employment and revenue growth in the economy (Acs *et al.*, 2008b). Acs *et al.*'s conclusions support Birch's observation that gazelles account for almost all the job creation in the economy, although their measures were not entirely comparable. They also had comparable findings with regard to firm size, but not firm age. High-impact firms are not new firms and they are found in all firm size-classes.

Parker *et al.* (2005) have taken the study on gazelles further by developing a theory of dynamic management strategies of these high-growth firms. Based on a data set from Britain containing information on over 100 gazelles, they advance a framework that emphasizes dynamic, rather than static, management strategies as key to high growth (Parker *et al.*, 2005). Another recent paper by Acs and Mueller (2007) found that business start-ups with fewer than 500 employees have persistent employment effects over time and across large, diversified metropolitan regions.

We are left with a certain degree of uncertainty about the specific organizational context of innovation. Entrepreneurship is, therefore, a function of small, medium and large firms. But perhaps what matters more are the mediating factors of their location or the impact of government policy. Acs and Mueller's (2007) conclusions suggest that the characteristics of the region are important for employment growth and the creation and growth of innovative firms.

The regional dimension

Is it countries or the regions within a country that are truly entrepreneurial? It is almost by reflex action that we think of the USA as the heartland of entrepreneurship. Between 1996 and 2004 it created an average of 550,000 small businesses every month (*The Economist*, 2009). This is also a country where little-known names burst into the economic firmament and remain leading organizations in their industry for decades to come. Walmart was founded in 1962, and only went public about ten years afterwards. Google, Facebook and

YouTube were the minnows a decade ago. The apparent deep-rootedness of entrepreneurship in America is attributed to its flexible employment structure (the ease of hire and fire), structural advantages created by the world's most mature venture capital industry, close working relations with universities, open immigration policy which allows for 52 per cent of Silicon Valley start-ups being founded by immigrants, and the willingness of consumers to try new products. But India and China are also creating billions of entrepreneurs today, and in rather different ways. While the former draws on the top end of its higher education system, the ideal of meritocracy, and its technology-savvy expatriate entrepreneurs, China relies on both its relentlessly fast-moving state machinery and state enterprises, and its highly innovative, technology-based new entrepreneurs, to boost its entrepreneurial mettle. Israel, Denmark and Singapore also rely on a focus on technology, foreign investments and systematic government intervention to promote entrepreneurship (*The Economist*, 2009).

The reference to the geographic spread of entrepreneurship across different countries masks the differences in entrepreneurial opportunities and outcomes in various parts of those countries. Certain regions are seen to be more entrepreneurial than others. Critical to the idea of the importance of any region to entrepreneurship and innovation is that one defined region is different from another, even in the same country. Detroit is not California in the USA, Berlin is not Essen in Germany, and Bangalore is not Patna in India!

The particularity of the regional environment that is conducive to entrepreneurship can be studied from various perspectives using a number of theories and concepts. One such theory is based on the idea of 'knowledge spillovers'. The knowledge spillover theory highlights the significance of local linkages for a firm's generation of its own knowledge (Jaffe, 1989; Acs, 2002; Stuart and Sorenson, 2003). Localized knowledge spillovers are defined as 'knowledge externalities bounded in space', which allow firms operating in proximity to key knowledge sources to introduce innovations at a faster rate than rival firms located elsewhere (Breschi and Lissoni, 2001). Knowledge takes the form of local human capital, business R&D and government R&D (Acs, 2002; Stuart and Sorenson, 2003; Krudsen *et al.*, 2007). This idea of knowledge spillover is discussed in more detail later in the book. What can be noted here is that levels of innovation and new firm creation can be distinguished by the extent to which knowledge is created and spilled over from one firm to another or from a university to a business. This notion of spillover gathers momentum when there is a concentration of similar or related firms, as in business clusters, because they can better share knowledge, technologies, talent and services owing to their close proximity. A concentration of successful firms in a cluster also attracts venture capital and other service firms in clusters till they reach a threshold where it is no longer economic to have such concentrations because of congestion or negative path-dependent factors such as 'lock-in', which prevents firms from seeking new knowledge from elsewhere.

Knowledge spills over not only because there is a concentration of firms. Available and appropriate physical, institutional social and socio-psychological factors are the basic building blocks of entrepreneurial environments, characterized by a concentration of creative firms with creative talent. These factors help to establish relevant and suitable framework conditions, which are then used by firms to create wealth. Sometimes it is difficult to establish what comes first. Is it the creative environment of artists, musicians architects and their bohemian consorts that provides fertile ground for creative entrepreneurs to pursue their new venture ideas, or do the success of the latter attract the former to the 'safe' haven of a creative hunting ground? There are not necessarily any clear cause-and-effect relationships that can be detected; neither is any linear logic obvious in the emergence of different sets of activities.

However, the association between different forms of creative talent and their joint contribution to economic prosperity and civic well-being has a long history, from the flourishing communities of the Indus Valley civilization to Medici Florence, right down to today's Berlin in Germany or Hoxton in London.

Mini case study 1.2: Creative environment and entrepreneurship: Berlin case study

There are artists, designers, musicians and writers who form part of a creative environment that is as attractive to them as it is conducive to entrepreneurial activity. Take Berlin! Mitte was once a drab district in central Berlin and is now becoming one of the world's centres for creative people. The supply of inexpensive accommodation is a major attractor. Cheap apartments and abandoned factories from the eastern, previously communist half of the city helped to depress prices throughout the city.

However, it is not simply cheap property that is the big draw. Berlin is still a city redefining and re-creating itself. The very act of redefinition is in itself an entrepreneurial act. This is manifest in migrants coming into the city to switch careers (such as a doctor from near Bremen becoming a consultant on environmental issues). The opening up of the physical space is accompanied by the availability of what many describe as 'mental space'.

The newness is part of a tradition in Berlin, creating a kind of path-dependency based on creativity and counter culture. During the Cold War era it was a magnet for West German punks, gays and pacifists who objected to military service and moved there. With the transfer of the government from Bonn in the 1990s some of that anarchic sparkle may have gone. The individual creativity still remains as the $400 Trippen boots testify, but these are symptomatic of a movement of upward economic trajectory! The city might be harking back to the days of East Berlin when Unter den Linden, a tree-lined boulevard, was Germany's answer to Paris's Champs Elysees. The war and the Wall devastated all of that, and there are still reminders of grotesque concrete blocks from the communist era. The re-creation that is taking place is located in this tension between the old and the new, between a conscious desire to be different, to be environmentally correct, where according to Time reporters the most used adjective is 'sustainable'!

The arts and the world of underground music and the renovation of over 170 museums have boosted tourism. As Florida (2002) has noted, creative economies attract and give space to immigrants, and Berlin has seen a remarkable rise in the population of foreigners who now make up 1 in 7 of its 3.5 million people. In Mitte district alone nearly 30 per cent of the inhabitants are from overseas. They populate the region and start creative businesses, and their value is being spotted by the city government which is encouraging local start-ups particularly in the fashion industry. And in the centre of it all is the slightly subversive culture of a city with its relaxed night life (Saturday nights start at midnight), the attraction of the annual 'techno' festival, 'The Love Parade' that drew nearly a million people to Berlin's streets annually till 2006, and the acceptance of a leisure principle in a place where 'artists gather and things spring out like nothing', something like Marshall's 'mysteries in the air' (Marshall, 1920).

(Source: *Time*, 2009)

Government policy

The creative environment and the framework conditions of that environment emerge from a mix of the evolving culture of a place and its ability to re-create itself. Some of this is achieved through effective government policy. But few if any nations have anything that may be loosely identified as entrepreneurship policy. Much of this is hidden in industrial, fiscal, monetary and even other operational policy areas such as health, transportation and foreign affairs. The extent to which these different policies create a facilitative environment that generates opportunities to create economic and social value in the form of new products and services through the creation of new ventures is central to the identification of a thread of policy measures and instruments that support entrepreneurship and innovation. The deregulation of the National Health Service in the UK created opportunities for different forms of service provision by hospitals, community organizations and the private sector, together with the possibility of tapping talent for new health products from within the community of doctors, nurses and paramedics often working with venture capital firms. This development has also created opportunities for unproductive entrepreneurship where new directions, such as target-setting and the creation of an internal market, have only exacerbated the difficulties within the provision of a unique social service.

Effective policy development is possible when governments and key stakeholders in society (individuals, social communities, industry, think-tanks, etc.) are engaged in institution building. Institutions do not just include organizations that represent specific functions or those that promote public and private causes, but perhaps more importantly the whole set of norms, practices and sanctions available in a civil society. These institutions set the boundaries for entrepreneurial activity and how they do it, what they set in terms of checks and balances, has a bearing on entrepreneurial activity in a particular environment. Perversely, and often because of its fluid presence in specific and defined territories of government functions, there is every chance of side-stepping the importance of opening up possibilities for new opportunities to be realized by new players. Incumbents in many industries have vested interests, often colluding with governments to nip any opportunity in the bud in order to retain monopolistic power. This is where anti-trust laws, transparency and other measures of governance can help to return entrepreneurship from its unproductive or even destructive side to its productive domain.

Socialization and entrepreneurship

Inherent in the creation of value, and in the realization of opportunity created by technological change or institutional intervention, is the interplay and relationships of people. As we shall see later, the very act of creating a new venture is immersed in the experience of the entrepreneurs, their previous occupations and skills development perhaps, in the networks of fellow entrepreneurs, family, business connections, and even contacts with the government. In seeking credit, for example, they perform more of a social act of establishing a relationship of trust with the creditor (in keeping with the etymological origin of the word). Both parties contract on the principle of 'I believe', which forms the basis of economic calculations of the value of such credit or indeed the due diligence checks necessary to grant credit.

The act of socialization is also evident in what the customer wishes to buy from a new venture, the associations of branded products pitted against the freshness afforded by a new alternative promising, for example, reduced gas emissions or a healthier diet. The entrepreneur's lantern in a dark world of uncertainty is lit to provide a pathway for others to follow and thereby illuminate the market for new products and services. The extent to which an entrepreneur interacts with other entrepreneurs and key stakeholders is a function some-times of the environment in which they operate – in concentrated business clusters, for example, where the mutuality of entrepreneurial effort and its outcomes is a function of what is often referred to as 'untraded interdependencies' or exchanges that do not necessarily involve typical business transactions. It is difficult to measure such 'untraded interdepend-encies' other than by creating loose measurement proxies. However, there is ample recog-nition of the value of social capital that is generated through such exchanges and through recognized forms of networking among entrepreneurs and other stakeholders. As we will see later, social capital is closely linked to the effective use of two other forms of capital – financial capital and human capital – that are essential to the formation and development of new ventures.

Socially motivated enterprises

Social value creation is inherent in all types of entrepreneurial activity. We now witness, however, a new type of hybrid organization that holds the achievement of social goals as its central mission while espousing business tools and methods to run its operations effectively. In doing so, such organizations are expected to attain economic self-sufficiency without compromising their social objectives. Their growth, if numbers are to be believed, has been phenomenal, and increasingly social enterprises have become the cynosure of public atten-tion as governments struggle to find ways in which they can promote job creation, public services, and self-sufficiency for their citizens. Public attention is as strong in developed countries as in their developing counterparts partly because of the phenomenon of jobless growth even in high-growth economies.

The growth and importance of socially driven enterprises can be attributed to other impor-tant considerations that have both historical antecedents in and long-term significance for many economies. Where social and economic circumstances leave a people disenfranchised from work and social amenities there is economic and social value creation in the independ-ent action of individuals and communities to regain their worth through opportunities that they own and manage directly. Where governments find it difficult to maintain high-end social services the possibilities of deregulation can allow community-based organizations to take ownership of local service provision. These are not easy options and sometimes gov-ernments can promote such enterprises as an excuse for cutting public expenditure in those areas. While withdrawal of public services can be a spur for new forms of activity, the test of governmental sincerity is to be found in the circumstances and in the time they give to promote such enterprises.

Mini case study 1.3: Entrepreneurial community development: McScience case study

There are many stories of social resolution of personal, social and economic problems of a community of people. The McScience Group in Mayfield, Midlothian, in Scotland, has a turnover of nearly £3m, it employs over 70 local people in an area of widespread social deprivation, and it returns a large amount of its profits to the community while also helping out with projects in developing countries.

As it syndicates its experience today to many other communities in Scotland and elsewhere, the organization and its members can reflect on the extraordinary mission of hope and determination of a former Scottish miner, Brian Tannerhill. When he was thrown on the scrapheap with the closure of mines in the 1980s, his resolution was to defend his community from the industrial and social carnage that was wreaked by the closure. He did so by raising only £7,500 but enough to start a business providing jobs, training, skills and facilities through five operating companies that offer managed workspace, property development, energy conservation, central heating, security installations and locksmith services, property maintenance, cleaning, recycling, call centre services, and conference and seminar facilities. The call centre, funded by the European Regional Development Fund, provides customized contracts for the voluntary and private sectors and helps provide financial support for industry-standard training facilities to accredited Scottish Vocational Qualification Level 2 standard.

(Source: *Observer*, 2007)

The multidisciplinarity of entrepreneurship

Even a cursory reading of this introduction would suggest that entrepreneurship and innovation help to create economic, social, personal and collective value through a variety of means, disciplines and methods. Recognizing the multiple identities of entrepreneurship and innovation means giving up on the silo-based singularities of thought and analysis! It means dropping neat little packages of definitions, of existing discipline-based explanations, and of singular tools of analysis with which to justify specific outcomes. It means embedding economic analysis in social structures, in understanding that economic equilibrium goals and effective allocation of resources are always affected by social activity and errant human behaviour, which in turn generate new opportunities. It means drawing new knowledge on the subject from social anthropology, the arts and technology. It means that the patterns of growth and development of new opportunities that find new, small ventures at the helm of new economic activity being swallowed up by larger firms as soon as such activity is consolidated have given way, at least for now, to very short life cycles for products and services, defying traditional approaches to achieving economic equilibrium. It means recognizing that the genie of new product and service development and new venture creation is out of the bottle. The sources of technological change, of new business models with which to harness such change, can be found in unusual settings not based on traditional models of development theory. It means providing a base for a new approach to the better understanding of opportunity identification, opportunity creation, opportunity realization and value creation.

This book tells this story of value creation through opportunity identification, the harnessing of technological change, socialization, institution building and development and government policy in particular environments. The narrative assumes the role of the individual entrepreneur but does not demand from him or her the role of the narrator. In this sense, the entrepreneur is unknown even if various writers have provided us with fascinating insights into their characteristics, traits and psychological make up. Rather like Jovanovic (1982), who stated that an individual's suitability for entrepreneurship is unknown to them or for that matter anyone else until they actually start their new ventures, this author does not hazard any guesses about the type of entrepreneur who negotiates best institutions, socialization processes, and governments, or uses best the right technologies and the financial tools with which to start a successful venture.

If the environment for successful entrepreneurship is uncertain then the best an entrepreneur can hope to derive is optimal value with a given set of instruments and functions. The entrepreneur does so with different sets of skills, some acquired while in a previous economic activity or in previous business experience either directly in terms of running one's own business or through a family enterprise. Much emphasis is put these days on the supply of trained entrepreneurs equipped with the skills to read and write business plans and cash flow forecasts. There is perhaps a tenuous association between training and learning to carry out a function or a set of tasks, to acquire competencies to achieve a target. Entrepreneurs learn in different ways, through 'learning by doing or learning by imitating' and a set of heuristics. Most importantly, the learn from the judgements they make based on information they have and signals they receive about their venture and the location of that venture in a place, and within an industrial sector. Much of this learning is tacit. Often it is embedded in the processes and practices of their own organization. A lot of it is dependent on who they are and what they do in specific circumstances.

Various studies have identified different types or categories of the population and have focused on the peculiarities of the young entrepreneur (Blanchflower and Meyer, 1994; van Praag, 2003; Rosam 2003), the ethnic minority entrepreneur (Basu and Goswami, 1999), the female entrepreneur and even the futuristic nascent entrepreneur (GEM 2009 reports: Bosma and Levie, 2009). There are indeed interesting explanations of how these individuals carve out their own spaces of entrepreneurial activity. The focus of this book is less on who these people might be and more on what they do, the conditions and circumstances of their offering, and the nexus of institutions, policies and environments that impact upon or influence their working agendas. These agendas and the interplay of the areas of interest referred to above contribute to economic development, especially at the regional level. This book represents a search for such relationships and contributions.

The purpose and scope of the book

As a text, the book, and what it represents, enters relatively new territory. However, the passage of this engagement has been facilitated enormously by academic research and policy developments. Words (and some pictures), rather more than numbers, fill the learning void that this book purports to address on the subject of entrepreneurship, innovation and economic development. In that lie both its limitations and its advantages. The former are those of this author alone, while the latter are where he shares with others the commons of imagination, insight and understanding.. The purpose of this book is to look at those spaces in between individual entrepreneurs, to find the kind of meaning of entrepreneurship and innovation in the same way that Miles Davis, the great jazz legend, used to discover music in between the notes. It examines the structures and processes that lie outside the individual entrepreneur. It focuses attention on how entrepreneurs and the opportunities that they seek and find are influenced or impacted upon by the external environment, the institutional arrangements that are in place in specific circumstances, and how policies that governments create can open up or hinder opportunities. The book identifies the externalities that are generated as a result of technological change and by research or even entrepreneurial activities that other entrepreneurs capture and use. It explores the social relationships that entrepreneurs develop to use these opportunities, the inter-linkages between people, between different actors representing, for example business, cultural institutions, and government, and the forms of learning that they inculcate through these connections to start or grow their ventures.

In launching and developing their ventures entrepreneurs make direct and indirect use of their environments, thereby contributing to the economic fortunes and development, over time, of the regions in which they are located. This is dependent on whether their activities are productive, unproductive or destructive, and whether the environments in which they operate provide conditions that are conducive to their endeavours.

The book is based on the idea that theory and concepts are critical to our ability to make sense of the different scenarios of entrepreneurship and innovation. These theories and concepts help to illuminate, in Shackle's (2009) words, the 'features of the scene'; it 'gives them substance by eliciting a shadow, defines profiles and lends colour'. Theory and conceptual underpinning of the ideas and events help to support the discussions in all the chapters of the book.

Crucially, the outcome of all such exploration is to go back to the beginning where one can also find the end. The beginning is the location, the region and the environment that is the crucible for opportunity identification and entrepreneurial activity. In the end it is the creation and growth of new ventures and opportunity realization that enhance the capacity of regions and locations to achieve entrepreneurial development. This book is about entrepreneurship, innovation and regional development, their meaning, their polemics and their connected narratives.

The book will not deliver on Arvind Adiga's promise of offering everything you need to know about entrepreneurship. That is why you have fiction! Here we have a text about certain aspects of entrepreneurship and innovation and how they contribute to economic development. It is an attempt at directing the attention of the reader to new developments and relevant connections. In tracing these new developments, much is taken from the knowledge of and scholarship in the field and from multiple sources in various disciplines. It identifies opportunities for learning in between the spaces of different disciplines, creating openings unknown to fools but where angels might love to tread!

The structure of the book

The book is organized in terms of an elaboration of

- ideas, theories and concepts;
- constructs and structures;
- processes, instruments and policies;
- consolidation and synthesis of themes and issues; and
- future directions and the unending romance of entrepreneurship.

The book is international in scope; it draws on references, activities, events and ideas from across the globe if only to reflect the global character of entrepreneurship and to demonstrate its significant evolution in different environments. It uses 'mini case studies' in most chapters to illustrate ideas and concepts and sometimes to question them. It combines the demands of a text with discourse on the subject and topics that provide the make-up for the title. Each chapter (2–11) has particular learning outcomes that the reader could use to gauge his or her critical understanding of the topics which can then be tested by answering the self-assessment questions at the end of each of the chapters.

Ideas, theories and concepts

Following this introduction, the book provides a short essay on entrepreneurial opportunities, where they come from, how they emerge and what entrepreneurs do with them. That chapter provides the lead for a slightly elaborate discussion on some of the basic economic and social (sociological) aspects of entrepreneurship and innovation, drawing on the work of some of the pioneering theorists and their illustrious followers, in Chapters 3 and 4. These discussions provide the foundation for the chapters that follow. Theories and concepts continue to underpin all the chapters in the book.

Constructs and structures

Chapter 5 explores in depth different types of entrepreneurial organization following the line that it is in the creation of organizations that entrepreneurship gives life to innovation. Entrepreneurial organizations are to some extent dependent on entrepreneurial environments or locations that are conducive to the creation and growth of new firms, innovative activity and economic development. In these environments institutions play a critical role, as do the framework conditions and the evolving culture of a place in cultivating networks, alliances and forming business clusters or concentrations of similar or related firms and institutions. These issues are covered in Chapter 6.

Processes, instruments and policies

How organizations behave and how they interact with their environment is often part of a learning process for entrepreneurs and the organizations they try to sustain. Exploring the value of learning and how entrepreneurs learn informs Chapter 7. Chapter 8 then looks at another aspect of entrepreneurial organizations and their environments – internationalization – which helps these organizations to sustain their innovative capabilities. The capacity of local firms to internationalize is symptomatic of their ability to grow through the development of new products and services in new markets. Their growth helps to enhance local capacity of current and future employees by extending their skills base. It encourages knowledge exchange, which in turn facilitates the dynamic capabilities of firms especially in the face of competition. Internationalization highlights a paradox that underpins entrepreneurship and economic development. The greater the capacity of local firms to grow through internationalization, the higher is the prospect of the region in which those firms are located to develop. Much of this growth and development is made possible through engagement with many different institutions.

Institutions and the role of learning have attracted attention in both research and policy circles. The importance of higher education institutions in particular has acquired a particular significance especially in terms of their value to economic growth and development in a knowledge-based society. Good universities broaden the minds of people from across the globe. In that, they are the original multinationals of ideas and intellectual power. However, they are primarily local in their physical construct and identity, and they make major contributions to the learning process and the economic activity of the regions in which they are located. Increasingly, much of this contribution to economic development stems from their activities in carrying out research and development that can support industry, in transferring and exchanging knowledge with a wide group of stakeholders, in the spinning of ventures from ideas that germinate in the laboratories, in staff common rooms or in student halls of residence, and in syllabi that accommodate personal development opportunities. The role and value of universities is examined in Chapter 9.

Chapter 10 takes the reader away from the processes and institutions anddown the policy avenue to look at how, why and when effective policies help to create opportunities, to harness talent and to marshal resources with which to support new business creation, innovation and economic development. This chapter tracks the meaning, purpose, scope and mechanisms of government policies, their significance and redundancy in fostering different systems of innovation, the nurturing of learning environments, and the emergence and scaling up of new firms.

Consolidation and synthesis

The critical contents of these chapters are then woven into the fabric of the main tapestry of the book that can found in Chapter 11. This chapter brings together the key issues, concepts and empirical evidence, helping to make the connection between entrepreneurship, innovation and regional development.

Future directions and the romance of entrepreneurship

Finally in Chapter 12, the author engages in a bit of romance with the emerging trends, preoccupations and attractions in the field of entrepreneurship and innovation in the middle of a stubborn recession and significant social and environmental problems. This romance is in the new opportunities that are exploding across an enormous, global canvas of technological change and innovation, offering us the chance to avail ourselves of them in unusual ways that challenge our knowledge and make redundant the tools with which to make use of such knowledge. The romance is also to be found in the exploration of territories of entrepreneurship and innovation that transgress our limited scoping of entrepreneurship as new business creation and innovation as technology-based new product development. Like most romances, this one will be left incomplete as its necessary consummation within the limitations of a book can only leave one with the hope of more.

2 Entrepreneurial opportunity

Conditions and circumstances for innovation and new firm creation

Learning outcomes

In this chapter the reader will:

- obtain a critical appreciation of the different sources of entrepreneurial opportunity and new business creation;
- link critically the different sources of opportunity to various theoretical insights and concepts;
- obtain a critical insight into the relationship between technology-driven opportunities and entrepreneurship;
- understand critically how opportunities can be shaped by different stages of a product life cycle;
- obtain an overview of the role of government in generating entrepreneurial opportunity.

Structure of the chapter

Following the introduction, this chapter examines the different sources and types of opportunities that lead to new product development and to the creation of new firms, including the impact of demand and supply side issues. In Part II we examine how technology – its availability and use – influences opportunity creation, identification and exploitation through new business formation. Part III then makes the connection between different opportunities and the stages of a life cycle of a product, showing how different stages yield various opportunities for innovation and new firm formation. The final part then explores ways in which institutions and especially governments influence the generation of new opportunities for innovation and entrepreneurship.

Introduction

This short chapter introduces the reader to the world of opportunities. Opportunity identification, creation and realization lie at the heart of innovation (as in new product, service and organizational development) and entrepreneurship (as in new firm formation with which to manage innovation). Opportunities are identified, created and realized in different ways in varied environments. This is due, in part, to what are called framework conditions. Framework conditions represent the composite set of institutions, culture and attitudes of people supporting or hindering entrepreneurial and innovative activity in a particular environment.

Against the backdrop of the framework conditions and the role of institutions in entrepreneurship development and the variety of situations (discussed in detail in Chapter 6) within which entrepreneurship is manifest, we also need to examine the demand- and supply-driven conditions for the realization of new opportunities. This means that while certain framework conditions may hold or evolve in certain contexts, it is important to see how entrepreneurs engage with those conditions and create possibilities for new ventures. For example, Richard Branson's decision to open Virgin Records was based on his search to find an alternative way of making his records available to his customers when his mail order business was threatened by a postal strike in the early 1970s. Earlier he had set up his mail order business selling records from shops with excess stock, taking advantage of the new legal situation of the 1960s (Clydesdale, 2010).

The example of Richard Branson suggests that while framework conditions may be important for understanding entrepreneurship development, the actions of entrepreneurs are a function of change. Entrepreneurs thrive when there is change, irrespective of the state of the economy. Riding the crest of a middle-class market wave in the United States, Henry Ford responded to the need for personal mobility among members of that class who wanted to distinguish themselves from others. Nirma Soap in India responded to the changes in lifestyles especially among the urban and rural poor by making a previously luxury cosmetic products available in affordable, smaller packs and sachets. Changes in populations due to increased birth rates, decreased mortality rates and immigration led to the growth of baby products in the 1950s, toys in the 1960s, the housing market in the 1970s (the impact of baby boomers), increased housing stock (to cater to needs of immigrants), and health care and retirement markets in western economies (allowing for ageing populations) (Clydesdale, 2010). Opportunities for entrepreneurial activities, for something 'new and different' are dependent on change. The purposeful organization of the search for change, and the systematic analysis of the opportunities such change might offer in both economic and social terms, is what systematic innovation all about (Drucker, 1985).

PART I: SOURCES AND TYPES OF OPPORTUNITY

Search and organization

Peter Drucker in his seminal book *Innovation and Entrepreneurship: Practice and Principles* (1985) identified seven sources of opportunity resulting from the exploitation of change. This view suggests that change may have occurred already and that the consequent asymmetries in information and resources among people is what leads to innovative activity. Identifying these sources means carrying out a diagnostic test of the specific areas of change – those that lie within a firm and others that can be found in the external environment. Table 2.1 shows these two categories of sources of opportunity – the internal or firm-specific sources, and the external or ex-enterprise or industry sources – that encapsulate Drucker's seven sources of 'innovative opportunity'.

The sources of opportunity identified here do not represent a hierarchy in the sense that any one opportunity is not necessarily more important than another. But as Drucker (1985) states, there are wide variations between these sources in terms of their reliability and predictability. New, scientific knowledge, for example, is the most time-consuming, expensive, high risk and least reliable source of opportunity. This may explain why new firms, created in the form of spin-offs from universities, are often not as successful in their emergence as

Table 2.1 Varying sources of innovative opportunity

Sources of opportunity	Types of opportunity	Examples of opportunity
A. Internal sources		
1. Unexpected	Unexpected success or failure	The choice faced by retail stores Macy's and Bloomingdale's when faced suddenly and unexpectedly by the growth of sales of appliances; Branson's entry into the music business due to a prolonged postal strike; use of titanium in costume jewellery inspiring its use for dashboard panels in cars
2. Incongruity	Between reality as it actually is and reality as it is assumed to be or as it 'ought to be'	Emergence of private heath care insurance to protect against rising costs and need for increased health care; the popularity of Netbook computers in western countries when they were originally designed for developing economies
3. Innovation	Based on process need	Incremental innovation arising out of conversion of enzyme that dissolves a ligament in cataract surgery by ensuring that the enzyme is kept fresh by way of refrigeration; touch screen technology on mobile telephones replacing keys for easier use
4. Changes in industry or market structure	Catches everyone unawares	Changes in the automobile industry for less energy-consuming, smaller or electric cars; changes in market structure, as in the global production process of various forms of manufacturing, supply chains and logistics because of the increased use of the Internet; changes in WTO membership and entry of new players in the pharmaceutical industry from developing countries challenging the R&D hegemony of larger companies
B. External sources		
5. Demographics	Changes in population	The making and use of robots to offset for an ageing population in developed economies
6. Changes in perception, mood and meaning	Attitudinal change	Attitudes to health and fitness providing opportunities for fitness centres; health care products
7. New knowledge	Scientific and non-scientific	Nanotechnology in manufacturing; biotechnology as in Genentech founders Robert Swanson of Kliener Perkins and Professor Herbert Boyer of University of California setting up a new firm to use bioscience to synthesize human insulin in 1978

Source: based on and adapted from Drucker (1985).

firms established elsewhere. While the former might be relying on perfecting the technology that emanates from the science in universities, the latter might be simply filling a market gap in terms of additional demand for an existing product.

To Drucker's list we could add perhaps another source of opportunity which lies simply in the recognition of differences in economic, social and natural environments. The clock radio's success in African and other developing countries was carved out of a conscious attempt to make radio available using simple forms of energy and its availability in particular environments. It was made available at a price that was affordable by the consumer because it did not need to rely on the unnecessary sophistication of technologies. Cost alone is not the factor of its success, but an informed approach to 'what works' best in specific markets. Similarly, the eradication of malaria in poorer nations is in part not necessarily dependent on the availability of expensive drugs but on the supply of good-quality mosquito nets. These examples represent conscious forms of enlightened intervention, either on the part of individuals or firms, and sometimes even of governments. We can review the different opportunities that arise as being either demand or supply led.

Demand-led opportunities

Typically, demand-led opportunities can stem from

- demographic changes (see above for examples on ageing or the effect of immigration);
- alterations in lifestyle, consumer taste and behaviour (new markets in sports and high-fashion leather products for a firm making saddlery products in a declining market);
- future expectations (productive opportunities such as the buying and selling of shares or unproductive ones in the securitization of mortgages);
- spillovers from changes in complementary industries (potential growth in the tourism industry as a result of cheaper air fares or new energy sources as a result of a hike in oil prices); and
- improvements in economic conditions (the rise of consumption among the increasing middle classes in China and India).

These changes can be identified in business cycles and the levels of investment associated with different stages of the cycle. Investment tends to follow confidence levels in the state of the economy, quite often leading to irrational behaviour on the part of investors. Levels of investment by both government and business have an impact on opportunities available in the marketplace. At a time of economic buoyancy when confidence levels are likely to be high, businesses may invest if they can take advantage of a growing market. Investment in plants and factories could lead to new jobs, which in turn will fuel growth in consumption expenditure. However, a fall in economic output and any resulting decline could have the opposite effect, dampening opportunities. In a downswing, opportunities that are hit hardest tend to be in capital-intensive industries, which are most vulnerable because of both the drop in value of capital items and the drying up of capital because of loss of investor confidence.

Often, the fall can be a sharp and prolonged one, especially if the preceding stage of economic growth occurred on the back of a speculative bonanza, as we have witnessed in recent times and since 2007. The speculative trade-off between real productivity and the increase in the value of investments, generally favouring the latter outcome during such unproductive bull runs, can leave investors and ordinary savers with very little purchase as they find it difficult to choose between a safe and a secure investment (Clydesdale, 2010). During such times, it is usual to find government spending rise as they try to bail out various institutions and their respective economies. Any quick reversal of such action leading to cuts in public expenditure could have serious and damaging consequences for opportunity creation and growth since there is no other form of finance available to boost demand and generate new opportunity.

Supply-driven opportunities

Almost all industries and businesses depend on a reliable and efficient source of supplies to enable them to realize newly identified or existing opportunities. Such supplies are affected by the price of resources necessary for production purposes. If there are a number of users of the same resource, their combined and conflicting needs can lead to an increase in the cost of the resource, especially if the resource is in short supply. Equally, their demand for the resource could influence industries dependent on such a resource to push for cost-saving technologies to be introduced by the providers so that economies of scale and scope can be exploited. The recent deliberations over the cost and dangers of carbon emissions, for example, are compelling users of fossil fuels to consider alternative technologies such as hydrogen, and the producers of high-emission-bearing sources of energy such as oil to explore new cost-saving technologies or various forms of manipulation of supply and price. The higher the number of sellers in the market, the greater is the likelihood of prices coming down in that market. This is demonstrated currently by the high levels of turbulence in the consumer car market. In such a buyers' market, and with high rates of competition, business failure is more likely to occur, thereby driving down opportunities for new ventures.

Other market-based strategies include forms of hedging, such as holding stocks of commodities in expectation of future gain or selling high in anticipation of a drop in prices. Such opportunities are predicated on knowledge of the market and indeed on the nature of the products or services being traded. As Clydesdale (2010) notes, such activity is unlikely to take place when, for example, perishable products are under consideration.

A major driver of opportunity creation is technology. Lack of competition might prevent identification of technological opportunities as complacent oligopolies and large firm players raise the threshold of entry for new firms. Their slowness to adapt to technological change eventually brings the barriers down as nimble new operators take the market away from the incumbents. The next section examines the different forms of technological opportunities that are created at the interstices between science, technology and the market.

PART II: TECHNOLOGICAL OPPORTUNITY AND ENTREPRENEURIAL FIRMS

Klevorick *et al.* (1995) have argued that the set of technological opportunities available in any one industry is a fundamental determinant of technical advance in that business. They postulate three distinctive sources of technological opportunities:

- advances in scientific understanding;
- technological advances originating in other industries and in other private and governmental institutions; and
- feedbacks from an industry's own technological advances.

Generic and specific advances in scientific understanding

Advances in scientific understanding account for major developments such as the radio, the atomic bomb, nano technology and biotechnology. In other words, major pieces of scientific research such as Maxwell's work in fundamental physics (leading to the development of the radio) provide the bedrock of such developments. But direct and simple or linear linkages may not be the rule, mainly because of varied time lags between the research, the invention and the innovation, intricate and complex feedback mechanisms and flows, with information on opportunities emerging at unexpected stages of development. Moreover, unlike applied R&D activity where the emphasis is on problem-solving, basic science does not set such objectives. Where basic and advanced scientific understanding does provide for opportunity is in the replenishment of the stock of knowledge that diminishes over time in technological application. Universities and colleges, therefore, produce new graduates with new sources of knowledge with which to support technological development.

With regard to specific scientific and engineering disciplines, such as metallurgy, materials science, electric engineering or computer science, research at any level is often focused on supporting technical progress and enhancing problem-solving capacity. It could, therefore, be argued that advances in scientific understanding plays two distinctive roles in generating opportunities: one by way of increasing the stock of knowledge and the other as a flow of directly relevant knowledge (Klevorick *et al.*, 1995).

External origins of technological opportunities

There are numerous examples of technological opportunities in one industry opening up or advancing the cause of other industries. The invention of the transistor has unleashed considerable opportunities in radio, television, calculators and computers, even though the inventor was working in a telephonic equipment firm. Antecedents in technological development account for such spillovers. Watt's steam engine, for example, would not have been possible if the accurate and uniform cavities that such an engine required were not developed earlier in the form of machinery used to bore metal (Klevorick, 1995).

Government laboratories conducting research in specific scientific areas have also contributed to the generation of opportunity in technologies, as have universities and various private research institutions. The work done by Tim Berners Lee in CERN was directly instrumental in the eventual rise of what is now the ubiquitous Internet.

Hippel's research on end-user innovation (1976, 1977, 2003, 2005) has documented systematically the significance of user feedback and user-led innovation, leading to what he refers to as the 'democratisation of innovation'. This trajectory of innovation offers considerable advantages over traditional manufacturer-centric innovation, according to Hippel (2005). The relationship between the manufacturer and the user, as between the seller of a product and the user, is often blurred within an existing organization. Hippel (2005) refers to Boeing as a manufacturer of aeroplanes but also as a user of machine tools. It is a manufacturer-innovator when it develops innovations for its aeroplanes. However, when Boeing considers innovations in metal-forming machinery which it has developed for in-house use in building aeroplanes, it operates as a user-innovator. This mix of users (who benefit directly from the innovation) and the manufacturer or service provider embraces individuals, businesses and sometimes non-governmental organizations in a range of industries from software development to manufacturing, and across global, networked platforms, as the development of the Linux operating system demonstrates. Some of these forms of interaction are part of what are described as open innovation systems; others take the form of closely coupled or integrated network systems (Chesbrough, 2008).

Feedback-based technological opportunity

Opportunities generated through feedback from the use of technology for a particular process to potential application in another have been described by Rosenberg (1969) as 'compulsive sequences'. Innovative efforts in industry are often focused on a set of distinctive problems and their solution. When such problems are resolved they generate new technical problems that require new solutions so that the benefits from the original breakthrough can be fully realized.

The adoption of new materials for advancing a technical process, such as in the use of ceramics to replace parts made previously by metal in building aircraft engines, can indicate that there might be wider applications for ceramics. The alternative use might help to reduce not only the cost of materials but also maintenance costs. Under these circumstances, new research and technological enquiry into the properties of ceramics can be considered together with the possible replacement of other parts of the aircraft made from metal (Klevorick *et al.*, 1995).

Production strangleholds by larger firms on their smaller suppliers can drive the latter to consider alternative outcomes. This author worked with several small manufacturing firms in the UK supplying high-quality metallic paint to large car manufacturers in the UK who were concerned about such a grip on their capacity to make paint products. Their strong belief in other applications of their products and the need to break out of rigid contracts led them to ask a simple question: 'How do we find a better customer?' The technological opportunity was being compromised by a constraint on organizational arrangements for better access to market opportunities. This led to a search for both new opportunities and an action-learning-based R&D project with these small suppliers with which to change direction for business activities in the immediate future.

Central to the discussion above is the learning process that underpins the realization of benefits from all three forms of technological opportunity referred to by Klevorick, *et al.* (1995). Such learning affords a triangulation of different conditions – opportunity, appropriability and demand – to enable entrepreneurial firms to reap the best advantage from the innovation process. Many of these opportunities and the conditions referred to above are also a function of the stage of development of any particular product in any industry. Different opportunities and varied constraints obtain during specific stages in any product life cycle.

PART III: ENTREPRENEURIAL OPPORTUNITIES AND PRODUCT LIFE CYCLE

Low and Abrahamson (1997) suggested that not all entrepreneurs can take advantage of opportunities at different points in the product life cycle because of the need for differentiated strategies for each stage of the evolution of the market for the product.

When a new product is made available in the market for the first time we see the emergence of an industry. The pioneers are essentially creative people who have broken down various barriers and made new combinations to meet the needs or wants of the user of such a product. These are hugely uncertain times, and the greater the emphasis on technology in the making of the product the more likely it is for this uncertainty to be exacerbated. Finance may not be the motive for bringing the product to the market, but rather the creative impulse to solve problems and in some cases the desire to acquire a reputation in society. Opportunities in such circumstances are circumscribed by uncertainty and ambiguity, which as Knight (1921) observed combine to pose a greater challenge than the risk of investing money in the business. These are moments of rare opportunities, which Bhide's 'promising' Type B entrepreneurs can recognize too well because they cannot secure financial capital from either venture capitalists or banks (Bhide, 2008).

Opportunities at the growth stage are more likely to surface when managerial responsibilities are combined with entrepreneurial nous. The sharp, intelligent observer of the market rather than the creative entrepreneur is more likely to make use of these opportunities. The market is more competitive, and there is less ambiguity and more information with which to make judgements. Interestingly, venture capitalists are specifically interested in these situations because they seek track records of both the entrepreneurs and the industry within which the new product is being launched. The entrepreneur derives advantage through more information gleaned from networks and associations of existing players. The making and selling of a product that differentiates itself from similar products in the same market becomes a viable proposition when there are enough buyers who demand something different in the characteristics or the make-up of the product. Their collective strength in the market is an opportunity for an entrepreneur to capture a niche in that market.

Markets that have reached maturity tend to stop growing any further. Intense competition characterizes the operation of such a marketplace, and only limited opportunities are available to those entrepreneurs who can take real advantage of profound knowledge of that market and the product on offer. Such opportunities are generally available to insiders with considerable experience within an industry who seek to detach themselves from their existing place of work. They are often late entrants, such as Dell in the PC market, which distinguished its business through customized, mail order distribution channels (Clydesdale, 2010). Anticipating changes in the market to seek and convert opportunities to real business activity is not an easy task as the structure of the market shifts.

Consideration of the different stages of the product life cycle raises questions about the right timing for entering a particular business and starting a new venture. We note a fairly complex set of circumstances and motivations that interact with each other to determine what could be achieved and when. The individual or team-based entrepreneur's motivations for starting a new venture is as much a function of his or her environment, the conditions that prevail in the environment (see Chapter 6), and the type of product and the stage of its evolution in the market. To this cocktail we can add the role of government in shaping or directing entrepreneurial opportunities.

PART IV: GOVERNMENT-INFLUENCED OPPORTUNITIES

The role of government is generally seen to be at odds with entrepreneurship and opportunity creation or realization. Rather like the value of higher education, government action does not appear to accrue any benefits for the entrepreneurial class. Or so some critics would observe! While the role of government policy is the subject of separate chapters (see Chapters 6 and 10), it is worth mentioning here that changes in government policy can have major effects on entrepreneurial opportunity. The Chinese government's decision to open up the Chinese market for foreign direct investment and mass manufacturing has made China the factory of the world with both state-owned and private enterprises basking in the opportunities created and realized in a breathtakingly short period of time. The Indian government's belated realization of the value of the Indian software industry has led it now to pass a range of favourable legislation to boost this highly successful, globally based software outsourcing and development industry. Similarly, the various European governments' interventionist strategies in the telecoms industry have enabled telecom operators in Europe to be leaders in the global telecommunications market.

Governments manage significant resources and set rules for both the deployment of these resources and the way in which the markets operate. Incentive-oriented strategies and policies, which could include prioritizing certain forms of expenditure, can be highly productive and lead to favourable entrepreneurial outcomes. On the other hand, an over reliance on market forces that ignores the travails of market failure can produce the most unfortunate results. The recent openness to financial services-led light regulatory mechanisms could not withstand the high levels of rent-seeking and destructive business activities in that sector (Baumol, 1990, 2007).

At a relatively mundane level, governments use legislation and other policy instruments to change behaviour. Strict laws on drink-driving have created a climate of much greater caution among drivers, while the absence of enforcement of relatively 'looser' legislation on the use of hand-held telephones while driving has not had any impact on driver behaviour. These laws opened up opportunities for entrepreneurs to produce alcohol-free drinks and various Bluetooth-based devices for car drivers and their mobile telephones. At another level, the reorganization of the National Health Service has meant opportunities for the private sector in various forms of diagnostic and health care services.

Conclusion

This brief excursion in opportunity land has helped us to track the sources of opportunity and the ways different types of opportunity are identified, created and realized. Different opportunities and the ability to take advantage of them lead to change. Change has implications for entrepreneurs who create new firms with which to both manage the change process and generate wealth through new products and services. Both demand- and supply-side factors impinge on the opportunity-creation process as do technology and the different points in the life cycle of a product. The intervention and action of governments attempting to facilitate entrepreneurs to best realize opportunities for productive economic outcomes also contribute to new opportunities.

Opportunities abound in all sorts of environments, and economic prosperity is not necessarily a provider of entrepreneurial opportunities. We can find in deprived conditions greater incentives for identifying opportunity without need for the provision of special support. Survival and necessity can engender unusual entrepreneurial outcomes, especially when they are clearly identified by entrepreneurs engaged in seeking opportunities for social change. Not all such opportunities and the various forms of intervention lead necessarily to productive gain or positive economic outcomes. Quite often, as Baumol (1990, 2007) has shown, opportunities are directed towards rent-seeking or rent-destroying activities, or unproductive and destructive entrepreneurship. Often such negative activities use the same opportunities, resources and institutions to realize personal gain only. We shall address this issue later in the book.

The multiple sources of opportunity provide for a complex and uncertain environment, which entrepreneurs need to navigate. They do so by creating firms. In the chapters that follow we will be examining the wide range of economic, social, institutional and other factors that drive, facilitate, restrict and in some cases hinder opportunities and the ability of entrepreneurs to make best use of them in productive ways.

Mini case study 2.1: Nuru Energy and lighting-up opportunities in Africa

Some years ago Rwanda was known for a particular wave of notoriety at a certain point in time of its recent history. It remains an economically poor country but there is change in the trajectory of its development. The Bugesera region of the Rwanda is known for its sorghum farming. It is also known for its poverty. Most villagers in this region use kerosone lamps for their lighting, and as a result their poverty is accompanied by air pollution and lung disease. But the availability of a generator and LED lights has opened up new opportunities for economic and social change.

At the centre of the change process is an entrepreneur, Sameer Hajee, the co-founder and CEO of a London-based start-up, Nuru Energy. His vision and actions support a widow, Annonciata Mukandekwe, a 50-year-old basket weaver who spends an hour a day pedalling a small generator charging LED lights. She sells the lights to her fellow villagers, and in her first 2 weeks in business she has sold 140 of the $6.58 lamps. She earns $3.78 per day, more than triple the daily income in rural Rwanda. In the process she helps her fellow villagers to obtain safe and clean lighting at about one-tenth the cost of kerosene.

Mukandekwe's angel, Sameer Hajee, has an Insead MBA. While working for at the UN and especially at Freeplay Energy, a successful London enterprise selling crank-up radios around the world, Hajee was inspired to act. At Freeplay its Foundation was piloting a micro business model to provide foot-powered generators to the rural parts of Africa. Instead of the usual transfer of technology to Africa through donations, Hajee and Freeplay thought of getting technology into the hands of as many people as possible by creating sustainable businesses managed by local people. He left Freeplay and formed Nuru a for-profit organisation with 11 employees, in 2009. He obtained seed money of $200,000 from the 'World Bank Lighting Africa' initiative and started arranging microloans for entrepreneurs to buy the lamps and an additional $200 to buy Nuru's bike-pedal electric charger, which it manufactures together with the patent-pending LED lights in China.

The typical African business owner of the bikes takes about 6 months of pedalling to earn enough cash to pay back the loan together with the interest. Any extra earnings is pure profit for the entrepreneur. Nuru also provides entrepreneurs with accountancy training. In 2010 Nuru helped to establish 70 businesses in Rwanda which provide lighting to the equivalent of 7,000 families.

Hajee envisions a move from lighting to enabling African entrepreneurs make a living out of charging cellphones, radios and other domestic appliances using his pedal generators. As long as Hajee is able to attract fresh capital for the microloans, he is bound towards creating a genuine platform for entrepreneurial opportunity in Africa. In exploring demand led opportunities together with those influenced by technology and supported by institutional finance, Nuru and the case of LED lights and pedal generators demonstrate the power of entrepreneurship in sezing on productive opportunity for economic and social change.

(Source: adapted from Dumaine (2010); *Fortune*, 5 July 2010)

Self-assessment questions

1. How are opportunities for new venture creation generated?
2. What are the different sources of opportunity identified by Drucker? Consider each of them to identify new opportunities that have opened up for entrepreneurs in the past two years.
3. What role does technology play in providing opportunities for entrepreneurship?
4. Can government policy be a source (or a hindrance) for innovation and entrepreneurship?

3 Entrepreneurship theories
The economic arguments

Learning outcomes

This chapter will enable the reader to:

- identify and specify critically the elements of key economic theories of entrepreneurship;
- explain the foundations and limitations of economic theories of entrepreneurship;
- explain critically the differences in assumption and the approaches to the analysis of these theories;
- recognize the range and depth of economic analysis of entrepreneurship; and
- identify ways in which the theories can help to illuminate and explain the practice of entrepreneurship.

Structure of the chapter

This chapter introduces some of most important explanations of entrepreneurship drawn from different economic theories. It starts with an explanation of the rather difficult emergence of entrepreneurship in economic theory. It traces the historical roots of economic growth theory and the glimpses of entrepreneurship that can be found in the writings of the early theorists and their interest in equilibrium theory, concepts of risk, arbitrage, the political economy, marginal utility and the prescient Marshallian ideas of knowledge, learning, partial equilibrium and organizational collaboration. Part II then offers a critique of the traditional approaches through brief references to leading figures such as Hayek before examining in some detail the work of the masters of entrepreneurship theory including Israel Kirzner and, especially, Joseph Schumpeter in Part III. Part IV explores some of the key concepts of risk, uncertainty and ambiguity that inform a considerable amount of modern writing on the subject together with references to insights from major economists such as Keynes and ideas of information and arbitration propounded by Mark Casson. Part V then covers briefly three relatively new areas of theory: the evolutionary approach to entrepreneurship with its focus on existing organizations, routines and choice based on the work of Nelson and Winter; the idea of incentives and productive, unproductive and destructive entrepreneurship as developed by William Baumol; and the idea of large firms, connected firms and networks of enterprises. The chapter concludes with signposts for other critical theoretical work explaining different manifestations of entrepreneurship in our economic and social lives.

PART I: INTRODUCTION

While a large number of economists have made significant and interesting contributions to the subject of entrepreneurship, mainstream economic theories have tended to ignore the role of new venture creation and indeed the entrepreneur in making sense of the dynamics of economic progress and development.

> Surely, this neglect must give us pause? It is a scandal that nowadays students of economics can spend years in the study of the subject before hearing the term 'entrepreneur', that courses in economic development provide exhaustive lists of all the factors impeding or accelerating economic growth without mentioning the conditions under which entrepreneurship languishes or flourishes, and that learned comparisons between 'socialism' and 'capitalism' are virtually silent about the role of entrepreneurship under regimes of collective rather than private entrepreneurship. (Blaug, 2000)

Yet the many problems that economists deal with – the allocation of scarce resources, markets and their efficiency, choice and behaviour – are all highly relevant to the study of entrepreneurship. Entrepreneurs make economic decisions about entering markets, producing goods with the right mix of materials and other ingredients, source supplies at the optimum or least cost, price their products in a competitive marketplace to optimize, if not maximize, value, and most importantly generate custom with a view to creating value.

PART II: ECONOMIC THOUGHT AND ENTREPRENEURSHIP: THE TRADITION

The concept of equilibrium and entrepreneurship

Let us consider why entrepreneurship has been ignored in economics for a long period of time. It is the concept of equilibrium, or the maintenance of established patterns of demand and supply, around which most economists have built their analyses and work. Frank Hahn (1984) argues that an economy is in equilibrium when it generates messages that do not cause agents to change the theories or the policies that they hold or pursue. Thus 'agents' make decisions for resource allocation, growth, pricing, product portfolio development and service delivery according to previously formulated plans and routines, centred around two critical questions – one that explains how markets work and the other that evaluates how well they work. To deal with these questions economists depend upon

- full information (on individual choices, resource availability and constraints, production and production processes);
- the rational human being, based on maximizing any opportunity available for oneself;
- circumstances where no one at the end of the day can really improve themself because if they have full information and if everyone is into maximizing opportunities, then paradoxically no one gains unless they make someone worse off; and
- where there is perfect competition (where everyone buys or sells at a given price).

Under the conditions stated above, the entrepreneur, who generally upsets the apple cart (the equilibrium), either does not have any role to play or is someone who simply tinkers with entrepreneurial possibilities based on what is already available in the marketplace. Equilibrium theories ignore issues such as the distribution of income or the type and nature of preferences individuals make, which can be critical in decisions about the purchase or sale of products and services. In fact, an entrepreneur introducing a new product or service poses a threat to the equilibrium structure.

In trying to explain the absence of the entrepreneur in microeconomic theory, Barreto (1989) has investigated this 'disappearance' in detail. He traces the historical basis of the concept of entrepreneurship in various schools of economics and compares them with the evolution of the theory of the firm in economics. He concludes:

a) the theory of the firm is based upon the production function, the logic of rational choice and the environment of perfect information, while entrepreneurship is made up of innovation, uncertainty bearing, and coordination and arbitrage;
b) the entrepreneur enjoys the same amount of visibility (or invisibility) in modern microeconomics with the maturation of firm theory as the orthodox framework of modern microeconomics gives exposure to the tenants of firm theory;
c) innovation does not fit in with the concept of firm where the production function is given and where the logic of rational choice demands adherence to an ends-means framework;
d) the concept of uncertainty, the hallmark of the entrepreneurship process, is difficult to conceptualize, but with the theory of the firm perfect knowledge of present and future exist because of perfect information;
e) the process of arbitrage arising out of asymmetric information that entrepreneurs engage in cannot be allowed in an environment of perfect information and the logic of rational choice.

But where did these ideas come from? To answer that question we need to delve into history. Although no attempt is being made to capture the depth and breadth of economic thought through the centuries, a quick overview is worth considering if only to try to locate the entrepreneur in a historical context.

The political economy and entrepreneurship

Casting our minds back to what may be described as the first great period of classical economic thought, we find in the work of Adam Smith, Thomas Malthus, David Ricardo, John Stuart Mill and even Karl Marx a preoccupation with issues of distribution of income and power among social classes and its relation to social and economic change, production and value underlying market exchange and the allocation of resources in a competitive, private enterprise economy. In essence what these philosophers and political economists were attempting to do was to connect economic behaviour to its social and political context. Many of these questions about resource allocation and economic behaviour were being dealt with in a given context, where change and the *role of entrepreneurs were a function of what was available to them.* Entrepreneurs would mediate with these available resources to ensure that best value was obtained from such allocation in a given political and social context. What mattered were the institutions that governed the processes and the methods by which these functions took place.

In his seminal work, *Inquiry into the Nature and Causes of the Wealth of Nations* (1776), Adam Smith (1723–1790) established the conceptual foundations for the analysis of how the market economy works. In doing so, he also influenced the way economists considered the role of the entrepreneur. For Adam Smith there was no difference between the *capitalist as the provider of stock and the entrepreneur as the ultimate decision maker.* The function of entrepreneurship in the economy was also ignored by Smith, and it was this lack of distinction between the capitalist and the entrepreneurial functions that provided the basis for classical economists. The entrepreneur or the capitalist earned their profits as long as the worker wanted less than what he/she added to production. As a reasonable and rational human being, such a worker would rather remain in employment than seek higher wages. However, as we shall see later, Smith's pioneering ideas about the division of labour and specialization were to have a profound effect on our understanding of how new firms are created.

The French economist Jean Baptiste Say (1767–1832) had already argued that higher levels of yield generated by the production process resulted from the smooth functioning of the market exchange process. In this environment the entrepreneur 'shifts economic resources out of an area of lower and into a higher productivity and greater yield'. Say went further than other economists of his time by arguing that the function of entrepreneurship in the economy was that of combining the means of production into an organism.[1] The role of the entrepreneur was that of a *broker who organizes and combines the means of production with the aim of creating goods and services that have value or utility.* The entrepreneur carried out this role of production on his own behalf, implying that he/she also took on the risk of doing so.

Say's observations had long been anticipated by an Irish-born banker, Richard Cantillon (*c.* 1680–1734), who recognized that imbalances between demand and supply and prices create opportunities in a marketplace. The entrepreneur identifies these opportunities by *arbitraging* (buying cheaply and selling at a higher but unpredictable price in an uncertain environment). His or her actions eventually lead to the realization of equilibrium, but this does not happen without the entrepreneur having both foresight and the willingness to take risks. While Cantillon probably fleshed out the concept of equilibrium, he was less concerned with the bigger picture of changes in production conditions and social and economic relations.

Marginal utility function

It was in the latter part of the eighteenth and mid nineteenth centuries that another group of Europeans, Stanley Jevons, Leon Walras, von Thunen, von Mangoldt, Bohm-Bawerk, Carl Menger and Weiser, moved the focus of economic thought to the question of allocation of resources and distribution of income among individuals. Instead of the broader concept of the political economy, what now gained currency was a quantitative approach to formulating ideas of 'marginal utility'. Instead of costs of production and supply, what became prominent first were subjective factors of utility and demand to help determine values of market exchange, and then incremental benefits and costs of alternative individual decisions, based on rational choice. 'Economic men' continued to be concerned with seeking economic gain through exchange of supply and demand in markets that were competitive and made up of many small-scale industries. Competition was dependent on access to technologies and enterprises grew if they could overcome the problem of diminishing returns and scale diseconomies.

The methodological subjectivism (and indeed Menger's methodological individualism) of the main Austrian and German economists examined economic phenomena as relations among people, as opposed to objects. This relationship was among *individuals* who were the main actors in any economy, not their group or class. Consequently, and unlike the natural sciences, economic theory is dependent on various social, cultural and economic conceptions that govern human actions, and cannot disregard the perceptions, wishes, desires, idiosyncrasies and views of the subject of its study – people. What individuals do, based on their awareness of particular situations, determines changes in the economic and social landscape. In this context, the entrepreneur is a change agent who by being aware of given situations and discrepancies in the marketplace transforms resources into useful products and services.

Thus far the idea that the equilibrium position is the most satisfactory position for all individuals and organizations in the economic system went unchallenged. Suggestions of any profits over and above those necessary to reward owners of enterprise for their productive resources were excluded from any possible consideration. Changes were affordable in the equilibrium model but the necessary and rational mediation of capitalists and entrepreneurs ensured that resource allocation was optimized and that imbalances were corrected quickly. There was perhaps some contention over the primary unit of economic or entrepreneurial activity – an individual or a class of people – but the broad parameters of economic analysis did not ask questions about why certain changes occurred when they did and why there were uneven patterns in such change processes.

Alfred Marshall and local production

Back in the nineteenth century Alfred Marshall (1842–1924) continued to ignore any possible distinction between entrepreneurial and other forms of economic activity. Human beings were 'impelled' to change and progress, so change was integral to life and business. Despite using 'marginal utility' theory, Marshall's focus on supply and cost issues enabled him to observe that sellers can use customer loyalty to enjoy a degree of local monopoly and that attempts to increase sales beyond that market required additional marketing costs or lower prices. The local factor of production and market exchange were key concerns of Marshall who also believed that while rational people might have spending power they might not use their power in certain circumstances. Changing preferences, the use of human potential and increases in productivity and innovation became his main concerns alongside the actions of the state and voluntary ones of individuals.

Marshall (1920) argued that new activities gave rise to new wants in the long run. This meant that activities were not strictly linked to wants as most economists believed in his time, but that specific goods and services were used as alternative means of satisfying different general desires, including variety, distinctiveness and excellence. Self-reliance, independence of thought and action, mediated choice, forethought and prediction were the main characteristics of modern industrial life, and these characteristics were to be found in both competition and collaboration among people. These characteristics enabled better use of human potential, which in turn encouraged prudent consumption, higher levels of productivity and innovation. The proper use of human potential meant that factors of production systems, resources, technologies and the products could be changed incrementally and cumulatively involving all people. The basis of change and that of the effective use of human potential was *knowledge*.

Knowledge, learning and organization

Marshall first wrote about the knowledge that an individual needed to have of his or her own trade, including the ability to forecast movements in the patterns of consumption and production, understanding of customers, suppliers and competitors, and identifying an opportunity for making and supplying a new commodity that either meets a real new want or improves the processes of producing an old commodity. In other words, being alert to opportunities and circumstances based on knowledge of one's trade were key, daily requirements of the business person. *Experience* was critical. As experience helped improve products and processes, the new knowledge base generated new activities, leading to new wants.

Complementing the capacity for knowledge of one's trade was Marshall's requirement for the business person to run and manage an organization. Choice of and trust in people, the catalytic power to encourage the power of enterprise and creativity among such people through the creation of an information and learning system, are the hallmarks of a successful business person or entrepreneur.

The significance of *learning* in an organization and the time that it takes for such learning to truly embed in and influence organizational activities pose difficulties for equilibrium theories. Learning may not take effect in time to enable a return to equilibrium that traditional economists hankered for at that time. Instead, Marshall proposed the idea of partial equilibrium that allowed for business people, economists and policy makers to focus on a part of the economy at any time. In looking at things in part and in enabling increased productivity, incremental change is a central consideration. Trial and error, close observations and alertness to modifications are all based on prior knowledge, and it is this process that helps to increase business profits.

Many firms and collaboration

There are of course many firms and organizations in the same and in other trades. Within each trade, various individual businesses organize and increase their knowledge incrementally, but their actions and wants are all different. The individual's perceptions and temperament together with those of external opportunities and resources influence such actions. Scale advantages might help the larger firm to introduce new products and services, but Marshall was of the view that the dominance of an industry by a few large firms could only lead to stagnation. It was as if a strong moral imperative underpinned Marshall's thinking. He was conscious of the distinction that firms that thrive in a competitive environment may not be those that benefit that environment the most.

To mitigate the loss of 'beneficial' businesses it was necessary to look at ways in which to support enterprises (as for example retail co-operatives supporting their more vulnerable producer co-operative counterparts). To this end collaboration was a foil to Darwinian natural selection, and this was possible with increased specialization of businesses. The more there was specialization and the break-up of stages of production, the greater the possibility for smaller firms to counter the advantages of larger enterprises.

Marshall did not stop at the level of a single industry to explain the relationships between businesses and the value of collaboration. He was also interested in inter-industry linkages that increase the knowledge base. Such linkages were both horizontal, across different industries requiring use of a similar skills base, technologies, and materials, and vertical, along the value chain connecting the supplier, producer and distributor. Both formal structures and informal arrangements (including networks, and what is often referred to as 'untraded interdependencies') were the outcome of the links between firms, and these structures and arrangements were to be best found in a particular nineteenth-century phenomenon, the industrial district.

Marshall's unique elaboration of the structure of business at the level of the firm, the industry (similar firms) and the industrial district (complementary firms) was a distinctive contribution to economic theory. In explaining the organizational contexts of firms and business or entrepreneurial activity based on incremental change, Marshall's economic system was not dependent on either external data or induced, internal creativity to maintain or disturb the equilibrium process.

The other significant part of Marshall's unique elaboration was, first, the value that he placed on knowledge and especially on different knowledge streams that flowed with individual firms, from one firm to another in the same industry and across different industries. Many a modern conception of the firm or indeed of economic growth draws from Marshall – ideas of externalities, traded and untraded knowledge, local and global networks, clusters of similar and related firms, which taken together constitute an innovation ecosystem. This amazingly modern view of how a firm operates in terms of its capabilities, competencies and other resources paved the way for significant new developments in entrepreneurship and the economics of entrepreneurship and innovation.

Business life cycles

It was the life cycle of the individual firm, and the birth of new and the death of old firms, that generated improvements in both products and services and the quality of business. This Darwinian approach to the life cycle also embraced the ability of the firm to create, absorb and use knowledge. The firm's capacity to vary its capacity to do so depended on the initial but imperfect knowledge base that the entrepreneur had at his or her disposal. The new founder of a business might not have sufficient knowledge but could rely on drive, energy and ambition to compensate for the lack of experience. Thus psychological issues of motivation were real in Marshall's reckoning. Marshall shows much faith in the new founder (and especially those who were 'born elsewhere') learning through trial and error and allowing the firm's organization to evolve and structure the learning process. This view has remarkable correspondence with modern writings on and the prevailing wisdom about minority or ethnic entrepreneurs on foreign shores with what Florida (2006) refers to as global creative talent, who are the architects of the development of cities.

The ability of the new firm to grow was dependent on the time it took to expand the organization together with the knowledge base and the difficulties associated with developing a market. The further a business was from its consumer, the greater the extent of difficulty in forming and building a market. To overcome this problem firms needed to enter into collaboration with other firms, horizontally and vertically, and acquire legitimacy and recognition among peers and competitors. In networks and through collaborative engagement in business clusters, firms learnt the value of mutual interdependency and were, therefore, able to grow. Marshall was a strong believer in systems, first at the level of the network and of firms interacting with one another, but also in terms of how he interpreted the various functions of firms. Marketing and production were closely related as part of the process of adjustment of supply and demand, even if they were separate activities in an organization. To make a customer buy a product could be part of what we know as marketing, but all that was necessary to satisfy a customer and make the product available makes marketing part of the production function.

In understanding how growth takes place and the barriers to such growth, Marshall was acutely aware that products and services declined over their life cycle as new technologies were introduced and new markets emerged. This had a multiplier effect on knowledge. What Marshall also recognized was the psychology of those who had built up a successful business and who after both the passage and the ravages of time decided to call it a day. Succession in Marshall's time as it is today, was a serious concern. For him, many a child of a business person going to university to improve their life chances meant a death knell for succession, as the child learnt to despise his father's trade (the male was dominant in this debate during Marshall's time!).

One way of avoiding decline was to transform the business into a 'joint stock' company, even though Marshall acknowledged that the bureaucratic nature of these companies did not always compensate for the availability of capital. In other words the real, entrepreneurial business could not be found in the larger firm.

Marshall's preoccupations did not sit comfortably with the growing popularity of the larger joint stock company and the changing economics of his latter days. Subsequently, much of what he wrote was abandoned by economists. Yet his insights into the role of the dynamic enterprise, the process of learning and continuous improvement not only echoes the view of Schumpeter but has particular resonance in modern economic thinking. The idea of collaboration alongside the need to build the individual firm, the mutuality of incentives within the network, and the dispersal and localization of knowledge have all been part of recent theorizing and relevant policy formulation.

PART III: CRITIQUING THE TRADITIONAL APPROACH

Critics of the 'grand tradition' of economic thought were not slow in calling into question some of the ideas of the market economy. Socialist thinkers, including Marx, linked the market economy to inequalities, poverty, the exclusion of the working class from the fruits of their labour, and various contradictions in the process of capitalist transformation. Others, such as Veblen and Rogers, paid much greater attention to the technological, cultural, psychological and institutional factors of economic life. The idea of business cycles challenged Say's proposition. Intellectual ferment was more the order of the day over the next few decades as new ideas about market structure, value and capital, and the legal and institutional foundations of capitalism were developed by economists such as Joan Robinson, John Hicks and John Commons. A significant development occurred with the publication of some of the most compelling work on money, employment, public expenditure and the irrationality (or 'animal spirits') of human beings, by John Maynard Keynes.

Despite the creation of hugely meaningful and varied landmarks of economic thought over two centuries, the defining feature of such thinking was that of life governed by given circumstances and the necessary adjustments to the interrelationships among different economic variables, all under static conditions. The stationary, general equilibrium model helped to match demand with supply in both product and resource markets, enabled individuals to maximize economic gain by adjusting demand and supplies at given market prices. Land and labour and the market value of the marginal utility of these two resources allowed for the distribution of income in the form of 'rent' or 'wages'. The preferences of consumers helped to allocate resources. Rational assumptions about competition and equal credit eliminated surplus values, and all profits and interest were the result of productive and profitable investment.

Everything has its price and all prices are known to everyone. As the economy moves along this steady course, small, marginal and incremental increases in the work force, savings and capital accumulation, adaptation to consumer preferences and external data became the order the day. Consumers determine changes; business people respond passively to demand and cost conditions, deriving no special income beyond that of rent for the use of their land and wages for their services. In this equilibrium-driven environment, the entrepreneur is at best subsumed in the economic process, like any other business person, or at worst is seen as a threat to the economy.

Neo-classical thinking has its intellectual merits. It offers an analytical framework for the search for a solution to a perfectly formulated economic problem, namely how best to allocate resources based on who knows what and when. In other words, information is a given resource. However, in entrepreneurship the very search for such information about 'who knows what and when' is a central activity of the entrepreneur. The dynamic approach of the entrepreneur does not find house room in the static environment of the equilibrium state where decision-making becomes a mechanical application of mathematical rules for optimization. Instead of a theory of the competitive process in any economy, what we have is a theory of the outcome of that process in an equilibrium state (Blaug, 2000).

The ideal state of equilibrium, like the perfect goal in football, may be possible but that does not mean it is necessarily attainable. The question that then arises is as to how equilibrium is achieved. Was it possible that all the data was publicly available so that either central planners in a state-driven system or economists could draw on that data to allocate resources efficiently?

It was Hayek (1937) who explained that in reality the data that was used for analysis was randomly distributed in people (in their heads and written notes), in organizations and elsewhere in society. Obtaining and organizing this knowledge was as important as developing techniques to reach the ideal state. Enforcing people to part with their knowledge secrets is one possibility, but perhaps a better way is to allow people to make their own effective and productive use of it. It is the latter approach that allows for the development of entrepreneurs. So the real value of entrepreneurship in economics lies less in ruminations about the equilibrium state and more in exploring ways in which the process of 'discovery' of knowledge takes place, or in its coordination to achieve equilibrium. By doing this, the entrepreneur is welcomed back to the world of economics!

Israel Kirzner and the perspicacious entrepreneur

Markets enable and facilitate the 'discovery' process. Emphasizing the role of the entrepreneur in this market-based activity was what Israel Kirzner (1973, 1985) was concerned with as he argued against the typical focus on equilibrium as a guide to public policy-making and a reflection of how an economy works. Kirzner states that as knowledge is widely scattered in the economy, making equilibrium difficult, people can only do their best with inadequate information and knowledge resources. Traditional economic theory suggests that if knowledge is so dispersed then people will gain from this non-equilibrium state. However, people are aware of such gains to be made because they have the necessary information, and therefore they will do everything possible to realize them to ensure that there are no excess profits to be made. Kirzner argues that people are actually ignorant and not aware of the opportunities for beneficial exchange. Consequently, these opportunities are missed by both buyers and sellers.

For every ignorant person there is one who probably sees things more clearly than others, and this 'someone' is Kirzner's entrepreneur. The entrepreneur is alert to these opportunities and takes advantage by arbitraging between buyers and sellers in different markets. Similar or the same goods and services are sold at different prices in various markets. Whoever buys in the cheaper market and sells in the more expensive one engages in arbitrage and, according to Kirzner, in entrepreneurship. With each act of buying or selling based on superior knowledge, the entrepreneur makes choices and incurs an opportunity cost of for the discarded option.

Every time the entrepreneur engages in this process, he/she generates awareness of such possibilities to other sellers and buyers. The shared knowledge creates increased opportunities for entrepreneurship, and in turn greater levels of competition. Higher levels of competition help to distribute the profits and reduce the original arbitraging entrepreneur's gains, following a pattern of activity that returns the economy to its equilibrium position. Even if the individual, and especially the original entrepreneur, may not have any interest in sharing the benefits, his or her self-interest is part of a cycle of socially desirable outcomes as more and more entrepreneurs pursue economic gain.

The eventual return to equilibrium is not a one-off or a permanent state once it has been achieved. Changes in the data, information and knowledge base generate new problems. Such changes do not take place because of the introduction of new products or services by entrepreneurs but because the latter are alert to the fact that the new introductions in the market are not known to others. For Kirzner, the equilibrium system remains intact but the process of reaching that state matters more because of the continuous availability of external data from outside the system. The entrepreneur does not really create anything; he/she is simply more perceptive or alert to the changes than are others.

Where does the external data come from in the first place? The economy when not in equilibrium generates messages about goods, services, prices and sources. Does the entrepreneur require any particular skill to be alert to these messages? Such a requirement is unlikely because being alert relates to specific circumstances and situations; the entrepreneurial outcome is in the use of knowledge which may apply as much to a producer of goods and services as to a consumer.

Kirzner's ideas about entrepreneurial arbitrage inevitably led him to extend his views in terms of issues related to differences between current and future prices. Given that he did not consider investment resources to be of any importance for the entrepreneur, or that such resources could be used for arbitraging into the future, the extension of those original views appears to be a bit suspect. It is one thing to coordinate resources, namely superior knowledge, in reality as it appeared; quite another to assume maintenance of such superior knowledge into the future even through 'imaginative, bold leaps of faith and determination' (Kirzner, 1985, p. 56). Kirzner appears to be calling into question his original view that the entrepreneur is a passive agent of changes in external data by suggesting that he/she could anticipate change. It is this problem of speculative insight that has given entrepreneurship a bad name in the current economic crisis of the twenty-first century.

Against this looseness of Kirzners's latter-day observations, his original formulations help us to fully appreciate questions of relativity, namely that the value of making a product or providing a service in one environment renders the product/service unsuitable in another market, and that there is an opportunity cost associated with every choice that is made. This means it is possible for everyone to become an entrepreneur, with perhaps the new entrant being more perceptive to change than existing firms which are required to be conscious of their own internal environments.

Kirzner acknowledged his debt to Ludwig von Mises (1881–1973) and Fredrick von Hayek (1899–1992). For Mises, entrepreneurship was about anticipating the market correctly, being useful to the customer and realizing a profit. The entrepreneur's calculations were based on making the most of opportunities, the concept of 'human action' (Mises, 1949) describing such behaviour.

In Hayek's market economy the stock of knowledge is divided unequally among individuals, with no one individual possessing the same knowledge as another. The interplay between those with access to privileged knowledge about shortages of resources and others who lack it results in entrepreneurship. Those who have the knowledge obtain the benefits because they create such knowledge through the process of entrepreneurship and by virtue of their individual situations, occupations and social network. Those who lack such knowledge do so because they are unable to create it. Entrepreneurship is, therefore, a 'discovery process'.

Despite variations to the equilibrium theme, namely in terms of, for example, 'marginal utility' and 'partial equilibrium', models of neo-classicists and Marshall, respectively, or Kirzner's attempt to understand the process that leads to it, there is no deviation from the equilibrium position itself in our explanation of economic theory so far. This position, which relies on firmly established prices for goods and services and inputs to the production process, enables the entrepreneur to compute costs clearly and precisely. There is no uncertainty. These prices helps to set optimal prices for new goods and the sales that can be expected at that price. Comparisons between similar products that exist in the marketplace can, therefore, be made systematically. In other words it is the stable environment of the equilibrium model that provides the foundation of an entrepreneur's action. This explanation provides for a brief insight into Joseph Schumpeter's starting point, which he termed the 'circular flow of economic life'.

Enter Schumpeter

The idea of the circular flow

In describing and analysing the 'circular flow' of the equilibrium model economy, Schumpeter acknowledged the value of such a model by recognizing that there were times when systems needed to draw towards equilibrium. Where prices are known for all inputs, the entrepreneur can calculate costs. But unlike his predecessors who did not provide any explanation of why changes occurred to any system, and simply assumed that 'external data' influenced or impacted upon an existing economic, equilibrium-driven model, Schumpeter had other ideas. Discarding the apparent triviality of minor adjustments to data and simplistic notions of learning, Schumpeter believed that the change process needed a thorough explanation.

The learning process did not simply lead to adjustment, as Marshall may have implied. The learning process was also a creative process that led to development, and in particular economic development. Creativity and learning were internal processes engendered by initiatives within an economy. These initiatives are taken by entrepreneurs. Instead of reacting to data, the Schumpeterian entrepreneur causes them to change. He/she does not rely on the market or the consumers to state their preferences, and then adjust to them; the entrepreneur enables those changes to occur in the first place. The entrepreneur educates the consumer, who learns from that process.

Three critical publications of Schumpeter covered his essential theses of economic development and the significance of entrepreneurship. These works were *The Theory of Economic Development* (1926; 1934), *Business Cycles* (1939) and *Capitalism, Socialism and Democracy* (1942). These three publications plus the numerous articles and reviews by Schumpeter introduced the idea of the dynamic properties of capitalism – the corollary to the evolutionary process of capitalism that Karl Marx had identified long ago.

Schumpeter's creative entrepreneur

Progress is linked to the activities of creative entrepreneurs. In the process, winners and losers emerge to disrupt the model of Pareto efficiency, which prevents anyone from gaining at the expense of another. This disruption is acceptable to Schumpeter because the entrepreneurial process yields a higher number of better-off people than those who lose out. In creating something that does not exist, in having a vision for newness, the entrepreneur opens up opportunities for all. The rhetoric is advanced on the basis that intuition helps with the capacity for seeing things totally differently from others. This is not simply the superior knowledge that Kirzner's entrepreneurs have, but rather the creation of new knowledge from within underlined by the need for

- the dream and the will to found a private kingdom;
- the impulse to fight, to prove oneself superior to others, to succeed for the sake not of the fruits of success, but of success itself;
- the joy of creating, of getting things done. (Schumpeter, 1934, p. 93)

The entrepreneur is self-centred but is not just a profit-seeking Kirznerian arbitrager. Entrepreneurs are driven by a mission to achieve, even if their calculations for economic gain are made coolly in a stable environment. Psychologists may have more to comment on regarding the mix of these characteristics, but Schumpeter is concerned with the process of discontinuity from the past and anticipating the impact it may have on the economy and in the wider society.

Entrepreneurship and economic development

The entrepreneur makes the event of change happen. Therefore, he/she cannot simply be alert to changes. Neither can the entrepreneur anticipate any impact of his or her actions operating within the 'circular flow' of routines and equilibrium systems. The new event is a shock to the system. New possibilities are created that threaten the status quo and the viability of existing products, services, processes and organizations. These processes are discontinuous and destructive, but as a process destroys it creates new possibilities based on new combinations. Such a concept of economic development has, as Elliott (2008) suggests, 'three salient characteristics':

1) it comes from within the economic system and it is not merely an adaptation to changes in external data;
2) it occurs discontinuously, rather than smoothly; and
3) it brings qualitative changes or 'revolutions', which fundamentally displace old equilibria and create radically new conditions. (p. xix)

Growth accompanies economic development in that there is a long-term and positive impact on national income, savings and the population. But such a conception of growth is not merely a version of typical fixations of quantitative growth. In other words, what matters is not a curiosity of more factories, more enterprises, and more jobs and more mail coaches, but the new products made in those factories, new forms of organization that enable those products to be made and improved upon, and a 'railway system' that transports people easily, safely, effectively and economically.

Entrepreneurship and innovation

Unlike monetary, financial, and fiscal stimulus to boost the economy (much bandied about in our current times), the Schumpeterian stimulus took the form of innovation. Innovation was defined as the commercial application of

- a new product, process, or method of production;
- a new market or source of supply; or
- a new form of business or financial organization.

The commercial application could also involve the acquisition and redirection of current means of production. The three typologies of commercial applications rested on five cases of development or the 'carrying out of new combinations':

1) the introduction of a new good, that is one with which consumers are not yet familiar, or of a new quality of a good;
2) the introduction of a new method of production, that is one not yet tested by experience in the branch of manufacture concerned, which need by no means be founded upon a discovery scientifically new, and can also exist in a new way of handling a commodity commercially;
3) the opening of a new market, that is a market into which the particular branch of manufacture of the country in question has not previously entered, whether or not this market has existed before;
4) the conquest of a new source supply of raw materials or half-manufactured goods, again irrespective of whether this source already exists or whether it has first to be created; and
5) the carrying out of the new organization of any industry, like the creation of a monopoly position (for example, through trust) or the breaking up of a monopoly position.

Innovation is different from 'invention' in that the latter is concerned with new ideas and developments of a mechanical or a technical nature, whereas the emphasis on the commercial application of a new idea is what distinguishes 'innovation'. Schumpeter also went on to explain the role of diffusion by stating that the commercial application of a new idea was not complete unless the market had adopted the new product/service through imitation.

Innovation needs financing, but this could not be done within the equilibrium or steady state 'circular flow' model because the revenues generated in that system are meant to cover existing costs only. New combinations and new ways of doing things require new net investment and cannot bank on investments for replacement needs only. The commercial bank, which stands as a source of credit outside the circular flow, can create new money and new purchasing power above existing saving and current income. In this equation the capitalist (or the owner of money) is different from the entrepreneur or innovator even if they can be the same person; their functions differ. The capitalist charges interest for any loan that he/she may provide to help finance the innovation; the entrepreneur needs to assure the capitalist that the innovation will yield profits that will cover the cost of the principal sum advanced by way of a loan, the interest that accrues on the advance and a net surplus profit.

In identifying the need for appropriate forms of finance for innovation, Schumpeter recognized the importance of credit creation for economic development. However, the ability to carry out new combinations, by putting into practice the entrepreneurial ideas, was significantly more crucial for economic progress.

Schumpeter's entrepreneur is also different from capitalist owners of money, inventors and business managers. In distinguishing the three categories of people, Schumpeter departed sharply from the classicists and their apologists who did not make any such distinction. Entrepreneurs do not necessarily run established businesses, and not all managers pursue entrepreneurial activities because of their engagement with routines in established businesses.

In our attempt to appreciate Schumpeter's work, we need to consider the writer's own evolution. His first forays in theory development in 1911 led him to consider internally generated change in all phenomena – economic and social. All such phenomena could either have creative activities or be characterized by repetitive ones within closed systems of circular flow. By the time of the publication of his second edition of *The Theory of Economic Development* (1926) and *Business Cycles* (1939), innovation was defined as the setting up of a new production function (p. 87).

Creative destruction

The Schumpeterian entrepreneur is a harbinger of economic development and change. In attempting to construct a theoretical model for the process of such change and 'how the economic system generates the force that incessantly transforms it', Schumpeter, in common with Marx, was of the view that the 'source of energy within an economic system would in itself disrupt any equilibrium that might be attained'(Clemence, 1951). Both Marx and Schumpeter broke from the tradition of the stationary economic model. However, while Marx believed that capital accumulation is the main force of economic development in capitalist societies, Schumpeter argued that the primary cause of economic development is innovation and that capital accumulation is a significant outcome of that process. Schumpeter's belief that in later stages of capitalism innovation is the mainstay of large and established businesses, rather than new gazelles of creativity, echoes Marx's analysis of the capital accumulation process.

The creative destruction process is the beginning of the evolutionary process. The success of entrepreneurs stimulates and encourages both initiation and competition. The outcome, which is one of increased flow of goods and services and the growth in the demand for property and capital equipment, results in an economic boom. Booms do not last, as increasing competition reduces the value of profits as well as profit levels, discouraging additional investment. Additional flows of goods and services dampen prices, and rising costs and interest rates choke profit margins. The economy falls into a recession. The disruptive process cannot be continuous and, therefore, there is the cyclical process that Schumpeter addressed in his theory of business cycles (Schumpeter, 1939).

Entrepreneurship and Schumpeter's business cycles

Schumpeter's theory of business cycles was predicated on the idea that discontinuity through innovation and the associated technological, organizational and resources changes is the cause of cyclical fluctuations. The changes provide the basis of economic growth and prosperity. While the cycle may be interrupted by recessions or depressions, the latter are part of a normal process of adaptation. Without prosperity there no depressions! Contractions from depression force reorganizations of production processes. They can generate greater efficiency as a result, lower costs, and squeeze out inefficient businesses. At the same time, new products, services, processes and methods replace the old. This evolutionary process of change is what Schumpeter described as a 'perennial gale of creative destruction' (1939, p. 85).

Schumpeter referred to three types of business cycles – short, medium and long cycles. The short cycle of 3 to 4 years was referred as the 'Kitchen Cycle', the medium one of 9 to 10 years was called the 'Jugular Cycle', and the longer fluctuation of 54 to 60 years was identified as the 'Kondratieff Cycle'. In accordance with the 'Kondratieff Cycle', Schumpeter dated three waves, the first from the 1780s to 1842 (associated with the industrial revolution), the second from 1842 to 1897 (linked with the development of railways), and the third from 1898 to 1930s (connected with innovations in the chemical, electric power and automobile industries). The cyclical movement was characterized by a clustering of innovations rather than any movement in outputs, suggesting that specific innovations appear and are absorbed over half-century cycles.

Schumpeter's ideas about clusters of innovation developed in *Business Cycles* (1939) was further developed by Erik Dahmen (1950, 1970) who came up with the idea of 'development blocks'. These 'blocks' described an integrated industrial system within a country where different institutions and businesses support each other because of their dependence on the same or related raw materials or production processes. This dependency or complementarity was generated by new innovations, for example in railways and electrification, and the 'blocks' have enabled old firms to consider new locations while letting new firms be formed as part of the change process.

While Schumpeter was mainly concerned with the work of the entrepreneurial individual, after 1940 and during the inter-war period he came across the corporate world of large American businesses with extensive capacity for research and development activities. Innovation in existing organizations attracted his interest from then onwards, and this combined with his interest in economic history. While musing on the prospect of socialism eventually replacing capitalism in *Capitalism, Socialism and Democracy* (1942), he also predicted a decline in the importance of the role of the individual entrepreneur. Increased routines and rationality in societies, adaptability to change and the rise of big corporations developing innovative technologies in a routine fashion were all signs of the decline of entrepreneurship as he knew it.

Schumpeterian lessons

What, then, are the lessons that we can draw from Schumpeter's vision and theories of the dynamic process of economic development and the significance of entrepreneurship in such development?

The first important consideration is that of the value of the dynamic process of economic development, and especially of the dynamic innovations generated by entrepreneurs constituting a powerful competitive force.

The second, perhaps paradoxical, lesson is that innovation can lead to both prosperity and a subsequent recession. A slump can be avoided by preventing innovation because the latter process disrupts the status quo and decouples people from knowledge associated with a steady state. The development of a new portfolio of knowledge for the next wave of innovation takes time and is dependent on trial and error. The pace cannot be forced through, for example by artificial price fixing by government.

Third, a monopolistic situation may be good, at least temporarily, for economic progress. The innovator may require protection of his or her new products/services through patents and licences, which could result in the generation of pure economic or above-normal profits through the manipulation of price, quantity and production techniques. This form of support may lead to short-run inefficiencies in income distribution and resource allocations. If government intervenes in this process through anti-monopolistic measures, innovators may be discouraged.

Schumpeter was aware of the charge that monopolists have little incentive to innovate once their position is secure. His view was that even such established positions cannot prevent major innovations from upsetting the monopoly. This raises problematic questions for policy makers and believers in free market competition. But if we understand Schumpeter as well as we can, we find that his was not an attempt to replace a flawed notion of perfection by another concept of a perfect economic system. Rather, it was an explanation of the evolutionary character of economic life. In his later writings he went on to celebrate the role of R&D for innovation and entrepreneurship and the particular capabilities of large, monopolistic firms to manage the innovation process. The capacity of larger firms to be more innovative than their smaller counterparts has been challenged by many writers since, but it has certainly opened up possibilities for a better understanding of entrepreneurship in the corporate environment. Recent studies on theories of the firm and on corporate entrepreneurship (topics that we shall examine later) bear this out.

Monopolies reflect Schumpeter's idea of the dynamic process of competition. Unlike the beliefs of Adam Smith and John Stuart Mill in competitive markets as a mechanism for economic coordination and control of business activities, Schumpeter's interest lay less in the competitive market and more in the creative daring of entrepreneurs. Developing new products and processes was far more important than price-fixing or price competition.

A fourth consideration is the critical distinction that Schumpeter drew between those in possession of money or capital (capitalists and bankers) and those who had creative vision to make new products and services (entrepreneurs) and who could sway the former group to part with their money. Evidence of this distinction is more than apparent in the roles that business angels and informal finance providers (in many cases family members) play in financing the 'dreams' of those making and offering the prospect of returns from new combinations of ideas, resources, goods, services and technologies.

Fifth, by 1939 Schumpeter had clearly introduced the concept of the organization of new production functions, which suggested that there was something systemic in the process. Not only were creativity and newness important but their substance lay in the entrepreneur's ability to set things up, to organize new activities in ways that led to productive outcomes. But Schumpeter writes about the organization structure of industries, not of individual firms.

What Schumpeter was attempting to do in exploring a dynamic economic theory was to complement what his Austrian predecessor Leon Walras (1834–1910) had established through his static economic model. Schumpeter's ideas changed over time, and at best his approach is interdisciplinary in nature, using psychology, sociology, history and economic history to add to his insights into economic theory (Swedberg, 2000).

But who is this daring visionary of an entrepreneur? What makes them special and able to obtain advantage in terms of controlling resources? Is the growth of knowledge in the economy limited to entrepreneurs only? Their simple dependency on money from external financiers and their need to obtain legitimacy or acceptance of their operations suggests a form of outsider check on their visionary ideas. How does the entrepreneur negotiate or interact with these outsiders? Schumpeter does not really answer such questions. His preoccupation was not with either the factors of change or the specific motivations of the change agent, but rather with the mechanism of change: 'The entrepreneur is merely the bearer of the mechanism' (p. 61n).

There are no clear guidelines in Schumpeter's work on how the entrepreneur should behave. Although Schumpeter's entrepreneur is driven by the dream to find a private kingdom, the will to conquer and the joy of creating, pursuing the entrepreneur's motivations was not considered to be a legitimate part of his work on economic theory. Business schools, business trainers, policy makers and support service providers looking to Schumpeter for guidance on how to create entrepreneurs may not find any! Therein lies a paradox. Schumpeter's entrepreneur is different from ordinary people and their economic behaviour. In doing something different and new entrepreneurs have to proceed ultra carefully in uncharted and uncertain territory. Common sense tells us that it is probably in such uncertain conditions that an individual needs the most of any practical advice that is possible. But who provides such advice? Is it the intervening adviser and counsellor, or the market and the lessons learnt in the marketplace through trial and error?

Finally, Schumpeter's theories of entrepreneurship are virtually context free unless one considers his leaning towards the larger firm as the bearer of true entrepreneurship. Contexts define the environment in which new combinations are made, and each context provides different opportunities for new products, services and organizations. To ignore this aspect of development leaves the reader with no understanding of how and why entrepreneurship differs from one place to another. Why is the USA referred to as the bastion of new venture creation and why do some countries find themselves at the bottom of league tables such as the Global Entrepreneurship Monitor (GEM)? Why do regions, even in the United States, have different levels of entrepreneurial achievement? To answer such questions one has to dig deeply into the varied contexts in which entrepreneurship occurs and the ways in which these contexts shape or influence the practice of enterprise creation and innovation (see Chapter 6).

PART IV: RISK, UNCERTAINTY, AMBIGUITY AND ENTREPRENEURSHIP

Ten years after Schumpeter's first edition of *Theory of Economic Development* (1911), Frank Knight had lit a different fire by questioning the relative unimportance of entrepreneurship at that time. In his book *Risk Uncertainty and Profit* (1921), Knight drew a clear distinction between 'risk' and 'uncertainty'. 'Risk' had an objective probability attached to it. One could be uncertain about the specific time or nature of the outcome but there was a certainty about an outcome. A race would have a winner and a loser, life would end in death by a certain age, a specific return on a bet or on an investment could be hedged or any other risk insured. What would be incurred would be a cost. As far as the production process is concerned that cost would be a deduction from profits and losses incurred; it cannot be the cause. Unlike 'risk', 'uncertainty' does not have any precedent. There is no objective probability because it is impossible to know what will happen as a result of taking any action. Such activities cannot be insured, capitalized or salaried.

Only real uncertainties about the future allowed the entrepreneur to earn a profit. The entrepreneur engages in the production process because he/she anticipates that the end products will be consumed. The expected demand of consumers for a product helps to determine the price the entrepreneur will pay for the factors of production. But the price he/she will charge is unknown and all that can be done is to speculate. The only thing possible under the circumstances is guesswork – guessing the final selling price.

The entrepreneur may stand to make a windfall gain if the receipts from the sale of the marginal products exceed those forecasted. But this profit is not the same as the price that is paid for a specific service; it does not have any relationship to the burden of uncertainty. In fact the 'profit' that Knight refers to is not even attributable to businesses that do not start under novel circumstances, as for example a small bakery or a hairdressing business that starts and remains small. Rather, novel circumstances are found with high technology start-ups requiring venture capital or business angel funding, or exclusive goods and services such as luxury handbags, where customers are buying something ineffable such as a cool brand.

Such uncertain environments deter the average 'ambiguity-averse' individual, and as this outcome results in reduced competition, the entrepreneur who is prepared to enter uncharted territory stands to gain more. Playing with such uncertainty does not of course guarantee profits because of the need to second-guess the price, but where it does work, the rewards are high (Bhide, 2006).

A Keynesian overview

A major rival of Schumpeter, John Maynard Keynes is not often referred to in the context of entrepreneurship. This is because almost all the attention that Keynes has attracted since he wrote his ground-breaking *The General Theory of Employment, Interest and Money* (1936) was given to his fiscal and monetary policy ideas of how credit-worthy governments, like those of the United States and the United Kingdom, could borrow and spend and help put the unemployed back to work. As Ackerloff and Schiller (2009) have explained, beyond Keynes's theories of deficit finance there was a deeper analysis of how the economy really works and the role of government. Eschewing the idea of purely rational agents, Keynes believed that most economic activity was also governed by 'animal spirits' or the non-economic motives of people. These 'animal spirits' were the main cause of fluctuations in the economy. Also, in uncertain times decisions can only be made as a result of spontaneous action, not 'the outcome of a weighted average of quantitative benefits multiplied by quantitative probablities' (Minsky, 1982).

The five different aspects of these 'animal spirits' are 'confidence', 'fairness', 'corruption and antisocial behaviour', 'money illusion' and 'stories' (Ackerloff and Schiller, 2009). Keynes identified their role in the calculations that business people made and how they influenced the operation of the market. The entrepreneur's actions are redolent of 'the urge to act', the combination of animal spirits with information, skills and resources in realizing new opportunities and creating a business. More significantly, with fluctuations in the economy, and the absence of full information, the entrepreneur could seize opportunities for realizing those opportunities and gaining from superior information. Keynes's apparent solutions for the economic crisis of the depression of the 1930s overshadowed Schumpeter's own work, but there is probably room to accommodate some degree of commonality in their arguments.

Information and arbitrage

Mark Casson's attempt at a synthesis of the works of Knight, Schumpeter, Kirzner and others suggests that a possible unifying theory of entrepreneurship could emerge at some point in the future. Such a theory may not of course help anyone else apart from theorists, but it could help us to consider what we should be focusing our analysis on in order to obtain a better understanding of the entrepreneurial phenomenon. For Casson, the entrepreneur is an individual person who enjoys a comparative advantage in making decisions. The entrepreneur makes judgemental decisions about how resources should be coordinated. The decisions that are made by the entrepreneur are different from those of others because of access to better information or the ability to interpret it better than most people. The ability to make these judgemental decisions distinguishes the entrepreneur from the norm, but this distinction could be found as much in political and social life as in an economic counterpart. What matters are 'non-routine' decisions and actions, and therefore, in economic terms and in a capitalist system, anyone making such decisions is effectively an entrepreneur. Also, entrepreneurship, according to Casson, is closely tied to ownership of capital or assets. This is because the entrepreneur cannot depend on the external capitalist financial agent who may not trust his or her non-routine, non-conformist views.

Casson's central argument is concerned with the success and failure of the individual, the firm or even the nation. It is not because people make wrong choices in decision-making or lack resources, which is what optimal decision-making is concerned with in traditional economics. Such success or failure is attributable to the efficiency with which resources are used, which is a function of correcting errors due to wrong judgements. Individuals may wish to make optimal decisions, but they do not often get it right. Therefore, their errors need correction. There is no notion of Schumpeterian creativity here; attention is given to the correction of mistakes made by others. Errors are made because individuals do not pick up signals in the economy and because they rely on outdated information. As long as these mistakes are perpetuated, the entrepreneur enjoys the opportunity for profit through arbitrage. Indeed, the individual who perceives and takes advantage of such an opportunity is an entrepreneur.

The entrepreneur engages in arbitrage when he or she mediates between two people who wish to trade with each other but do not recognize the possibility for doing so. The entrepreneur enables them to make the deal. All parties benefit, even if the entrepreneur walks away with most of the gain. When there are different preferences of risk, adjustments are made so that everyone is satisfied. This is a role that banks, brokers, manufacturers and service providers can all play. However, the entrepreneur becomes a speculator when the trade-off between risks is not agreed because of differences in judgement. For example, hedging one's bets on the sharp rise in the cost of wind power in the future might make the entrepreneur buy fossil fuel for the time being till there is an adjustment to the price of the former. Till such time, the entrepreneur will gain by making alternative resources available.

Unlike Kirzner's entrepreneur, Casson's counterpart needs resources even if they are limited and even if reliance on a capital market is necessary when information is not freely available, or is incomplete or dispersed. Moreover, in such markets, who you know matters considerably, so a new entrepreneur may only be able to obtain limited support. So the entrepreneur needs to move between arbitrage and speculation and to rely on speed of access to improve his or her stock of information with which to make gains. The entrepreneur does so by piling up stocks of either goods or cash. If the price of goods is stable then stock-holding is beneficial; if the market is unstable then using stocks as a safeguard against price variations enables a return to stability.

How does Casson's entrepreneur act when there is either competitive threat or loss of value of information once it is released? If competing entrepreneurs do not collaborate when they have the same information then profits are likely to be minimal or zero. As rational people, entrepreneurs will either want to outpace their rivals or not seek any information at all if they believe they will end up with nothing. So a monopoly situation may be the only way that an entrepreneur can protect his information, and this can be achieved by setting up a business. In some situations, Casson believes that an entrepreneur can only gain from superior information by creating a new market.

Creating a new market for goods and services is an expensive proposition. Taking control over that market is another big problem that cannot be solved easily. The alternative for the entrepreneur is, therefore, to establish an organization, a firm, making him or her an owner-manager. Relying on 'transactions cost theory', which assumes that all transactions have costs, and that these costs refer not only to methods of production but also to the organization of production, Casson's entrepreneur makes optimal decisions about market-creating activity through the firm. For example, the entrepreneur makes contact between the buyer and seller when there is none, negotiates to arrive at an acceptable price when there is no agreement, monitors quality of products to overcome any lack of confidence about the specification of goods, and holds stocks or inventories to avoid the cost of renewing contracts (Casson, 1982).

The complexity of the products, time lags between the making and implementation of contracts and between payment and supply, and problems in possession of goods and quality monitoring have an effect on costs. Some of the costs relate to start-up activities (initial capital costs) while others are fixed costs associated with a transaction. The higher the cost of start-ups, the greater the incentive to have sustained, long runs of the product that is made by incurring those costs. The higher the fixed costs of operation, the more beneficial it is to run a large volume of each transaction. By being first in the market, the entrepreneur can drive down average costs by generating a high volume of business activity. The follower will still have to incur set-up costs. In reality, such an argument poses a problem for entrepreneurs in that they have to rely on customers to define what activities they should pursue and how, and not just their own judgements. Moreover, the follower may well find that in an established market the original pace-setting entrepreneur actually helped to reduce start-up costs. Additionally, incremental changes in the use of an established product may give the second and subsequent players a bigger advantage. It does not always pay to be the first mover.

The creation of a firm could help to reduce the costs of interaction and trade in the marketplace, an idea that was first developed by Coase in 1937. Instead of dealing with a number of tradesmen or, for example, carpenters in the open market, a furniture maker could offer standard contracts to a group of people. For a specific sum of money, secure holiday periods and other conditions of payment, the carpenters agree to make the type of furniture the entrepreneur wants. Instead of buying or hiring tools and equipment every time there is a new job, the entrepreneur could buy a set of those tools. These tools and equipment can then be controlled and the cost of their wear and tear could be accounted for over a period of time before they are replaced.

Typically, as the business grows, the decisions about who to hire and what equipment to buy are delegated to managers. This could cause problems for the entrepreneur who believes that he or she knows better, and more than the managers employed to do the task. The tasks cease to be entrepreneurial, in the sense that they are no longer about creating the firm and the business but about managing and maintaining it. Such activities need to be routinized. Casson does not recognize routines as being part of the repertory of the entrepreneur in the same way that Schumpeter or even Kirzner did in their accounts of what an entrepreneur needs to do to create and realize new opportunities.

PART V: NEW AREAS OF THEORY

Entrepreneurship: an evolutionary approach

Economic arguments for entrepreneurship have also been influenced by evolutionary theory. Here we have entrepreneurship being examined from an organizational perspective. Organizations are essentially considered as a set of routines because of the idea of bounded rationality. Nelson and Winter (1982) developed the idea of routines by focusing on entrepreneurship as a process of economic change. They did so by combining the ideas of Schumpeter (as stated above) and Herbert Simon (1976, 1979), who studied human decision-making assuming that human beings were rational. However, they also have to deal with complex problems that can be too much of a burden for the human brain. Their rationality is, therefore, incomplete or bounded.

Based on Simon's ideas about behavioural rules and how they are influenced by organizational design, Nelson and Winter followed Schumpeter in first rejecting the idea of routines as merely a set of operations that convert particular inputs into a specific set of outputs. According to this latter idea of routines, a decision maker may choose between different routines but having selected a routine no further choices need to be made. This rather deterministic notion of choice and routines, where the former is not affected by the other, does not necessarily hold in any given system. Choices are often affected by routines because following a specific routine may not yield expected outcomes, which may result in different choices being made.

In defining routines as the skills of an organization, Nelson and Winter (1982) were acknowledging the fact that trial and error often help to develop skills and that some of these skills may not be explicitly identified. Organizational skills are associated with particular roles rather than specific individuals; even if the latter sometimes shape those roles, they often involve joint or collaborative actions and they need to be linked to other sets of skills in the organization. In an organization consisting of a collection of routines, not many of them are clearly specified mainly because of bounded rationality. Local knowledge often helps to define a particular set of skills. In these circumstances, how one set of routines are linked to others in some form of structure is of crucial importance to the organization. Three kinds of routines – operating, investment and search – capture the activities of an organization, and it is this three-dimensional structure that Nelson and Winter use to explain economic development.

Nelson and Winter follow Schumpeter in suggesting that economic development is generated from within, but their focus is on existing organizations and not the new 'creative destroyers'. According to them, change is possible only when routines are established. New routines are created within organizations and selected as a result of better performance in their environment. However, not all selection and change is necessarily beneficial or successful. Entrepreneurs may wish to maximize their ability to earn profits, but bounded rationality prevents them from doing so, and in some situations routines can be adopted and practised that are inferior to other choices that could have been made. A typical organization has a memory of such routines that embody the knowledge endowment of the organization and form a repertoire maintained by practice. If a stable environment prevails then familiar routines can be practised effectively.

Under the hypothesis of imperfect information and bounded rationality, organizations are dependent on behaviours that produce satisfaction. In other words, as long as the objectives and performance of the organization are achieved satisfactorily, the routines are maintained. When such targets are not met, the organization follows a process of change during which new routines are searched and developed. Sometimes unsatisfactory routines are preserved because they cannot be perfectly specified. In these circumstances, those who take the decisions to select certain routines attempt to hold on to power by sticking to them. Under such circumstances and due to such attitudes change may not be welcome, with the consequence that unsatisfactory routines are preserved within the organization.

Entrepreneurial activity involves decision-making 'with regard to whether the new pattern of routines is to be a new creation or an adaptation from an existing pattern' (Glancey and McQuaid, 2000). Such decisions form the basis of the search process for new routines that leads the organization to identify and realize new opportunities. Unlike Schumpeter's emphasis on discontinuity, the evolutionary approach suggests that new ways of doing things are based on decisions that are dependent on adaptations or new combinations of old ways. In this sense an established or incumbent organization always has an advantage over new ones because of its familiarity with what came before. This may also explain why new firms are not necessarily a threat to existing firms.

Previous knowledge, experience and past history influence the current features and knowledge of the existing organization that seeks change. In their search for legitimacy, new firms also try to subscribe to systems, behavioural patterns and ways of doing things within specific environments. Knowledge spillover sometimes enables other firms (including new ones) to avail themselves of the opportunity of sharing established knowledge and experience. This complex interdependency leads to the emergence of the phenomenon of path-dependency. The emergence and evolution of industries are shaped by historical events.

For an existing entrepreneurial organization, path-dependency means setting up routines that facilitate and do not impede novelty. Their organizational memory, history and experience may help them not to sacrifice future opportunities for current necessities, although this sense of vision may elude or not be within the grasp of many firms. For the new firm, the absence of any organizational memory may make it difficult to consider future opportunities as the intensity of the start-up process may preclude them from doing so. However, it is in their challenge to incumbents that start-ups help to activate new searches in the economy. The function of entrepreneurship is crucial and, in the end, economic evolution is determined by the entrepreneurial activities of both new and existing entrepreneurial organizations.

Incentives, different forms of entrepreneurship and Baumol

It was William Baumol (1990, 2002, 2007) who drew attention to the varied social value of entrepreneurs. The importance of entrepreneurs in any society was dependent on the rewards they received. The supply to any society may be constant, but the variable conditions of different societies foster different types of entrepreneurship – productive and unproductive. Unproductive entrepreneurship is associated with 'rent-seeking' or those activities that in generating handsome rewards for the rent seekers reduce the level of resources available for innovative activity (Murphy *et al.*, 1993). Such activities also include tax evasion and tax avoidance.

The highest levels of private returns may not yield the highest levels of social returns. For example, more of the same type of undifferentiated businesses activities may help to redistribute wealth but not actually create new wealth through innovation. Thus entrepreneurship varies in its allocation, and its impact is not always positive. Depending on the nature of incentives provided and the motivations of the entrepreneurs, the outcomes could be negative and exploitative of consumers and the community. This is typically the case when an individual entrepreneur pursues personal gain at the expense of his or her customers and the wider society. In recent times we have witnessed considerable numbers of 'destructive entrepreneurship' activities taking the form of highly 'innovative' financial instruments (such as credit swaps and securitized assets that mortgage lenders and banks created), which though not illegal have had a hugely adverse impact on the lives of ordinary people and the working of institutions.

Baumol makes three distinctive propositions about entrepreneurship. First, he suggests that the 'rules of the game' (based on conditions, incentives, legislation) affecting new venture creation and growth can change. If so – and here he makes his second proposition – entrepreneurial behaviour responds to these changes. Third, how entrepreneurship is distributed between productive and unproductive activities affects the economy's capacity for innovation and development.

How a society can control unproductive entrepreneurship is dependent on the relative strength of the institutions that govern economic and social activities. The absence of strong institutions is not limited to developing countries as is commonly understood. It is often argued that in fast-developing economies such as Brazil, China, India and Russia, the acceleration of profit-making opportunities through deregulated markets is out of step with institutional reform. This may indeed be the case. However, as we have seen in the current financial and economic crisis, technological advances, extreme forms of human ingenuity and sheer 'animal spirits' can outpace even well established institutions in developed countries. Under these circumstances, entrepreneurship can take the form of corrupt business activities.

In a recent paper, Desai *et al.* (forthcoming) have suggested that there is an absence of any conceptual framework for destructive entrepreneurship. Formalized structures do not always help to generate economic growth. They refer, for example to the requirement for and practice of business registrations in some countries. Such a process is not always attractive to all businesses, and consequently there is widespread 'hidden entrepreneurship' or an informal economy operating in parallel to the formal one. But not all forms of 'hidden' entrepreneurship are illegal or destructive. It is the existence of property rights, high stocks of social capital and informal agency work that can, on the one hand, help to tackle both unproductive and destructive entrepreneurship and, on the other, realize the value of hidden but productive entrepreneurship. What we need to understand better is why and how productive and unproductive or even destructive forms of entrepreneurship co-exist at any time in any society, and what needs to be done to mitigate for the negative outcomes of the latter two on economic and social development in a society.

A review of the theories that we have examined so far suggests both closeness of ideas and explanations and considerable differences. Knight's ventures into uncertainty and a proper explanation of profits may not have actually questioned static economic equilibrium theories, but the implications about the 'special reward' could be seen as the corollary of Schumpeter's creative destruction, the force that comes from within. Both are unexplained, but we know that they have little to do with the traditional economists' obsession with the pricing of factors of production. Hayek's ideas about creative knowledge and the 'discovery process' also has some similarities with Schumpeter's ideas about new combinations, even if the former does not refer to the introduction of new knowledge from outside the system. Kirzner's idea of alertness and the realization of knowledge, which suggests that the entrepreneur reacts to unknown data, does not mean that Schumpeter's ideas of creation were radically opposed to Kirzner's or those of the Austrian school. As Noteboom (2000) states, there is an overall process of discovery that concerns all of these thinkers, and creation and realization are complementary and mutually dependent. This is because realization requires prior creation while providing the basis for the next wave of creation.

The wider world of innovation and entrepreneurship

Large firms

For some years, and especially after Schumpeter's Mark 2 phase, the larger firm or corporation became the focus of entrepreneurship, and especially the critical role that technological innovation played in promoting economic growth through these organizations. Schumpeter had in part rued the change in economic and social conditions that favoured the larger firm as the source of innovative activities. In his view, increased rationality and routinization can weaken entrepreneurship especially as far as individual effort is concerned.

Examining the corporate scene in the USA and based at Harvard, Schumpeter observed that only large organizations with a capacity for routines and organized effort could perform innovative activities. These firms were, therefore, more important for the economy. By this time Schumpeter had developed a particular interest in economic history and on the institutional structure of society, as illustrated in his book *Capitalism, Socialism and Democracy* (1942). His prediction about the possible decline of capitalism corresponded with his view that the entrepreneur's economic significance would diminish as well. If the entrepreneur's role was to become less important then capitalism as an economic system could be displaced by socialism. It is unclear whether Schumpeter was suggesting that the growth of the large firm as the innovator was a sign of declining capitalism, but it would be misleading to conclude that he was either prescient with his views or that he had a change of heart. We continue to see the importance of individuals and small firms as innovators in most economies. Also, as Noteboom (2000), referring to Langlois (1998), notes, Schumpeter's later ideas about corporate innovation were already present in his earlier work. It is suggested that the emergence of the larger firm was part of the evolutionary process.

Schumpeter had an important ally in John Kenneth Galbraith, who in his two major studies, *American Capitalism* (1956) and *The New Industrial State* (1967), argued that economic policy needed orientation towards larger corporations. Both original and incremental innovations were, according to Galbraith, part of the domain of efficient large corporations. The important role of both technology and innovation in an economy emanates from larger corporations and not from struggling small firms in a highly competitive marketplace. The former could dictate how they wished to engage with both buyers and suppliers, and this power would generate a response from consumers and workers leading to a countervailing check on such powers. These checks and balances were to be provided through the balance of economic power among the three institutions in an 'Iron Triangle' – big business, labour and government (Auerswald and Acs, 2009).

Acceptance of this view might mean the acceptance of a paradox, namely that on the one hand Schumpeter is referring to the creative destruction capability of the entrepreneur (Mark 1), while on the other he is referring to organizational integrity and routines for innovation being particularly important for economic growth. The point is not to ruminate too much about this paradox but rather to accept a framework of entrepreneurship that allows for different types of entrepreneurial activity following innovation at different stages and in varied forms in any business cycle.

Entrepreneurship and job creation

Interest in the importance of the larger organization has enveloped the study of economics and business management, and many still hold true the view that such organizations are the mainstay of economies. They form the proper subject of study as they continue to influence government policies and institutional engagement. The myth persists even if the facts of our times suggest that the reality is somewhat different. Ironically, as this book is written, the problem for government, as far as larger firms are concerned, is not that they pose a challenge in terms of monopolistic or oligopolistic power, but that they are in desperate need of being kept afloat (Auerswald and Acs, 2009).

Turbulent economic conditions in the 1970s had already taken care of the inadequacies of a reliance on larger corporations. These organizations were seen as inflexible, slow in terms of their ability to respond to market signals and conditions. Increasing global competition, developments in new technologies, especially information technologies, and demographic and structural changes led to greater uncertainty and market fragmentation. The period immediately after the depression of first the 1970s and then the 1980s saw major new break-throughs in information technology and biotechnology, in particular. Both as a reaction to the deficits of the larger firm and the ability to commercialize new inventions, the smaller firm captured the imagination of policy makers. The 'iron duo' of Ronald Reagan in the United States and Margaret Thatcher in the United Kingdom promoted small businesses and entre-preneurship in a variety of interesting, productive and not-so-productive ways. Job creation was uppermost in the eyes of politicians and small businesses were the engines for new jobs in this era of change.

The conditions were ripe for new work on job creation and the creators of these jobs –just as they are now! One enquirer, David Birch, was interested in understanding how jobs are created. There were two critical parts to his seminal work, *The Job Generation Process* (1979). The first part investigated the nature of job creation. Birch found that

- the movement or migration of firms from one region to another did not really affect jobs; and
- job losses, including death and reduction/contraction rates did not vary much between one region and another. There were changes in the net rate but this could be attributed to variations in the rate of replacement, not the actual rate of loss. So the rate of job replace-ment is a crucial determinant of the growth or decline of a region.

But who creates these jobs, and who is responsible for these rates of replacement? Birch's results showed that independent firms, especially firms with fewer than 20 employees, cre-ated about 60 per cent of all jobs in the USA, while independent small entrepreneurs helped to create 50 per cent of all jobs. However, once small, young firms had been in existence for over four years, they failed to sustain their job creation capability; in fact, they declined! Large firms were responsible for less than 15 per cent of all net new jobs.

The two issues of job creation and small firms has dominated the field of entrepreneurship, especially in terms of critical analysis of issues related to economic development, ever since Birch's path-breaking work. The small firm as a unit of analysis of economic development has been taken on board by leading writers such as Acs (1984), Acs and Audretsch (1990), Storey (1994), Kirchoff (1994) and Wennekers and Thurik (1999), among many others.

Zoltan Acs (1984) found small firms as agents of change based on empirical data drawn from the US steel industry. Small mills in this industry were capable of producing different products with different inputs and production processes. In partnership with David Audretsch, Acs investigated in depth the role of small firms in innovative and technological changes in the economy (1990) based on the question: 'What determines innovative activity at the industry level?' They found that while there is a higher level of innovative activity in industries con-sisting of larger firms, small firms tend have more innovative advantage in those industries dominated by larger firms. Furthermore, the innovative advantage of small firms is promoted in innovative industries utilizing high levels of skilled labour. Where there were no concentra-tions and where industries were capital intensive, larger firms were more innovative. However, capital intensity did not preclude small firms from joining these industries, and in fact the more innovative they were, the more likely they were to challenge the hegemony of larger firms. Their conclusion was that what matters is not whether small firms were more innovative than their larger counterparts. Instead, we should consider that both have a role to play but that they are different and vary according to sectors. However, what small firms can do is to develop strategies of innovation to compensate for their size and resource-related constraints.

The critical role of small firms, and their share of economic activity, has been well documented. The Bolton Committee report in the UK (1971) was a turning point in the recognition of the size of the small firms sector. For a detailed appreciation of the importance of small firms the reader is directed to three key studies (among others): Storey (1994), Bannock (2005) and Johnson (2007). This chapter is less concerned with the specific role of small firms and more with the identification of the economic arguments about small firms as key agents (among others) of entrepreneurship.

Further work by Bo Carlsson demonstrated how economic activity in manufacturing firms had moved from larger industries to small firms (1996). David Storey (1994) pointed out that small firms were more important in terms of contribution to GDP and employment growth than was the case 20 years ago. By examining different data sets, he argued that small firms in the United Kingdom were more important in the early and late years of the twentieth century. However, he warned of the error in believing that countries with firms with a higher proportion of employment in small firms were necessarily better performers than countries with a high proportion of employees in larger firms. Similarly, he argued that increases in self-employment are not related to increases in employment. Referring to Acs *et al.* (1991), Storey (1994) also observed that economic development is generally associated with lower self-employment, and that between 1980 and 1986 the rapid increase in self-employment was associated with increased levels of unemployment together with an abundance of government schemes to promote enterprise at the expense of benefits for the unemployed.

Entrepreneurship, networks and other constructs

The chapter cannot be concluded without at least a short reference to yet another stream of thought enabling a better understanding of the economic value of entrepreneurship. Italian economists developed the original arguments of Alfred Marshall's industrial district by exploring the links between the wider community and interrelated firms in specific regions. In doing so they shifted the arguments about industrial districts away from concentrations and clusters of firms to social processes, learning regions (developed later in terms of the 'innovative milieu'), networks, and small firm interaction in communities. Entrepreneurship and innovation were central to these processes, and in moving attention to these issues Becatini and Brusco began to ask serious questions about the importance of regions, and geographical space, in our understanding of new venture creation and innovation. Their work has been the inspiration of a growing literature on the subject of entrepreneurship and regional development, to which we shall turn, in part, later in this book.

Conclusion

The economic arguments and related theory development continue apace. Any chapter on an overview of economic issues pertaining to entrepreneurship can only end abruptly because

a)   the theory-building process continues with increasingly new insights into contexts, size, sectors, units of analysis and methods; and
b)   understanding entrepreneurship is not the same thing as investigating the nature and scope of the development of entrepreneurial activities.

The incomplete story of entrepreneurship from an economic perspective is almost a tautology. Each age will discover its economic perspective. The strength of this perspective lies in the fact that the explanation of many phenomena has been provided by economists who have explored the value of entrepreneurship, and indeed the idea of value creation in entrepreneurship in different economic conditions, environments, and organizations. These explorations will be discussed in various chapters throughout this book. The purpose of this chapter was to highlight the essential concepts of equilibrium, change, creativity, learning, knowledge, organization and innovation that help to define and explain entrepreneurship. Later chapters will draw attention to some of the new ideas, theories and concepts created by numerous authors but notably by Zoltan Acs, David Audretsch, Roy Thurik and a few others, with particular reference to topics such as 'entrepreneurship and growth', 'entrepreneurship and development' and 'entrepreneurship and public policy'.

There is also the need to introduce the reader to other ways of exploring the idea and the phenomenon of entrepreneurship. Explaining entrepreneurship is one thing; developing entrepreneurship is another. The growth in the importance of management studies has created new avenues of critical research about motivations, behaviour and social relationships, together with prescriptions about how to achieve entrepreneurial success. The latter is concerned with a repertoire of 'how-to' manuals and texts teaching and training people to develop business plans, marketing strategies and the like. Our focus is on the former set of issues and the growing interest of social science analyses in entrepreneurship. To this end, sociologists, psychologists, behavioural scientists, anthropologists, economic historians, economic geographers and economic planners have provided unique insights into the subject. It is to their efforts that we turn in the next chapter.

Self-assessment questions

1. Explain why economic equilibrium theories may not help with our understanding of entrepreneurship.
2. Identify the different ways in which neo-classical theories touched on and laid the ground for entrepreneurship theory development.
3. Identify the extent to which Marshall's idea of learning, knowledge and collaboration help us to understand developments in the economy today.
4. Explain the concept of creative destruction and how it relates to Schumpeter's ideas about business life cycles.
5. Briefly account for the emergence of new ideas and theories of entrepreneurship.

4 The social dimensions of entrepreneurship

Learning outcomes

In this chapter the reader will:

- obtain a critical overview of the social science perspective of entrepreneurship;
- distinguish between social and economic approaches to entrepreneurship;
- assess and examine critically some of the underpinning theories that help to explain entrepreneurship in society;
- examine key concepts of social capital, networks, social contexts and culture critically, with a view to understanding the role of the entrepreneur in society.

Structure of the chapter

This chapter is divided into six parts. Starting from a broad delineation of the scope of social values and the social domain of entrepreneurship in Part I, the Part II examines social tools and artefacts with a particular focus on the technology life cycle and how technology-led innovation and entrepreneurship are informed by social values and created in their peculiar social contexts. Part III then moves on to explore the implications, influences and relevance of culture in society and how the specific ingredients of culture shape entrepreneurship in different environments. A significant social and cultural asset, social capital is considered today to be a major input for entrepreneurial activity and an outcome of entrepreneurship in any society. Social capital is the subject of the Part IV. Social capital is closely tied to networks and networking, and these issues are discussed critically in Part V. Before the chapter is concluded, Part VI reflects briefly on the emergence of a new type of hybrid enterprise, the social enterprise, where social value creation takes centre stage in the activities of the firm while it uses business tools and methods to run its operations.

Introduction

While scholars from other fields may dispute this contention, it is difficult to find anywhere outside economics a strong and cohesive theoretical underpinning for the study of entrepreneurship. There are variants, as we have noted in the previous chapter, and theory-building concerning entrepreneurship in economics has indeed taken many different routes. But it is the preoccupation with economic growth and development, and with the necessary agents for such activity, that has given us a sound basis for our understanding of entrepreneurship. However, entrepreneurship, like so many things in life, does not live by economics alone.

Our understanding is enhanced considerably by explorations into the development of entrepreneurship, the social relationships between different economic actors, and between such actors and institutions, and not just by way of explanations of its economic rationale.

The purpose of this chapter is to examine what social factors have a bearing on our understanding of entrepreneurship. To this end we explore concepts of social capital, networks, culture, technology cycles, trust, legitimacy and a few other issues that are concerned with the way people interact, socialize and create environments for new venture creation. Many of these concepts have gained a considerable amount of prominence these days in determining:

- how and why new ventures are formed;
- the circumstances and the environment in which new products and services are made and developed; and
- how and in what ways the social interaction of people and institutions contribute to the creation of a culture that is conducive to economic development.

Pioneers such as Schumpeter had recognized the role of the other sciences, such as psychology, in explaining entrepreneurial motivations but avoided any search in that area; he considered the latter subject to be well outside the reach of economists. We have also seen from our short review of economic theory as it applies to entrepreneurship that many writers and thinkers have forayed into territory occupied by other social scientists, but without, sometimes, the necessary acknowledgement of their contributions. The advent of behavioural economics and economic sociology as new areas of study has also given us new room to manoeuvre as far as explanations of entrepreneurial activity are concerned.

Optimum resource allocation is crucial to economic thinking, but social relationships, why and how individuals behave entrepreneurially, and organizational and locational factors that affect the entrepreneurship process have thrown new light on the subject. Additionally, cultural and ideological views have been connected with social insights into entrepreneurship. Various early studies on populations in Britain (Booth, 1983; Rowntree, 1913) referred to the economic and social role of the small business strata. Marxist studies, entrenched in class dynamics, have been concerned with the shopkeepers, artisans, small-scale landowners or Marx's 'petty bourgeoisie'.

Entrepreneurship is now firmly embedded in the social sciences, outside economics. Let us examine some of the more important thinkers and the critical ideas about society, social connections, culture and networks that can help to enrich our understanding of entrepreneurship.

PART I: THE SOCIAL CONTEXT

Societal values *v.* the individual entrepreneur: Weber and the entrepreneur

We can start by reflecting on Max Weber (1864–1920) and the numerous complex insights into entrepreneurship that are scattered throughout his work. It is Weber's theory of 'charisma' and the special type of 'charismatic person' that is often linked to ideas of an entrepreneur: such a special type of person makes others follow him because of the strength of his personality. This type of thinking still prevails widely in many quarters as entrepreneurs are seen as heroic leaders and risk-taking agents of economic change. Charisma could also account for other types of leaders. Leonard Cohen's Jesus was a sailor and he said all men would be sailors, even though he was better known for his spiritual leadership and for his incredible charisma that eventually led to the creation of a new religion. Gandhi and Mandela are political leaders whose charisma has changed the way we think of the world.

Weber's idea of charisma was relevant for the early stages of human civilization. Interestingly for him, economic change in a capitalist society was a function of enterprises geared to profit in the marketplace. It is in this exchange economy that Weber finds the entrepreneur, and it is in the actions of the enterprises, rather than those of the individual, that he finds entrepreneurial activity contributing to economic change.

Weber's (1947) thesis on the protestant ethic and the spirit of capitalism provides most students with the main arguments about entrepreneurship. This work shows how attitudes towards entrepreneurship started to change from hostility and alienation to acceptance and even promotion after the Reformation in the Western world. He also analysed how a certain form of ascetic Protestantism (Calvinism, Pietism, Methodism and Baptism) was responsible for developing a positive attitude towards moneymaking and work. This association with commerce, moneymaking, hard work and entrepreneurship was unleashed from within Christianity, influencing favourable attitudes towards business. The gradual erosion of the value of religion did not, however, result in a corresponding fall in the popularity of entrepreneurship; rather it was set free (Swedberg, 2000).

The ascetic Christians changed the way the economy worked. The traditional link between greed and business activity had been cut methodically by merchants who were among this pious and controlled group of Christians and who influenced the way the enterprises designed to make profit worked, changing the effective course of the economy.

In his later work, Weber discusses the relationship between bureaucracy and entrepreneurship. The rationalization of society led to higher levels of bureaucratization, which could bring about the death of entrepreneurship and the economy especially if there were a socialist revolution. Capitalist economies afforded a check on such forms of bureaucratization. Weber argued that this tendency could be observed with an individual enterprise as well, and if that occurred then rent-seeking would replace profit-making, resulting in either the slowing down or the corruption of the economy. Possessing superior knowledge, the entrepreneur could predict and understand the pitfalls of routinization and bureaucracy. The entrepreneur, through his enterprise and his special responsibilities, could provide a countervailing power to such excesses.

Weber's focus on Christianity does not necessarily help with our understanding of the entrepreneurship process in countries where other religions are dominant. Can and should religion play any part in realizing entrepreneurial opportunity? Braudel (1979) rejected the Weberian idea by showing that early forms of capitalism occurred in places where religion did not play any important role. The confluence of trade and religious ideas, as between Akbar's India and Elizabeth's England in the sixteenth century, or the Venetians and the Arabs, enabled countries or groups of people to imbibe different values and ideas with which to pursue their business goals. Over time, as different cultures have given way to others (the Venetians to the Genoans, Genoans to Armenians, and Armenians to Protestants in Europe, or the Hugenots to the Jews to the Bangladeshis in the East End of London), they have left legacies of ideas, belief systems and values that have become embedded in particular environments and across communities for others to pick up and apply in their working lives. Only further research on the value and impact of different religions on entrepreneurial economic activity can help us to answer such a question. Unless we attribute a single identity to the entrepreneur, the idea of any religion having a positive or negative influence on entrepreneurship will remain unknown and probably suspect. The entrepreneur's plural identities suggest that he or she is influenced by many other factors.

There appears to be a degree of commonality in Weber's ideas and those of Schumpeter, especially when we note that both writers were equally concerned with the rapid encroachment of routinization and organizational bureaucracy stifling innovation. The comparisons he makes with the bureaucrat and the entrepreneur still hold true. It is also the notion of the outsider that brings Weberian thinking into line with many other views (for example, Kirzner and Marshall's, or even Knight's) of the entrepreneur. However, Weber's emphasis on the organization and society rather than on the individual entrepreneur offers a different perspective on entrepreneurship. Weber was less interested in the free individual and more in societal values, while Schumpeter's theory of entrepreneurship was directly concerned with individual motivations without necessarily any social ethic. They offer different perspectives.

The wider social domain of entrepreneurship

Schumpeterian echoes can also be found in the deliberations of sociologists such as Durkheim, who referred to the idea of 'collective effervescence' resulting from social interaction and the power of new institutions and new values in society. This effervescent spirit enables a new dynamic to take root in society, causing radical social, political and economic change. Revolutions, such as the French, American and Industrial revolutions, are examples of such change. On a quieter note, the dynamics of places such as Silicon Valley, Bangalore, Munich, Taipei and elsewhere, and the rise of the information society in other parts of the world, are examples of significant change. Here new ideas based on the development and use of information, and communication technologies create opportunities for new business creation based on networks, constant innovation and the high density of similar or related organizations located in the same place. Significant change occurs because of the change in the way business is done locally, nationally and globally through different types of connected organizations. They change the environment from a sleepy, salubrious summer resort to a hive of knowledge-based businesses. Perhaps what preceded Barack Obama's election as the first Black President of the USA, what endured during the elections and what is now being sustained in disparate communities to bring about radical change in American society – in terms of health care, care for the environment, better forms of education – could also be a sign of such 'collective effervescence'. Time will tell.

There is a connection here between considerations of social change in and out of institutions and the idea of social movement that helps to create social, moral and political entrepreneurs (Becker, 1975). These considerations raise issues about the varying cultural, social and organizational contexts of entrepreneurship (see Chapter 6 for a detailed explanation of contexts of entrepreneurship). In other words, we can find here the seeds of a different understanding of entrepreneurship; forms that relate entrepreneurship not only to new small business creation but also to changes in organizational structures, changes in how people live and work, and how new economic, social and cultural values are forged. This takes us to a wider arena of entrepreneurship and its meaning, where we are able to explore different social connections and links between people, organizations and cultures.

The previous paragraph ends on a positive note about the creative elements in different types of entrepreneurship. The creative spirit often, however, has unfortunate outcomes. Predicting Baumol's (1990) ideas to some extent, Robert Merton (1968) suggests that entrepreneurship could be linked to crime in some societies. If people's aspirations to achieve do not have corresponding means by which they may be achieved, the result could be deviance from the norm. Such deviance could either take the form of productive, innovative behaviour, or crime if the legitimate means are not available or affordable. Baumol's 'incentives' and Merton's 'means' share a common thread of argument. We discuss issues related to productive and rent-seeking or unproductive and destructive entrepreneurship in Chapters 11 and 12.

So how do social factors have a bearing on the creation of new ventures? Let us spend a little time exploring this familiar territory of new business or firm formation and the social aspects that underpin the creation of new firms. How firms are created, the social contexts in which they are created, and the various dynamics at play influencing people to act in entrepreneurial ways are some of our concerns, and this is why we start with examining the social context of new firm formation.

The social context of new firm formation and opportunities

How do firms emerge and where do they come from? Do certain conditions prevail and are such conditions more important than others? In attempting to answer such questions we find that personal, social, cultural and economic theories all have something to contribute to the discussion. However, each of them tends to provide a basis for isolated arguments generating a wide and fragmented body of knowledge. What we do know and what matters are the organizational contexts for new venture creation and the range of entrepreneurial activities that change these contexts from time to time (Schoonhoven and Romanelli, 2001).

The two issues of organizational context and entrepreneurial activity are interdependent in that new firms can be created both out of the existing knowledge base of different industries and by the change (entrepreneurial) process itself. The real question, however, is that about the sources of entrepreneurial opportunity (Venkatraman, 1997) leading to the creation of new firms.

Schoonhoven and Romanelli (2001) suggest that individuals learn about opportunities for new business formation from their work environments and from their educational organizations. Furthermore, the nature and character of existing organizations and the environments in which they are located influence the individual and the firm formation process. The local source of entrepreneurial ideas and of opportunity, especially the work environment of putative entrepreneurs, is considered to be critically important for our understanding of new business formation (Jacobs, 1969; Aldrich and Widenmayer, 1993). Using empirical evidence to test these ideas, they formulate ten different propositions in five categories of information centred round the importance of the source, and especially the local source of new business formation:

Category A: Organizational origins of new organizations

1. The majority of new organizations will be founded to exploit new opportunities identified on the basis of a founder's work and expertise in a previous organization.
2. Major changes in the strategy or governance of an organization will be positively related to the organization's production of entrepreneurs who will found new organizations (the authors refer to the formation of Intel in the Silicon Valley being directly related to the changes of Fairchild's California subsidiary).
3. The growth of an existing organization will be positively related to its rate of production of entrepreneurs who found new organizations that replicate the primary work of the existing organization (suggesting that the creation of these new organizations helps to soak up the additional demand for products and services of a growing, existing organization).

Category B: Local population origins

4. The number of different kinds of work in an existing organization will be positively related to its rate of production of entrepreneurs who found new organizations, especially organizations that do not replicate the primary work of the existing organization (meaning outgrowth stemming from current activities as from research and development or work that adds value in different ways, as in the growth of credit reporting agencies which came out of the growth of retail industries (Aldrich, 1979), or where the focus of expertise is outside the immediate remit of the existing firm).
5. Rates of founding in local organizational populations will be curvilinearly related (in an inverted U-shape) to the density of the local population (here the possibility of new firms emerging is dependent on both the existing level of firms in the area and the capacity of the area to absorb new firms with new products and services).
6. The density of an exiting organization's population will be positively related to its production of non-replicating organizations (this proposition goes back to Adam Smith's ideas about specialization resulting from a fragmentation of skills which in turn occurs as the size of the market increases).

Category C: Local community origins

7. The number of populations in a local organizational community will be positively related to the number of organizational foundings in the community (this idea is closely linked to the notion of knowledge spillovers and clustering that was referred to previously and is developed later under the theme of contexts in Chapter 6). In essence it suggests that the characteristics of a community with different types of organizations often attract new and innovative firms in the same region).
8. The diversity of populations in a local organizational community will be positively related to the number of organizational foundings in a community (in other words, it's not simply the concentration of organizations in any one sector that matters, but rather the spread of concentrations of different sectors in any one region).

Category D: New population formation

9. The number of organizational foundings in a local organizational community will be positively related to the number of new populations established in the community. (Reference is being made here to the positive impact of new ideas emerging from new businesses giving rise to even more new developments. Together they create new markets.)

Category E: Local community boundaries

10. Founders will most often establish a new organization in the same geographic region as the existing organization from which the founder came.

Much of what is stated above marks an important departure from the study of entrepreneurship that concentrates on its meaning and the personality of the entrepreneur, and the behaviour and socio-economic influences on the individual. Schoonhoven and Romanelli (2001) take the discussion about entrepreneurship to a different and vitally important area.

They explore the impact of entrepreneurship on a region, on technological innovation, on organizational growth and on competitiveness, and ask why, and what gives rise to entrepreneurship and the emergence of innovative new firms in specific contexts. More specifically, they argue about the nature and form of the local origin of entrepreneurship, examining the critical connections between existing populations, its stock and diversity, and the reality of new firms being created. By organizing the information in the five categories stated above, they show the link between local founders, their previous organizations, the local population of organizations and the local community.

What happens in any given economy or society is not simply confined to the relationships and influences described above. The origins of entrepreneurial activity are not always dependent on the personalized location of the individual entrepreneur and the relationships he/she has with the immediate or wider environment. A large part of this relationship is mediated through the tools and resources, the technologies, that entrepreneurs use or develop, how and when they use them, and the stages of development of those technologies.

PART II: THE SOCIAL ASPECTS OF THE TECHNOLOGY CYCLE, SYSTEMS AND SUB-SYSTEMS

Technology, discontinuity and opportunities

What is known about a particular technology, or the stage of development of a product in a particular market, can have a serious impact on entrepreneurial activity. Murmann and Tushman (2001) have argued, for example, that the connections between the technology cycle (invention, development, commercialization, implementation, diffusion, growth and adaptation, maturity and decline) of the product, the knowledge industry associated with that technology and the role of the University in the same context can have a profound impact on new business creation. Technologies evolve after a first stage of newness and dominant design, and through gradual improvements generate further new technologies. Entrepreneurship is often concerned with the creation, development and application of new technologies, and as Schumpeter has observed (1950), technological breakthroughs open up opportunities for entrepreneurs. But these opportunities are available both at the time of the original breakthrough and at each stage of the development of that technology, whether they take the form of variations in or incremental improvements of the technology. Improvements to the dominant design can lead to applications not imagined at the original breakthrough stage.

Following Schumpeter, variations occur as a result of major discontinuities, during which time many competing technologies emerge. Murmann and Tushman (2001) refer to the automobile industry, which during its early period was characterized by competition between three motor technologies that competed with one another – steam, internal combustion and electric engines. The similarity with our times and the competition between petrol, diesel, hydrogen fuel and electric engines suggests a cyclical pattern for car engines as for many other technologies. In the early period, the internal combustion engine won the day and what followed were many years of incremental change till the time appears to have come for a new period of variation, selection, and retention of relevant and effective technologies.

Nested hierarchy and systems

Tushman and Murmann (1998) designed the concept of systems, subsystems, linkages and compenents (refered to as a 'nested hierarchy' model) to explain the evolution of technologies. A car for example is a system, the engine and the cylinder constituted sub-systems, the chassis a linkage mechanism, and the screws and bolts are described as compo-nents. Their critical point was that while technological discontinuities could occur at the linkage mechanism level, a dominant design may prevail at the subsystem level. What makes dominant designs emerge is dependent on socio-political and economic processes in society. This could mean that the best technologies do not always win. Both markets and governments can enable a dominant design to arise. The VHS dominated the Beta and Video 200 formats even though it was considered an inferior format to the latter two. Political processes in the USA have helped to set the high definition TV as a standard, just much as the digital system is being 'imposed' over and above analogue in the UK. Standards are also negotiated within industry.

Entrepreneurs with contacts with diverse groups of stakeholders, including other industry players and government, help to push the dominant design in the market. This is more likely to be the case with high-technology products. Moreover, these developments could occur within a country or a region or at the international level. Murmann and Tushman (2001) refer to the links between German dye firms and University professors to campaign for changes in patent law. This suggests the importance of networked communities across different systems and subsytems (see below for details on networks and networking). Similarly Mitra and Natarajan (2011) refer to Indian software entrepreneurs and their connections with US software and information technology hardware product firms that helped to promote the IT software entre-preneurs of India. In the Indian example we find the software firms offering niche capabilities at the subsystem and linkage mechanism levels of a wider network of a software development system, through outsourcing and offshoring activities for firms across the globe. This mix of capabilities across regions has helped foster complementary competencies between one region (for example, Bangalore in India) and another (for example, Seattle in the USA).

The social context of technological opportunities

At all three levels of the firm, the industry and the region or country, we find differences that suggest that the dynamics of the technology cycle and the emergence of dominant designs vary according to their social contexts. The dominant design of Swiss watches lasted more than 100 years till the Japanese watch industry offered quartz technology that overthrew the Swiss regime across all parts of the system and subsystem of suppliers (Murmann and Tush-man, 2001). Similarly at the national level, Chesbrough (1998) observed that institutional differences supported entrepreneurial endeavour in the disk drive industry in the USA. In the mobile telephone industry the difference between the USA and Europe was evinced in the latter's GM standard being negotiated between firms and the regulatory authorities while in the USA a number of incompatible designs were left to fight for market share because no such negotiation occurred (Chesbrough, 1998). The absence of any patent restrictions in the German and Swiss synthetic dye industries in the nineteenth century allowed entrepreneurs in large numbers in those countries to copy innovative British dyes and produce them without any threat of legal sanctions or reprisals. A quirk in the legal system that banned a covenant on competition in California allowed high-technology firms to learn more from one another than their counterparts on the East Coast in Boston where the covenant prevailed.

Social systems, sub-systems and networks

We appear to be moving quickly from one conceptual area to another. So pausing briefly, we can recall what we have examined so far. Starting with Weber and the importance of social values forged in specific contexts, we have found that different social dynamics and organizational and environmental contexts impact on the entrepreneur and his/her ability to start new ventures. We have also noted the connection between the technology life cycle of a product and the knowledge that is acquired and developed in specific systems. These systems also provide a social context for the development of new products and services and the establishment of new firms.

Connections with social actors, existing conditions, negotiations and arbitrage, the establishment of new conditions through mediation between actors, asymmetrical paths in technological systems and subsystems, are different manifestations of the importance of the social context. We look deeper into the importance of contexts of entrepreneurship in Chapter 6. For now, we note that Murmann and Tushman's (2001) idea of different forms of entrepreneurial opportunity being available within systems and subsystems is of considerable importance to practitioners and policy makers.

The tendency to look at whole systems, for example the car or the automobile industry and the entrepreneurial opportunities related to these systems, ignores the possibilities that arise within subsystems (car components and the car components industries). Logically, we could extend the argument to examine different kinds of systems and subsystems, and the nature of the entrepreneurial opportunities that arise within them. We could, for example, consider networks of businesses or clusters of businesses in regions where interconnectivity between businesses and other organizations helps to create such a system (as in a regional innovation system). While firms in such environments depend on each other for their growth and development, this networked-based relationship does not stop them from exploring individual pathways for innovation. In these circumstances, any decision to support prospects of entrepreneurial development will need to mediate between what can be done for all firms and what needs to be accomplished to encourage individual businesses.

Another way of explaining the differences in entrepreneurial capability of individuals, organizations and environments is by examining the impact and importance of culture. Issues relating to cultural attitudes, norms and practices have shaped some of our thinking on the importance of entrepreneurship, and culture is believed to have a profound impact on all facets of entrepreneurship in societies (George and Zahra, 2002).

PART III: CULTURE: ITS INFLUENCE AND IMPACT

But what is culture? To answer the question, we need to rely in part on other disciplines such as anthropology, sociology, philosophy, cultural studies and even literature. By doing so and by adapting what we find to entrepreneurship, we can enhance the richness of the subject. For our purpose, however, only a short journey through these domains is permitted.

The meaning of culture

Bourdieu (1972) refers to the complex of meanings, symbols, assumptions and motifs that underpin the norms and practices in any society. Shared beliefs and values of people in a society are also supposed to define a culture. Looking at the evolution of the word 'culture', Williams (1963) noted how it moved on from meaning 'the tending of natural growth' and a process of human training (suggesting a culture of 'something'), to culture as a thing in itself incorporating other meanings such as a 'general state or habit of the mind' and the general state of intellectual development in a society as a whole. The various associations of the word were raised by historical changes in industry, and the idea of democracy and class, as well as art. To this end, Williams argues that the development of the word 'culture' is a record of the number of continuing reactions to changes in our social, economic and political life – almost a kind of map with which to explore these changes.

In essence, culture could be regarded as a whole way of life (Williams, 1963). How a society encourages, embraces and practices entrepreneurship could be interpreted as being first part of this whole way of life, and also as being affected by other parts of the same way of life. To this extent, entrepreneurship could also be seen as part of a shared system of values, beliefs, aspirations and ideas of a people (Hofstede, 1980, 2001).

Social psychology

In his highly influential work, Hofstede (1980) provides psychological insights into the significance of psychic distances for people's ability to demonstrate individual entrepreneurial capability. Similarly Lipsett (2000), in his explanation of the relative unimportance of commerce and industry and technological education in Latin America and the contrasting Puritan values of work and science and engineering education in the USA, tries to explain how attitudes affect entrepreneurship. Attitudes differ even when it is believed that all societies have the basic issues and problems to tackle in order to support and control human activity. The culture of a society is, therefore, its response to these specific issues. The cultural orientations of a society are expressed through these responses (actions, symbols and traditions) which explain how different institutions function in different societies. Variations to and the adaptation, socialization and retention of actions, symbols and traditions enable the evolution of culture in society.

It is possible to find certain features of individual entrepreneurship in specific cultures, lending credibility to the idea of specific types of cultures and the idea that individual characteristics have cultural roots. Hofstede's four cultural value dimensions – individualism/collectivism, power distance, uncertainty avoidance and masculinity/femininity – have informed numerous studies on cultural orientations of entrepreneurship. Low uncertainty avoidance implied a greater willingness to enter unknown ventures, the type of ventures that Bhide (2008) identifies as Class B ventures (promising start-ups which could become gazelles but fail to attract venture capital funding and are, therefore, dependent on bootstrapping their activities with personal funds, friends/relatives and individual investors). These entrepreneurs (in the computing field or in luxury items) operate in higher levels of uncertainty than either common start-ups, which serve known consumers with a relatively known set of requirements, such as hairdressers or greengrocers. Similarly, they are different from 'high ticket' entrepreneurs who attract venture capital funds because the latter need to offer the VCs some degree of objective evidence of their markets. Using an epidemiology argument, Bhide suggests that VCs invest 'when the epidemic has plainly started but much of the population has yet to be affected' (Bhide, 2008, p.46).

Hofstede's idea of uncertainty avoidance can be studied together with Frank Knight's (1921) idea of entrepreneurs earning 'real, residual profits', not by taking quantifiable risks but by playing with unmeasurable risk (or 'unmeasurable uncertainty'). Hayton, *et al.* (2002) argue that the whole set of Hofstedian value dimensions are conducive to entrepreneurship, but this evidence is mixed. High individualism and low uncertainty avoidance appear to be the commonly agreed variables in this context. Such ideas may hold in terms of describing a state of affairs in any one place or two or more comparable/contrasting nations, suggesting something almost fatalistic as far as development is concerned. They do not explain how change occurs in different societies at different times. Neither do they provide a sufficiently robust historical explanation of conditions and attitudes when life was different in those economies. Crucially, not all forms of entrepreneurial value creation and the cultural-personal characteristics are found in the canons of Schumpeter, Kirzner, Marshall, Knight or others who by and large valued the role of the individual entrepreneur.

The cultural environment

It is argued that the collective and community embeddedness of values can have equally significant impact on entrepreneurial activity, as recent developments in entrepreneurship in China and India suggest. These developments include public sector or state-owned entre-preneurship in China. By way of contrast, private sector individual entrepreneurship is more common in India. Even in societies that value individual autonomy, the advent of social and community-based entrepreneurship suggests that there is a need to examine the subject of entrepreneurship outside the domain of individual business activity. Rather than an emphasis on individual discovery or an individually led change process, certain societies may well prefer a cultural emphasis on change.

Mention was made earlier of the rather static nature of the debate on the implications of cultural environments. The idea of homogenous people in particular environments with particular characteristics of power distance, individualism or collectivism and uncertainty avoidance becomes questionable when reference is made to Silicon Valley, regarded by many as the crucible of entrepreneurship and innovation. A key feature of the Valley is its mutlti-cultural character, its openness to ideas, technologies, the flow of talent and knowledge, and its connections with the rest of the world. Anna Lee Saxenian has studied extensively the role of migrants – English, Italian, Eastern European, Irish, Chinese, Indian, Russian and others – who are the pioneers of new technologies, innovation and new venture creation (Saxenian, 1994, 1999, 2002, 2006).

Through a wealth of stories about immigrant entrepreneurs, Saxenian identifies a curious cultural mix of people who have contributed to 'profound transformations in the global econ-omy', who are foreign born and technically skilled entrepreneurs and who travel back and forth from Silicon Valley to their home countries in Taiwan, Israel, China and India. Not only do they contribute to the Valley's extraordinary economic statistics of growth but their activi-ties challenge the basis of traditional economic development theory. Traditional theoretical views assume that new technologies emerge primarily in developed industrial countries that harbour high levels of skills and research capabilities, high income markets and mass produc-tion. Once the product is standardized, it is shifted to less developed nations, so less in the periphery follows more in the core. While the periphery can reduce its levels of deprivation, it can never catch up with the core. This view, which relies on the trinity of large firms, govern-ments and financial institutions working together in developed nations, has been undermined by the mobility of high-skilled workers, information flows and the fragmentation of produc-tion, especially in information and communication technology sectors. Peripheral regions now provide fertile breeding grounds for entrepreneurs who are skilled and connected (Saxenian, 2006; see also Chapter 11 for an overview of how global production networks operate).

The regional geography of culture

Saxenian's insights throw considerable light on the importance of regional geography and cultures that are globally connected through talent, technologies, financial capital, forms of learning, cross-cultural networks and social capital. Two critical issues are important to consider in any discussion on culture and entrepreneurship. The first issue concerns an understanding of culture at the regional level. It was in the regions of the developed world, such as the Third Italy, Germany's Baden Württemberg, New York, Boston Route 128, Philadelphia and the Santa Clara Valley, that a dynamic new model emerged (Saxenian, 2006; Putnam, 1993; Piore and Sabel, 1984). This new model is made up of financial and technical institutions and social structures that allowed for decentralized production and employment specialization. But it is not confined to the West.

Networked culture, international culture and diaspora communities

Networks of small and medium-sized firms of bicycle footwear and eventually high-tech semiconductor and software firms have also been responsible for the economic miracles in central Taiwan and Bangalore in India, respectively. The rise in international economic networks of production has transformed the cultures of regions and their ability to generate billions of entrepreneurs (Khanna, 2007). The social structures of these networks are characterized by entrepreneurship, information exchange, shared equity notions in venture financing, and the fragmentation of markets and industries (Saxenian, 2006).

The second point is concerned with the international mix of people and firms and in the systems of production that have now produced open innovation models, further intensifying the global networks (see Chapters 1 and 11). Silicon's Valley's global network of technologists and venture capitalists form a unique human tapestry of ethnicities. We find a similar mix of regional cultures and languages in Bangalore and Hyderabad in India. The shared common value system that defines a culture is different in such places from perhaps the more homogeneous forms found in Taiwan or China. The nature of path dependency in entrepreneurship that cultural values are sometimes stated to induce is not necessarily singular in style or nature. Melting pots can induce as much entrepreneurial value creation as monotone cultures. The real effects of positive entrepreneurial outcomes lie in the openness of all forms of culture to the dynamics of change and in the acceptance of varied influences often from people travelling vast distances, migrating to different countries, settling down there and establishing diaspora communities away from their original homes.

Silicon Valley houses what is part of long line of diaspora networks, including trade, entrepreneurial elite and classical migrating diaspora communities. The history of the diaspora community and its commercial adventures is a rich one, marked by the spirit of entrepreneurship. The three classical diaspora groups of Armenians, Greeks and Jews have been joined by scores of others. From these communities, organized groups of diaspora merchants carried out cross-cultural trade mostly confined to the Eurasian continent in the early modern period and, in the main, within Muslim environments. The main axis of 'trans-territorial', 'trans-ocean', 'trans-cultural', 'transnational', 'international' or 'multinational' network-based activities was the Muslim, Hindu and Chinese connectivity. Included in these cross-cultural activities were the Bahdadi Jews, the Chinese, the Gujaratis and the Parsis. Religion and culture have been offered as explanatory variables for the success of these diasporas (Weber's Protestant ethic, the Zoroastrianism of the Parsis; see McCabe, 2005).

For such diaspora communities, a common culture of commercialism sustained the networks. Such a commercial culture is defined in terms of the elaboration of a common commercial strategy relying on the organizational structure of the firms and methods of trading, rather than the interconnectedness between different commercial establishments (Baghdiantz *et al.*, 2005). The flows of knowledge, talent and human relationships that characterized these networks presage many of the developments that are often, and perhaps mistakenly, attributed only to the knowledge economy of today. High levels of confidence, great trust among members of the same community, reduction in transaction costs through a dispersed but tightly knit international community with a distinctive culture, were largely shared by the diaspora peoples (Chaudhury, 2005). Entrepreneurial activities flow from these new combinations of cultural identities because of this overriding common culture or belief in a certain kind of commercialism and a set of institutional values. It is as if such combinations produce a completely new and synergistic culture of enterprise creation and development without the necessary loss of independent cultural inputs from each group.

The breadth, depth and variety of culture and its influence on entrepreneurship

Disentangling the exclusivity of profit-making from entrepreneurship could help to obtain an understanding of social effects and benefits linked to entrepreneurship. The important issue here is to examine the varied cultural impact on value creation and change. This means that the realization of opportunities for making new products and services and setting up new forms of organization is possible in scenarios that value individual autonomy and collective interests. As seen previously, this idea has been well developed by Baumol (1990), who argues that societies rarely have a shortage of entrepreneurs. There may well be a constant supply of entrepreneurs, but if in certain environments individuals obtain a higher utility from being something else other than an entrepreneur – perhaps being a lawyer, a doctor or even a criminal (!) – then they will do so unless the rules of the game are changed to make the productive entrepreneurial action more attractive than other economic pursuits. Baumol (1990) was referring to the set of institutional values and incentives in society that encourage or discourage entrepreneurship. The argument is moved further here in terms of the cultural influence on these institutions and incentives.

It is difficult to find causal explanations of the influence of culture on entrepreneurship because culture relates to a wide set of social responses in the way people live and behave in society. Different societies will display different codes and varieties of social conduct, which to some extent will reflect the stage of their economic development. Therefore, while certain environments may be more conducive to individuals starting their own business, others might favour the innovative growth of existing businesses. Mediation through government policy favouring certain types of activity at specific times may also affect the cultural orientation of those societies. For example, in the UK and in most Western economies, large firms were deemed to be particularly important for wealth and job creation and innovation in the period 1950 to 1980. Schumpeter (1950) referred to large firms as being the main vehicles for technological innovation after the war. He did not necessarily argue that this was good for entrepreneurship, but he saw it as an inevitable consequence of economic growth and development. It did not prevent small new ventures from emerging, but they were not seen as important units of economic activity and government policies were aimed at that time towards the development and consolidation of large firms.

The nexus of time and space in culture is particularly important when it is noted, as it is by certain authors, that economic ferment tends to produce a larger crop of new businesses ready to burst onto the scene with their new technologies and ideas, while the growth of larger firms is best observed in stable economic conditions (Schumpeter, 1934; Murmann and Tushman, 2001). The roles of government and other institutions and how they are used to mediate the influence of culture on entrepreneurship is discussed in Chapters 6 and 10.

Social interactions, social networks, cultural influences and local institutional factors all generate the kind of wealth that is deemed productive as far as entrepreneurship is concerned. They generate a form of capital that has gained a lot of currency in government circles and in the social sciences as a model for capturing the contributions of social elements in explaining both individual and collective behaviour (Lin and Erickson, 2008; Lin 2001). This form of capital is described as social capital.

PART IV: SOCIAL CAPITAL

Forms of capital

Social capital is perhaps best understood in the context of the concept of capital itself and by reference to other forms of capital. The term 'capital' represents investments and possession of resources of value. In theoretical terms, it refers to a mechanism by which resources of value, such as land and labour, are produced, reproduced, accumulated and allocated (Lin and Erickson, 2008; Lin, 2001). Human capital is concerned with the skills and knowledge base of individuals and its theory suggests that their use could generate economic returns (Schultz, 1961; Becker, 1964, 1993). A third form of capital is cultural capital. Bourdieu (1972) refers to cultural capital as routines and rituals and as valued resources that could be invested in the production of specific codes of practice by the ruling classes. These codes of practice could then be used to educate and indoctrinate the masses and form a specific set of beliefs, values and institutions with which to control them.

The valued resources that generate returns to individuals and collective groups in society and that are captured in the social relations of people is described as 'social capital'. Advantage by individual and collective actors is gained through the investment and use of social relations obtained in social networks. The network base of social capital is widely acknowledged (Bourdieu, 1980; Lin, 1982; Coleman, 1988; Flap, 1991, 1992; Burt, 1992; Putnam, 1993). However, Lin (1982, 1999, 2001) argues that social capital cannot be possessed by individuals. Rather the valued resources are actually embedded in the networks and are accessible through direct and indirect ties. Crucially, what matters is not the specific social relationships that individuals have but rather the different social links that are found in different social locations.

An example of a social location is workplace – a factory or an office. How many links an individual has at different levels can help him/her find a new job or move up the ladder. Other locations outside the work environment include, for example, business federations. This approach helps in the measurement of social capital, and measures of this kind are referred to as 'position generators' (Lin and Erickson, 2008).

Social capital, institutions and entrepreneurship

But in what way is social capital important for entrepreneurs? Entrepreneurs are expected not only to set up new ventures but to navigate their way around markets, trade associations, rules and regulations, and other institutions in the wider society. How these institutions are governed has considerable implications for entrepreneurs. Weak legal and governance systems can leave investments and new products unprotected and prevent the sharing of technologies and resources that will remain appropriated by larger, monopolistic organizations. If societies and economies allow privileged and well-endowed larger firms to dominate one industry with their resources, the economy will show a bias for these firms often at the expense of undifferentiated products and services, with no choice for the consumer. Weak institutions also force businesses to negotiate institutions and select strategies that enable them to have access to outside markets and investors. While such barriers may help the more innovative firms to get the better of the system, they can also create conditions for corruption. The idea of the 'licence raj' in India before the deregulation of the market in 1991 is a case in point. Restrictions on market entry for foreign firms and capital often meant that firms had to spend more time obtaining licences from bureaucrats for the purchase of technologies, for example, than on developing the business. The social capital was tied up in these limited and bureaucratic networks of government departments, agencies and firms.

Reputation building

Social capital is also linked to the idea of reputation-building (Litch and Seigel, 2008) and legitimacy (Aldrich and Fiol, 1991). The higher the level of reputation of the firm and the entrepreneur, the greater is the opportunity for the firm to access resources, suppliers, distributors, suitable employees and even financiers. Trust plays a big part in such reputation-building, but trust and social capital are not enforceable in court. The intangibility of social capital also makes it difficult to contain in terms of specifying its time span and its use. Siegel (2005) suggests that 'reputational bonding' strategies can be adopted by entrepreneurs. This is possible when the latter associates or embeds themselves deeply within a social network (Aldrich and Zimmer, 1986), where access to other members offering custom or supplies is based on their record of trustworthiness in business dealings.

Reputation-building helps to create possibilities of mutual support through investment, distribution, custom and supplies, but without legal enforcement measures. Collectivist cultures help to create such systems, as in the Korean Chaebol or the Japanese Keiretsu, where members monitor one another's behaviour and where community-level enforcement or sanctions are used to punish any form of transgression. Increasingly from the latter part of the twentieth century, high-technology entrepreneurs have depended on such mutuality of support and sanction to attract investment and make their businesses work. Licht and Siegel (2008) refer to Powell (1996), who showed that biotechnology firms were often started by scientists without managerial experience, access to finance or distribution channels. They depended on external collaborators to help with the management of their businesses. Frequent changes in technologies, and the mix of technologies in specific products and services and especially in the sources that generate the knowledge associated with these technologies, force entrepreneurs to both consider and trust different partners with whom to develop products and services.

Trust

But how is trust gained by entrepreneurs, especially those who provide resources from outside? Licht and Siegel (2008) identify four sources of social capital that constitute the mechanisms by which social capital generates trust:

- *value introjection*, or identity from birth with a group leading to altruistic behaviour towards members of that group;
- *reciprocity exchanges*, or acting generously towards members in a particular group based on ideas of mutual support;

- *bounded solidarity*, or sharing a common event or set of events during the course of a life with a defined group of people;
- *enforceable trust*, or the expectation of punishment of a member of a group if he/she has acted inappropriately against another member of that group.

The ideas of 'reciprocity exchange' and 'enforceable trust' fit in well with theories of rational utility maximization, the cornerstone of neo-classical economics, and these two ideas have gained more attention than the other two.

To understand how such trust can be formed and how individuals use trust or its absence to manoeuvre their way through society, we should consider the idea of 'structural holes'.

Structural holes

Ronald Burt (1992) came up with the idea that any individual's network contains entrepreneurial opportunities, which he described as 'structural holes'. A 'structural hole' is 'a relationship of "non-redundancy" between two contacts'. By 'non-redundant' contacts, Burt means those contacts that lead to different or a diverse group of people who provide different information benefits. The benefits that are derived from links with 'non-redundant' contacts add to the entrepreneur's reserves of knowledge, information and skills. The entrepreneur (rather like Casson's entrepreneur combining information from various sources) enters the structural hole between two players as a 'tertius' brokering the relationship between them and generating a profit from such action.

While Burt refers to opportunities and motivations, the question that we also need to ask is how these non-redundant relationships are mediated by entrepreneurs. To what extent are there external and internal factors within social locations and social groups that explain how productive relationships are created? How do such relationships help with the formation of new ventures?

Granovetter (1973, 1985), in his much celebrated articles, discusses trust as an important element in establishing new ventures, especially where people are isolated from one another. Examining the small scale of enterprise formation and especially minority groups, he outlines a solution to the problem of enterprise creation based on trust and limited liability. There is an inevitable limit to the number of family members of representatives from the minority community that an entrepreneur can trust. The number is usually small. In such situations, they put their trust in other individuals by starting another business, which explains why entrepreneurs in developing countries have a wide set of interests in various businesses. The placing of trust is often dependent on the kind of ties that people have with others in their own community and outside. Some of these ties are inevitably strong while others are weak. Do such ties matter?

Strong and weak ties

One of the most important contributions that Granovetter (1973, 1985) made was the distinction between strong ties and weak ones and how they contribute to successful entrepreneurial outcomes. 'Strong' ties are formed from kinship and other community-based ties including membership of groups. 'Weak' ties refer to contacts that are remote or vague. Quoting Aldrich and Zimmer (1986), Granovetter (1973) points out that the conditions 'that raise the salience of group boundaries and identity, leading persons to form new social ties and action-sets, increase the likelihood of entrepreneurial attempts by persons within that group and raise the probability of success'. Therefore entrepreneurs with a wider network of weak ties with individuals from outside their local area are more likely to be successful. This network could include members of the same community living in areas outside the entrepreneur's own or from outside communities. The Armenians, the Parsees and the Marwaris in Calcutta, India, the Gujuratis in various parts of the world, the Chinese in Indonesia, the Philippines, Italy and the USA, have all shown how this form of networking has helped them to establish successful ventures (Granovetter, 1985; Chaudhury, 2005).

Understanding the use of social capital in specific contexts, the different forms of networking and the influence of culture (inclusive of religion, social mores, customs) helps us to obtain a clear idea of the social context of new business creation. But do all new ventures follow the same pattern of business formation activities? Does our understanding of how firms are formed improve when we examine what individual entrepreneurs do with specific reference to the establishment of the firm? In setting up new firms in a well-established industry sector, the tendency is for entrepreneurs to follow the behaviour of their forbears. However, when it comes to completely new firms (i.e. those that are the first of their kind), it can be argued that the creation of a firm is not enough for its sustainability even in the short term. Making other people aware of their existence and their unique value can help them with their longer-term survival. This translates into a quest for legitimacy.

The search for legitimacy

The higher the level of innovation, the greater is the uncertainty in creating and growing new firms. By imitating other firms and following in the footsteps of incumbents, new business owner-managers take advantage of the range of available social connections and examples of good practice that exist. The social construction process is relatively easy even if the information from existing sources may be suspect sometimes. In creating completely new ventures, not only do entrepreneurs set up new organizations where they didn't exist before; they also create new knowledge about their product or service, about the technologies and competencies that they use, about the organizations they establish and about themselves. In developing new knowledge, they seek legitimacy from incumbents of existing knowledge.

Types of legitimacy

Aldrich and Fiol (1994) identified two types of legitimacy: cognitive and socio-political. By 'cognitive legitimacy' they refer to the acceptance of a new kind of venture as something a specific environment takes for granted. In such an environment there is an existing knowledge base that takes the form of routines, structures, products and strategies. 'Socio-political legitimacy' means the acceptance by key stakeholders (including governments, decision-making institutions and opinion formers) of the new venture in terms of regulatory, moral (acceptance) and cultural (norms) standards in a society. Brand new entrepreneurs with radical new products or services need to negotiate these two types of legitimacy at all levels – that of the organization, industry, the wider economy and in society. Much of the negotiation process occurs as part of a collective process of cooperation between and within different communities. This is where social capital and networks involving weak and strong ties come in handy (Aldrich and Martinez, 2005). The process does not stop at the level of firm formation. For the new firm to survive with a new product or new industry, it also has to consider the possibility of creating a new community of firms making the same or similar products. This process of diffusion is what embeds innovation in the economy. Aldrich and Martinez's explanation provides for some valuable insights into Schumpeter's idea of creative destruction brought about by entrepreneurs with their new products and services. The latter pointed to the trajectory of entrepreneurship but not to the ways in which it is sustained for the period of time that it flourishes and stabilizes before declining. With this explanation of the difference between what the average new start-up and the innovating start-up do in terms of seeking legitimacy, we obtain a clear picture of the firm creation process (see also the Chapter 5).

PART V: NETWORKS AND NETWORKING

Interspersed in the discussions on social capital, legitimacy, culture and social connections is the idea of networks. Networks and networking have acquired a legendary status in modern times. Granovetter (1973) suggested that networks are an organizational form, an institution, but rather different from firms and markets. Extending this definition further, economic sociologists (Granovetter, 1985; Aldrich and Baker, 1990; Mizruchi, 1992) describe networks as a form of organized economic activity that involves a set of individuals and organizations (referred to as 'nodes') who are linked together as a result of formal and informal relationships including contractual obligations, membership of trade associations, transfer of funds kinship and family ties (Gulati, 2007; Nohria and Eccles, 1992). These definitions reinforce some of the points made earlier in this chapter about economic activities being influenced by their social contexts and in connected systems, subsystems and linkage mechanisms. The position of the different 'nodes' or network players influences their economic activities and outcomes. Firms and other organizations are not atomized entities but are part of an interactive environment of networked nodes. This idea of networks can apply to organizations at any level of analysis – trade federations, regional and national business clusters, and global institutions such as the World Trade Organization.

The popularity of networks and networking has spawned a large volume of literature, and has engaged the interest of economists, sociologists, managerial scientists, policy makers and practitioners in various ways. It is not within the scope of this book to cover that huge literature. However, a brief review of the reasons for networking's popularity and its contribution to new business creation and innovation is worth some consideration.

Nohria and Eccles (1992) suggest three reasons for the growing interest in the concept of networks:

1. the competitiveness of the small, entrepreneurial firms of Silicon Valley, the industrial districts of Modena, Prato and Faenza in Italy, of new high-technology industries such as computers and bio technology in Taiwan, Japan, and Korea. The organization of these firms and industries is characterized by lateral and horizontal linkages, alliances within and outside the firm that represents a marked contrast to the large, Chandlerian hierarchical firm. The influence of the former on the latter today is seen in the way larger organizations are seeking higher levels of cooperation with vendors, customers and even competitors;

2. technological developments that have created a set of higher levels of disaggregated, distributed flexible production arrangements, links with other firms and new forms of organizational change. The new technologies of telecommunications work on the principle of networks and in turn have created various forms of organizational networks;

3. the rise of network analysis as an academic discipline, evolving as it has from an esoteric mathematical subject to considerations of social structures and structural analysis, cooperative behaviour, and voluntary and formal strategic alliances. Typically, answers have been sought for such questions as: What motivates firms to enter into alliances? With whom are they likely to enter into such alliances? What types of governance structures and contracts are used to make these alliances work? How do these alliances evolve over time? What factors influence the performance of firms in these networks? (Gulati, 2007)

To this list we can add three other reasons for the importance of networks, rather than just their popularity:

*   the need for new firms to seek legitimacy (Aldrich, 1999), protect their new products and services, acquire new knowledge and attract investmen;
*   the critical importance of sound governance structures that actually work and are not simply there to ensure transparency of business activities. Entrepreneurs establishing new firms need to work their way through systems and institutions to establish themselves. In developing countries with weak institutions (especially legal systems) and in developed countries with inadequate institutions, the development and sharing of technological, financial, human and other resources by new firms becomes difficult as a few monopolistic and even corrupt firms try to dominate the market. The recent financial crises, especially in Western economies, point to the inadequacy of regulatory bodies that has led to even more severe consequences for small entrepreneurial firms than for the banks themselves. The absence of fully fledged property rights in some developing economies make it difficult to protect firms with new products from piracy;
*   the emergence of the Internet, which not only connects millions of people, entrepreneurs, users and others together, but appears to have changed the way assets are valued, and value chains are disaggregated, with increasing reliance on intellectual capital for the creation of new products and services. This has enabled a firm like Microsoft to become a world leader and a major corporation in less than twenty-five years; it has also enabled the emergence of open networks and what Tuomi (2006) refers to as an informal self-organizing social community. Firms such as Linux pose a serious threat to Microsoft's dominance of the operating systems market. Linux and Apache operate as highly networked, open source networks where individual and organizational developers interact outside the scope of well-defined markets and hierarchies. In this scenario, the importance of nodal points changes continually as each point can come up with new ideas for connected services.

What we can observe now is that networks evolve in the same way as organizations, and markets evolve in order to provide a specific forum of activity (or activities) for the wide range of connected players. Together they create an open-ended organization that defies the logic of economic structure especially in its extreme forms, as in their interconnected existence and roles on the Net.

The idea of virtual networks (networks based on the Internet) has captured the imagination of all who are interested in the idea of networks. These networks lie at the heart of the growth of e-business, e-commerce, B2B, B2C and C2C, and a range of other forms that are increasingly tying producers, distributors, suppliers, customers and end-users in new networks of innovation. Their growth has led to numerous contributions on the subject, with books and articles dedicated to the topics of the 'knowledge economy' and/or the 'new economy' and the development of new business models. Their popularity demands separate attention.

Network resources and network value

No examination of networks (however cursory) is meaningful without a discussion of the resources used in such networks and how networks are measured. It should be observed that while we are treating concepts such as networks, network resources and social capital separately, these terms are often used either interchangeably or in conjunction with one another. Theoretical and analytical constructs that separate such concepts help us to try to probe the depths of meaning of different terminologies. However, in practice their interdependency is evident in their manifestations and in the measures adopted to quantify their value.

Network resources are different from the material resources available to any firm. Most studies on organizational behaviour and the firm draw on insights from the resource-based view (Penrose, 1959; Wernerfelt, 1984; Barney, 1991), which highlights the importance of material resources such as hard and soft firm assets (including physical assets, competencies and capabilities) that lie within a firm's boundaries. The subject of resources that lie outside the firm and in the environment in which firms are located, especially the social network, context or embeddedness of firms, has only attracted recent attention. Gulati (2007) and Nohria and Eccles (1991) have argued that firms are able to leverage valuable resources of information and capital and through these networks. Such resources lie within the social network, and taken together the resources constitute network resources. Apart from easier access to information, the use of network resources helps firms with the shape and direction of their actions, the development of new skills and the use of joint competencies or capabilities through alliances. Developing close links with members of the network also helps firms to access additional or new material resources.

Simple questions related to problems bring firms together to share resources. This author's personal experience with manufacturing firms in the West Midlands shows how component firms came together to find an answer to the question: 'How do we find better customers?' All these component manufacturing firms were tied stringently to large players in the automobile industry without being able to explore new custom for their products. They believed their products had several applications outside the auto industry, but their contracts with large end-users limited their search. They worked together with this author to explore, first, new ways of negotiating with their customers, and second, innovative ways of saving existing customers while developing new ones.

Using longitudinal data from a sample of American, European and Japanese firms in three different industries, from 1981 to 1989, Gulati (2007) showed that:

- the greater the extent of a firm's network resources that originate from its network of prior alliances, the greater the likelihood that it will enter a new alliance in the subsequent year;
- the greater a firm's alliance formation capabilities, the greater the likelihood that it will enter in the subsequent year.

Gulati's research suggests that prior association and knowledge and the capabilities for forming links developed from previous connections are ideal resources. This indicates that firms combine both internal and external resources to take advantage of network resources.

Denser networks create clusters of highly connected firms, and it is expected that in such concentrations firms make better use of networked resources. Concepts such as 'knowledge spillover' have been used to describe what firms use from the external environment; smaller, entrepreneurial firms make use of such spillovers to develop their firms. These 'knowledge spillovers' include the know-how and resources that are surplus to individual firms, and that, being intangible, are difficult to retain or trade. Yet they flow into the system and are used randomly by firms without paying for them. In a recent study, Abubakar and Mitra, (2009) have shown that while the knowledge spillover process defines networks of firms, the spillover effect is not limited to a local network. In other words, firms at the cutting edge of high technology make equal if not greater use of wider networks than their local ones. Additionally, network links are not necessarily characterized by knowledge spillover functions but also by hard, material pecuniary transactions (see Chapter 11).

PART VI: SOCIALLY DRIVEN ENTERPRISES

Networking and relationship-building is not just restricted to the creation of new businesses and their innovative growth. Often social value creation and utilization define the nature and scope of entrepreneurial activity. This helps to spawn a new community of entrepreneurs who are not necessarily motivated only by turning opportunity into economic gain; they are driven also by the desire to take ownership of the lives they lead as part of a community where social objectives are larger than personal ones. They form socially driven opportunities.

Social enterprises emerge and grow thick and fast today as they seek different forms of legitimacy, both in the marketplace and in the social communities that they serve. We do not explore social enterprises in any detail in this chapter, but certain features of their special make-up are worth highlighting. The Social Enterprise Coalition (2009) in the UK suggests that:

- social enterprises are run at a wide variety of scales but their economic impact is growing all the time;
- social impact is the main objective behind social enterprises and a routine fact of life for such enterprises through profit-oriented investment;
- social enterprise represents a diverse sector, and there are not many business sectors that do not include social enterprise. Many of these enterprises focus on the development of human capital through training activities;
- the diversity of social enterprises is also manifest in the wide variety of legal forms that they choose. However, most enterprises (roughly 60%) are companies limited by guarantee;
- entrepreneurial individuals, former public sector organizations and voluntary and community sector organizations are the key sources of social enterprise activities;
- the scope of the operations of social enterprises is mainly local.

Social enterprises are varied in size and scope. While some are very large with turnovers in excess of £100 million, the majority of them are small with a median turnover of £175,000.

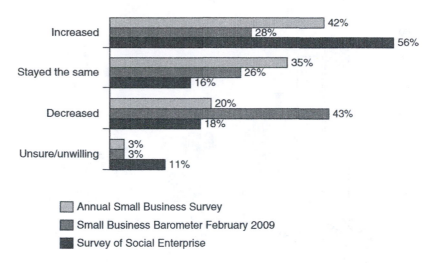

Figure 4.1 Social enterprise growth in turnover compared with SMEs

Source: Social Enterprise Coalition, 'State of Social Enterprise Survey 2009' (London Social Enterprise Coalition, 2009).

What is particularly significant is that their profile suggests that they have more in common with business enterprises than with charities and other voluntary sector organizations with whom they are often associated in a welter of definitional confusion. At a time of considerable economic constraints, it is in the statistics of growth that we can find evidence of the strength of these enterprises as Figure 4.1 shows. Allowing for differences in the methods used in the surveys, we find that social enterprises have increased their turnover compared with SMEs and a smaller number have either reported decreases in sales or maintained their turnover in comparison to SMEs.

The fact that social enterprises can be found in numerous business sectors and that their business-led functions confirm their status as key economic actors might account for their prevalence in regional economies where economic growth is strongest. As the graph from the Royal Bank of Scotland survey (2010) shows (Figure 4.2), the London South East region has the highest representation of social enterprises.

At the global level, the GEM (2009) report indicates that the rate of social enterprise activity (SEA) is higher in efficiency-driven and innovation-driven economies, reflecting possibly the better affordability of such enterprises where there are relatively higher levels of economic prosperity. It is not so much a matter of 'charity beginning at home' but rather of entrepreneurial activity with social objectives being closely intertwined with enterprises that have business objectives. Where the latter set of enterprises flourish there appears to be a greater likelihood of financial resources, a stronger skills base, and the possibility of more direct engagement with socially driven opportunity realization.

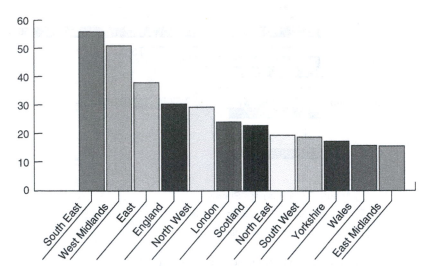

Figure 4.2 Which region/country is growing the fastest?

Source: RBS SE100 Data Report: Charting the growth and impact of UK's top social businesses (RBS, 2010).

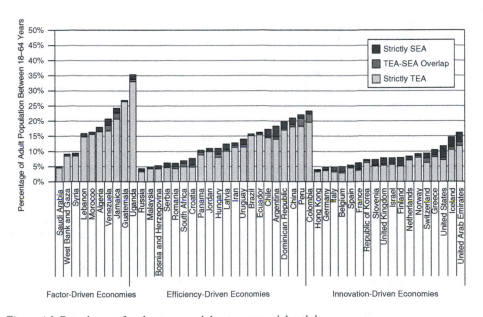

Figure 4.3 Prevalence of early-stage social entrepreneurial activity

Mini case Study 4.1: Socially motivated enterprise: Eating Divine chocolate

When 2,400 African cocoa farmers danced on a sun-baked parade ground to a brass band in Kumasi in the Ashanti heartland of central Ghana, they were celebrating the success of Divine Chocolate Ltd as the overall winner of the Enterprising Solutions award for 2007. Divine Chocolate Ltd is a 16-person company based in South London in the UK which is 45 per cent owned by 45,000 farmers of the Kuapa Kokoo (KK) co-operative in Ghana. When Divine was launched in 1997, the farmers owned one third of the company and the rest of it was divided between Body Shop International, Comic Relief, Christian Aid and Twin, the alternative trading firm behind Cafedirect.

Two of the KK members sit on the board of Divine, and as the farmers own the business the profit is distributed among them – all this as part of a mission to couple farmer ownership with profitability.

Divine's business success is manifest in the turnover that they generated for their enterprise – a cool £10 million in 2007, with a profit of £500,000 after tax. The company's range of dark, milk and white chocolate bars and eggs sell in well-known supermarkets, such as Asda and Morrisons in the UK, and has also penetrated the US market. The social ownership and value consolidation is evinced in the fact that Divine pays a fair price for cocoa (guaranteed to be higher than the market price) plus a Fairtrade premium that helps to fund social projects including the sinking of wells and building schools and health centres. This is augmented by interesting initiatives such as 2 per cent of turnover being invested in securing the firm's supply chain by funding activities including co-operative training in agricultural practices, health and hygiene, and gender development. Divine offers a solution to the Kuapa farmers through both opportunity identification, innovative organizational and operational arrangements and ownership of the opportunity – the innovative organizational practice that turns these opportunities to a package of solutions with which to overcome poverty.

In the local Twi language, Pa-pa-paa' means 'best of the best', a message that the Kuapa farmers never fail to chant when they meet, when they eat, and when they pass each other – an expression of the spirit of creating and growing a new venture that they own to realize opportunities.

(Source: *Observer*, 2007)

Conclusion

This chapter has provided key insights into the literature on the different social dimensions of entrepreneurship and innovation. The overall objective was to enable a clear understanding of the social context of new firm formation and innovative growth. To gain such an understanding, the establishment of social contexts, embedding of technology and innovation in those contexts, the critical components of culture, social capital, reputational building and bonding, and networks were examined with a view to confirming their relevance to the study of entrepreneurship. Finally, the chapter touched upon an emerging and burgeoning new arena of entrepreneurship – social entrepreneurship – as it struggles to seek an identity of its own and a meaningful place in economic development activity through its unique organizational arrangements, marrying the social with the business dimensions of a hybrid organization. It was noted that many of the economic concepts have either an explanation or an elaboration in the related disciplines of sociology, anthropology, and management and organizational studies. The fusion of ideas to create a new field of study – entrepreneurship – is in keeping with the meaning and spirit of this field. There are of course other insights. The role of institutions in society, especially the rule of law, property rights and norms and practices, also has a strong social context. Its importance demands a separate consideration, and this is achieved in the chapter on entrepreneurial contexts (Chapter 6).

We started this chapter by referring to the significance of the economic aspects of entrepreneurship and the substantive body of knowledge about entrepreneurship that the field of economics has helped to develop. A reading of this chapter should, it is hoped, widen the horizons of the reader to consider seriously how an examination of the social aspects offers different conceptual and practical insights into the process of entrepreneurship, while illuminating the economics of the subject.

Self-assessment questions

1. To what extent do Weber's ideas about the individual, society and religion shed light on your understanding of entrepreneurship?
2. If opportunity recognition is central to entrepreneurship, to what extent does a person's work environment and educational background provide clues to how opportunities are identified and realized?
3. Explain how technology life cycles are determined socially.
4. Why is investing in social capital important for entrepreneurs? What are the key features of social capital?
5. Identify the critical features of networks, and show networking helps to build social capital for entrepreneurs.

5 The entrepreneurial organization

Learning outcomes

In this chapter the reader will:

- explore in depth the meaning, scope, structure and components of entrepreneurial organisations;
- distinguish critically between different types of entrepreneurial organisations;
- assess critically the relative merits, disadvantages and values of various types of entrepreneurial organisations;
- obtain a thorough understanding of collaborative forms of innovation that help to define modern entrepreneurial organisations;
- derive a critical appreciation of the changing landscape of innovation and the role of entrepreneurial organisations in a global economy.

Structure of the chapter

We start this chapter with an attempt to explain the meaning and scope of entrepreneurship and innovation in business organisations. Understanding what entrepreneurship and innovation mean in an organisational context helps us to distinguish entrepreneurial firms from ordinary, run-of-the-mill businesses. It also helps us to appreciate how these firms represent change and the ability to change and adapt as dynamic organizations in continually transforming environments. This appreciation stems from a consideration of the features and structures of entrepreneurial organizations, leading to a review of different types of organizations in the second part of the chapter. As part of this review, Part II of the chapter takes the reader on a journey of entrepreneurial processes in an adaptive organization where ambidexterity offers a way of dealing with the randomness and diversity associated with uncertainty and disruptiveness in technology life cycles. An in-depth look at the types of change generated by innovative activity reveals the need for ambidextrous organizational capability.

As the third part of the chapter shows, complexity in uncertainty environments requires more from organizations than ambidexterity. Networking has emerged as a strategic tool for organizations which now make products and provide services based on inter- and intra-firm alliances and relationships. Networked firms are concentrations of business units connected with one another and coordinated by market and non-market mechanisms. How networking, ambidextrous and other entrepreneurial processes work in different types of firms is the focus of the fourth part, which looks at the distinctiveness of small, medium and large entrepreneurial firms. Their evolution and the key drivers of innovation in these firms now find new directions in the changing landscape of innovation in a globalized world. How organizations retain their entrepreneurial features in this world is discussed in the fifth part of the chapter before it is concluded.

Introduction

We have introduced the idea of entrepreneurship as value creation in the form of discovery, evaluation and exploitation of opportunities to produce new goods and services (Shane and Venkatraman, 2000). Inherent in such a definition is a conflation of the two terms, entrepreneurship and innovation. As we discussed in the Chapter 1, a great deal of writing on the subject assumes such a conflation and does not distinguish between the two terms. For most students of the subject, this is not necessarily a satisfactory outcome because the two words are not synonymous. The other conflation found in the vast body of literature – namely that of entrepreneurship and small businesses – provides us with a clue, which is that there is an organizational component in entrepreneurship. Individuals who are entrepreneurs create new organizations (Gartner and Carter, 2003; Acs and Audretsch, 2005). So organizations and the process of building up suitable organizations are central to entrepreneurship.

New organizations are most likely to be small organizations but they do not necessarily take the form of totally independent small firms. As we shall see later in this chapter, large businesses often spin out new firms. Crucially, larger firms often demonstrate the ability to reinvent themselves to pursue entrepreneurial activities. These entrepreneurial organizations identify and create new business models with which to carry out new activities and generate revenue streams that were not imagined before. Other types of organizations have completely radical missions, such as the fulfilment of social objectives through their business activities. These are the so-called social or community enterprises. All of these organizations:

- create different forms of economic, social, cultural and personal value; and
- contribute to the social and economic development of the regions in which they are located.

Our focus here is on the entrepreneurial *business* organization. Such an organization is not necessarily a *new*, small firm. *Existing* firms that are able to adapt, change and create value through new products, new services, new markets and organizational transformation can also be regarded as exemplars of entrepreneurial activity. This chapter describes and analyses these firms and their organizational capability to run entrepreneurial and innovative firms.

What makes an entrepreneurial organization, how they create such value, their constructs and purpose and their role in entrepreneurship development is what we explore in this chapter. This exploration takes in organizations of different size – small, medium and large organizations – their respective characteristics, constraints and approaches to innovation, their relative strengths and weaknesses according to the sectoral context in which they operate, and quite importantly the way they collaborate and network to optimize their innovative potential. Different types of entrepreneurial organizations come together to contribute to economic development through a variety of innovations following distinctive processes. Mixing the micro with the macro level issues is a hazardous exercise! We, will, however, take up that challenge if only because how different types of firms carry out and manage their organizations in an entrepreneurial way is as important as the contribution they make to the wider economy. Understanding how these entrepreneurial organizations establish and grow their unique ventures is the main objective of this chapter.

PART I: INNOVATION AND ENTREPRENEURSHIP IN ORGANIZATIONS: MEANING AND SCOPE

We are referring here to particular types of existing organizations that are deemed entrepreneurial. In doing so, we are distinguishing them from other types of organizations. The distinctiveness is achieved by virtue of these organizations being vehicles for change. Change is exemplified in the form of developing new products and processes, and in using technologies, money, talent and other resources to do so, creating appropriate platforms for their production, their development, promotion, sale and diffusion in the marketplace. In short, these organizations harness and generate innovation.

The way innovation works in organizations and the strategies necessary for successful innovation is part of the process of creating new products and services. The innovation process is a complex management issue in organizations involving defining the process within an organization, exploration and exploitation, search and routines, forecasting and implementation, learning and diffusing – all in highly uncertain environments. These processes have been studied exhaustively.[1] For the process to be effective enough to yield positive results, an organization needs a culture and structures that can support innovation. The organization needs to be created and maintained as an innovative organization (IO). An IO is not simply the opposite of, for example, a non-innovative bureaucratic organization with loose structures and informal environments, but is one that has appropriate structures, mechanisms, routines and a culture to support the type of innovation it produces. The appropriateness of such structures and mechanisms is contingent upon the type of innovation the organization is able to generate and the industrial sector in which it operates. In many cases the innovation is not only found in the new products and services that are created but also in the management processes and even in the re-creation of the style and building blocks of existing organizations. In this sense the entrepreneurial organization not only produces new goods and service; it is also innovative in terms of its evolution as an organization. The entrepreneurial organization, is therefore, an innovative organization.

Components of an entrepreneurial/innovative organization

Tidd and Bessant (2009) argue that the innovative organization is characterized by an 'integrated set of components that work together to create and reinforce the kind of environment which enables innovation to flourish' (p. 101). They identify seven components, as shown in Table 5.1.

The set of components is a mix of personal and impersonal elements including:

- people – vision; leadership; teams;
- structure and organization – organizational design; team working; high involvement; and
- environment – internal culture and external focus.

Structures

The components shown in Table 5.1 represent an eclectic and complex mix, requiring a high level of management attention. Typically, cognitive, behavioural and structural ways of maintaining the status quo coupled with core rigidities quite often come in the way of change

Table 5.1 Components of innovative organizations

Component	Key features	Meaning and scope
1. Shared vision, leadership and the will to innovate	Clearly articulated and shared sense of purpose; stretching strategic intent; 'Top management commitment'	The idea and practice of innovation is not limited to a few people – for example, managers and technocrats – but shared across all levels and encouraged through different types of activities
2. Appropriate structure	Organizational design that enables creativity, learning and interaction. Not always a loose 'skunk works' model; key issue is finding appropriate balance between organic and mechanistic options for particular contingencies	Adapting and experimenting with varied forms, structures, mechanisms and responsibilities to allow for proper understanding of change through new products, services and organizational practice
3. Key individuals	Promoters, champions, gatekeepers, and other roles that energize or facilitate innovation	Believers, supporters, providers and implementers of innovation who facilitate and make innovation happen
4. Effective team working	Appropriate use of teams (at local, cross-functional and inter-organizational level) to solve problems; requires investment in team selection and building	Individuals working within groups and across different functional activities to harness capabilities to best deal with the varied pressures of uncertainty
5. High-involvement innovation	Participation in organization-wide continuous improvement activity	Together with structure to keep innovation on a level of meaningful alertness at all levels of business activity
6. Creative climate	Positive approach to creative ideas, supported by relevant motivation systems	Generating, harnessing and using creative ideas through tensions and cooperation of people across the organization and through networks within which organizations operate
7. External Focus	Internal and external customer orientation; exclusive networking	Recognizing and valuing the role of the organization within its sector, its geographical location, its network of stakeholders, as part of its strategic and operational focus, imbibing ideas from outside and influencing external environment with ideas generated within the firm

Source: Adapted from Tidd and Bessant (2009).

brought about by innovation. The limiting behaviour is reinforced in organizations that have mechanistic structures characterized by rigid hierarchies and highly defined routines, job classifications and standard measures of accountability. Organic structures allowing for flexibility of purpose, use of convergent and the divergent skill sets of people are more suited to innovative change in organizations. The higher the uncertainty in the environment, the greater the level of flexibility that is required in both structures and processes. There is evidence of such flexibility in the fast-moving electronics, information technology and biotechnology sectors, which appear to have highly adaptive and organic modes of operation. Their counterparts in the traditional industries often need to have twin and differentiated structures within the organization with specialist groups to meet the needs of a diverse marketplace (Tidd and Bessant, 2009).

The type of structures appropriate for innovation is then a function of the type of industry in which entrepreneurial firms are located and in some cases the size, age and strategy of the firm in question (Child, 1980). The necessary mix of large and small firms in a particular industry could also have implications for both the type of firm and the structure and processes that are best suited for innovation (Acs and Audretsch, 1994).

PART II: THE ENTREPRENEURIAL PROCESS IN ENTREPRENEURIAL ORGANIZATIONS: THE EMERGENCE AND MANAGEMENT OF NEW IDEAS AND THE NEED TO ADAPT IN UNCERTAIN ENVIRONMENTS

Entrepreneurial firms are growing firms. Successful innovation helps them to grow, with the production of new goods and services and new forms of organizational management practices. Growth manifests itself in terms of turnover, increase in market share and in the ability to create jobs. But non-innovative firms can also grow, and the metrics of turnover, market share and job creation can apply equally to these firms. There are, however, crucial differences.

Innovative firms not only compete with their non-innovative counterparts, but in doing so they stretch the scope and content of existing markets. New products and services offer greater choice, allowing for imitation, refinement and changes to the use of the products and services. Other innovative firms pursue 'Blue Ocean' strategies (Kim and Mauborgne, 2005), identifying markets that do not exist either by challenging the boundaries of existing industries or through operations in new industries created by new technologies such as the Internet.

Kim and Mauborgne (2005) refer to the interesting example of a Canadian firm, Cirque du Soleil, a circus industry firm created by street performers who achieved a level of revenue in 20 years that the industry global champions took 100 years to achieve. Cirque du Soliel did so in a declining industry where interest in circuses was fading fast, and curiously by opening up new market space appealing to corporate customers and adults rather than just children and their accompanying parents. Here is an example of a firm that:

- made the competition irrelevant by not entering into the same competitive market space; and
- created and captured new customers and their demand for the spectacular.

Uncertainty and adaptation

Innovation and entrepreneurship are context driven (see Chapter 6 for a full discussion of the importance of contexts). In specific environments and at certain times, the pressures on organizations vary from country to country and from region to region. In the highly globalized environment of change, product life cycles are difficult to forecast and turnover levels are difficult to maintain. Uncertainty, rather than risk, with all its concomitant difficulties of assessment, poses problems for growth. Growth is necessary, but this can be achieved only through renewal and innovation. Part of this uncertainty is caused by the change in the structure and composition of the industry. Interviewing the CEO of Egmont, a big media firm in Denmark, Muzyka (1999) observed this twin pressure of renewal and growth. In the video containing this interview, Jan O. Froshaug, the Egmont CEO says:

> I believe it's simple: either you grow or you die! If you do not take the opportunity, someone else will. In our industry . . . the media industry changes very fast and the time horizons of all new products are very short. It's becoming like the fashion industry.

Analysing the new media industry and the internet base of the music industry, Chris Anderson observed the long-tail phenomenon occurring. Smaller and relatively unknown products (CDs and DVDs by relatively unknown artists) earned a higher level of aggregate revenue than, for example, hit records by established names. The Internet had opened up new music to a wider audience, and innovative firms responding to this change have had to adapt to compete and grow.

The nature of adaptation is a far cry from restructuring through fairly standard procedures of cost-cutting, downsizing or streamlining, including the laying-off of employees, selling so-called non-core aspects of a business, and re-engineering – management buzz words of the 1980s that have not gone away! These traditional processes do not change the status quo of management in 're-engineered' organizations; they function as transactional organizations concerned primarily with only those adaptations that are necessary for the implementation of an immediate activity. Invariably, their main focus is on cutting costs and rationalizing the activities they pursue.

> It seems as if management tries to either control, acquire, cost reduce, focus, rationalise, reorganise and hence finally shrink their way to success. (Muzyka, 1999, p.7).

Transactional organizations that work round single opportunities or projects offer a temporary alternative to the traditional form of restructured organization. But these organizations face the higher transaction cost of pursuing single opportunities and closing and opening up, with all their displacement problems, every time there is a new opportunity. Organizations which, however, build and leverage organizational processes, capabilities and systems to meet the demands of an evolving set of opportunities by learning how to grow from within are self-renewing innovative organizations. They are also referred to as 'Adaptive Entrepreneurial Organizations' (AEOs) (Muzyka, 1999). For these firms, growth and new business creation are not options. Their scorecard is that of value creation, and this scorecard is made up of two essential parts:

a) managing the *performance gap*, which consists of improving performance across multiple dimensions of quality, cost, cycle time, productivity and profitability; and
b) focusing on the *opportunity gap*, which means using resources effectively and profitably to create new markets, new businesses and a sense of broad strategic direction.

These parts are managed simultaneously through an aspiration for innovation and the development of an open, strategic architecture (Prahalad, 1997). Deploying these twin elements in management practice enables firms to develop core competencies so that they can bundle multiple technologies, customer knowledge and intuition creatively, allowing a firm to look both within and outside the firm (Prahalad, 1997).

AEOs are distinguished by their design and 'dynamic balance'. They appear to be at least marginally different from other organizations, allowing for communication and collective endeavour to manage dilemmas while focusing on growth. This focus on growth is possible only when organizations move away from simply reinforcing the management of existing resources and assets and tying up their organizational identity to an existing portfolio of products and services. A greater emphasis on the capabilities of the organization linked to opportunities and the competencies of people differentiate them from the ordinary. Pervasive innovation – that is, innovation at all levels of an organization – and the establishment of an open architecture that allows for the search for opportunities outside the immediate knowledge horizon are typical features. Good examples include firms such as Nokia, which switched from being timber merchants to telecommunications, and 3M, which embraced the development of Post-it notes even when it was not in the paper business.

Ambidexterity and multiple modes of operation

What we can bank on so far is the idea that an innovative organization is one that is specifically designed for that purpose. Its structures, processes, rewards and people are combined in a special way to do something for the first time. Other organizations also have structures, processes and reward systems. They too manage people effectively. But whereas their goal is to produce more of the same (perhaps with some modifications), the innovating organization creates and manages opportunities for producing goods and services for the first time. In typically large organizations there is a need to do both: to manage an 'operating organization' that looks after routine production, and an innovating organization that develops new lines of activity (Galbraith, 2004). Often new lines evolve into standard products and services over time and their development then becomes the preoccupation of the 'operating' firm. The components of these two types of organization are different, as Table 5.2 shows.

Managing the two types of organization makes a single organization an 'ambidextrous' organization (Tushman *et al.,* 1997), the type of organization necessary to emerge as a 'knowledge-creating company'.

Technology cycles and ambidextrous organizations

A major imperative for the creation, establishment and management of ambidextrous organi-

Table 5.2 Comparison of components of operating and innovating organizations

Organization design components	Operating organizations	Innovating organizations
Structure	Division of labour Departmentalization Span and control Distribution of power	Roles: Orchestrator Sponsor Ideas generator (champion) Differentiation Reservations
Process	Providing information and communication Planning and budgeting Measuring performance Linking departments	Planning/funding Getting ideas Blending ideas Transitioning Managing programmes
Reward systems	Compensation Promotion Leader style Job design	Opportunity/autonomy Promotion/recognition Special compensation
People	Selection/recruitment Promotion/transfer Training/development	Selection/self-selection Training/development

Source: adapted from Galbraith (2004).

zations is the nature of technology cycles. Technology cycles are made up of technological discontinuities. These discontinuities generate both technological and business competitiveness turbulence, because an existing technology fights against the introduction of a new technology while businesses using the old and new technologies also compete with one another in the marketplace. In some cases many new technologies compete with one another and with the incumbent one. Tushman *et al.* (1997) refer to early radio transmission and how continuous wave transmission was a disruptive technology challenging spark-gap transmission. The former initiated competition not only with the latter but also between different versions of continuous wave transmission itself, including alternating wave, arc and vacuum tube transmission, with the last-mentioned technology emerging as the dominant design. The emergence of dominant design induces incremental changes to the dominant technology and some degree of 'architectural' change in the way the technology itself is created till such time as another, substitute product breaks its hold in the market. This analysis of the evolution of technology and its consequent disruptive capabilities is in line with Schumpeterian thinking of entrepreneurship and economic development.

The interesting issue is not so much the emergence of the dominant design itself but rather how it emerges! Tushman *et al.* (1997) argue that competitive organizations, strategic alliance groups and sometimes governmental regulators, each with their own political, social and economic agendas, initiate and push dominant designs into the marketplace. Organizational imperatives come to the fore as product innovation gives way to process innovation. An organization's capability in managing the internal/external influences and dynamics is, therefore, crucial for innovative firms. What is equally important to understand is that, depending on where they are located in the technology cycle, organizations will innovate accordingly. In eras of ferment requiring discontinuous product variants, firms will be associated with fundamental process innovation, while at times of incremental change organizations will follow streams of incremental and architectural innovation. The outcome of these dualities is that organizations need to be ambidextrous in handling both strategic and innovative diversity. A single organizational unit hosts multiple cultures, structures, processes and human resource capabilities. Such multiple tasks and structures can create contradictions and tensions between disparate sub-units of activity.

How does an entrepreneurial, ambidextrous firm know how best to align its competencies and assets with changes both in its industry and in the technologies that it uses? An incoherent approach to any form of alignment can result in failure for the firm adversely affecting its resources, knowledge base and brand capital. Quite often a misjudgement in the type of innovation to adopt in certain circumstances can result in significant problems for the firm, especially in the consequent misallocation of resources.

Westland (2008), building on Conner and Prahalad (1995), identifies four types of change – intermediate, progressive, creative and radical – and the threat of obsolescence or the need for preservation associated with them. Figure 5.1 shows these trajectories of change.

Westland (2008) suggests that different capabilities are required by the innovative firm to meet the challenges of change, thus making the case for appropriate alignment of strategies with which to manage the change process:

- *Radical change-oriented strategies*: Radical change occurs when an industry's core assets and core activities, including knowledge and brand capital, are threatened with obsolescence. Internet-enabled mobility of the digital media such as MP3s and DivX files have, for example, introduced radical innovations in the music and network television industries;

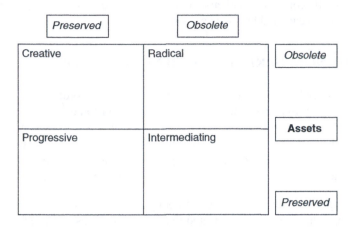

Figure 5.1 Trajectories and the threat of obsolescence

Source: adapted from Westland (2008).

- *Progressive change strategies*: Progressive change does not threaten the core assets or competencies of a firm, and the past 20 years or so, before the real impact of internet technologies, have seen most firms indulging in gradual change because the basics assets, technologies and activities remained stable. If firms lost market share or their commercial base, it was because rookie firms had a better understanding of the way in which best advantage is secured from existing technologies. Efficiency is the by-word for such changes!
- *Creative change-based strategies*: Creative change results in the accelerated depreciation of core assets but not necessarily the core competencies of a firm. Telephone equipment manufacturers, such as Ericsson, Motorola and Nokia, have for example faced serious competition from consumer electronics firms. In Ericsson's case, it was a partnership with a consumer electronics giant, Sony, involving the transfer of its handsets protection to the latter that left it free to focus on the operator equipment market.
- *Intermediate change strategies:* The exact opposite of creative change, intermediate change takes place when core competencies are threatened with obsolescence even when core assets continue to generate value. A classic case is that of Swatch and its enormous success, which was formed by Swiss makers who saw the sales of their analogue watches decline rapidly with the advent of their digital counterparts. Teaming up with designers from many countries, the group of Swiss watchmakers reduced the number of components and the production time.

Increasingly, in a highly uncertain and globalized environment, optimization strategies indicate that it is no longer profitable or effective to manage so many multiple functions independently. This is because of the speed with which technologies are emerging, the highly competitive and architecturally different channels of production, marketing and sale of products and services (as in physical forms of production and internet-based design and development activity), dispersed sources of know-how and talent, and radical changes in the structure of consumer preferences. So, in addition to managing disruptive and operational technologies, firms have to manage different processes within the dualities referred to above, search for technologies and talent elsewhere, and respond to new deliberations of the ethical and environmentally conscious marketplace. Here, the efficacy of the single firm gives way to the opportunities generated by a network of firms.

PART III: THE NETWORKED ENTREPRENEURIAL FIRM

Networked firms can be defined as clusters of business units coordinated by market mechanisms instead of layers of management and multiple decision makers within a single organization (Snow *et al.*, 1993). These firms are not reliant on scale economies, centralized planning and control systems, and resource accumulation associated with the more traditional firm of the first three quarters of the twentieth century. Their focus is on doing fewer things better with less (with a smaller management team and/or a smaller portfolio of activities):

*   exploring opportunities and resources globally;
*   maximizing returns on assets dedicated to a business – irrespective of whether they are owned by their firm or by partners, associates and even competitors;
*   performing functions for which they have specific expertise and competencies;
*   outsourcing activities that can be performed more quickly and more effectively.

(Snow *et al.*, 1993)

Table 5.3 shows the demands of the new business environments and the organizational responses to these demands, as explained by Snow *et al.* (1993).

Table 5.3 Organization responses to the new business environment

The new competitive reality

Driving forces:	**Interactive forces:**
Globalization	Deregulation
Strong new players at every stage of the value chain (upstream and downstream)	Legal and policy change produce uncertainty and increase competition
Competition has reduced all margins – no slack left in most economic systems	Public services are being privatized
Technological change and technology transfer:	**Changing workforce demographics:**
Shorter product life cycles	Domestic workforce is becoming more mature,
Lower barriers to entry	diverse and less well-trained and educated
Economies of scope as well as scale	Global workforce is becoming more mobile
	Facilitating forces:
	CAD/CAM and other manufacturing advances
	Faster, lower cost communications and computer technologies
	(The Internet)
	More social and political freedom

Organizational imperatives

Product and service demands:	**Managerial requirements:**
Focus on distinctive competence	Build smaller, better-trained permanent workforces
Reduce costs and accelerate innovation	Develop and use links to part-time and temporary human resources
Hold only productive assets	Develop and use links to global technological resources
Reduce overall time cycle	

The allocation of skills and business activities across the network of designers, producers, brokers, suppliers and distributors in the market enables the members of the network to bring competitive forces to bear on each element of the product or service value chain, with market factors influencing the resource allocation decisions.

Network structures

Snow *et al.* (1993) refer to three types of network structures – internal, stable and dynamic – each appropriate for particular competitive environments. In common with organizational structures in general, network-based structure are dependent on the context of their operations.

Internal networks are created within organizations to encourage managers of different units and assets to work to the logic of the marketplace. The idea is that innovations are more likely to occur as a result of the pressures on internal units having to operate with market-based prices instead of artificial transfer prices. Car and component manufacturers such as GM have over time reduced the number of components divisions with each division pursuing their own speciality, and converted a relatively rigid and inefficient components division into a group of well-coordinated and flexible subcontractors with clear performance measures (Snow *et al.* 1993). A public sector model of internal networks can be found in the United Kingdom's National Heath Service, with its internal market, although there are unanswered questions about the applicability of private sector models in the public sphere.

Stable networks are characterized by particle outsourcing allowing for the introduction of some degree of flexibility in the overall value chain of a business. Assets are owned by many firms but dedicated to a particular business, which enables the ownership of assets and associated risks to be spread across independent firms. A large core firm, such as BMW, has a set of vendor firms either providing inputs or distributing its outputs, or both.

Dynamic networks are the meta networks of discontinuous innovative and highly competitive environments. Extensive outsourcing is the order of the day, and firms in the film, music, publishing and fashion business are typical carriers of dynamic networks. The lead firm in the dynamic network relies on a core skill (such as manufacturing, R&D, design, assembly or brokering), identifying and assembling assets owned by other companies.

Snow *et al.* (1993) provide the interesting example of a broker-led dynamic network. Lewis Galoob Toys has approximately 100 employees and its primary function as the lead network player is that of brokering. While independent inventors and entertainment firms conceive Galoob's products, outside specialists carry out the design and engineering work. A dozen or so vendors are contracted for manufacturing and packaging in Hong Kong, who in turn pass on the more labour-intensive manufacturing to China. On arrival in the USA, the toys are distributed through commissioned manufacturers' representatives. Galoob's accounts are handed over to a factoring company that also sets Galoob's credit policy.

The network as a whole provides for both specialization and flexibility while running the risk of variations in quality, loss of expertise and proprietary knowledge or technology. If design and production cycles are short then dynamic networks can work effectively because of a lower level of dependency on quality variations. Similarly, if proprietary rights can be protected and outsourcing is limited to specific elements of the manufacturing or development process, the risks of a 'collective deficit' are reduced (Snow *et al.*, 1993).

The stakes of dynamic networking have been raised, thanks to globalization and a business model response in the form of open innovation. The dynamic, network-centric open innovation models are now permeating a wide variety of business structures, defining a new way of working across countries and regions and raising questions about the nature of policy that can support business activity across global value chains. This process is accompanied on the one hand by flows of capital, technologies and talent across borders in a cluster of industries often related to each other through common and transferable technologies and skills. On the other hand, it is characterized by a level of connectivity of ideas and people (both producers and users working together).

How do these changing landscapes impact on organizations? How do organizations respond, and what entrepreneurial strategies and processes do they use to cope and to derive advantage for their organizations? Answers to such questions are to some extent dependent on whether we are referring to small, medium or large organizations. Examining the differences between these firms, their varied influences and how they manage the innovation process through, for example, ambidexterity or networking, can throw light on different types of organizational capabilities necessary for different types of firms.

PART IV: EVOLVING FIRMS AND THEIR TYPES

Innovation and large firms

So far an overwhelming part of the discussion has ignored the size question and the respective capabilities of small and large entrepreneurial firms. However, much of the deliberation on different types of entrepreneurial firms is based on the literature of innovation, which to a great extent relies almost blindly on the peculiarities of the larger organization. Larger firms are able to accommodate ambidextrous units, run parallel activities of specialized innovation and routine business practice, and take full advantage of the networked environment. Economies of scale can enable a large firm to benefit more from innovation, given the levels of investment in R&D, taking out Intellectual Property Protection (IPO), the attraction of venture capital,[2] and the percentage cost reduction that can apply to the larger volume of a bigger firm. They have the market power to do so. This view lies at the centre of conventional wisdom and it is, therefore, believed that the larger enterprise capitalizes on its market power and is the main driver of technological change. No less a person than Schumpeter (1942) argued that:

> There cannot be any reasonable doubt that under the conditions of our epoch such superiority is as a matter of fact the outstanding feature of the typical large-scale unit of control, though mere size is neither necessary or sufficient for it. These units not only arise in the process of creative destruction and function in a way entirely different from the static schema, but in many cases of decisive importance they provide the necessary form for the achievement. (Schumpeter, 1942, p. 101)

Seduced by the rise of the American corporation in the middle of the twentieth century, Schumpeter was referring to the larger firm especially in the context of monopolies where the monopolist firm is likely to generate a larger supply of innovations because there are advantages that, even if they are not unattainable on the competitive level of enterprise, are realized only on the monopolistic level. This suggests that unless a firm dominates a market it cannot undertake the risks and uncertainties associated with innovation. The evidence backing the dominant role of larger firms in innovation is especially strong when the R&D aspect of technological change is considered. Acs and Audretsch (2005) refer to Scherer (1984), who found evidence among US firms of increasing returns to scale for about 20 per cent of the industries he studied, constant returns to scale for a little less than 75 per cent, and diminishing returns in less than 10 per cent of the industries. The case with patents is slightly different in that various studies, including one by Scherer (1982), show that the number of patented inventions increases less than proportionately with firm size.

Innovation and the small firm

Over time various pieces of research have found compelling explanations for the innovation advantage smaller firms have over large firms. The management structures of small firms where there is less bureaucracy (in comparison with larger organizations) and a smaller decision-making team is conducive to a culture of innovation in the firm. Additionally, as Acs and Audretsch (2005), referring to Scherer (1988), point out:

> many advances in technology accumulate upon a myriad of detailed inventions involving individual components, materials and fabrication techniques. The sales possibilities for making such narrow, detailed advances are often too modest to interest giant corporations. An individual entrepreneur's juices will flow over a new product or process with sales prospects in millions of dollars per year, whereas few large corporations can work up much excitement over such small fish, nor can they accommodate small ventures easily into their organisational structures. (p. 20)

All of these components also tends to have their own technology cycles, as Tushman *et al.* (1997) found in their study of the innovation process of firms. If smaller firms are able to cash in on the initial indifference of their larger counterparts to these products and processes they could gain a distinctive advantage over the larger firm as far as the innovation process is concerned.

The spillover effect and spin-offs also help smaller firms to overcome the limitations of R&D expenditure in their organizations. Differences in expectations between the value of an invention to the scientist inventor in a firm and the management of the firm could lead the former to consider a spin-off if the costs of doing so (i.e. setting up a new firm) is lower than the return from the prospective innovation. The knowledge generated in the large organization of the researcher-inventor now flows into the spin-off where it is commercialized. Similarly, knowledge as public good created in universities can also spill over to private enterprises where it is commercialized (Jaffe *et al.*, 1993; Acs and Audretsch 2005). In fact Acs *et al.* (1992) found that spillovers from universities contribute more to innovation in smaller firms even if larger firms are more active in university-based or sponsored.

The seminal work of Acs, Audrestch and others on the role of the small firm in the innovation process is based mainly on data relating to US firms. However, corroborative evidence has also been found in Europe, Asia and other parts of the world (OECD, 2009; Tidd and Bessant, 2009). What is particularly important to note is that it is not simply a matter of either large or small firms being more innovative than the other. Instead, what matters when we try to understand the nature of the entrepreneurial organization and its ability to innovate includes:

- the type of innovation – different types of products, services processes;
- the industrial sector in which the innovation is taking place;

- the measure of technological change generated by innovation; and
- the management processes in those firms that help to nurture and support innovation.

When we attempt to measure technological change we can find a proper analytical basis for arguing about the size of entrepreneurial organizations and their relative association with or impact upon the innovation process. Technological change can be measured using 'input' measures such as R&D. Here, the Schumpeterian Mark II theory holds sway. However, when 'intermediate' measures such as patents are considered, the results are somewhat ambiguous. But when a direct measure of innovative output is used, the reality is more complex. Using this last measure, entrepreneurial firms contribute more to innovation according to the industries in which they belong. For example, small firms generate more innovations in computers and process control instruments while large firms are the main innovators in pharmaceuticals and aircraft industries where significant capital outlay for new product development is essential (Acs and Audretsch, 2005).

Acs and Audretsch (2005) suggest that the best measure of innovative activity is the total innovative rate, which is explained as the total number of innovations per 1,000 employees in each industry. For larger firms, it is the total number of innovations made by firms with at least 500 or 250 employees (depending on whether we are referring to the US or Europe, for example) divided by number of employees (thousands). For small and medium-sized firms, the reference is made to firms with fewer than 500 or 250 employees divided by the number of employees (thousands). This innovation rate allows for a proper accountability of large and small firm innovation relative to the number of these firms in different industries.

The above picture gives us some idea of the contribution that different types of small firm make to the innovation and technological change in the wider economy. But what about how such firms are managed and the determinants of innovation in these firms?

A survey of 2,000 SMEs by the Small Business Research Centre in the UK found that 60 per cent of the sample had apparently introduced a major new product or service innovation in the previous five years. This statistic could be interpreted as a demonstration of the view that innovation is indeed important for the majority of small firms even if we do not really obtain any picture of the type and value of any such innovation, the impact on the market in terms of dominant design or end-use, or even financial results. Given their traditional internal resource constraints, smaller firms are more likely to use external sources including individual firms, personal contacts and social networks to provide leads for developing new products and services. MacPherson (1997) suggests that there is indeed a positive connection between the performance of a small firm and the level of external scientific, technical and professional support. This finding corroborates in part the evidence of the beneficial impacts of spillovers from universities that Acs *et al.* (1992) found. However, these benefits are circumscribed by the legendary limitations of small firms, such as their constrained technical and managerial competencies and stretched financial resources that prevent them from making relevant expenditure for innovation (Oakey, 1993).

Tidd and Bessant (2009) challenge some of the findings from early studies on small firm innovation which found that, adjusting for size, smaller firms made more new products than larger firms. They refer to methodological shortcomings in those studies, including the inclusion of subsidiaries and divisions of larger firms, and inappropriate weighting of the technological merit and commercial value of firms. They go on to explain that formal R&D is weakly associated with growth and profitability but found other factors, such as the founder's level of managerial experience and technological know how, pro-activeness and propensity to engage in innovation, to have stronger associations with innovation performance.

Small firms, large firms

Different sectors are likely to show different factors affecting the success of small firm innovation. Underpinning these success stories are the relative behavioural advantages that small firms enjoy over their larger counterparts which tend to rely on resource advantages (Rothwell and Dodgson, 1994). Flexibility, the ability to respond rapidly to demands and changing circumstances, and experimentation are some of the behavioural advantages induced by internal conditions, namely the size of the small firm. Conversely, their size constrains smaller firms in accessing easily critical resources, competencies and capabilities for innovation. Scale and scope factors associated with larger firms equip them for realizing innovations dependent on specialized teams or high-value equipment (Cohen and Klepper, 1992).

A large part of this debate on the relative value of large and small firms is centred around the link between size, survival and growth and the implicit connection that is made between innovation and growth. This debate takes place in the context of the industry life cycle. Firms grow because they innovate, and their ability to innovate may have something to do with their size. Gibrat's Law assumes that firm growth is independent of size (Sutton, 1997). However, Geroski (1995) and Sutton (1997) claim that the likelihood of firm survival is not independent of firm size, and other writers (Doms *et al.*, 1995; Agarwal, 1997; Audretsch, 1995) have followed suit by suggesting that there is a positive relation between firm size and the likelihood of survival. Why is this point important? To answer this question we need to review briefly what Jovanovic(1982) wrote about entrants facing costs. Costs are not simply random; they vary according to different sectors and across firms. Typically, an entrant does not know its own cost structure but it gains its relative efficiency through a process of learning and discovery from the actual marketplace. Survival is possible if abilities exceed expectations. Geroski (1995) points out that small-scale entry is relatively common in most industries but that there is a shorter life expectancy, suggesting that abilities do not match expectations.

Other writers (Porter, 1979; Caves and Porter, 1977) have argued that because they occupy strategic niches in specific industries small firms do not need to grow to survive. In other words, these firms are spared the trials and tribulations of survival if they remain small, in strategic industrial niches. This view is likely to hold in the mature phase of t an industry life cycle and with high-technology products. Utterback and Abernathy (1975) pointed out that in the formative stage of a life cycle there is no dominant design or product. Firms experiment through short production runs, making changes as they go along and after receiving responses from their customers. By contrast, at a mature stage of the life cycle of an industry the product is more standardized as markets grow at a more predictable rate, innovations tend to be limited, and connections between suppliers and customers shore up any form of potential volatility in the market. Innovation, where it occurs, is relatively routine and incremental. In broad terms, therefore, innovative entry is favourable in an entrepreneurial regime found in the formative stage of the industry life cycle, while a routinized regime reflecting a mature stage of the life cycle favours established firms (Winter, 1984).

Rogers (2004) has argued that smaller firms have access mainly to smaller pools of knowledge and human capital. To overcome part of this problem, smaller firms – especially high technology-based firms that rely on research and development activities – appear to obtain value in information exchange, acquisition of resources, technology transfer and risk management from cooperative R&D to improve their competitiveness and innovative capabilities (Rogers, 2004; Noteboom, 1994). Collaboration does not offer any form of equalization for small firms. The outcomes are often patchy and vary according to sectors, the technologies and the innovations involved (Freel, 2003).

Inter-firm alliances, networks and collaborative arrangements are often the main sources of innovation, according to Hippel (1988). Apart from the fact that these forms of activities and the experience of using external networks has grown sharply over the past two decades (Hagedoorn, 2002), smaller firms have derived considerable benefits from these networks (Zahra *et al.* 2000), including access to new knowledge, capital and other resources, technology and market requirements.

In addition, geographical factors, including those of spatially-based networking and clustering (see Chapter 6 and Chapter 11), appear to have beneficial effects even though the innovative firm is likely to outgrow and leave behind its local cluster as it searches for new resources not available in the vicinity of its location. However, the fact that innovative firms operate outside the rational logic of growth and rely on both local knowledge spillovers and national or global resources is borne out by the empirical evidence provided by various writers such as Saxeninan (1994), Florida (2002) and Acs *et al.* (2005).

Small firms and innovation in recent times

So how important are innovative small firms to the wider economy today? To try to answer this question, we need to explore the circumstances in which they function and innovate. According to the OECD (2010), the environment for innovation has changed and the importance of new and small firms to the innovation process has increased. A combination of new technologies, niche forms of market demand and increasing incomes have reduced the 'structural disadvantages' of smaller firms. In the so-called knowledge economy of today, and open and distributed forms of innovation, greater reliance on non-technological forms of innovation (as in organizational forms and social innovation), have created a period of formative change – the rise in the Schumpeterian innovation curve favouring the smaller enterprise.

With new firms entering the market and SME growth prospects, a contribution is made to upgrading the aggregate levels of productivity as incumbents are challenged and firms with lower levels of productivity are displaced. Spin-off ventures enable early commercialization of research, and breakthrough innovations are more likely to occur with smaller niche firms.

Yet there appears to be an uneven distribution of small firm innovation between a few high-impact or high-growth firms and a vast majority of SMEs that innovate less. OECD data also indicates that SMEs innovate less than large firms across a range of categories including product, process, non-technological and new-to-market product innovation. They also appear to occupy a smaller share of collaborative innovation activities. The OECD report on SMEs, Entrepreneurship and Innovation (2010), shows for example that in Sweden only one-in five SMEs (compared to nearly one half of larger firms) had introduced a product innovation in the last three years. Even after adjusting for size, there is a marked difference – albeit the gap is smaller (8% of turnover for SMEs compared to 14% of turnover for larger firms).

The burdens on SMEs remain. Access to financing – internal and external sources – and availability of qualified personnel are still thorny issues. In Italy, 20 per cent of smaller firms cite lack of external finance as a barrier to innovation (compared to 15% of larger firms), while 11 per cent of small firms refer to a lack of skilled personnel as being a hindrance to innovation. This last figure compares to 6 per cent for larger firms (OECD, 2010).

While collaboration and knowledge flows through alliances and networks feature strongly, the advent of globalization has created new opportunities, especially for domestic knowledge to be exploited overseas, together with possibilities for tapping into knowledge generated abroad. The other interesting finding from the OECD (2010) study is the smart use of 'Knowledge Intensive Service Activities' (KISA) by SMEs. This activity involves SMEs bringing in outside firms and consultants to enable the implementation of change in operational matters such as quality control, marketing and product development.

Innovation and the medium-sized firm

Lumping together small and medium-sized firms does not always help. The markets for these firms are often different, as indeed are their capacities for innovation, their management functions, and their routines and technologies.

One of the ways in which the distinction between firms of various sizes can best be studied is by observing them during crisis periods such as the recent recession. For example, the year 2009 started bleakly for most 'mid-market' firms which struggled to cut costs and refinance, but over the course of the same year firms managed to raise cash, improve their share prices, and generally recovere more quickly than either their FTSE 100 or small firm counterparts (FT, 2010). The winners of the FT 2009 PLC awards had demonstrated consistent growth as reflected in their share values; they all had long-term growth strategies and strong management capabilities focused on their customers. This combination of 'virtues' is not restricted to any particular type of firm. The diversity of the winners was represented by a retail chain, a pizza-delivery franchise and a defence manufacturer.

> ### Mini case study 5.1: Pizzas, Homeware and Mobile Telephones
>
> Essential to their success was a readiness to innovate, and relentless attention to quality. Domino Pizza, for example, excels in this determination to stand above others as far as quality is concerned. This includes their attention to ingredients, the ordering process, delivery times with smart on-line delivery systems (worth 20 per cent or more on average) to the nearest outlet, paring down delivery times and encouraging repeat orders. Another firm, an out-of-town homewares retailer, provides 'simple value for money' by appealing to all customers, from high end to budget, offering a wide product range, and providing skilled and knowledgeable staff combined with good service. In the year to July 2009, they improved their pre-tax profits by 9.7 per cent against sales growth of 6.7 per cent with £31m of cash in the bank, even as other retailers felt the impact of the credit squeeze. A third firm, CSR, a Cambridge-based technology company designing chips for Bluetooth wireless headphones used with mobile devices, mixed both corporate and entrepreneurial experience to navigate the business to productive shores. The prize-winning entrepreneur Joep van Beurden first took CSR out of the crowded mobile networks market with the aim of focusing on Bluetooth, Wi-fi and GPS, and also acquired a US-based satellite navigation business during what he describes as the 'deepest, darkest part of the nuclear winter of the economy'.
>
> (Source: *Financial Times*, 2010)

What these three examples show are the particular competencies that characterize organizational and market-oriented innovation. While new technology is used in the business, it is not in their development that these firms show their unique capabilities but rather in the organizational management processes based on simple customer-facing propositions. At a time of recession thrifty customers are both more careful and more sophisticated in the choices they make in buying goods and services, and firms that recognize this change. The act of financial commitment in the heart of an extremely inclement economic climate is made possible by a combination of organizational routines, high-level knowledge of the market and a concentration on niche products, services and markets – a distinctive basket of capabilities, knowledge, careful strategizing and organizational arrangements that sets them apart from many of their counterparts.

It is this basket of capabilities, knowledge, strategizing and organizational arrangements that distinguishes medium-sized firms as innovative leaders in terms of export performance, which in turn contributes to the export dominance of certain countries over others. Simon (2009) has found that countless mid-size firms are world leaders in exports and that the exporting success of German-language and Scandinavian countries is attributable to these firms. While he found that such firms are to be found in the USA, Brazil, Japan, South Africa, Korea and New Zealand, approximately 80 per cent of all mid-size world market leaders come from the German-Scandinavian countries.

A quick scan of some of the mid-size leaders reveals the list shown in Table 5.4.

What makes these export-oriented firms so distinctive and what is it that they share in common? Simon (2009) quantifies the criteria for these firms in terms of:

- their position in the global market – they are either number one, two or three, or number one on their continent;
- their revenue is below \$4 billion; and
- there is a low level of public awareness of these firms. In other words, these firms are 'hidden' from the glare of media with their owners and managers preferring instead a 'sustainable approach towards global excellence'.

As innovating firms, the way they approach their goals and visions for growth, how they define their markets especially in terms of diversification and globalization, hoq they consider their customers and ways in which they organize their financing for expansion are

Table 5.4 Midsize global leaders in their field

Country	Names of firms	Product/service
Iceland	Baader	Fish-processing systems
USA	McIlhenny;	Pepper sauce ('Tabasco');
	3B Scientific	Anatomical teaching aids
Singapore	International SOS	International emergency services
Sweden	Tetra	Aquarium and pond supplies
New Zealand	Gallagher	Electric fences
Norway	Tandberg	Video-conferencing technology
UK	De La Rue	Printer and maker of security paper
Germany	Arnold & Richter; Sachtler;	ARRI camera and tripod;
	CEAG	charging devices for cell phones
France	Petzel	Harnesses, rope-blocking snap links, front lamps, etc. for vertical sports such as rock-climbing, mountaineering and cave exploration
Italy	Technogym	Fitness equipment
India	Essel Propack	Laminated tubes for toothpaste and similar substances
Austria	Plansee; Jungbunzlaeur (Austrian-Swiss)	Manufacturer of high-performance materials made with refractory metals and composites; citric acid supplier for Coca-Cola
South Africa	Sappi	Coated fine paper and dissolvable pulp
Brazil	Embraer	Regional jets
Japan	Nisha	Small touch panels
Portugal	Amorim	Cork products and cork flooring

Source: adapted from Simon (2009).

critical issues pertaining to entrepreneurial management processes within the firm. An entrepreneurial approach to their local business environments and institutions also distinguishes these firms as innovative organizations.

Organic growth rather than growth through acquisitions characterizes high-flying medium-sized firms. What drives their growth is innovation, internationalization and diversification. Innovation often takes the form even of creation of their own markets, as the examples of Brita (for household water filters), Karcher (for high-pressure cleaners) and SOS international (for global rescue services) demonstrate. A sharp focus on process and marketing innovation, key elements of organizational (as opposed to technological) innovation, is another feature of many of these firms. The genuine religious conviction of its founder, Claus Hipp, guides Hipp's successful organic image in the baby and children's food market (Simon, 2009).

The organizational arrangements referred to above are essential capabilities of the medium-sized firms. But in making such arrangements the key players are not necessarily different from other firms. What distinguish the firms that are of interest to us (namely those that grow rapidly) are that they use these capabilities to foster and manage innovation. Achieving world market leadership and sustaining capabilities to maintain that position is a function of continuous innovation. By 'innovation' we are referring here to the wide range of technological, process, systems, marketing, services, high levels of R&D intensity, patenting and production of high revenue-earning products. The mid-size enterprises often handle their innovative activities in very different ways than their smaller or larger counterparts. Table 5.5 shows how entrepreneurial mid-size firms manage their innovation strategies, processes, people and resources.

Table 5.5 Approaches to innovation and the mid-sized firm

A. The scope of innovation:	B. Levels of innovativeness	C. New product development
Leadership in technological innovation with high market share (e.g. 'Rational' with a share of 52% of global markets) *High level investment in R&D* (e.g. Omicron, leader of tunnel-grid microscopes –40% of people in R&D) *Innovation in business processes* and ongoing improvements of processes; *Innovation in distribution, sales & marketing* (e.g. Wurth, world leader in direct trade with assembly and fastening products – core competency in sales and logistics systems of order, system and automation; or Bosch Power Tools' shop-in-shop concept in large DIY stores enabling extension of existing value chains); *Innovation in pricing* (Ryanair's charges for per-checked-in-item of baggage enabling price reduction of 9% for those not checking in any baggage)	*R&D spend*: approximately 5.9% of revenue (twice the average of average innovators in Germany, and 50% more than the top 1,000 R&D firms in the world, and 68% more than mechanical engineering firms) *Patents*: main reasons include own use and blocking of competition, but most firms don't use patents because of red tape, costs, time taken to file them, and unenforceability (cost of patent disputes for Blackberry in 2006 was $202 million, 27% more than their R&D budget). But high intensity for those who consider it important (one patent per week since inception of Claas). Number of patent applications per 1,000 employees is 5.8% for large corporations, and 30.6% for mid-sized hidden champions but the latter have lower level of R&D expenditure per patent	*Higher levels of revenue* attributed to new products (e.g. AL-KO, world market leader in mobile home classics, hardly have any products less than four years old; Putzmeister, market leader in concrete pumps, earns 80% of its revenues from products less than five years in the market) *Definitional issue* creates problem of making comparisons (e.g. some manufacturers produce individual products as for example builders of technical plants) *Key technologies*: many groundbreaking examples in microelectronics and nano technology (e.g. coated bonding wire that enables connection of semiconductor chips at room temperature) *New products in mature markets*: Claas's Lexion model is the most innovative and powerful combine harvester

Table 5.5 Continued

A. The scope of innovation:	B. Levels of innovativeness	C. New product development
Design-led innovation: combining function and appearance and incorporating technology into design (e.g. Hansgrohe, the leading bathroom fittings manufacturer with 310 applications for patents in 2007) *Systems integration*: working with partners to serve a common or different sectors (e.g. Behr, world market leader in engine cooling and air-conditioning works with partners to develop and produce comprehensive systems modules for the automotive sector		*Global scope and push of international markets*: 56.1% of respondents of Simon's survey focus closely on foreign markets; only 9.9% depend primarily on home markets

D. Stimuli for Innovation:	E. Origins of innovation	F. Management leadership and strategy
External: customers, competitors, affiliated enterprises, suppliers and science – in that order *Internal*: top management; other company departments; R&D department Practice of *both* resource driven *and* market-oriented strategies (markets and technology are equally important; with objective of achieving optimal synergies)	*Identification of customer problem* (e.g. Weckerle, the lipstick machine manufacturer, the breakthrough for which came after discovery of manual production methods) *Technological innovation finding different markets* (ion exchanger made originally by Bayer with no markets but a furniture seller sold product to gas stations to be used for producing water for batteries; this eventually led to birth of water filters produced by Brita) *Application of problems and solutions from personal experience* (organic food production by Hipp grew out of Claus Hipp's grandfather mixing a porridge of milk, rusks and water in an emergency for the feeding of his twins *Meeting customer need*	*Critical role of top management* – through entire process of innovation; *Small budgets but greater reliance on quality of budgets* (e.g. Vitrionic, a leading player in image processing, making the groundbreaking European toll collection system – Toll Collect; small budget of $7million in R&D but has greatest concentration of specialists. *Quality of employee* affects both final result and speed of innovation *Focus and continuity Shared values and cooperation between functions*: *Co-development with customers Significant role of women in management*: assuming leadership after husband's death; supervisory or advisory board membership; operational management as CEOs (e.g. Maria-Elsabeth Schaeffler has managed INA-Schaeffler, the world's second-largest manufacturer of ball and roller bearings, since her husband's death in 1996, increasing revenue from $2.1 billion then to $12.2 billion in 12 years. *Internationalization of management*: reflecting the high proportion of revenues generated abroad *Entrepreneurial managers and founding entrepreneurs*

Source: adapted from Simon (2009).

What is abundantly clear from the points made above is that medium-sized firms carve out a special place for themselves as entrepreneurial firms. They are defined by their ability to grow, but this growth is buttressed by innovation in all its rich variety. The capacity to mix modes of practice and different approaches, often defying theoretical conceptualization of their actions, as in combining internal resources equally with external stimuli and market focus, is a distinctive attribute.

To be mid-size means to be in the middle between large and small firms. It is, therefore, appropriate that they steer the path between their larger and smaller counterparts, often combining the advantages of both for their development. They appear to effect this combination admirably. They are better operators than larger firms in the international stage yet their flexibility of operation is similar to that of smaller firms. They fuse the internal resource capabilities (which in part they share with larger firms by virtue of higher number of employees and more financial resources than smaller companies) with the reliance on external stimuli that their small firm counterparts depend upon to survive and grow. They remain 'hidden' (as many of the names of market leaders referred to above suggest) because they choose to shy away from publicity. Their reliance on organic growth makes fewer headlines than the flamboyant mergers and acquisitions. That they do not attract publicity is perhaps welcome for them. By way of contrast, there seems to be little value in the media hype surrounding most mergers and acquisitions as they tend to either fail or lead to a reduction in the market value of the merged firm.

We find that there are indeed differences between large, medium and small firms and their approach to innovation. We have examined some of the factors that differentiate these firms and their ability to innovate. What is particularly interesting today, however, is the way in which many of these firms interact with one another to be part of an integrated system of innovation. Such a system is different from the one that is sometimes mechanistically driven by policy. It is rather an outcome of and a response to changes in the landscape of technological development, emerging organizational forms with which to harness such technologies for productive use, and the evolution of labour markets in different parts of the world.

PART V: CHANGING LANDSCAPES AND EVOLVING ENTREPRENEURIAL ORGANIZATION FORMS

The changing landscape of business today, especially for high-technology and innovative firms, is characterized by how these businesses pursue entrepreneurial activities in the way that they:

- source, produce and develop the ideas, skills, technologies, intermediary products and services as part of a collaborative ecosystem, often made up of networked centres of excellence, where access to resources require a high level of computational and organizational skills (as in supply/demand chain management; IT-enabled logistics). It is argued that the 'confluence of connectivity, digitization and the convergence of industry and technology boundaries are creating new dynamics between consumers and the firm' (Prahalad and Krishnan, 2008), and between producers and end-users (Hippel, 2005); and
- involve the development of global, network-centric, open innovation environments consisting of large and small firms, and a host of other organizations participating in 'free' mode to enhance technologies, services, the development of new products and, crucially, business models (as in Skype, Linux, Kazza, Rhapsody) for a wide variety of 'verticals' (industry sectors).

These activities are entrepreneurial in the sense that they seek to identify opportunities in previously unknown and highly uncertain environments, and engage in different modes of production and exploitation of resources, and in the process generate economic value that is not simply associated with growth, for example, in terms of market share, but also in terms of better value propositions for users of such products and services. This approach to value creation is accompanied by new configurations and business models based on ideas of open innovation, convergence, knowledge spillovers and global delivery platforms.

Open innovation, convergence, knowledge spillovers and global delivery platforms

The open innovation model of dispersed distribution involves inflows and outflows of information (Chesbrough, 2003), technologies, knowledge and talent across borders. It relies on connectivity, convergence of technologies, knowledge spillovers (Krugman, 1991, Jaffe, 1986) between different organizations, end-user involvement in the innovation process (Hippel, 2005), the development of new, iterative business models (Chesbrough, 2006, 2008) centred round vertical disintegration, outsourcing, modularization, niche technological expertise, global delivery platforms (Gartner, 2001, Mitra and Natarajan, 2008) and access to resources, personalized, co-created experiences, and flexible, resilient business processes (Prahalad and Krishnan, 2008).

All types of firms have a role to play in these scenarios or platforms of open innovation. Moreover, large and small firms are interlocked in their networked endeavours. In these circumstances, size is less important than the processes of networking and open innovation, and the outcomes resulting from these processes for all businesses involved in the networks. These processes are characterized by features of socialization, collective learning, and the emergence of different business models than we may have been used in the past.

Socialization and open innovation

The nature of connectivity among firms in global delivery platforms also involves a significant socialization process at the organization and individual levels, especially with producers, intermediaries and end-users (Hippel, 2005), creating a social life of information and knowledge production (Seeley-Brown and Duguid, 2002). This social life is manifest in both the development and the use of technologies, especially the Internet (Tuomi, 2008) and through the spillovers described above.

Collective learning and open innovation

The connected, socialized, open innovation environment also engenders different forms of learning about technologies, business processes, accessing resources and products and services. The open environment of learning is characterized by tacit forms, involving individuals (Polyani *et al.*, 2007) and action learning 'on the job' by firms. Understanding of the informal processes characterizing learning in firms (Mitra, 2000) raises issues about the management process involved in capturing the different forms of learning especially in global environments and how that contributes to innovation.

Business models and open innovation

Finally, the combination of socialization in the global open innovation environment, with both individual and collective forms of learning, is manifest in the generation of business models that are networked on the basis that they connect individuals levels of expertise, often without transactional or pecuniary engagement. This is evident in the arena of internet and computing technologies and software development (as in Skype, Linux or Apache), or in traditional industries using embedded software (as in Indian software firms working across different industry verticals). These processes help to establish different network-based business models, some of which are confined to specific network players, while others are entirely open and organic.

The 'Global Delivery Platform' (GDP) model (Gartner, 2001; Mitra and Natarajan, 2008) applies more to traditional networks operating in modern environments. These networks connect centres of excellence in different parts of the world to one another. Although these are tightly knit networks with defined programmes of activity, they allow for creative outcomes from different nodal points to generate new products and services that may or may not be part of a portfolio. This author's own work with Indian software firms centres around the identification of appropriate business models that can support new product development in, especially, the software industry and where such software is embedded in different industry sectors (Mitra and Natarajan, 2011).

Brafman and Beckstorm (2006) use the metaphor of the 'starfish' to describe the other type of mutating, network-centric, organizational model that is often leaderless and dependent on both trust and security. Here both organizational and individual expertise is leveraged, often freely to enhance products and services and where business models are developed as outcomes of such 'free' exchange.

The significance of small firms and their role in open innovation environments

Much of the significant research in this area has focused on the role of mutating large firms and on the interplay between these firms, research organizations and universities. Yet the mounting evidence of the increasing share of industrial R&D spending, patent awards with global components and employment in small enterprises (especially in the USA – e.g. Acs and Ausdretsch, 1988, 1990, 1995, 2008; Acs, 2007, 2008), suggests that there is a need for greater understanding of the role of SMEs in the open, global innovation process.

The importance of SMEs in both regional and global knowledge spillover processes (Acs, 2008, 2007; Griliches, 1990; Jaffe, 1986; Krugman, 1991; Abubakar and Mitra, 2009) and in pecuniary transactions with other small and large firms (Krugman, 1991; Aoki *et al.*, 2006; Abubabar and Mitra, 2009) also suggests their role in offering new business models that embrace networked configurations of large and small firms. Part of the reason for the generation of new business models is the rapid obsolescence of new products owing to changes in technology and globalization processes. The effective management of such change often calls for the particular role of SMEs (Jovanovic, 2001). Scale economies in global settings may favour larger firms in terms of entry in globally connected sectors where the possibility of survival is considerably less (Audretsch, 1995; Geroski, 1995; Sutton, 1997). The specific role that small firms play in fragmented industry networks and in the organizational innovation process has not been examined in sufficient depth to help us with our understanding of the global process that involve SMEs.

Research in this new arena of economic value creation could pick these four essential components of new forms of entrepreneurship and address the following:

- the different types of networks that operate in distributed, open innovation environments;
- how the different networks and their operations yield various business models through the realization of strong and weak ties (Granovetter, 1985), the particular use of information and computational technologies; and
- the specific role of SMEs in these global, open innovation networks.

Entrepreneurship in the open innovation scenario brings together multiple levels of activity involving networked organizations and individuals, creating economic value at the level of products and services, social value at the level of the ecosystem enabling mixed forms of learning, and cultural value in terms of generating access to information, incorporation of cultural nuance and experiences of a wide variety of players across different environments. This is made possible by:

- access to resources – global access is more evident and critical than ownership because of the constantly changing nature of those resources and the use to which they can be put;
- co-creation with customers, distributors, suppliers and individuals outside the average business system as part of a process of socialization;
- personalization where the end product or service is geared towards the satisfying of the individual customer experience; and
- convergence of technologies, talent, business models even when each of these elements retain their individual character (see Figure 5.2).

(Prahalad and Krishnan, 2008)

These elements are influenced by and impact upon institutions. They are often mediated by institutions. The realization of their aggregate economic value takes place in the market or multiple markets for different products and services.

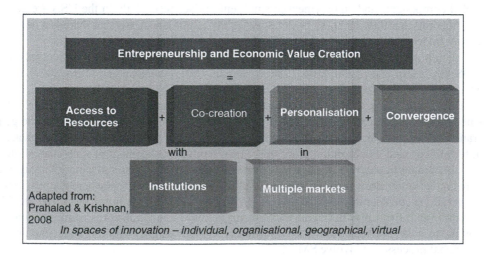

Figure 5.2 Economic value creation and entrepreneurship

Source: Mitra (2009).

Conclusion

There is much by way of variegated content in this chapter. Entrepreneurial organizations are varied in size, scope, style, approach, configuration and objectives. Consequently, small, medium, large, technological, non-technological and network-based firms, all contribute to innovation, growth and economic development. They do so differently according to:

- the organizational arrangements that evolve within the firm;
- the context in which they operate, which include industrial sectors, geographical regions and countries; and
- the type of firm.

Contexts have an impact on the types of firm that are best able to innovate. Contexts need differentiation. The impact of the industry life cycle in specific sectors is different from the spatial effects (stock of firms in a region, framework conditions, agglomeration and cluster effects) in geographical regions. Similarly, in exploring size and its bearing on a firm's ability to innovate, an entrepreneurial organization is distinguished by its features and structural advantages and constraints.

The competencies, capabilities and strategies that firms use represent internal or firm-specific resources which are harnessed and used to leverage external resources in the sector and in the region, but in different ways according to the type of firm, the level of its development and the stage of the industry or product life cycle. The evolving nature of entrepreneurial organizations suggests that they do not grow independently. Collaboration, alliances and networking have long been features of these organizations. In a globalized environment they take a different form in that the nature of the networking process is enhanced and re-shaped by open innovation processes and technologies which create possibilities of continuous innovation, often disruptive in scope and nature and in environments of increased uncertainty. These changes need to be supported by adequate business models that can make the most effective use of the changes. The productive interplay between these elements in enterprise and in the wider environment of organizations creates economic value, as shown in Figure 5.2. Studying all these complex, multi-layered issues is a difficult but hugely interesting exercise. Combining difficulty with curiosity and interest requires an extensive canvas!

Entrepreneurial organizations thrive in entrepreneurial environments and it is to these environments that we turn in the next chapter.

Mini case study 5.2: The adaptive, entrepreneurial and innovative wonder of Lego

If there is one product that binds children and adults together, it is the colourful shapes and interlocking bricks of Lego. Like many other extraordinary organizations that emerged in the last century, Lego owes its existence to the Great Depression of the 1930s, proving a point about the availability of productive opportunities even when we are in the middle of an economic slump.

Back in 1932, the construction sector took a nose-dive in Denmark. In the Danish town of Bilkund, Ole Kirk Christiansen, a carpenter, found himself out of work and with only scraps of wood. Instead of allowing social and psychological depression to accompany the economic one in which he found himself, Christiansen began making toys from the wood scraps. As the economy improved, he found that not only had he established a foundation for a new business but that it was in fact doing rather well. There was a need then to harness both his capabilities and the resources that he had managed to marshal till then to give his business an identity and a name – Lego, after the Danish words 'leg godt', which mean 'play well'.

As the business started growing, Christiansen hit upon the opportunity of shifting from a reliance on wood to plastic to make his toys. This move to new materials was made possible because of the increasing popularity of plastic as the material of choice for both industrial and domestic products. Christiansen was an early Danish bird with plastic technologies, buying his country's first plastic-injection machine and following that up in 1958 with the patenting of the interlocking bricks that have been part of children's playtime and the creative adult psyche ever since.

It is difficult to assess whether the creative spur that engendered entrepreneurial outcomes in the 1930s had become part of the firm's intangible asset portfolio or its DNA. However, the story as told so far suggests a continual drive for innovative change and growth. Lego did not simply rely on the success of its wooden toys but used its technology gate-keeping skills to shift is materials base from wood to plastic and make a genuinely new offering to its customers. Perhaps it is this DNA that has enabled Lego to recover again right in the middle of the current recession after posting $350 million in losses in 2004. Analysts had written off the firm as a 'casualty of the digital era'. In the early part of this century, its supply chain was in a mess as the firm tried to keep nearly 14,000 unique elements in stock. The firm continued to stick to model runs for sentimental reasons, even as deadlines were missed and retailers found their agents both gnostic and aloof.

How then did Lego change from almost an 'also ran' toy maker to a firm that has seen revenue go up 22 per cent last year to approximately $2.3 billion, enabling net profit to rise by 63 per cent to approximately $442 million? The fact that Lego has been able to turn around its relatively low-tech business, first in a recession and second in a world dominated by the virtual kingdom of the Internet and 'high-tech' toys, is all the more remarkable.

Lego's tactile toys may be a far cry from the virtual 'high-tech' toys that are thrust upon children these days. However, in tough economic times it is often traditional, tried-and-tested products that still give pleasure to customers. Parents are keen to save money but not deprive their children of fun. A trip to Disney World can be foregone, given the availability of the cheaper but attractive alternative of Lego toys. This mental shift on the part of cautious customers accounts for only a small amount of the change that took place in Lego.

Thanks to the introduction of a former McKinsey consultant, Vig Knudstrop (also a Dane), who succeeded Christiansen's grandson as CEO in 2004, a rigorous focus on the bottom line and on cash flow underpinned a major overhaul of the brand, a shift in focus on the type of user, the business model and the operational aspects of the business. Instead of chasing sales, the product line was refocused on the core consumers – the 'serious builders' of Lego. Operationally, Knudstrop introduced higher levels of efficiency in the firm's logistics, reducing by half the amount of unique pieces that were produced by the factories. Curiously, the emphasis was on not wanting to grow, an approach that it was possible to inculcate in a relatively small family-owned business. Lego struggled for a few years, but by the time the recession swept across markets it was reasonably well prepared for it. While most firms were in the middle of a 'horror show' in the fourth quarter of 2008, Lego 'sailed through it like it was no problem', according to a toy industry analyst at Needham and Co.

Beyond the financial tightening and the operational efficiency, the real change came in the re-organization of the product and business models. Without this change, the administrative measures would only have resulted in a leaner and possibly weaker, unproductive business. Instead of relying on studded bricks for its success, the company has moved from the business of selling construction toys to marketing highly developed models, even an entire 'toy world' where the interlocking blocks tell stories or help the children to build stories in the same way as books spur the imagination of the readers. Rather than individual plastic brick toy components, Lego has moved increasingly to selling themed boxes, starting in 1999 with its first licence deal to produce sets based on the 'Star War' movies. Licensed products account for approximately a quarter of the sales in the toy industry, and Lego has continued to offer products based on 'Batman', 'Harry Potter', 'Bob the Builder', 'Indiana Jones' and 'Spongebob Squarepants'. A multi-year partnership with Disney was announced in 2009, with Lego acquiring the rights to produce sets based on a wide range of the company's intellectual properties. In 2010 alone, new products based on 'Toy Story', 'Prince of Persia' and 'Cars' have been introduced in the market.

Not satisfied with having almost 'every license you want in the toy industry' (according to Lutz Muller of Klosters Trading Corp), Lego has created it own story lines. 'Atlantis' is a deep-sea adventure series which is sold on line with a 22-minute movie, mini games, a 3-D website and augmented-reality content. The objective is to provide children with triggers for them to play in the form of the main points of the plot, including the important battles and the discovery of the city. As Lego makes the product available on the web, developers will continue to update it with new features.

What we find in this embrace of the digital age is a real sense of adaptability centred around innovative use of key products. The adaptability of plastic toys in the pixel age is Lego's biggest challenge. The Lego website attracts 20 million unique visitors each month who can use a program called 'DesignbyMe' to put together a virtual Lego creation, then order a real, physical copy together with an automatically generated building guide that they can print off the site.

Lego has always been ingrained in the hearts and minds of adults. Anyone observing so many of our skyscrapers around the world would realize the extent to which architects and builders owe their fortunes to Lego! However, now the web has generated a new adult following. Lego bricks now have cult status among engineers and software developers. To this end, Lego launched a new series of architectural models of skyscrapers designed for Lego bricks by a fan!

Adaptability is possible, but only if the firm is willing to pay a price for it. Lego's online experience does not match that of its work with physical toys. To overcome this deficit, the firm is now preparing for the launch of 'LegoUniverse', a multi-user on-line rolling game in which participants evolve into Lego figurines fighting evil in a world overwhelmed by a dark energy called Maelstrom. All users will be able to design their personal space, while the greater part of the game will consist of combat, collection and the completion of missions. It is expected to attract in particular those who have played the Lego-themed video games for Wii or PlayStation, but the idea is to move the business to an era and to a point where freestyle construction and the little plastic brick might be a thing of the past.

Lego's evolving toy experience adventure is a creative adventure, where innovation, adaptability and the management of routines and networks have enabled the firm to adopt different strategies to move to a new, virtual world of games, without compromising the essence of the plastic brick that gives its essential value. Its high innovation strategy is evinced in its ability to drive change across its operational fronts, its technologies and its business model. It utilizes the driving, interactive and facilitating forces of uncertainty brought about first by economic depression and also by technological change through the clever use of the web world to open up new opportunities for itself and its users; to enter new markets where adults have a differentiated use of its products while children remain its core customers. Its continual emergence as an active proponent of change marks it out as an entrepreneurial organization.

(Source: adapted from Faris, S., 2010)

Self-assessment questions

1. What are the essential features of an entrepreneurial organization?
2. How would you define ambidextrous organizations, and how do such organizations carve out their capabilities for innovation?
3. How do networked organizations operate and in what way are they different from other types of entrepreneurial organizations?
4. Does size matter? Or are different types of firms noted for their own innovative capabilities?
5. Describe the changing landscape of innovation and the role of entrepreneurial organizations in this landscape.

6 The entrepreneurial environment

Context, institutions, constraints and framework conditions

Learning outcomes

In this chapter the reader will obtain:

- a critical appreciation of the key elements of an entrepreneurial environment;
- an in-depth understanding of underpinning contextual and situational issues as they apply to entrepreneurial environments;
- a critical understanding of the meaning, purpose and role of institutions in an entrepreneurship environment;
- critical knowledge and understanding of framework conditions and their application to different entrepreneurial environments;
- critical knowledge of key tools with which to develop a framework for entrepreneurial environment appropriate for particular conditions, contexts and organizations.

Structure of the chapter

The chapter starts with a brief consideration of the social structure of an entrepreneurial environment, the foundation on which suitable or ineffectual conditions prevail. The social structure of an entrepreneurial environment is determined by the interplay of a number of factors which could be broadly described as institutional norms and practices. A short review of institutions and their part in creating an entrepreneurial environment is undertaken in the second part of this chapter. A range of institutions and their evolution in formal or informal terms help to create or constrain the framework conditions that form the basis for entrepreneurial activity determining, shaping and influencing such activity in different environments. Framework conditions are explored in Part III. A discussion on different models and the contexts in which various models can be found takes place in Part IV of the chapter, while Part V poses questions on the possibility of the emergence of a consensus view of a favourable entrepreneurial environment. Part VI then returns to the broad question of contexts and signs off with a brief reflection on approaches to developing an environment conducive to effective entrepreneurship before the conclusion.

Introduction

This chapter examines:

- the connections between the social factors that support institutions and the entrepreneurial environment;

- the role of institutions, including various systems that enable entrepreneurship development in particular environments;
- institutions and issues of conformity, formal and informal constraints or limits that obtain in the varied contexts in which different entrepreneurs operate and that influence the governance structure of organizations;
- the plurality of stakeholders whose cooperation is required for successful entrepreneurial outcomes and who have certain rights and interests in the entrepreneur's and the firm's activities;
- the wider task-based or general environment that creates the framework conditions for entrepreneurship.

This chapter adds to the discussion of the social dimensions and the economic arguments (Chapter 4) by identifying the different contexts in which entrepreneurship emerges. The focus here is more on the locale and on reference points for new venture creation and less on the process which Chapters 2 and 11 are engaged with substantially. It creates opportunities for detailed discussion and understanding of the nature and scope of and the circumstances for entrepreneurship. In doing so, it opens up possibilities for further engagement with critical issues of space and geography or the wider context, which is dealt with in Chapter 11.

PART I: THE FOUNDATIONS: THE SOCIAL STRUCTURE OF AN ENTREPRENEURIAL ENVIRONMENT

Economic thought in the early days of classical and neo-classical thinkers reflected on the importance of the political economy, and the allocation of resources based on maximization of utilitarian value. Although subsequent economists, and especially Marshall (1920), had identified local factors of production and the importance of knowledge, the entrepreneur was not seen as operating in any distinctive context of activity. Early day sociologists such as Weber had not considered this possibility of such a unique environment for entrepreneurship either.

Schumpeter (1934) had clearly identified the cultural context of capitalism for the conduct of entrepreneurship, arguing that the strength of capitalism lay in its ability to support both:

- rational thought and action in terms of planning and forecasting; and
- emotional, autonomous activity to create something dynamic and new for its own sake.

The paradox lies in the entrepreneur's reliance on systems and structures in the economy together with his/her individual ability for out-of-the-ordinary, innovative actions. Society and the individual come together in the creation and sustenance of an entrepreneurial environment. The tension of rationality and creativity enables the entrepreneurial outcome, and the environment in which this occurs is a social one in which economic motives for profit are coupled with the social ones of fame and prestige, power and leadership. *Entrepreneurship is, therefore, socially and culturally embedded and the environment in which the entrepreneur operates is one in which he/she is in continual tension with its values and institutions.*

Social and cultural embeddedness

An example of a unit of social and cultural embeddedness is the family. The context of the family provides a micro setting for understanding the Schumpeterian entrepreneur. What we find in this context is the tension between mobility on the part of those members of a family who wish to create new things and consolidation by those who seek to reinforce the success of their family in their society. The latter follow established norms and conventions to strengthen existing values while the former ask questions of the norm as they wish to explore alternatives that reinvigorate rather than reinforce an existing set of values in the family and in society. The entrepreneurial spirit of the former is influenced to a great degree by the incentives available in society for pioneering any change. The incentive for the latter is the degree to which they can use existing institutions and values to sustain their dominance and control of their family in the society in which they operate.

It is possible to detect the idea of maximization of incentives among entrepreneurs. Such a maximization process works as long as disequilibrium and a degree of monopoly prevail. Gradually, however, rational processes, which include diffusion of ideas, wealth and information, restore equilibrium. How this works is as much an economic phenomenon as it is socially formed. Entrepreneurs seek to maximize both profit and social prestige, legitimacy and power. Much of this maximization takes place in specific contexts where:

- the social and cultural background of entrepreneurs influence entrepreneurial behaviour and actions including risk-taking, creative thinking and the search for autonomy (as discussed in Chapter 4); and
- the particular social and economic environment made up of institutions such as the market, rules, conventions, governance, framework conditions and codes of behaviour and practice (the focus of this chapter).

Entrepreneurship is distinguished by its capacity for delivering the benefits of different forms of innovation through organizational arrangements. Technological innovation, for example, helps to produce new technologies that could help to solve production problems and help to reduce costs and yield higher profits. But this process is dependent on either the availability of a market place where the entrepreneur can exchange the innovation for a profit, or support structures that help to create a new market where none exists. Aldrich (1999) argues that the search for cognitive and socio-political legitimacy in which the entrepreneur engages to convince or create the market is a social phenomenon constrained by economic conditions. Here relationships between buyers, suppliers, customers and other agencies become critical. These relationships can only be forged in stable environments and through the agencies of law and order, facilitative government policy, the availability of credit, the smooth operation of banks and financial institutions, and the incentives supported by government.

Stability or uncertainty?

The argument in favour of stable environments being a necessary condition for entrepreneurial activities is an interesting one, especially when opportunities often emerge in unstable conditions. It could be argued that one of the reasons why entrepreneurs succeed in seeking legitimacy is that they seek to stabilize relationships between different, interacting actors (employees, customers, suppliers, distributors, large form contractors, competitors and government), and therefore reduce the uncertainty associated with unstable conditions. The ability of entrepreneurs to do this is enabled by stable institutions, including government, laws, regulations and various codes of conduct. From this viewpoint, government is not an intrusive and irrelevant actor. Unstable conditions may generate opportunities for entrepreneurs whose creative and arbitraging actions, supported by institutional codes and conventions plus regulations, lead to a recovery of stability.

Regulations

The importance of the role of regulation has been highlighted perhaps most emphatically with the onset of one of the worst recessions in recent history. Both firms and society need intellectual property rights, patent, anti-trust, consumer protection and other laws, which it is essentially the government's role to manage as part of a regulated context for firm creation and growth. As Martinelli (2004) observes, 'Business misbehaviour, like that exemplified in the Enron and Worldcom cases (and perhaps more recently by Lehman Brothers, and Goldman Sachs among others), has a greater damaging effect than terrorist attacks because it shakes investors' confidence and citizens' trust in the fairness of the market mechanism.'

Regulatory actions can help to control the predatory behaviour of large organizations pursuing monopolistic-style dominance in their sector. But how do these actions have any impact on or relevance for small and especially entrepreneurial firms? How do these small firms acquire legitimacy in a predatory world?

Legitimacy and intervention

What engages the small firm community and entrepreneurial firms is their place in the nexus of other firms with whom they have open or close social relationships in regions, networks and clusters. The importance of the search for legitimacy and acceptance tends to override any private longing or individual gain at the expense of other firms. Social or even network-based sanctions come into play more quickly than legal actions. In any case, the size of these small firms limits the extent of damage that they inflict on the economy.

What perhaps matters more is the necessary protection that smaller and new entrepreneurial firms need from larger firms and organizations that can overwhelm them in business. A classic issue is that of late payment and enforced extended credit, which can have serious cash flow consequences for small firms. Problems arising from the absence of relevant information related to forms of appropriate finance, or financial services such as low-cost factoring to reduce the credit burden, can be mitigated by measured interventions by government and their agencies.

Status quo and incumbents

A stable environment could also imply the natural dominance of incumbents and majority or mainstream communities in societies. Historic accounts such as those by Mills (1956) suggest that most of the business elite during the period of American industrialization (1870–1910) came from landowning families or families with entrepreneurial track records. Lower classes with limited access to resources or networks contributed between 10 per cent and 20 per cent to business activity. Belonging to an established social community would tend to provide ready access to the networks, structures and institutions. Societies such as those in Britain France, Germany, Italy and Japan had fairly rigid class structures, where privilege was a function of entrepreneurial activity. As stated in Chapter 4, the social relations of production and the political economy favour the privileged, mainstream groups of merchants, landowners and wealthy artisans.

Deviancy, marginality and exception

The accounts of established social communities call into question notions of deviant behaviour or the idea of the self-made entrepreneur fighting against the odds to create a successful enterprise. Does this argument also call into question the Schumpeterian idea of the entrepreneur as an outsider (socially marginal) because he/she acts irrationally in a rational environment? The social marginality of the outsider can be understood in the context of societies (and their mainstream communities) that do not encourage entrepreneurial activity. In this seemingly hostile environment, greater uncertainty prevails among those who are innovative and entrepreneurial and who do not enjoy the patronage of political power. These 'deviants' include minority communities such as Afghans in Pakistan, Jews in Iran, Parsis in India, Indians in East Africa, Africans in the USA, Chinese, Indians, and Pakistanis in the United Kingdom, the Lebanese in West Africa, and women in all societies. They appear to face structural barriers of racism, sexism and class. However, their ability to develop or attract alternative institutional resources through personal and intra-community interaction, to make creative new combinations using exiting resources or bringing in new ones, and to capitalize on asymmetric information about people's needs explains their entrepreneurial behaviour.

The growth of businesses of many of these minority groups often takes them out of their original networks and environments. The change takes them into the mainstream, where entrepreneurial activity demands being associated with:

- the social networks, customs, conventions and codes of conduct; and
- structures and institutions variables such as social class, marriage patterns, solidarity with groups, power relations.

Entrepreneurs shaping environments

Examining how entrepreneurs deviate from the norm, and create their own, transform or blend into existing environments, moves the analysis to a consideration of the actions of the entrepreneur in specific situations. This removes the factor of uncertainty in the general environment and the entrepreneur's ability to cope with it in either cultural or social terms. There are no fixed types of entrepreneurs whose behaviour is determined by specific cultural contexts. *Entrepreneurs demonstrate diverse forms of behaviour according to the situations they encounter*. To this extent, the behaviour of entrepreneurs changes constantly as they interact with rather different social contexts, and some of these interactions produce innovations. Instead of one type of entrepreneur, we find 'improvisers', 'revisionists', 'reverters' and 'superseders' (Gibb and Ritchie, 1982).

Environments shaping entrepreneurs

Situations and circumstances shape entrepreneurs in different economies. Entrepreneurs interact with their environment in different ways according to the prevalence of particular conditions. In poor economies where there are limited opportunities for economic activity, people can be pushed towards self-employment or setting up their own small-scale business operations. Jobs are scarce, and so the only alternative mode of survival and income generation is self-employment or small (often micro level) business activity. By way of contrast, richer economies offer a range of opportunities between paid employment and business creation for people to make decisions based on utility functions. According to the Global Entrepreneurship Monitor (GEM) Reports, these conditions create 'necessity' or 'opportunity' -driven entrepreneurs. While the former is essentially a product of push factors in situations lacking choice, the latter is generally found in environments where there are numerous opportunities for innovation and entrepreneurship to flourish and provide many economic benefits.

It is questionable whether constant and universal circumstances of poverty prevail in some countries. The obverse is true of other nations. Regional variations within countries indicate considerable differences in economic conditions between those regions. Los Angeles is not the same as Detroit in the USA, Hyderabad cannot be compared to Patna in India, Wuxi is different from Tibet in China, and Lagos offers a business environment distinct from that of Kano in Nigeria. Changes in economic conditions also have an effect on the type of conditions entrepreneurs have to deal with when setting up or growing their ventures.

Tough times, recessionary conditions and environments for successful entrepreneurship

Uncertainty and difficulties abound in particularly problematic economic and social scenarios such as those that we find during a recession. These are times when funding dries up, when fear and a drop in confidence levels among both investors and aspirant entrepreneurs can take a nose dive. Yet there is almost a tradition of new ventures being founded in inclement economic conditions that then carve their way through a difficult environment to achieve extraordinary levels of success. The emergence of firms such as Microsoft, Genentech, Gap, Hewlett Packard, Texas Instruments, United Technologies, Polaroid, Atari, Apple and Revlon – all of whom were founded in the middle of a recession or during the tail end of a depression – are testimony to the possibilities of entrepreneurship in tough times. In the current recessionary climate, a number of highly innovative ventures have begun to claim their unique position in the marketplace around the world, against all the odds.

Spencer E. Ante (2009) has found some 'intriguing' new firms that represent a 'barometer of innovation trends in the global economy, with start-ups that are pioneering new markets in biotechnology, clean technology, health care and Web Computing' (p. 46). They include firms such as:

- 'Hunch' – a website that uses the experiences of others to assist people make decisions, started by Caterina Fake who had co-founded the photo-sharing site 'Flickr' before it was acquired by Yahoo;
- 'China Water Energy' – a Hong Kong-based firm developing huge wind-power farms in the Chinese countryside;
- 'Driptech' – a Californian start-up engineering low-cost irrigation systems for poor farmers around the world; and
- 'Epizyme' – a Massachusetts-based outfit which is making drugs that attack errant proteins to combat cancer.

(Source: Ante, 2009)

Innovation and entrepreneurship lead to job creation, productivity gains, wealth accumulation and new business formation from the effective and smart use of technology, products, services, people and global business models. In the very first decade of the twenty-first century we are both in the grasp of a severe recession and within reach of key new technologies such as wireless broadband, green technologies, stem-cell research, nanotechnology, VoIP, cloud computing, social networking – all offering opportunities for wealth creation, the solving of social and economic problems, and the better allocation of capital resources for their development and use in productive environments. The notion that benign or resourceful environments are the most conducive to entrepreneurship, and the models of necessity- or opportunity-driven entrepreneurship, is challenged by unusual outcomes or outlier effects.

Why do harsh and inclement circumstances provide a fertile ground for future entrepreneurial success? Is this promise attributable to heroic and visionary entrepreneurs and their particular mettle? Michael Moritz of Sequoia Capital, a venture capital firm that invested in Apple during the 1970s, refers to them as 'the genuine article' as opposed to 'pretenders' (Ante, 2009). It is not so much an understanding of individual characteristics that can help to determine the apparent mismatch between successful entrepreneurial outcomes and hostile environments, but rather how opportunities are created and used in such conditions.

In a downturn, a larger pool of talented staff is often made available because of redundancies. The cost of labour, materials and rent is cheaper. Competition tends to flatten as existing businesses tend to pull down their shutters, at least temporarily, instead of investing money in new products and services. Many start-ups looking for venture finance find it difficult to do so, as stricter conditions are applied to lending because of either regulatory constraints or a new regime of caution among lending institutions. Limited money may not, however, lead to risk-free lending. Stronger but high-risk propositions are more attractive options for lenders in hostile environments than mundane but weaker bids. Caution is wedded to better prospects of higher returns in these circumstances, although the logic behind this connection is not necessarily explained. The pressure on firms to revisit or sharpen their business models in recessionary times could also enable them to reach higher levels of profitability in the future when the cost of finance drops. Finally, new business models can help to steer firms to create better value for existing customers rather than seek new customers and gain market share. Such models lead to service improvement and entrepreneurial endeavour rather than just cost-cutting. Paradoxically, customers demand more when costs are being cut!

The particular phenomenon of entrepreneurship in tough times offers hope for citizens and governments. Instead of the expected drop in new business creation, bad times can create more new firms. According to a survey by the National Venture Capital Association, at the end of 2008 firms enjoying an injection of venture capital funding were responsible for generating 12 million jobs and 20 per cent of US gross domestic product (compared to 10 million jobs and 17 per cent of GDP in 2005). In the UK, more new business are being created while employment levels have dropped. This phenomenon is not restricted to developed nations alone. Entrepreneurship and innovation in emerging economies such as China, India, Brazil, Turkey and South Korea is rapidly gaining momentum. In emerging markets, 85 per cent of entrepreneurs felt the impact of crisis, and while 88 per cent thought the worst was yet to come they expected businesses to grow by 31 per cent and workforces by 12 per cent in 2010. To them, it is the importance of global links that is the source of such confidence (McKinsey, 2009).

Particular situations explain different forms of actions by and outcomes for entrepreneurs. Whether they are deviating from the norm and shaping environments or are being moulded by the cultures, norms and practices in their environment, entrepreneurs are interacting with the institutions in those environments. These institutions consolidate the status quo or encourage deviants; they call for different types of regulatory activity or allow for a greater reliance on informal networks, trust and socially constituted activity. *The context in which entrepreneurship thrives or perishes is that in which an institutional support system works or disengages with the entrepreneur.* The institutions in these contexts help to create the environment in which entrepreneurs operate.

What then are institutions, and what role do they play in supporting entrepreneurship?

PART II: INSTITUTIONS AND ENTREPRENEURSHIP

A good starting point is Douglass North's idea of institutions and institutional change. North (1990) suggests several characteristics of institutions and what they represent:

1. institutions are the rules of the game in a society 'or more formally, are the humanly devised constraints that shape human interaction'(p. 3) – they structure incentives in political, social and economic environments;
2. institutions change the way societies and economies evolve over time – thus enabling our understanding of prevailing currencies of behaviour and norms through history;
3. institutions reduce uncertainty by providing structures for human interaction; and provide a guide for day-to-day human actions and activities;
4. institutions operate in different ways with varying degrees of potency in different countries and environments;
5. institutions have constraints which are both formal (rules and regulations) and informal (conventions and codes of behaviour);
6. institutions are created by mediation or choice (examples include the Indian or the US Constitutions) or evolve over time (such as the Common Law in the United Kingdom);
7. institutions have constraints that either permit people to pursue activities (such as starting a legal businesses) or prevent/prohibit certain types of behaviour (for example, criminal activities) – these constraints taking the form of either written rules or codes of conduct or unwritten conventions and codes of practice;
8. institutions allow for monitoring of the behaviour of people and organizations depending upon the prevailing culture and circumstances of particular environments;
9. institutions are different from organizations – this is a critical difference. Organizations depend on strategies, competencies, skills, resources and models with which to operate within a set of rules or conventions that constitute institutions. Businesses need to compete within the rules of the game set in specific environments and the incentives offered for participation and winning. The creation, development, fine tuning, evolution and outcomes of the rules of the game follow a different and independent process from those of organizations;
10. finally, institutions are created and altered by human beings – institutions impose constraints on choice made by human beings.

An institutional approach to entrepreneurship helps us to understand how entrepreneurs can cultivate and express their creativity. The making of a new product needs to include the organizational capacity to make it work in the market. The market with its 'rules of the game' has to accept this new product, but between the making of the product and its acceptance in the marketplace there are several steps of individual and organizational ingenuity. The learning process, the search for legitimacy, the protection of intellectual property and the realization of an entrepreneurial profit constitute those steps. One of the rules of the game is that found in the legal structures that prevail in a society and in the establishment of the right to property of its citizens.

Rule of law and property rights

It is widely believed that the rule of law and property rights constitute the most important institutions in society and in a prosperous economy (Rodrick *et al.*, 2003; Easterly and

Levine, 2003; Baumol, 1990). These institutions help to stop corrupt actions such as bribe-taking, pure rent-seeking and destructive forms of business practice. They can also help to reduce the uncertainty associated with the development of a new venture by making transparent what it is possible to do or make in particular environments.

Among researchers exploring the issue:

- Johnson *et al.* (2000) found that the emergence of new firms in five formerly Soviet countries was subject to bribery, protection or inefficient courts. These conditions had less of an effect on the finding of finance but more of an impact on the actual setting up and establishment of the venture. In other words, finding money was not the problem but there was a bigger difficulty in obtaining access to information, skilled people, and markets.
- Desai *et al.* (2003) found that greater degrees of fairness and protection of property rights were conducive to higher levels of entry rates, the reduction of exit rates and skewed variance in firm size distribution in Eastern European countries.
- Arzeni and Mitra (2008) found in their study of youth entrepreneurship in Central and Eastern European countries that the pressures of being part of a linked European economy and globalization led to the abandonment of old skills, favouring youth employment. However, the preference for work experience, which only the older workers could supply, left younger people to consider self-employment as a possible option alongside education and emigration. The mix of these possible outcomes had an adverse impact on entrepreneurship.
- In non-transition economic settings, others found that the more effective the legal systems of specific states in a country, such as Mexico, the more likely the presence of larger firms (Laeven and Wooruff, 2004).

Different contexts and multiple factors

What these studies (among many others) suggest is that conditions and circumstances vary in different environments, creating multiple and different contexts for opportunities for new venture creation and innovative growth. This further suggests that key factors of culture, attitudes and behaviour influence different contexts. Anna Lee Saxenian (1996), in her seminal study of Silicon Valley and Route 128 in the USA, referred to the crucial difference between the former's pioneer entrepreneurial spirit and the culture of corporatism and secrecy of the latter. Explaining why this difference could have occurred, Gilson (1999) pointed out that legal rules allowing for the enforceability of an old covenant not to compete in Massachusetts, compared with the way California interprets its employment law banning such covenants, accounts for the development of Silicon Valley's dynamic culture.

The Californian example is particularly important for the better understanding of this interplay between formal and informal institutional arrangements. The pioneer spirit of its entrepreneurial people probably helped to prevent any re-emergence of the covenant not to compete, and this was complemented by its relaxed approach to intellectual property rights. The Valley's entrepreneurs carry a reputation for not fussing too much about such rights in the leaky environment of information, communication and other new technological developments. In such environments the strong 'informal constraints' tend to prevail over formal ones, and it is to the differences between these two types of 'constraints' that we now turn our attention.

Formal institutional constraints

It is often argued that as a society becomes more complex there is a greater need for properly written or codified rules and statements of practice. This view cuts across individual organizations and governments. As an organization grows, the routines, structures, codes of conduct and instructions for people working within the organization grow in importance. How these constraints are developed, communicated and implemented becomes part of the organization's governance system. Similarly, with governments, structural, technological, demographic and other changes demand a clear articulation of rules, social conduct and signals for collective and individual behaviour, civic responsibilities and issues of citizenship. These then are the formal constraints.

Formal rules include those that are decided by government, the judiciary, economic rules and contracts. There is a hierarchical pattern to these rules. For example, political rules explain how decisions are made in a political structure, by government, by parliament in democratic countries, or through committees and by fiat. These rules are handed down through the different layers of the political structure, with each layer being organized in order of its importance.

The reference above to intellectual and property rights, including the ability to generate income from such rights, is an example of economic rights. Contracts are concerned with specific agreements relating to the exchange of goods and services (North, 2002). There are five points to note:

- first, these rules or formal constraints are meant to facilitate exchange and the smooth functioning of relationships between, for example, government and citizens, the producer and the consumer;
- second, the rules are there to both maximize wealth creation possibilities and to rein in any abuse of power to exploit others in the process of maximizing such wealth;
- third, since it is human beings who determine the constraints, there is always the possibility of these rules being altered to suit particular interests depending upon status, power and the ability to influence action to reassign rights and responsibilities;
- fourth, the diverse nature of human interests is likely to be reflected in economic transactions. Such diversity can lead to complex forms of exchange and arrangements for their observation, sometimes leading to a blurring of formal and informal constraints;
- fifth, formal constraints can help to lower transaction costs, including the costs of the search for information, and monitoring, negotiation and enforcement costs.

Informal institutional constraints

Outside the body of formal constraints there is in society a massive set of complex informal constraints by which human beings organize, define and structure interaction between them. In reality, formal rules are only a small proportion of the institutional constraints in society. For example, families, business federations and community groups, are all expected to operate within the law in any society. Each of them also has its own constitution and code of conduct in the form of Memoranda of Association or various instruction manuals.

Norms of behaviour

Outside the formal arena there are the various norms of behaviour, organizational culture, that generate informal constraints. They are often tacit in character and understood by a community of interest that shares certain sets of values and behavioural norms. Interestingly, as North (2002) observes, even when major evolutionary and historical changes have taken place, various aspects of society remain unchanged. The establishments of supermarkets allows for convenient shopping in many parts of the world. However, in some places they have not been able to replace the attraction of local, daily or weekly markets. In Bologna in Italy, for example, the store of fresh cheese, ham, fruits and wine laid out in an opulent environment for fresh produce in the main square attracts both locals and tourists perhaps a shade more than the supermarkets outside the main city walls. The prices of products, the norms of ordering and collection of goods, and the mellifluous tones of conversation are all part of a culture of the Bolognese, defining the interaction between the shop owners and their customers.

Language and communication

Many of these informal constraints emerge from social communication between people, through the language they use to convey information. Noteboom (2000) refers to language as a 'paradigm example of an institution' (p. 92) Employing de Saussure's distinction between 'langue' representing the 'intersubjective order' and 'parole' as personal creative language use, he argues that they are connected to exploitation using rigorous rules of scientific meaning, and to exploration involving poetic licence, respectively. The play between these two forms of language enables the establishment and enforcement of constraints and their interpretation. Formal constraints are identified by the formal language of communication of information. However, since information is generally incomplete, the gaps are filled in by interpretation and informal means of communication about the meaning and use of such interpretation. This interplay of words, meaning and interpretations helps to create networks of people and organizations, which provide a structure for relationships between and among entrepreneurs and their organizations.

Networks

Making information available in a way that helps people in specific communities to establish informal rules and codes implies the existence of dense social networks where people have a close understanding of each other. Preserving the benefits of that close understanding means warding off threats to it from deviant behaviour either inside or from without! This is where theories of kinship ties come in useful, often explained in detail by anthropologists when they write about primitive communities. They are of course as valid in modern times as they have been in the past.

Implied codes of conduct

How do informal constraints work? They work through implied codes of conduct and sanctions. If in a network one member defies the odds and acts purely in his/her own interest at the expense of another, then word of mouth information communication can lead to the 'deviant' member being 'blacklisted' by others. In such an environment no one wants to lose out because the collective benefit (cooperation) tends to be for the longer term for all than a short-term individual gain (defection). There is a discernible echo here of game theory models of behaviour. In other situations where formal rules act against the interests of a community, the informal arrangements for resistance can be both a bulwark against formal encroachment on community territory and an incentive for entrepreneurial action.

Informal constraints tend to be quite visible in Asian societies and economies, although they are by no means exclusive to them. Some of the rapid growth of Asian economies over the past few decades has been attributed to the best mix of capitalist and socialist systems embracing Confucian, Buddhist, Hindu and Islamic value systems. Development theorists such as McKay (2008), Peter Evans (1995) and Chalmers Johnson (1987) have suggested that Asian societies have been entrepreneurial and energetic along Schumpeterian and capitalist lines by introducing new products and services, entering new markets and jettisoning unprofitable old industries. Yet their societies appear to have a strong egalitarian motive and purpose. This balance has been possible because of the combined roles of social and corporate networks such as Quanxi in China and Chaebol in Korea, together with high-level state intervention.

Evans (1998) suggests that East Asian states are both 'autonomous' and embedded. While they may have protected certain vested interests, they have also been autonomous enough to act on behalf of the nation. At the same time, close integration with society has meant that they have been able to share the language of the people, especially the business community, to help fulfil their needs and requirements. Putnam's (1995) account of Northern Italian industrial districts reveals similar approaches to the creation and use of informal constraints.

Uses of informal constraints

In the type of intricate and dense social networks described above, informal constraints take their own shape. The difficulty lies when they are not enforceable in any exchange. Such an outcome can lead to greater costs because of the need to find new methods of enforcement, and even to cancel the exchange. A further difficulty lies in informal constraints being used to protect a community of interest against innovation, change and new practices (see mini case study 6.1). This author's own experience of an old industrial conurbation in the UK shows how previously well-established manufacturing firms in one of Marshall's industrial district were reluctant to embrace new technologies and new working methods because they were direct descendants of those 'who knew how to do and make things'. The result is what economists refer to as a 'lock-in', where no one can break out for fear of being sanctioned by the rest of the community.

Cooperative behaviour

Informal constraints are concerned with cooperative behaviour. They work when the stock of social capital is high and they are most effective when they combine forces with formal constraints. Inherent in the use of constraints generally is the idea of learning because the flip-side of rules acting as a break on behaviour is their part in inducing different ways of developing new products and services within constraints. Knowing how to develop products and services in constrained circumstances necessitates the introduction of a learning process. Making learning meaningful implies that there is a knowledge base that needs improvement. Rules could also attract the kind of disruptive or unproductive behaviour that seeks circumvention through the breaking of the rules for personal profit.

Trust

A central feature of informal constraints shaping institutional activity is trust. Social interactions take place because there are informal constraints which are based on trust between the actors. This trust is not necessarily blind and irrational, with all personal interest sacrificed at the altar of a greater community interest. Trust is generated in two ways. 'One is ethical behaviour on the basis of tacit, socially inculcated norms in a society. The other is the build-up of routine perception, interpretation, and behaviour in specific relations, by which conformity of behaviour is taken for granted, and awareness of opportunism becomes "sub-sidiary"' (Noteboom, 2000, p. 107).

Trust, however, is an abstract concept, and therein lies a problem. Who can be trusted and what should be trusted? What break of trust can be condoned and what needs to be punished? Answers to these questions are dependent on particular circumstances and the cultural milieu in which they unravel. If a break is intentional then punitive measures can apply, but how are such measures going to be used if there are no formal constraints? Does a deviant firm or individual care if they are able to 'get away' by joining another community? Sometimes the apparent breach of trust does not occur out of vested self-interest; often it may be because of the need to either survive or be innovative. Growing firms in industrial clusters, deeply embedded in the regional networks in terms of their business transactions, may find better opportunities for their technologies or products in previously unknown markets. What action does the firm take under these circumstances?

Cause and effect

Constraints matter most when they are 'enabling' in character and scope. Noteboom (2000) argues that effective constraints direct people to make choices in one direction. Such a choice means the foregoing of other alternatives. In this sense there are opportunity costs involved in the use of constraints. Any organization developing a set of informal constraints or working to a set of formal constraints can make choices where the economic opportunity cost is higher than the alternative foregone because they are more amenable to the cohesion of a community.

In the implementation of constraints, institutions either encourage or impede action ands social interaction. This means that in societies and economies choices have to be made to ensure that they are sustained by the logic of causality. In any economy, or in any economic unit, there is a framework of actions that are held together by a certain logic of cause and effect. Noteboom (2000) refers to an Aristotelian theory of multiple causality where there are:

- final causes (as in goals and objectives);
- efficient causes (as in an agent or an agency);
- material causes (the inputs used to achieve goals);
- formal or exemplary causes (knowledge, skills, methods);
- conditional causes (those that enable or prevent the other causes from operating).

Take the example of a potter (Noteboom writes about the carpenter). The potter is both an agent and an 'efficient cause'. He uses clay (material cause) to make pots based on his knowl-edge and skills and a guiding model (formal and exemplary cause) in order to earn a living (final cause) subject to conditions of law, market and social structures (conditional cause). The potter's organization, or for that matter any organization, is an institutional arrangement enabling the set of Aristotelian causes to come together. The way these causes are combined in a particular environment is through a process of institutionalization.

Using the multiple causality theory of Aristotle, Noteboom (2000) offers us a taxonomy of institutionalization showing how institutional constraints can enable or restrict entrepreneur-ship. This taxonomy is reproduced in Table 6.1, which provides an analytical framework for the evaluation of the role of institutions in entrepreneurship development. What is particu-larly noteworthy is the distinction between 'surface' and 'deep' institutions, which reflects

Table 6.1 A taxonomy of institutionalization

Aristotelian cause	Institutional effects	Institutions
Final	Incentives for entrepreneurship	**Surface** Ownership and decision rights Tax and social security Financial markets and rules of corporate control Market entry and exit conditions **Deep** Categories concerning virtue, risk, responsibility, independence and 'locus of control'
Efficient	Labour	**Surface** Wage and labour conditions **Deep** Work ethic, voice/exit
Material	Material inputs	**Surface** Import conditions, capital markets
Formal	Knowledge/technology	**Surface** Education, training, science Dissemination/transfer **Deep** Categories concerning cognition, skill
Conditional	Time and space industry structure	**Surface** Physical and communication – infrastructure Supply chain, entry/exit barriers, and market concentration

Source: Noteboom (2000).

the complexity of the different kinds of institutions underpinning social interaction, and the mix of cultural influences and individual responsibilities. They also reinforce the role of formal and informal constraints. The former can be found in the cluster of incentives referred to as 'surface' institutions in that there are explicit rules and conditions that apply to anyone considering a new venture. The 'deep' category can be stated to house both the informal constraints and the personal perceptions, circumstances, motivations and evaluations that underpin entrepreneurial activity.

Bounded rationality

Cause and effect are of course not possible to determine in all circumstances. Bounded rationality (Simon 1959, 1976, 1979) prevents us from making decisions that are based on rational conclusions of cause and effect. What we know is limited, and the rationality of people is incomplete. At the level of an economy or a society, an 'aggregate of incompleteness' can lead to non-causal outcomes. Instead of cause and effect we see associations or certain patterns of attitudes, behaviour, practice and response. For example, we may find that in a particular region there is a high level of new firm creation and an abundance of entrepreneurial training and educational programmes. It would be difficult to ascertain whether the existence of these training programmes has led directly to a positive impact on new business creation.

This is because there might be other factors, such as the availability of R&D facilities, angel finance and specialist skills, which also have an effect on start-ups.

It is from first a consideration of this mix of constraints and influences on behaviour of entrepreneurs, and second the role of institutions in that mix, that we can find the emergence of certain conditions for entrepreneurial activity. These conditions will vary between regions and countries because of variations in the level of trust, the stage of development of institutions and an array of other factors. However, the logical or associative link between these factors can be examined within a framework. Framework conditions can help to explain which factors and what combination of these factors can help to create and establish an entrepreneurial environment. But before we examine any framework condition(s), it is worth reviewing briefly some of the additional literature on entrepreneurial environments that has attempted to bring together the different constituent elements of a framework referred to above.

PART III: ENTREPRENEURIAL CONDITIONS AND ENVIRONMENTS

Various studies have, in the main, listed or described various environmental conditions that could have an effect on the level or rate of entrepreneurship in regions and countries. These studies, as Gnyawali and Fogel (1994) suggested, can be grouped together into three broad categories or streams:

*   general environmental conditions for entrepreneurship;
*   descriptive studies of the environmental conditions of regions or countries; and
*   the role of public policy in shaping such environments.

Studies in the first category (Bruno and Tyebjee, 1982; El-Namaki, 1988; Gartner, 1985) have identified legal and institutional frameworks that can contribute to the efficiency of private firms, the effect of experienced entrepreneurs, the availability of skilled labour, suppliers and distributors, accessibility to customers and new markets, firm level competition, supportive government policies and appropriate infrastructure.

Descriptive and empirical studies of entrepreneurial environments point to the low levels of rules and regulations, a good range of tax and other incentives, and the provision of training and counselling services to promote the prospect of start-ups. Counterpoint studies have suggested that the lack of financial assistance, information on business issues, a high level or incidence of taxation, and inflationary conditions can have adverse effects on the ability of entrepreneurs to start new firms The existence of universities that provide research and training, and factors such as the large urban environment or numerous sources of financial assistance, can be conducive to high levels of entrepreneurial activity.

Finally, other studies that have addressed the role of public policy (Mokry, 1988; Westhead, 1990) have suggested how different policy options, such as venture capital fund provision, government procurement programmes, intellectual property protection, investment in education, and pronounced and explicit support for entrepreneurship, including entrepreneurship education, can help to foster entrepreneurship.

What do these studies help us to understand? First, there is a suggestion that new businesses are more likely to emerge in conditions that are conducive to a positive business environment. These conditions boost confidence among people because there are greater opportunities, and also because the combinations of skills, access to information and financial assistance can help to realize such opportunities. As we can see, the thinking here is in line with what was referred to above as a stable environment. These issues have been widely discussed in policy circles and in academia, spawning a large body of literature reaffirming the positive or negative impact of these factors in wide environments. The OECD (1998) study 'Fostering Entrepreneurship', together with the publication 'Entrepreneurship: A Catalyst for Urban Regeneration (OECD, 2004) and numerous other papers, has emphasized the central significance of the three key factors – framework conditions, well-designed government policies and supportive cultural attitudes – for entrepreneurship development.

Smaller firms, hampered by meagre resources (money, information, skilled personnel, networks) may require higher levels of intervention, as conventional wisdom would suggest. Consequently, within specific environments institutional arrangements may need to be organized to better support the work of smaller firms.

The studies referred to above have also indicated that an environment conducive to entrepreneurship may differ from one type of economy to another. These differences would account for the varied mix of factors contributing to this entrepreneurship process. Emerging market economies, for example, may be more dependent on a higher supply side driven set of factors because of low levels of recognized entrepreneurial activity resulting from poor governmental or institutional support. The issue here may be more about the need for institutional upgrading than entrepreneurial capability, and the need for better organization and arrangements of formal and informal constraints referred to earlier in this chapter.

Stages of development

In the GEM 2008 report, Bosma *et al*. (2008), using a varied set of indices to put together a super index of entrepreneurship and its relationship with economic development, suggest that an S-shaped curved can be found when different countries are categorized into particular types of economies according to the stage of their economic development. Following Porter (2002), three types of economies have been found by Bosma *et al*. (2008): 'factor driven' (to include countries such as Angola, Bolivia, Columbia, India and Iran), 'efficiency driven' (for example, Argentina, Brazil, Turkey, South Africa, Croatia) and 'innovation driven'(generally European countries and the United States of America, with the exception of Japan and the Republic of Korea). (See Chapter 11 for further details on the different stages of development.)

PART IV: FRAMEWORK CONDITIONS

Different conditions apply in particular environments, depending both on the state of development in that environment and on the critical elements in the venture creation process (Gnyawali and Fogel, 1994). These core elements in the venture creation process, as several authors (Gartner, 1985; El-Namaki, 1988; Specht, 1993) suggest, are as follows:

- *opportunity* – for new venture creation both in the environment (as in institutional arrangements, cultural attitudes, incentives) and in terms of the way in which entrepreneurs use their influence for successful outcomes;
- *propensity to enterprise* – the inclination or willingness to take risk and to achieve, psychological characteristics and behavioural patterns, internal locus of control levels

of confidence, capacity to innovate (Schumpeter, 1934; McClelland, 1961; McClelland and Winter, 1969; Brockhaus, 1980);

- *ability to enterprise* – technical, managerial and organizational capabilities.

Integrated models

These elements of the venture creation process need to be linked with the conditions to understand how those conditions interact with the critical elements. The resulting integration of conditions and critical elements helps us to create a framework for understanding the real value of entrepreneurial environments. To this end, Gnyawali and Fogel (1994) created an integrated model of entrepreneurial environments, as shown in Figure 6.1.

The model and our understanding of the constituent elements of entrepreneurial environments, including the relationships between the factors and the elements of the venture creation process, could lead to certain propositions. These propositions include:

- the higher the opportunity, propensity to enterprise, and ability to enterprise, the higher the likelihood to enterprise (P1);
- the more favourable the socioeconomic factors, the greater the propensity to enterprise (P2);
- the greater the entrepreneurial and business skills, the greater the ability to enterprise (P3);
- the more favourable the government policies and procedures, the higher the opportunity to enterprise (P4).

(Gnyawali and Fogel, 1994)

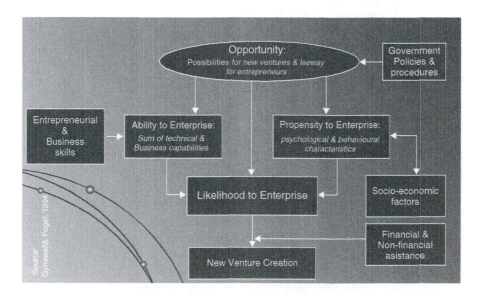

Figure 6.1 An integrative model of entrepreneurial environments

Source: Gynavali and Fogel (1994).

Various studies have carried out iterations of the model referred to above. One of the more recent variations can be found in the GEM 2009 Report, which built such a model for examining the framework conditions of different countries at different stages of development. The GEM model itself has gone through several mutations, from one that identified a Total Entrepreneurial Activity Index for various countries to a more sophisticated approach attempting to explore the connection between entrepreneurship and economic development. There are similarities between the Gnyawali and Fogel and the GEM models, even if some of the terminologies used to describe specific components of the models are different. Where the GEM model (Figure 6.2) departs from the Gnyawali and Fogel model is in the inclusion of two distinctive types of entrepreneurship – necessity- and opportunity-driven entrepreneurship, a wider set of factors (such as the presence of larger firms), the re-organization of the elements of the venture creation process, and, crucially, the consideration of different stages of economic development.

Examining the attitudes, activities and aspirations of respondents in their study, the GEM authors found different patterns of opportunity identification, fear of failure, associations and networks, skills and knowledge, expectation levels and overall country level attitudes as perceived by individuals. The breakdown into three categories of economies provides for a rich seam of information on the relationship between attitudes and perceptions of people and the economic conditions prevalent in the country. These are then represented in terms of the total, early stage entrepreneurship activity of the 54 countries surveyed by the GEM study group (2009).

The study of particular environments and their impact on new venture creation shows how entrepreneurs mobilize resources to follow opportunities and find new businesses with which

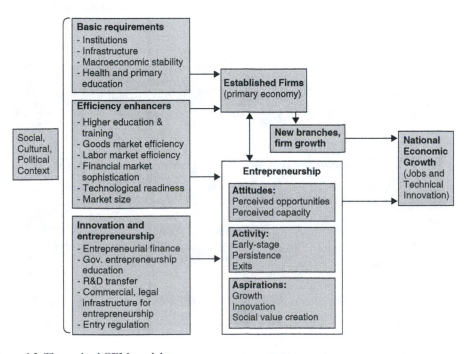

Figure 6.2 The revised GEM model

Source: Bosma and Levie (2009).

to develop products and services. Different conditions allow for both the varied rate and the quality or type of ventures that are founded. As the GEM Report suggests, 'necessity-driven' entrepreneurs are more likely to be found in factor-driven economies while 'opportunity-driven' entrepreneurship is more likely to emerge in innovation-driven economies.

An ecological perspective

Another conditioning factor is the experience and presence of existing firms and their impact on start-ups. Using an ecological approach to studying how organizations are formed, Aldrich (1990) found that, apart from the experiences of incumbents, the structure of the environment, prior foundings, dissolutions, density (intra-population processes) and the nature of competitive and cooperative relationships between populations of business, actions by existing firms including the distribution of resources and price controls (inter-population processes) have a profound effect on the establishment of new firms. Add to that cocktail the institutional factors of government policy, political and social events, and cultural norms, and we have the wider macro context that new venture founders have to negotiate to gain cognitive and socio-political legitimacy (Aldrich, 1990, 1999, 2001).

Creative environments and creative people

All the perspectives and approaches discussed above underwrite the importance of social capital and its key component of trust, networks and institutions that help to develop the entrepreneurial capital of different environments. These environments, especially in cities, attract creative talent. Talent, technology and tolerance account for a creative environment according to Florida (2002; 2003): the capacity of an environment to attract talent, and to tolerate the diversity of talented people irrespective of their gender, colour, race or sexual orientation, together with its capacity to invent and develop technologies and provide a good range of public amenities. Florida's 'creative class' includes artists, designers, engineers, entertainers, musicians, scientists, engineers and others. They bring new idea, new technologies, new resources and new content, thereby helping to stimulate an economy.

But is it creativity or is it talent that matters when the entrepreneurial or economic strength of a country or a region is evaluated? According to Glaser (2005), it is indeed talent or human capital that has more significance for driving economic growth, especially in urban areas. As Acs (2008b) shows, if Florida's 3Ts are included in a regression along with human capital, the creativity variables become insignificant. Education is, therefore, a key variable for creating a successful economic environment, and countries or regions making clever use of local factors together with the improvement or attraction of human capital demonstrate an innovative approach to creating a growing, entrepreneurial economy (see Mini case study 6.2).

Others such as Davidsson and Honig (2003) found that social capital probably plays a more integral role in the success of the entrepreneur than does human capital. Perhaps the real 'elixir' for an entrepreneurial environment lies in the interactions between social networking or social capital, its diversity and human capital. The presence of a diverse and rich pool of human capital, coupled with cultural diversity, facilitates the inflow of a particular kind of human capital that promotes innovation, accelerates information flow and develops new ideas, leading to a higher rate of new firm formation (Lee *et al.*, 2004).

Mini case study 6.1: Singapore: Talent and creativity capital

Recent interest in the dangers of the depletion of natural resources has engaged the minds of policy makers, researchers and business people from around the world. Of all the world's strategic resources – including oil, coal and land – water has probably attracted the most interest. It is likely to be the source of much political, economic and social controversy. While the rest of the world frets and argues over the water issue, Singapore, a country that may not have abundant water, has positioned itself to be a centre for water excellence.

Singapore's experiments with reclaimed seawater, waste water treatment and recycling, together with its positioning as a global hydro hub, has drawn in some of the biggest industry names including Siemens Water Technologies, Black and Veatch, GE Water, and the Norit Group. These companies have all set up R&D centres and regional headquarters in Singapore. They provide engineering, manufacturing support and services to a S$13bn regional market for water and water technologies. According to the Vice President of R&D at Siemens, Ruediger Knauf, Singapore's holistic approach to water management, competitive research programmes and testing opportunities, but most importantly its capacity to attract talent, are the key reasons for the establishment of its Singapore base. The talent pool is characterized by its diversity, both cultural and technological. The Dutch Norit Group, which purifies water for almost 9 per cent of the world's population, was specially attracted to Singapore's engineering and management talent. The Group's Managing Director, Duane Schilcht, states that Singapore is a know-how centre of knowledge and one of the few places in the Asia-Pacific region, if not the world, where he does not have any problems in recruiting quality staff. It is also a gateway to the Asia-Pacific region.

Singapore talent does not live by water alone. Its 'Fusionopolis' is an 'innovative cluster of futuristic temples dedicated to creativity'. The cluster is a state-of-the art hub for infocomms and media with most of the users of the hub dedicated to the vision of a digital future made possible by the convergence of info-communications and new media.

The French company Ubisoft, one of Europe's largest distributors of video games, was attracted to Singapore where it set up its eighteenth development studio. The studio creates and develops high-profile game titles. 'Teengae Mutant Turtles: Turtles in Time Re-Shelled' was the first independent production of the Singapore studio, rising to number one in the video games charts in August 2009. Other recent productions include 'Assassin's Creed 2 and Prince of Persia: The Forgotten Sands'. The studio employs 140 people – game developers, production and general administration personnel – and plans to increase this to 300 by 2013. It took the decision in order to have a presence in South East Asia and chose Singapore, because it has a strong commitment to this industry but more importantly because of the availability of talent. The expansion plans will make it the largest games development studio in the region.

Ubisoft is joined by Double Negative Visual Effects (DNVE), one of Europe's top providers of visual effects for films. The company, which was set up in Singapore in 2009, worked for the Hollywood blockbuster *Iron Man 2* with part of Lucasfilm, Industrial Light and Magic. What is DNVE's special interest in Singapore? According to its Managing Director, Alex Hope, it is its 'rich creative talent plus an education system focused on enhancing the skills of people coming into the industry'.

Traditionally, Singapore has excelled in the hard sciences and process-driven economies, but with its infrastructure and talent leadership it is fast becoming a major creative economy, especially in the world of digital media.

The Singapore environment is a fine example of entrepreneurial vision based on generating highly skilled human capital supported by a strong physical and learning infrastructure. This provision attracts existing entrepreneurial businesses from across the world. They identify opportunities in new markets based on demand-side pull (as in the rapidly growing youth market for video games) and a well-organized supply of creative talent, skills development and support for organizations.

(Source: talentcapital.sg; collectivecreativity.ft.com; *Financial Times*, 20 July 2010 and 4 August 2010)

PART V: A CONSENSUS VIEW OF AN ENTREPRENEURIAL ENVIRONMENT?

Institutions worldwide have tried to grapple with the question of how to provide a template for creating an entrepreneurial environment. The assumption behind attempting to reach a consensus view is predicated upon the belief that there are universal principles underpinned by a theory of entrepreneurship that could apply to different economic conditions. Therefore, irrespective of the stages of growth and the cultural peculiarities of countries, certain prerequisites prevail. The focus is mainly on macroeconomic issues, including finance and trade and institutional building. Policy makers are expected to concentrate on these issues and develop good banking systems, attractive interest and exchange rates, and stable tax structures alongside the need to deregulate, privatize and invest in infrastructure. Adopting these measures provides propitious environments for entrepreneurship to flourish according to what is known as the Washington Consensus and more recently, by Baumol *et al.* (2007) and Schramm (2006), as the necessary backdrop for such an environment (see the first two columns in Table 6.2).

Table 6.2 Models of building a consensus for creating a friendly environment

The Washington Consensus	The Baumol, Litan and Schramm (2007) framework	A developing country framework
• Fiscal policy discipline • Reduction of public spending on indiscrimitate subsidies • Tax reform • Maintain market-determined interest rates • Instil competitive exchange rates • Impose trade liberalization • Liberalize inward FDI • Privatization of state enterprises • Deregulation • Legal protection of property rights	• Ease of forming a business • Institutions that reward socially useful entrepreneurial activity – e.g. rule of law, property and contractual rights • Increasing economic pie, by government • Incentives to grow and innovate for both large companies and successful entrepreneurs – e.g. anti-trust laws, openness to trade	• Developing critical mass through innovation clusters and value chains • Leveraging pockets of dynamism • Cultivating innovation leaders and knowledge environments • Engaging diaspora networks • Changing institutions through innovation programmes • Using micro finance as an entry point and for development

Source: adapted from Schramm (2006).

Models of entrepreneurship and entrepreneurial environments

Despite being critical of the American template because it 'fails to reproduce a vital element of the US economy: support for entrepreneurship' (p. 154), Schramm (2006) recommends the four-sector model that drives entrepreneurship in the American economy. This model is made up of new firms, the symbiotic relationship between large and small firms especially in terms of outsourcing and buyer-supplier relationships, the government which fosters new business, and universities from which there is a constant flow of ideas that move into the entrepreneurial sector for eventual commercialization. Schramm (2006) suggests that the same model could be exported to other countries, especially developing ones where more pro-active attention needs to support each of the four components of the model.

Gainsaying the proposals about consensus models does not perhaps achieve much in the way of new, alternative insight. Most of the elements of infrastructure-building, government intervention, the role of higher education and small and large firm networks work or should operate in most countries. The question is, however, about specific contexts, the motivations of people in those contexts, the priorities that different contexts demand, and the novel, competitive advantages that ensue in those environments. There are, therefore, different models of entrepreneurial environments created by different approaches to the promotion of entrepreneurship, as Figure 6.3 and list of different models created by Cullum *et al.* (2002) in Table 6.3 show.

The points made above bring us back full circle to the underlying issues of social embeddedness, culture, institutions and framework conditions that shape different environments. According to the Accenture Survey (Cullum *et al.*, 2002), the majority of senior executives who were asked to name the entrepreneurial country of their choice opted for the US, with Japan a distant second. For these senior executives dreaming of US conditions while

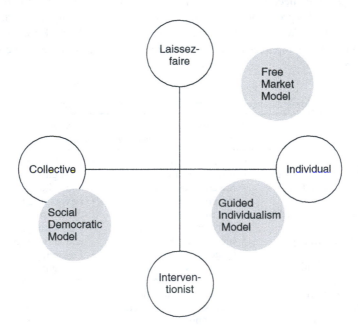

Figure 6.3 Entrepreneurship models

Source: Accenture Research (2002).

Table 6.3 Models for entrepreneurship

---

1. The Free Market Model

Examples: The United States and Canada

In this model, the role of government is fairly limited. Public policy can create some of the basic conditions required for an entrepreneurial culture to flourish, such as good telecommunications infrastructure, and can remove many of the obstacles that get in the way, but the rest is up to the private sector.

This model thrives in a culture in which entrepreneurial success is celebrated rather then denigrated. The tax structure rewards initiative and financial gain, but the degree of social protection is generally low.

2. The Guided Individualism Model

Examples: Singapore and Taipei

This model, too, is based on the encouragement of individual enterprise. Its distinctive feature, though, is the role of public policy in determining the broad sweep of entrepreneurial activity – in effect, signalling the sectors and industries in which entrepreneurial energies can most usefully be directed.

3. The Social Democrat Model

Examples: Sweden and Germany

This model combines the encouragement of enterprise with an emphasis on social protection. Countries that follow this model create a sort of social partnership, with key aspects of the economic and social framework determined by negotiations between the different social partners, such as employers, employees and government.

The collective nature of the social partnership system means that initiatives to encourage entrepreneurship – such as those promoting greater labour flexibility – can be accompanied by other measures (for example, retraining schemes and unemployment benefits) to offset any adverse impacts on particular sections of society. It thus becomes easier to gain the approval of society at large for the key measures needed to strengthen the productive base of the economy.

4. The Human Capability Model*

This model is different from the others mentioned above. It is based on the well-being of people stemming from their capability for, and freedom of, functioning The model implies that it is not enough for new technology to provide access to facilities but that it should provide the necessary knowledge for its uses and the opportunities generated by it to enable people to make informed choices.

The model is different from the 'consumerist' paradigm that focuses on the provision of clean water, food and shelter or even the 'entitlement' paradigm that advocates equitable distribution of the benefits of economic growth.

Source: adapted from Accenture Research: Cullum *et al.* (2002); Sen (1984, 1993, 1999); Alampay, 2006; Manimala, 2009).

* This model does not form part of Accenture's research findings. This model is provided by the author, based on the work by the Nobel Laureate Amartya Sen and others, as referred to above.

operating in different country environments, their wishes are unlikely to open up business opportunities. Rather their ability to adapt to the wider and specific contexts could provide new pathways for generating their firm's entrepreneurial behaviour activities.

PART VI: BACK TO CONTEXTS: DEVELOPING ENTREPRENEURSHIP

Specific issues relating to particular contexts are associated with the stages of development of a nation or a region. The type of entrepreneurship that is likely to work is partly a function of necessity and opportunity but is more importantly dependent on addressing critical priorities. As the third column in Table 6.2 shows, developing countries might need direct government intervention to create an environment where a critical mass of new ventures and larger firms can be built quickly, where champions and leaders are given pride of place, where it makes it easier for diaspora networks to invest in infrastructure, technologies and new firms. These environments should see intense human capital development activity take place, where the poor are engaged directly in the market place through mechanisms of micro finance or indeed enlightened large firms. The need for microeconomic strategies and interventions alongside broad macroeconomic measures are critical for change in such developing economies.

The last model (third column) in Table 6.2 is a major departure from the other ones provided by Accenture and others, and is of greater significance for local policy-making in developing countries which have different priorities and offer more challenging environment for other types of entrepreneurial activity. If an environment that is conducive to entrepreneurship for industrialized economies is promoted in developing countries then there is likely to be an inevitable asymmetry between expectations and possibilities in those countries. Yet, there are regular calls for fast-tracking pockets of growth in developing nations that mimic conditions in their developed counterparts. Creating such environments can serve the interests of rootless multinationals or a small proportion of firms catering to markets outside their home countries (as in special export processing zones) but not necessarily those of locally generated enterprise. In the long run both multinationals exploiting short-term advantages and local enterprises miss out on growth opportunities. Adjustments that large firms need to make to their business models (see Chapter 5) more adaptive to different types of local markets, to address both local and global needs, is as important as local capability development that can help nurture new ventures. Offering an environment where both outcomes are possible and where these outcomes can address key priorities is the main challenge for entrepreneurship in developing nations.

Engaging the poor in the market place has specific relevance to the world and to the particular role that entrepreneurship and innovation can play. The majority of the world's poor, who represent approximately 40 per cent of the world's population (or about 2.6 billion people), live on less than US$2 a day, surviving on subsistence agricultural activity or in informal enterprises in dreadful urban environments or in rural areas. For them, a propitious environment based on macroeconomic policy formulation is almost meaningless unless it is accompanied by local initiatives, developed and evaluated at the micro level through both public and private sector initiatives. Some of these policy initiatives are discussed in Chapter 10.

Conclusion

Understanding the status, depth, breadth and flexibility of institutions, their capacity to evolve in specific environments coupled with the mix of elements of the new venture creation process helps us to obtain a proper insight into factors that create, grow and hinder entrepreneurship and innovation in different economies. A fairly complex process of analysis is necessary to comprehend the various economic and social elements at play that are harnessed by governments, social institutions and entrepreneurs in particular environments.

Understanding the social structure of different economic environments, the tensions on the one hand between maintaining the status quo and the accommodation of deviancy, and between stability and uncertainty on the other, and the role of institutions in the management of these tensions provides us with clues about how people and organizations create their own entrepreneurial environment. The process of interaction between the people, organizations and environment within prevailing framework conditions helps to identify, promote, realize and evaluate various opportunities for productive change. The nature of this change process which defines entrepreneurial outcomes varies between different contexts, and a clear elaboration of those local contexts is necessary for the appropriate harnessing of ideas, resources, tools and structures with which to create and implement entrepreneurial policies and activities.

This chapter should ideally be studied together with Chapter 11 ('Entrepreneurship, Innovation and Economic Development') and Chapter 10 ('Entrepreneurship Policy'). A country or a region's approach to development, influenced by a range of factors, and the stage of development in which it is in at a given time, will have an impact on the kind of environment it creates for entrepreneurship and the policies it adopts to improve or change the environment to enable its development.

But how do these opportunities emerge? How are they identified and realized? How do these opportunities obtain in particular situations? Some of the answers to such questions might lie in the process of learning that people, organizations and regional environments engage in, and the learning cultures that they help to foster. We move on then to Chapter 7 to enquire about learning and its relationship with entrepreneurship and innovation.

Self-assessment questions

1. What are the dynamics of the social structure of an entrepreneurial environment?
2. Are institutions important for an entrepreneurial environment?
3. Institutional constraints affect the type of environment that is conducive to entrepreneurial activity. Discuss.
4. What are framework conditions, and why are they important for an entrepreneurial environment?
5. Is there a consensus view on the creation of an entrepreneurial environment?

7   Entrepreneurship and learning

Learning outcomes

In this chaper the reader will:

- obtain a critical understanding of the relationship between the concept and practice of learning and entrepreneurship;
- gain a thorough appreciation of the components of learning and the learning process, with particular reference to organization learning, and their connection with the process of entrepreneurship;
- examine critically the levels and significance of learning (individual, firm/organization and wider environment) and appraise their value as part of the process of entrepreneurship;
- apply their understanding to novel approaches to entrepreneurial decision-making at the level of the firm and also at the level of the region.

Structure of the chapter

This chapter is organized into five parts. It begins with an elaboration of learning and especially learning in an organizational context. Learning is central to the creation of new organizations and their growth. The process of organization learning contributes to the creation of adaptive, flexible, changing and learning organizations. These organizations work with different types of individual, collective, situated, endogenous and exogenous learning which can be managed within an organization to achieve innovative growth. The Part II makes the connection between organizations and learning on the one hand and opportunity identification and realization on the other, looking critically at some of the tools such as education and training, and the different stages or cycles of entrepreneurship that depend on different tools and instruments for them to take effect. It also examines the link between learning and innovation and how that connection helps to secure competitive advantage for firms. Finally, the chapter explores how innovation is enabled within the wider context of learning, often in clusters of industries or in regions involving the interplay of different stakeholders.

Part III situates the content of the chapter specifically in the context of SMEs, and discusses in detail how SMEs manage the process of formation and growth using different types of competencies and resources as part of an explicit or implied agenda of learning. It is argued that a proper understanding of this process is facilitated by the adoption of a 'learning system' that accommodates the flows of learning both within and outside a firm, and how the use of such a system encourages innovation. This is followed by a scrutiny of different forms of learning that inform entrepreneurial activity in SMEs and that can be incorporated into a learning system appropriate for particular types of entrepreneurial activity. Part V then addresses the question of entrepreneurial skills, making the case for a range of skills the development of which is dependent on the type of new venture, the absorptive capacity of entrepreneurs and the environment in which they are located. The chapter concludes with a summary of the essential elements of learning that illuminate the process of entrepreneurship.

Introduction

The act of creating a new venture, or that of growing an innovative organization, is a learning process. It suggests a movement from a previous position marked by an accumulated stock of knowledge, experience and ideas to another level characterized by a difference in that position that confers some advantage, gain and insight. It is tempting to dismiss such a movement as accidental or dependent on pure chance. Perhaps luck does play a part, especially when uncertainties hold sway in a changing world. But the involvement and mediation of the human agent(s) (the entrepreneur or a team of entrepreneurs) suggest that there is a process of discovery generating insight, and the use of tools and resources yielding results, which can be regarded as a learning process. Such learning takes place among individuals, within and among organizations, among networks of organizations, and in the wider environment. Our purpose is to understand how such learning contributes to the creation, growth and development of new ventures and how these ventures consolidate and spawn new forms of learning for the development of new products, services and other forms of innovation.

The centrality of the learning process is drawn from the contention that entrepreneurship has distinctive value if organizations and individuals 'learn' to move from one point to another in terms of generating new products/services, delivering new values, redefining organizational boundaries, and effecting change. This contention stems from a consideration of the well-rehearsed arguments that gained popularity among high-profile organizations as they set out to develop human resource strategies and production systems more adaptable to rapid socio-economic change (Matlay, 1997). This view propelled the concept of learning organizations into the forefront of strategic management and development thought (Dodgson, 1993; Kanter, 1989), and promoted the idea that learning is a key component of organizational development (Mitra, 2000; Moiengon and Edmondson, 1996; Senge, 1990).

In addition to the development referred to above, the term 'learning' has acquired an analytical value with the potential to unify various levels of organizational analysis: individual, group and corporate. Learning is perceived to underpin a proactive and interdisciplinary approach towards the cooperative and community nature of a new breed of highly focused and competitive twenty-first-century organizations (Dodgson, 1993), underlining the importance of innovation at the level of the organization.

Understanding the different forms of learning process (for example in large, medium and small firms; internal learning, learning from the external environment; individual, team-based and organizational learning) is a complex process. Many tomes and seminal pieces have been written on the subject (Argyris, 1996; Baets, 2006; Bennis and Wenger, 2004; Easterby-Smith *et al.*, 1999; Moingeon and Edmondson, 1998; Starkey, 1996, to name a few), concentrating mainly on the nature, systems, methods and implications for organizational learning and the role of management in deriving appropriate benefits from managing the learning process. Porter (1998) and Enright (1998) have in their work on clusters and industrial districts built on the notion of dynamic social learning (Becatini, 1984) and social embeddeness (Veblin, 1929), exploring the meaning and scope of learning in particular environments. But not much effort has been made in looking at the specific issue of capabilities, competencies and skills required to use socially embedded learning resources and the management of externalities, especially in the context of SMEs, and especially those creative small and medium-sized firms that are often celebrated as the main sources for job creation through innovation (Mitra, 2000; Cullen and Matlay, 1999).

Learning is critical in the fast-changing world of our times. Amplifying Drucker (1985), the systematic practice of innovation through learning, and the organization of knowledge generated by innovation through the learning processes, foster entrepreneurship. Such an imperative is perhaps most apparent in any meaningful consideration of the changes that characterize the new economy. The regularity of rapid change:

- calls for the availability of urgent learning tools and methods with which to cope with the change process;
- demands new products and services to reflect technological advancement; and
- requires advanced knowledge management techniques to make sense of constantly moving patterns of resources, processes and values.

(Christensen and Overdorf, 2000)

This chapter examines how theories, concepts and the practice of learning help us with our better appreciation of entrepreneurship, the entrepreneurs, the activities they engage in, and the organizational and wider environment in which they operate. We are, therefore, embarking here on a short journey to explore the connection between learning and entrepreneurship. Central to this examination is the connection we can make between key tenets of learning as a process and its link to innovation and entrepreneurship. We assume that learning takes place before, during and after new products and services are offered in the market. We also assume that learning is embedded in the firm creation and development process, and finally we expect that learning as an interaction process is made possible in the very 'act of doing' (making new products, establishing new firms, etc.) while providing opportunities for its renewal from the use of the outputs of innovation and entrepreneurship.

PART I: AN IDEA OF LEARNING, INNOVATION AND ENTREPRENEURSHIP

The learning process underlines different types of innovation. Innovation is often the result of interaction of various subjects, technologies, people and organizations, and it is the learning that is derived from such interaction that underpins innovative activity. Learning is defined as

> the process which changes the state of knowledge of an individual or organization. A change in state of knowledge may take the form of adoption of a new belief about causal relationships, the modification of an existing belief, the abandonment of a previously held belief, or a change in the degree of confidence with which an individual or individuals within an organization hold a belief or a set of beliefs.
>
> (Sanchez and Heene, 1997, p. 6)

Identifying the opportunities in the change process described above, organizing resources to enable the learning process to take effect, and making new combinations of knowledge, goods and services, and creating economic or social value lies at the heart of entrepreneurship. The learning process is manifested in the organization that is created out of it and its development through its continued use. This form of organization is based on the identification, acquisition and development of competencies that help to generate knowledge, establish a learning base for the organization, and support the innovation process. As an iterative, on-going process, what emerges is a form of learning that could be described as 'organizational learning'.

Organizational learning, knowledge, innovation and entrepreneurship

There is now a respectable body of evidence that connects sustainable competitive advantage to three strategic elements: *organizational learning, knowledge management* and *innovation* (Matlay, 2000). In the specialist literature, successful business outcomes are often linked to workplace learning, knowledge management and process or product/service innovation. Large organizations manage to combine these strategic elements into successful corporate drivers to maintain or expand their market share. It is not yet clear to what extent SMEs are becoming more adept at combining these strategic factors to create and sustain niche-based competitive advantages, despite their traditional reputation for being flexible, adaptable, less constrained by hierarchy and bureaucracy, and innovative.

Underpinning themes of organizational learning

Organizational learning can be best understood in terms of three underpinning and related themes or sub-sets of learning (Lumpkin and Lichtenstein, 2005):

- *Behavioural learning* – the repetition of behaviour that has been successful and the cancellation of that which has not, leading to the establishment of routine-based systems. These systems help to acquire, distribute, retrieve and store information and knowledge, and allow for adaptive learning through trial and error which in turn leads to the establishment of routines. A focus on antecedents and changes in structures, technologies, routines and systems of an organization is tied to the incremental responses of an organization's own experience and those of others (Huber, 1991; Levinthal and March, 1993; Lundberg, 1995).
- *Cognitive learning* – related to the resource-based view of the firm and strategy, the focus here is on the content of learning through the aggregation, translation and use of the cognitive maps of individuals so that they become part of the organization's own cognitive learning and knowledge base (Brown and Duguid, 1991; Kim, 1993; Weick and Roberts, 1993). Processes are put in place to improve such knowledge and to aid creativity, quality management and performance in general. Knowledge (or 'thought-process assets') is sourced and exploited both internally and externally as part of its dynamic capability.
- *Action learning* – here the emphasis is on practice and on filling the gap between what organizations think and proclaim they do and what they actually do, so that effective action is taken in real time (Argyris 1990; Senge *et al.*, 1994). There is a strong connection and alignment between what an individual learns in an organization and what the organization benefits from as a result. This is achieved through what Argyris and Schon (1978) and Bateson (1972) referred to as 'single and double loop learning'. While with the former incremental changes help to improve the efficiency of on organizational process,

'double-loop learning' generates challenges by raising questions about the appropriateness and effectiveness of the actions taken. Commitment to such a form of learning helps to establish a community of learning practice that improves communication, innovation and performance (Senge *et al.* 1994; Wenger, 2004).

Analytical and critical aspects of organizational learning and strategy development

As a dynamic and integrative concept, organizational learning involves analytical and critical aspects that shape individual and team values into successful business strategies (Moingeon and Edmondson, 1996; Senge, 1990). The management of knowledge, which involves the acquisition, creation and transformation of strategically relevant information (Ruggles, 1998; Mitra, 1999), enhances organizational performance and promotes people management practices that are more responsive to rapid socio-economic changes (Scarbrough *et al.*, 1999; Goh and Richards, 1997). Innovation is critical to sustainable business competitiveness (MacPherson, 1997). It involves the continuous development of new business processes, products and services that consolidate and reinforce the systematic practice of strategic and competitive management (Mitra and Formica, 1997b). These three organizational components of learning, knowledge management and innovation involve continuous internal transformation and improvement which, when combined into a cohesive business strategy, have the potential to significantly enhance a firm's competitive advantage. Inherent in this process is the idea of incremental innovation and, from time to time, radical innovation. This form of innovation is realized especially when the cohesive strategy is challenged by dynamic changes in the external environment because of new entrants in the market or by the introduction of new technologies that alter the rules of the marketplace. The occurrence of organizational learning enables a firm to adapt, change, re-organize and augment its capabilities. The motivation and demand for the regular occurrence of such learning leads to the establishment of learning organizations.

The learning organization

The idea of the 'learning organization' evolved from the 'Organizational Development' school of management, which proved popular during the late 1960s and early 1970s (Starkey, 1996). It places work-based learning and knowledge management at the core of sustainable competitive advantage (Senge, 1990). A learning organization is able to support consistent internal innovation, having as its immediate objectives the improvement of quality, the strengthening of relationships between clients and suppliers, and the achievement of a more effective corporate strategy (Mills and Friesen, 1992). More than three decades since its emergence, the theoretical principles and practical applications relating to organizational learning remains confused, fuzzy and difficult to comprehend or implement (Scarbrough *et al.*, 1998; Goh and Richards, 1997; Hitt *et al.*, 1996).

Sustainability of and continuity in learning

Continuity in organizational improvement and transformation through work-based learning is advocated by Pedler *et al.*, (1991), Senge (1990) and Cunningham (1994). Typically, however, this can only be achieved through intentional learning processes occurring at individual, group and systems levels (Dixon, 1994; Mumford, 1995; Fisher and Torbert, 1995). The continuous development of a learning organization is deemed conditional upon the quality of individual and collective learning in an organizational setting (Lank and Lank, 1995; Dixon, 1994). In competitive terms, de Geus (1998) argues that the ability of a workforce to learn faster than their counterparts often defines the only sustainable advantage at the disposal of a learning organization. Scarborough *et al.* (1998) point out that the focus of a learning organization should be upon the individual development of all its employees, regardless of their position in the corporate hierarchy. In practice, it appears that the competitive edge of a learning organization is dependent upon the way in which individual development is valued, managed and enhanced in order to ensure its continuous strategic transformation (Pearn *et al.*, 1995) and, critically, its contribution to collective learning and knowledge.

Individual and collective learning

Most influential writers on the topic of learning organizations differentiate between individual and collective learning (Romme and Dillen, 1997; Huber, 1996). As larger business entities rely upon the performance of various categories of employees, work-based individual learning becomes an important and necessary condition of sustainable competitive advantage. Collective learning in this type of organization takes place in addition to learning processes occurring at individual level. Importantly, however, although collective learning can occur independently of each individual, it cannot take place if all the employees in an organization are prevented from learning (Romme and Dillen, 1997; Kim, 1993). Both individual and collective learning can be significantly hindered by, for example, a multitude of stress-related problems. In small businesses, the crucial role that owner/managers invariably play in the daily operation of their firms often results in individual learning and development at managerial level. As a direct result, the need for collective learning is significantly reduced or even displaced entirely (Matlay, 1999).

A learning organization could also be defined or measured in terms of the sum total of accumulated individual and collective learning (Hyland and Matlay, 1997). Indeed, some pertinent research studies in this field were based upon the detailed analysis of learning practices and their effect upon overall business competitiveness (Huber, 1991; Sterman, 1989). Learning at work can be seen as a product of corporate values, internal competition and personal ambitions (Harrison, 1993). Organizational factors such as working conditions, management styles and employee relations play an important role in shaping learning and knowledge management processes specific to each business entity. It appears that only fragments of the knowledge gained through individual learning are actually recorded or disseminated, either formally or informally, for corporate use. Knowledge emerging from collective learning is much more complete and is usually recorded formally for corporate access and benefit.

Situated learning

Learning is not only concerned with specific activities. It is also connected to or embedded in social communities. This means that learning implies becoming a full participant, a member, a kind of person. As Lave and Wenger (1991) suggest, learning from this perspective suggests being able to be involved in new activities, to perform new tasks and functions, and to master new understandings as part of and within a socially constructed environment. It is this newness and the outcomes of perceived change that come from such newness that contribute to our understanding of the link between learning and entrepreneurship.

All activities, tasks, functions and their related understanding do not exist in isolation. They can be seen to be part of broader systems of relations in which they have meaning (Lave and Wenger, 1991). These relations, the people who form these relations through learning, and the meaning they generate constitute 'communities of learning'. Novice entrepreneurs enter at the peripheral edge. Gradually their engagement deepens through stages of learning and entrepreneurial activity. They become full participants, and will often take on organizing or facilitative roles within such communities. In this sense both learning and knowledge are not decontextualized, abstract or general' (Tennant 1997), but are situated in a specific context and are at the heart of the creation of a new organization, or the development of a new product or a service. What happens in these communities of practice is 'situated learning'.

Difficulties with individual and collective learning

Some commentators stress the conflict of interest that can exist between individual and organizational learning (Probst and Buchel, 1997; Starkey, 1996). It appears that those researchers who favour personal development also recommend the acquisition of 'transferable' skills. This is more likely to be the case in large organizations with internal labour markets that offer opportunities for both personal development and corporate progression (Thomson and Mabey, 1994). It is now widely acknowledged that that micro and small businesses do not offer development opportunities commensurable with those found in larger organizations (Storey, 1994). Progression is very limited and employees are more likely to leave employment and start their own firms. Consequently, small business owner/managers prefer their employees to acquire firm-specific, non-transferable knowledge, which is easier to manage and which also curtails individual opportunities in the external labour market. Work-based learning is closely controlled by small business owner/managers who fear that their competitors would poach their key employees. Bomers (1989) argues that organizational learning is most likely to be constrained in organizations where most of the knowledge and skills are dependent upon fewer individuals. As most small businesses fall into this category, organizational learning in this type of firm is likely to occur sporadically, as a reactive strategy, rather than as a proactive drive to enhance the quality of the workforce (Kim, 1993).

Endogenous and exogenous learning

In entrepreneurial terms, the strategic pursuit of economic profit is often perceived in terms of a struggle to match internal resources and skills to external opportunities and risks (Grant, 1999). At the microeconomic level, issues related to knowledge management and the skills base of an organization fall largely within the influence and competence of the entrepreneur and/or the firm. Easterby-Smith and Prieto (2008) refers to this form of learning as 'endogenous learning', where the organization learns from its own resources.

At a macroeconomic level, factors such as prevailing economic circumstances, size and component of the labour market, supply and demand of goods and services and overall risks operate largely outside an entrepreneur's control. These are 'exogenous sources' that provide resources for learning to the firm from outside. Given the crucial role of an entrepreneur in the organizational decision-making process, the match/mismatch of entrepreneurial knowledge and internal/external factors can significantly affect strategy and ultimately determine the success or failure of a business venture. Thus learning at the business strategy level can be viewed as the relationship between internal resources and external circumstances where 'entrepreneurial success' largely depends upon the economic equilibrium generated by sustainable competitive advantage. Definitions of 'entrepreneurial success' can vary considerably among individual entrepreneurs. They could, typically, include wealth creation, lifestyle maintenance, social usefulness and personal satisfaction. Whatever the objective, the entrepreneur learns to recognize opportunities for innovation and growth through learning.

PART II: OPPORTUNITY RECOGNITION, LEARNING AND ENTREPRENEURIAL ACHIEVEMENT

A well-recognized competence or ability of a successful entrepreneur is the ability to identify and develop business opportunities. Ronstadt (1988), Shane and Venkatraman (2000) and others have all identified these issues as being critical to our understanding of entrepreneurship. Success or failure contributes to the richness of experience. The acquisition of knowledge, competencies and contacts that accompany that experience are believed to advance the ability of the entrepreneur to discover and take advantage of opportunities that emerge in the market. This way they enjoy primacy of place in the market over novice entrepreneurs (McGrath and Macmillan, 2000), even to the extent of gaining access to what McGrath (1999) referred to as 'shadow options' or unrecognized opportunities. What they acquire over and above anything else is an entrepreneurial mindset (Politis, 2008) to search for and realize opportunities.

What is it that makes particular individuals discover opportunities where others do not? Some researchers have suggested that prior information of opportunities and cognitive properties (of knowing, learning, tacit knowledge) necessary to assess and evaluate these opportunities provide the key (Shane and Venkatraman, 2000; Busenitz and Barney, 1997). These two factors suggest that there is a stock of information that is available exclusively to individual entrepreneurs and that the latter know the nature, scope and possibilities of the relationships between what is to be achieved (the ends) and how best to achieve specific commercial ends (the means). The legitimacy acquired through prior experience provides the necessary boost for experienced entrepreneurs who combine entrepreneurial flair with insight into routines and codes of practice unknown to new entrepreneurs.

Liability of newness and smallness

What does learning help to achieve? Various writers have written about the liability of newness (Stinchcombe, 1965; Starr and Bygrave, 1992; Aldrich, 1999) and also about the liability of smallness, which plague entrepreneurs and small firms. Lack of funding, and the absence of any foundation for trust, are hindrances that generate the liabilities referred to above. Prior experience and the knowledge base acquired through such experience together with a diverse background could help to stimulate creativity and provide a strong basis for coping with uncertain situations. Refer back here to the idea of networks and social and cognitive legitimacy discussed in Chapter 3, which should augment the statements made here. In that chapter we also learnt how previous work experience, contacts and networks can have a positive impact on the entrepreneurial experience, especially for new players.

Experience encapsulates the idea of 'learning by doing' and the tacit knowledge that facilitates entrepreneurial decision-making in uncertain conditions (Sarasvathy, 2001). This suggests that while education can provide for objective information and knowledge, it is essentially the actual and direct gathering of information for making a buying or selling decision or the setting up of a firm that helps entrepreneurs to understand the activities.

Education or experience

Previous experience constitutes the stock of general knowledge that an entrepreneur is believed to posses. Education appears to have a lower value than experience, but this is not necessarily the case. Education can also be considered to be part of the entrepreneur's stock of knowledge, and some writers have argued that it can be a source of ideas for new ventures (Vesper, 1979), and that without education experience only could cause a higher likelihood of failure. The jury seems to be still out on this matter as studies have produced mixed results, with some indicating that education has little or no effect on firm formation (Sandberg and Hofer, 1987) and others suggesting that higher profitability rather than higher growth was the more likely outcome of education (Jo and Lee, 1996).

The role of education can be understood more clearly in today's environment where opportunities are often derived in the global market place as a result of new technologies and the opening up of new markets. First, the issue is not simply about acquiring new technologies and using them in a specific context. New technologies, including the Internet, nano and bio technologies, often require or result in the sharing of know-how and applications for further use across different organizations. Second, advanced technologies often have a strong scientific base requiring the direct involvement of engineers and scientists in the production of goods and services. It is not surprising to find the vast number of highly qualified engineers, computer scientists and business graduates who are behind the phenomenon of Silicon Valley or the less fêted but highly powerful economic success stories in Israel, China, India and Taiwan. However, education also has its fair share of drop-outs in Gates, Allen, Brin and others who simply managed to combine their alertness to opportunities with their skills a bit earlier than their 'fully qualified' counterparts!

These debates continue apace. And what do we learn from them? One way of answering such a question is to locate the learning issue first in terms of what Noteboom (2000) refers to as the cycles of entrepreneurship, and then in relation to entrepreneurial outcomes, especially competitiveness.

Learning and cycles of entrepreneurship

Entrepreneurship is associated with innovation, novel combinations leading to creative destruction, the identification and utilization of different possibilities for consumption and production, the management of different factors of efficient production, and the provision of capital (Noteboom, 2000). These associations result in different roles for entrepreneurs, all with varied characteristics and competencies. Risk-taking, alertness, perceptiveness, open-mindedness, absorptive capacity, ability to make judgements, achievement motivation and leadership are some of these characteristics or competencies. Noteboom (2000) suggests that rather than being fixated with any specific notion we can make better sense of what entrepreneurs do by linking some of these characteristics with different stages in the cycle of entrepreneurship.

Entrepreneurship is a process of both discovery and development. We can identify the different stages of discovery that an entrepreneur or a firm goes through, including:

*   *differentiation* –differentiating from existing products or services in response to a diversity of demand. This step requires certain degrees of perceptiveness, imagination and initiative;
*   *reciprocation* – adding novel combinations resulting from drawing elements from other related practices, resulting in better application of those services, which requires routines and structure together with dynamic capabilities, including alertness;

- *accommodation* – making novel combinations drawing elements from other products or services but generating new value; which require a high degree of autonomy, courage and unusual levels of imagination;
- *consolidation* – carrying out trials of new combinations, which require seeking acceptance through social and cognitive legitimacy, a strong sense of realism and judgement, networking, the establishment of large scale production facilities; and
- *generalization* – stretching the products, the firm and the capabilities to new horizons through internationalization, standardization, scale and scope economies, demanding different forms of experience, courage, and higher levels of networking and co-ordination capabilities, plus cultural sensitivities.

(Noteboom, 2000)

Each of these stages provides for different opportunities. The fulfilment of these opportunities requires discrete sets of skills and the capacity to learn. The competencies necessary to engage in this learning process do not necessarily reside in any individual entrepreneur. There is inevitably a need for combinations of skills across different individuals or through networks and in the creation or development of the firm, which makes the process itself the embodiment of evolutionary learning. What we obtain at the beginning or the end is a mix of the Schumpeterian movement away from equilibrium (through differentiation, reciprocation and accommodation, for example) between supply and demand, with a Walrasian process of arbitration that allows for holes to be filled in the market, thus exerting a movement towards equilibrium, or a sense of alertness to opportunity in the Kirznerian sense of utilizing novel possibilities to satisfy demand and regain the equilibrium position (Noteboom, 1999, 2000).

Learning, innovation and competitiveness

Since Schumpeter introduced the bi-modal concept of innovation in the early 1930s, this topic has enjoyed periods of cyclical revival and decline. The critical connection between innovation (defined as the successful transformation of an idea or knowledge into new products, processes, services and organizational forms) and productivity is best understood in terms of economic productivity, the essential fuel for a nation's competitive advantage and prosperity. Fostering an environment where innovation flourishes requires recognition of both efficiency (brought about by technical change) and 'value' (brought about by learning and entrepreneurship derived from the change process). This, as Porter and Stern (1999) argue, manifests itself not only in what a nation produces but in how it goes about it.

Competitive advantage in firms of various sizes operating across all sectors of an economy can be established and sustained by innovative strategies. According to Porter (1980), two generic strategies can be distinguished: process innovation and product or service innovation. By the use of process innovation, a firm may be able to secure competitive advantage or even be at the forefront as a cost-leader. Similarly, competitive advantage can be achieved through innovation aimed at ensuring higher quality products and/or services. In the case of smaller firms, scales of economy are difficult to achieve and cost-leadership in most sectors of economic activity is a rare and often short-lived occurrence. Non-price, quality-related strategies are more frequently observed in smaller firms and are increasingly based upon innovative processes initiated and sustained by owner/managers in search of the 'added value' competitive edge (Roper, 1997).

The influence of the wider environment for learning and innovation

While Schumpeter (1942), Solow (1956) and Abramovitz (1956) were the early proponents of the importance of innovation to economic growth, it was Rosenberg (1963; 1982) who pointed out the importance of the interaction between the wider environment, national institutions and microeconomic processes for economic growth. These processes influence innovative activity in the macroeconomy (Porter and Stern, 1999). Government support through public investment in a country's science and technology base and the transfer of knowledge generated from such a base bring together the three players – government, higher education and industry. The three-way involvement defines the activities of the institutions, and resources and capacities of various organizations in an innovative environment. Such an environment is made up of interconnected industries and supportive infrastructures, best exemplified in clusters or industrial districts.

Clusters of learning and innovation

The cluster-based innovative environment's three-dimensional structure is completed by the social and human component. What binds the three dimensions is the interdependency between them. As cluster-based firms draw on the resources of the common infrastructure, their investments through training, grants and R&D support replenish the infrastructure, while the social and human component engenders a dynamic interaction process of formal and informal learning. The majority of the players in these environments, or indeed outside clusters, are small firms. How learning enables new firms to be created to manage innovation and how the learning process takes shape inside these firms to foster growth are, therefore, inevitable subjects of enquiry.

PART III: SMES, LEARNING, ENTREPRENEURSHIP AND INNOVATION

Lacking in size, adequate resources and market power, SMEs have little direct control over their environment. They are, therefore, fundamentally dependent upon a series of critical relationships with both individuals and disparate organizations within a transactional or task environment, and in a social milieu. The management of this externality is a highly complex process, and unlike with large firms, there is an absence of formal strategies for coordination and communication, and considerable dependence on supply chains and subcontracting. The organization and reorganization of competencies becomes a function of the relationship with the outside world and of the learning process.

Part of the management of learning processes in SMEs is based on both the 'negative' and 'positive' presumptions about SMEs. The 'negative' suggestions are that SMEs are too small and too resource constrained to develop adequate competencies within the organization. Hence they are naturally dependent on externalities, with their wellspring being within the firm and the domain of the firm. In these circumstances, the core capabilities of the SME lies in its ability to learn, generate sufficient internal knowledge and leverage its competencies with other firms, resources and institutions available externally.

Most small firms face the problem of resource constraints in both the creation and the early growth stages of their business. Recent research has established that networking and clustering (seen in terms of close geographical proximity of firms in a region) are important entrepreneurial tools for new owner-managers because they help them to draw upon 'firm addressable' (see below) resources from the region in which they are based (Birley, 1985; Shaw, 1997; Mitra *et al.*, 1999). Through interactive social relationships in particular contexts, entrepreneurs obtain information, resources and social support (Aldrich and Zimmer, 1986; Saxenian, 1990; Hakansson and Johannisson, 1993). Thus, it is likely that the smaller the firm is, the more urgent the need for that firm to draw on external resources. This in turn demands more active networking on the part of the firm.

Successful outcomes of social relationships and networking do not emerge without considerable endeavour from the parties involved. On the one hand, as Birley *et al.* (1991) pointed out, entrepreneurs have to work hard to develop relationships: they have to persuade, socialize, bargain and reciprocate with others to create a relationship and maintain it. The commitment of entrepreneurs to firm-building will be dependent on their attitudes towards networking and their perception of specific benefits. The growth of technical-operative knowledge, supported by processes of learning by doing and learning by using, combined with the idea of 'dynamic socialization' (Capello, 1999) processes, produces very important innovative results. In this context an adaptive learning process, characterized by incremental improvement of products, services and technologies, enables firms to generate competitive advantage. In generating products and services, firms develop learning resources or competencies. Building and using these competencies both within the firm and through social relationships is at the core of the learning process for SMEs. The motivation for this learning is the acquisition of legitimacy both within the industry and in the wider society.

Competency building competency leveraging and socio-cognitive legitimacy

Competence building (to achieve qualitative change, e.g. new firm creation, new product development), and *competency leveraging* (applying competencies to market opportunities or shared activities) are the actions taken by firms to generate learning resources. These competencies can then be utilized by *firm-specific assets* (assets exclusive to and tightly controlled by a firm) and *firm addressable assets* (assets that it is able to draw on through networking) to manage 'causal ambiguities', resulting from asymmetrical and ambiguous data gathered from an uncertain environment, and innovation (Mitra, 2000).

For new firms in relatively new industries there is the other dimension to the learning and growth process, namely the legitimization that firms go through to establish themselves. Legitimization of their identity, their products and services (Aldrich and Baker, 2001) is symbiotically linked to the learning process. Thus the firms are not only establishing critical relationships within existing and accepted norms of business practice and convention but are creating new forms of learning among established organizations by demonstrating the value and legitimacy of their products and services.

Schuman's (1995) and Aldrich and Baker's (2001) notion of legitimacy as a 'generalized perception or assumption that the actions of an entity are desirable, proper or appropriate within some socially constructed system of norms, values, beliefs and definitions' appears to be particularly relevant for the purposes of understanding small firm behaviour.

Aldrich and Baker (2001) argue that in seeking this form of *cognitive legitimacy* new entrants are likely to copy existing organizational forms. This involves the use of strategies for use of firm-specific and firm-addressable assets. Where there is an established population of businesses in a particular industry, new ventures manipulate those assets through tried and tested feedback mechanisms (Mitra, 2009).

Socio-political legitimacy refers to the acceptance by key stakeholders and the general public of the appropriateness of new ventures. In the context of regions, this form of recognition is not simply a static process by which legitimacy is gained by a firm when it subscribes to existing norms and traditions only. Socio-political legitimacy is also a dynamic process, in that stakeholders create environments conducive to the development of new industries. The development of a regional innovation system could be considered to be an example of a facilitative environment for supporting new industries. Entrepreneurs identify opportunities in this state of flux and work with stakeholders to establish successful new ventures (Mitra, 2009).

Cognitive and socio-political legitimacy were considered in detail in Chapter 3 when we examined sociological theories of entrepreneurship. Here we make the connection between the process of learning, the resources of learning (competencies), the objectives (innovation, competitiveness and legitimacy), and the environment (organizational and wider environment, as in a region). Bringing these components together, we can develop a framework or a system of learning and innovation for SMEs.

Developing a framework of learning and SMEs

In considering the idea and value of learning, it is appropriate to make some key assumptions. For our purpose, these assumptions help to provide the necessary framework for testing some ideas on learning and its concomitants, namely innovation and competitive advantage, with particular reference to small and medium-sized enterprises (SMEs). The key assumptions include the following:

* Learning for SMEs is closely associated with innovation (in all its forms) because of the need for SMEs either to survive through incremental innovation or grow through dynamic change processes.
* Small (early stage) entrepreneurial firms (SEFs) are local/regional firms.
* SEFs are resource constrained; therefore, they seek cognitive and socio-political legitimacy (Aldrich and Baker, 2002), essentially in the regional environment (though not restricted to it).
* SEFs' route to acquiring legitimacy is based on different learning forms ans methods using different types of 'learning' assets.
* Learning at the level of the firm, or organizational learning, is concerned with systems, based on early Schumpeterian notions of specialist, science-based research and formalized coordination in large firms, on the idea of more intensive forms of participation by small firms, or on collective innovation processes in industrial districts or clusters.
* Systems of organizational learning and innovation are location- and culture-specific, suggesting the need for an evolutionary and socially constructed approach to its study.
* Learning at the international level reinforces the types and forms of connectivity between technologies, skills, organizations and people that can be observed within specific regions, especially in industrial clusters, confirming the paradox of the more international scope and character of business activity among firms in regional clusters.

Typical 'learning' assets are the knowledge resources of the firm, which can be either *firm-specific or firm-addressable* assets (Mitra, 2000). Both types of learning assets are located in the region, in that the firm-specific ones are characteristic of the peculiarity of the specific firm in the region, and the firm-addressable ones are either drawn from within a particular

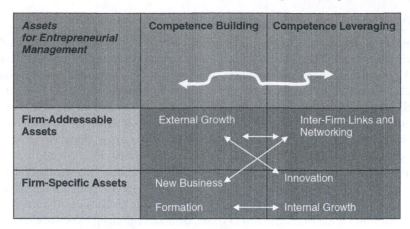

Figure 7.1 SME entrepreneurial capability building and the learning system

Source: adapted from Mitra (1999, 2000) and Bellini et al. (1997).

geographical construct or brought in to the recipient firm's region from further afield. The assets absorbed from outside the region then become part of the pool of knowledge resources of the region. The use by firms of such learning assets is a function of their competency-building or competency leveraging. The acquisition of appropriate competencies leads to realization of cognitive and/or socio-political legitimacy. If these assumptions hold then what emerges is a 'learning system' within small firms and in the nexus of interacting firms within a geographical space (see Figure 7.1).

As Figure 7.1 indicates, the use of different assets can be associated with different stages of growth in the early years of a small firm. Specific competencies can be detected at each stage commensurate with the use of particular learning assets. An inherent factor of growth is the interplay between these assets such that each stage of development inevitably reflects a mix of usage of these assets and competencies. Competency building and competency leveraging occur in non-linear fashion, with one often spawning the other as firms organize themselves in terms of the reliance on internal and external resources.

The learning system, innovation and entrepreneurship

The generation, codification and transfer of knowledge are the essential elements of the *learning system*. Within a region, the system is operational within and across firms through the dynamic exchange afforded by 'competency building' and 'competency leveraging'. If the regional environment is conducive to innovation because of the availability of essential innovation 'attractors' (skills and knowledge base, information access, capability of market conversion of ideas, knowledge and technological spillovers), then learning for innovation is concerned with:

*   the creation, adaptation and fusion of new ideas among firms and across the region (generation and competency building);
*   re-use and reference of knowledge through continuous learning (codification and competency leveraging); and
*   moving knowledge from one firm to another or between institutions and firms (transfer and coordination, and the move from firm-specific assets to firm-addressable assets).

Convergence and paradox in regions and the innovation process

The learning system approach helps us to identify a few other important features of a learning environment. The first feature is that of *convergence*. Convergence may be detected in sectoral structures through diversification, combination of technologies, and the rise of new micro clusters such as biotechnology, information and communication technologies, internet applications, image processing, multimedia and computer applications. Different levels of industrial/sectoral and technological convergence also provide for both increasing and diminishing returns, depending on the industry, within the same regional environment.

The second extended feature is that of *paradox*. SMEs located in an environment featuring a high concentration of similar or related firms innovate through the management of paradox (Mitra, 1999). Paradox is evident in the globalization-regionalization tensions inherent in these regions of high agglomeration. Successful regions and business clusters such as in Silicon Valley, in Emilia Romagna and in Basle, balance regional productive excellence with international market positioning. In fact empirical studies (Keeble *et al.*, 1997, in Cambridge and Oxford; Formica and Mitra, 1996, in London) have found that firms with above-average international links have higher local linkage intensities and frequencies than their nationally oriented counterparts.

The learning process involved in the building and use of competencies and assets helps firms to identify issues of convergence and paradox, and manage the complexity and uncertainty of the external environment. The organization and management of these competencies vary from one stage of development to another even as each set of competencies appropriate to a particular stage of development of a firm feeds or mutates into another form of learning at a different stage. The formation stage of a firm, for example, is more likely to be associated with generating competencies (competency building with firm-specific assets) inside a firm, while the early growth period may be more concerned with leveraging competencies from outside relying essentially on firm-specific assets. Codification of learning might be more important at this stage because of the need to use an established learning base from which to venture into new markets and generate new products. Competency leveraging continues through maturity and wider market participation using assets from or transferring them outside the firm. These capabilities are enhanced in networks. Stability and legitimacy gained through the stages so far help to consolidate internal competencies through new forms of competence building. This is not a linear process. Firms may move from one stage to another in unplanned and non-linear ways, resulting in unique combinations of firm-specific and firm addressable assets. Every attempt at developing a new product, a new process and a new market opportunity is a function of this learning process.

Figure 7.2 illustrates the learning system approach to cluster based innovation (Mitra, 2000) incorporating the above-mentioned elements discussed above.

How can learning be organized, promoted and used systematically within and by, especially, entrepreneurial small and medium-sized firms? What forms of learning do SMEs have at their disposal and how do they make use of these forms?

PART IV: FORMS OF LEARNING AND SMES

The dearth of skills in SMEs is often considered to be a barrier to their development. But this is a contentious issue. Entrepreneurs and owner-managers often refer to the value of informal training, which is seldom understood or codified either by firms or by researchers simply because of the difficulty associated with formalizing any of the training that goes on.

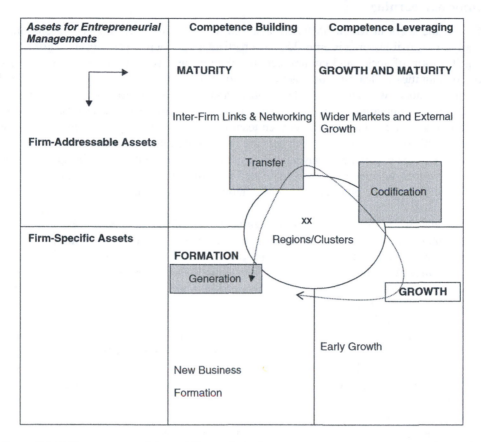

Figure 7.2 SME entrepreneurial capability and the learning system: From start-up to innovative growth

Source: adapted from Mitra (1999, 2000, 2001) and Bellini et al. (1997).

A large part of such informal training is either tacit or informal. It is generally carried out as part of a job ('learning by doing'). Entrepreneurs and owner-managers often refer to the value of relevant training carried out in and as part of the job and the importance of instant measurability given that survival of the firm is often the order of the day (Averill and Hall, 2005; Atwell, 2003).

Our understanding of learning in SMEs is based on the knowledge that we acquire through traditional surveys and other explicit forms of data gathering. These techniques help us to know that what SMEs provide space and time for are essentially acquiring and growing technical and organizational skills such as information processing and management, deduction and analytical skills, decision-making skills, creative thinking and problem-solving skills, communication skills, language skills, leadership and teamwork, team-based learning, strategic thinking, management and business, and customer services. Various studies about skill development in enterprises focus on formal training practices provided by education or training institutions, usually leading to a certified qualification. However, anecdotal evidence and common sense tell us that given the constraints SMEs have they use both formal and informal methods.

Informal learning

One of the ways in which SMEs are assumed to offer possibilities of learning is 'informally'. Informal learning is embedded in a particular community (organization/firm), making it a form of social and cultural activity. Within these settings 'learners' become part of communities of learning or practice (CoPs). These communities are made up of voluntary members who share knowledge, ideas and interests, mentoring one another. They generate new opportunities for knowledge management and learning processes by using new forms of social interaction between team members, and fairly loose contact between these members or actors. New members are incorporated into the culture of skills and informality of the experienced players, which in turn helps to produce new insights into their work practices. Members are also motivated to participate through opportunities to learn new skills and work practices in collaboration with local colleges (Hamburg and Hall, 2008).

Dale and Bell (1999) refer to informal learning as learning that takes place in a work context, without any formal organization of a programme or a curriculum. This form of learning relates to a person's performance and employability and it may be recognized by all who are involved in it. What defines such learning is essentially the context and the administration of such learning together with the kind of sponsorship it attracts. At the formal level learning takes place within often a defined physical space, is clearly structured and enjoys organized funding support and championing.

Coombs and Ahmed (1974) also identified the unorganized nature of accumulating knowledge, skills, attitudes, insights and experience in various informal settings, such as the home or in recreational environments. They identified various processes of informal learning including imbibing knowledge while spending time with the family, or reading a newspaper or watching television, pointing to the unorganized, unsystematic and even unintentional nature of such learning.

What tends to distinguish informal learning from its structured and formal counterpart is the organizational and administrative arrangements. The latter is associated with formal institutions – schools, colleges, universities and private training organizations – while the former is part of the activities of communities of practice or interest and takes the form of interactions with friends, family and work colleagues.

The form and context of learning provides some explanation of the nature and scope of informal learning. Small and especially entrepreneurial firms are distinguished by their chaotic and unstructured environments. These environments are more conducive to informal processes of all kinds of learning than structured alternatives as problem-solving and task-orientation acquires a sense of immediacy in terms of both their learning and their doing. But what lies behind this form of learning? What could be the motivation or intention for such learning?

Here Eraut's argument is of interest, especially when he examines intention in learning. He creates a continuum with implicit learning – first with the idea of 'the acquisition of knowledge independently of conscious attempts to learn and the absence of explicit knowledge about what was learned' (Reber, 1993; quoted by Eraut, 2000, p. 12). At another extreme, Eraut writes about 'deliberative learning' where time is specifically set aside for learning. Between the two is 'reactive learning'. Here, although learning is explicit, it occurs spontaneously and in response to recent, current or imminent situations but without any time being set aside for it. These categories come very close to Donald Schön's categories of 'knowledge in use', 'reflection on action' and reflection in action.

Tacit knowledge

Another way of exploring the idea of informal learning is to view it simply as implicit learning. Such learning results in the acquisition of what Polanyi (1967) calls *tacit knowledge* – 'that which we know but cannot tell'. The topic of tacit knowledge has featured widely in the development of organizational knowledge and learning theories. Attributable to Polyani, the concept of 'tacit knowledge' probably has earlier antecedents in a fifth-century Indian, Bharthari: 'the expert's knowledge of the genuineness of precious stones and coins, incommunicable to others, is born of practice and not of reasoning' (Ayer, 1965, p. 46). Referred to as knowledge that cannot be coded, tacit knowledge can be made explicit (and explicit learning can lead to tacit knowledge). It is also associated with procedural knowledge or what the Greeks referred to as *techne*, or practical knowledge, as opposed to *episteme*, or the knowledge about things (Noteboom, 2000).

Tacit knowledge provides much of the basis for the way we interact with people and situations. It is embodied in people, rather than in any codified form or in tangible objects. In most cases it is difficult to transfer such knowledge between people even if it can be acquired by a firm through hiring people, R&D and interpersonal networking. The problem is in the 'telling' of what knowledge has been acquired or shared. In most organizations good practice is based on rich experience that cannot possibly be codified into written forms. In small firms with fewer resources and with higher levels of reliance on informal processes and contacts, it is even more difficult to displace tacit forms of learning. But once it is exposed, there is a possibility for testing such knowledge with a view to harnessing and developing it. However, there are difficulties with this process. If we follow Polanyi's definition it may not be possible at all to carry out those tests.

Fortunately, Nonaka and Takeuchi (1995) offer some suggestions to develop mechanisms for transferring tacit learning and knowledge to general situations. They refer to the idea of shared space (or 'ba' in Japanese) as being central to the relationships of knowledge creation. In this space, knowledge is generated through a spiralling process of exchange and interactions between tacit and codified or explicit knowledge, including:

- socialization
- externalization
- combination
- internalization.

'Socialization' between people helps to make sharing of such knowledge possible, and this form of interaction can take place within the firm or outside with those not directly connected to the firm. 'Externalization' occurs when tacit knowledge is expressed for transmission to others, and 'combination' takes place either when tacit knowledge is transformed through sharing into explicit knowledge or when explicit knowledge is converted to even more complex knowledge through a mix of tacit and explicit forms. Finally, 'internalization' is a manifestation of the conversion of newly created knowledge into the organization's collectively understood and accepted tacit knowledge base.

How is such interaction and knowledge creation achieved? It is made possible through the availability of shared space or, more precisely, four types of shared space – face to face, peer-peer, group to group and on-site – with each space making possible the conversion of an individual's knowledge to a shared platform of knowledge for a group or organization, and the conversion of the latter to a form understood by the former.

The often time-constrained entrepreneur or small business owner-manager reverses the process by making explicit knowledge tacit and develops heuristics based on previous know-how or experience. They learn and develop routines and habits to deal with situations. These can range from developing the ability to operate a laptop to adaptive responses to emergency situations – for example, dealing with a problem with a sole customer or supplier. The response can often become part of a pattern of actions without any significant deliberation, where responses are made to specific characteristics of a situation. Unlike employees of a large firm, smaller firm owner-managers quite often create similar 'ba' or spaces outside the firm with peers and counterparts in similar or different firms. Their reliance on such external platforms can increase their transaction costs, and a trade-off between such costs and the benefits of network-based learning is often a key consideration for entrepreneurs.

If we are to accept the different stages of entrepreneurship referred to above and the varied forms of entrepreneurial activities and outcomes, we can see that the learning process in different spaces is a significant variable that needs to be taken into account to better understand the development of and outcomes from innovation and new venture creation.

Training

Formal training activities are generally associated with the acquisition of vocational skills and competencies linked to a specific function, task or a job. In this sense training has a specific context, is time bound and requires an output in the form of, for example, better performance, and sometimes an outcome in terms of a more knowledgeable employee. Incentives and rewards for taking up and completing a successful training programme are evinced in qualification certificates, salary increments, job mobility and bonuses.

The task orientation of training is at odds with the idea of a holistic, tacit knowledge-based and informal form of competency development that entrepreneurs might be expected to champion. The vocational content is more suited to the learning of crafts and techniques necessary for pursuing such crafts, including those of plumbers, carpenters or electricians. Many of these people are self-employed and are classified as entrepreneurs in most public databases on firm formation and by researchers around the world. These self-employed people learn their skills through vocational training colleges or through apprenticeships with employers.

Apprenticeships

Apprenticeships have a long pedigree. Crafts guilds in the Middle Ages supervised the apprenticeship system, which involved a master craftsman employing young people. The latter were often provided with food and lodging and formal training in a specific craft for a substantial period of time (between five and seven years. Today's apprenticeships combine classroom teaching with on-the-job training. A recent OECD report (2010) indicates that apprenticeships are popular in countries such as Denmark, Germany and France. Germany in particular is hailed as an excellent example of a country where the demand for the VET (vocational education and training) dual system of on-the-job or in-company training has constantly exceeded supply in both eastern and western Germany (OECD 2010). Ever since the second industrial revolution, the German model of skills training has been closely tied with innovation, helping to nurture skills directly associated with new product or service development and organizational change.

While entrepreneurship is holistic in scope, specific elements of problem-solving or learning-on-the-job are typical of entrepreneurial activities. The use of tacit knowledge in 'learning by doing', which Stenstrom and Tynjala (2009) argue is the natural way of learning for entrepreneurs, might suggest that apprenticeships provide fertile ground for entrepreneurial training. However, tacit knowledge implies (since there is no way of really knowing!) a wider field of knowledge acquisition that both covers specific training issues and provides the motivation for self-determination. Indeed, if we are to accept sociological analysis that suggests that many people emerge as entrepreneurs from their previous employment equipped with both the skills related to such employment and the inspiration to offer better products and services, then apprenticeships can be considered a vehicle for promoting entrepreneurship. Note, however, the difference between the formal and explicit organization of apprenticeships and the more informal, self-orientation of entrepreneurial learning suggested by sociological analyses (see Chapter 4).

But what skills are acquired by entrepreneurial firms? Do entrepreneurs need to acquire particular skills that make them better entrepreneurs, or should they focus on general management and other competency-building skills necessary for running and growing a firm? What constitutes entrepreneurship skills?

PART V: ENTREPRENEURSHIP SKILLS

If entrepreneurship can be defined in terms of value creation by identifying opportunities for new products and services and realizing them through new firm formation, then it is the process of transforming identification to realization of opportunities that forms part of the entrepreneur's learning experience. The skills that are necessary for such an experience are cumulative. They are acquired over time, compressed or stretched depending on the type of entrepreneurial activity. They can take tacit forms with serendipitous outcomes or they can be understood best in terms of a codified process involving the generation of ideas, a business-planning process, the raising of funds and other resources, and eventual implementation of the business proposal. Whatever their form, the skills that are acquired are those that are required and used by the entrepreneurs. In an increasingly institutionalized world, with higher levels of uncertainty and complexity accompanied often by jobless growth, there is possibly a greater demand for the identification and provision of particular skills that can be acquired through education, training and experience.

Basic, advanced, converging and entrepreneurial skills

The OECD (2010) distinguishes between basic, advanced and converging skills. Basic skills refer to generic or routine skills common to most industries and organizations. Advanced skills have a higher component of knowledge intensity of both the 'hard' (technical) and 'soft' (human, social and communication) variety, while converging skills include a combination of the first two categories plus skills associated with creating and managing new ventures and innovative projects (strategic thinking, risk assessment, use of networks, etc.). Entrepreneurship skills also include the propensity of the entrepreneur to drive innovation and recognize and welcome innovation (Green et al., 2007), suggesting a mix of Schumpeterian creativity and Kirznerian alertness. Green et al.'s (2007) list of core characteristics of entrepreneurs includes:

- identification and extraction of relevant knowledge that can be tuned in to recognize available opportunities;
- strategic thinking, self-confidence, ability to deal with uncertainties and challenges plus co-operation with others, leading to (a) planning, organizing and communication; (b) project development and implementation; team building and attribution and rewarding of success; (c) recognition and proactive orientation to change and innovation; (d) risk assessment and warranting;
- use of initiative and a positive approach in the face of positive or adverse change, and an adaptability to learn and unlearn from life situations.

This list of almost superhuman capabilities, combining basic, advanced and converging skills, is a compendium often touted by researchers to provide a comprehensive analytical construct to make sense of the magical world of entrepreneurs. Idealized portraits of entrepreneurs can show all of the characteristics at work. It is, however, questionable, whether any one entrepreneur or all entrepreneurs have these characteristics which can then be codified for the purpose of effective training in entrepreneurship skills. Entrepreneurship is often a social activity involving teams of people with complementary skills. Alas, there is no ideal entrepreneurial team to determine what perfect match can be organized!

Entrepreneurial skills for the entrepreneur or the firm?

A number of questions arise from the discussion above. First, if entrepreneurship skills training were to be offered, would it be more appropriate to provide increased awareness of, on the one hand, economic, business, social and technological history, together with multidisciplinary insights from the arts and sciences on the other? Second, is it more appropriate to offer practical, task-oriented skills necessary for generating and validating an idea, identifying resources, negotiating these resources, understanding administrative and regulatory issues, and prospecting for growth? Third, should entrepreneurship training focus on the individual entrepreneur (or teams of entrepreneurs) or on the firm in both its pre-formative and post-formation stages?

Almost all the discussion preceding the questions raised above gives the entrepreneur(s) premium attention. This is inevitable in view of the simple fact that learning and training are concerned about existing or prospective trainees who may be entrepreneurs. However, the third question highlights an important consideration, especially at the development stages of an entrepreneurial venture or the re-organization of an existing business into an entrepreneurial organization. In these scenarios entrepreneurial outcomes are not just dependent on the founder of a business but rather on a wide range of people who can come up with new ideas and be equipped to turn them into smart, adaptive and innovative firms developing new products and services continually. The set of entrepreneurial skills necessary for such organizations and their employees will be different from those for individuals forming new start-ups for the first time. This differentiation is enhanced when we examine internet-based or networked organizations and open innovation systems that offer mind-boggling opportunities for the creation of new ventures requiring a range of fast-tracking, problem-solving and organization-building skills, creative scenario development, convergent technology adoption and adaptation, and other skills.

Variations in the levels of uncertainty surrounding specific types of entrepreneurial activity will require corresponding skills for coping with, first, the peculiarly volatile environment, and then attracting resources for new ventures. Bhide's (2008) 'B-Class' ventures, which tend to provide high-unit-price goods and services to a small number of customers from other businesses, generally bootstrap their ventures from personal funds and fail to attract funding from VCs. These firms obtain rewards for assuming unquantifiable risks because of the novel circumstances of their business. Starts-up selling fancy handbags or high-tech equipment fall into this category, the latter because of the uncertainty caused by constant innovation in that industry and the former because of the absence of any clear direction in the sales of goods, which are a function of the emotional responses of customers (such as the desire to be 'cool' or 'trendy') (Bhide, 2008). The entrepreneurial skills sets necessary for Bhide's B-Class entrepreneurs depend on obtaining granular knowledge of types of customers, changing trends and innovations, and technology-watching, rather than any generic qualities required by other types of entrepreneur (Bhide's C-Class entrepreneurs starting beauty salons, auto repairs, and painting and decorating businesses, or the elite A-Class category which enjoy rapid growth and receive venture capital funding). Preparing each group of entrepreneurs accordingly will, therefore, be best accomplished by ensuring the correspondence between the objectives of learning and the type of venture activity in question.

Yet another set of entrepreneurial skills are required for social and community enterprises where the balancing of 'enterprise' and 'social objectives' and the organization of social championing skills with employee management, the attraction and use of volunteers plus the acceptance of a 'community' of stakeholders, demands a rather different portfolio of cognitive capabilities and competencies associated with such an organization.

The features of entrepreneurial organizations and how they function are discussed in Chapter 5. What is critical for the purpose of this chapter is the recognition of different sets of entrepreneurial skills necessitated first by different types of venture creation and innovation. Identifying or acquiring entrepreneurship skills is not simply a matter of pinpointing a specific set of competencies. Apart from the variation in skills sets associated with different types of ventures, there are two other points that relate to the provision of entrepreneurship skills that are worth mentioning:

- the absorptive capacity for receiving and learning entrepreneurial skills among beneficiaries of training; and
- the appropriateness of providers of entrepreneurial skills.

Receiving and providing entrepreneurship skills training

The nature of skills training, including cognitive, analytical, reflective, social and pedagogic skills necessary for entrepreneurship, is likely to vary according to the type of enterprise in question. Prospective entrepreneurs will emerge from different social and economic backgrounds, calling for a scalable form of training provision from the 'basic' to the 'high impact' variety requiring very different sets of tools and pedagogies. Where they receive such training has often been cited as a constraint. Access to provision, given their employment or unemployment status, geographical locations and technologies will have an impact on the take-up and effectiveness of the training programme. Who provides such training also has a bearing on the appropriateness of imparting skills. While new and potential entrepreneurs might be more amenable to receiving inputs from a combination of trainers, educators and practitioners, existing business people seeking new knowledge are more likely to favour peer group and professional interaction. Entrepreneurship training in the social and community enterprise sectors is unlikely to be complete if it does not combine the involvement of business training providers with perhaps community enterprise activists and champions who can inspire commitment.

The range of entrepreneurial skills referred to above form part of a learning system in different environments. Entrepreneurs navigate their way through competency channels within relevant systems of learning that originate from their particular circumstances, backgrounds, experiences and social structures, involving a process of competency building and leveraging with resources specific to their venture and those obtained from outside the venture. Learning to create and grow organizations to constantly produce innovations is, therefore, a kind of social algorithm that is derived as much from formal processes as much from heuristics and various informal modes of 'doing'.

Mini case study 7.1: How small firms learn to grow

Firm A

Organizational profile – key products and services

Firm A is a software development business established over eight years ago in a major science park in Birmingham in the UK. It specializes in harnessing new media technologies (software-driven technologies) to produce powerful marketing tools for business, from 3D visualization and animation through to CD-ROM design, software development and e-business solutions. Firm A has built a client portfolio that spans industry, commerce, education and government, from small and medium-sized enterprises right through to multinational corporations. The business has met every challenge and opportunity since its inception, and has pushed the boundaries of multimedia. It has already established an international reputation. In 2000, Firm A was recognized as the one of the top 50 fastest-growing technology companies in the UK and Ireland, by Deloitte & Touche, the UK's fastest growing professional services firm.

Core competencies, proximity and externalities

Firm A has ambitious strategic goals and already competes with the best in the international market. Its decision to locate in the science park was based in part on the need to have a good image to operate in the international market, and also to obtain the benefits of shared office facilities and free business advice. As the business has grown, it has equipped itself with state-of-art but low-cost office facilities, but seeking business advice has become less important as their demand for 'customer-tailored' services is unavailable in the park. However, being local, they are able to tap into talents and resources available locally. Their members of staff are competent and highly qualified in their chosen field of employment. The business has benefited from its close proximity to local higher educational institutions, and these links have enabled them to build particular competencies and to develop their business. However, the experience of the business and its owner-managers suggest that effective networking is a function of people and their own contacts, and institutional mechanisms to promote networking cannot supplant personal links. The difficulty facing the business is knowing how to find the right people in the university (and in other institutions) with whom they could engage for the development of their business.

Critical success factors

In managing externalities, the business has demonstrated that location advantage is important, for it can draw upon skills and labour locally, interact with local businesses, and watch the market and competitors. However, its own market is not necessarily local. Therefore, one of the firm-specific competencies is the ability to organize its own position in the value chain, in the international context. For example, the making of one of its products requires Firm A to follow a triangular route to complete the whole process. Following the design and development of the product, it is sent for volume manufacturing in China in order to take advantage of low labour costs there. However, the materials have to be sourced from a Birmingham-based paper supplier and then sent to China. In this process, Firm A needs to bring a separate partner into the equation to deal with distribution of the manufactured product. Finally, the finished products are exported to Firm A's designated retailers in Europe. Five partners are involved in this value chain, and to bring these partners to work together effectively Firm A has collaborated and networked intensively, using a range of firm-specific and firm-addressable assets, with a view to gaining a mix of cognitive and socio-political legitimacy, and ensuring a successful business outcome.

For a high-tech business such as Firm A, the quality of human capital is an integral firm-specific asset. The business has recruited people with at least a first degree from the large pool of computer science graduates in Birmingham, thus ensuring a reasonably high-level skills base for the firm. However, the relatively limited supply of people combining management know-how and software development skills creates problems for the growth of a fast-developing business where a combination of these different skills is critical to its operations. This has prompted the owner-managers to concentrate on the recruitment of people who are excellent in particular, functional aspects of the business.

Strategy and competency building

Firm A's strategy is to be the best in the three fields identified above and to deliver people-based and high-quality products and services. However, the software industry is characterized by rapid change in products and fierce competition internationally. For large projects, decisions have to be made regarding in-house development versus outsourcing, and collaboration on the basis of delivery on time and within the budget. From the firm's point of view, the international dimension of its projects has given rise to the need for acquisition of new management competencies in project management. The early successes of Firm A have generated the kind of cognitive legitimacy that most new firms would desire. Such success has also helped the firm to acquire socio-political legitimacy in that key institutional stakeholders actively seek its products and services. Individual and collective strategies have thus been combined to support growth and recognition in both local and external markets.

The early transition to a managerial base and the corresponding speed of response to the needs of different forms of learning (from entrepreneurial to managerial know-how) also suggests a dynamic approach to the uses of cognitive and socio-political legitimacy.

Table 7.1 The competency framework for Firm A

Strategic goals	Managerial function	Working situation	Areas of responsibility	Existing competencies	Wished competencies
To be the best in the three fields identified above; people based and high-quality products and services	Strategic, financial, marketing and sales – all clearly divided and shared	Local firm, using location to derive best advantage in markets anywhere	Different functional responsibilities reflecting growing firm status	Knowledge • eight programming languages • animation and design Capabilities • new media technology • visual communication • e-solutions • training Motivations • proactive, collaborative work for mutual gain	Software development management in an international context

Firm B

Organization profile – key products and services

Firm B is a Cambridge-based innovative leader in plastic electronics manufacturing, a revolutionary new technology for printing electronic devices. The company will be the first to apply the new technology to a fully commercial application. It was originally spun out of a local university research laboratory. The plastic electronics industry is being forecasted by experts from IDTechEx to be a $30 billion industry by 2015, and could reach $250 billion by 2025. The firm is building the first commercial manufacturing facility targeted at flexible active-matrix display modules for 'take anywhere, read anywhere' electronic reader products. Its research shows that consumers are very reluctant to read on laptops, phones and personal digital assistants (PDAs) despite being in an age of digital content. People still carry around enormous amounts of paper, but are becoming more sensitive to the environmental impact of printing to read. The thinness and robustness of the company's flexible displays are therefore aimed at enabling electronic reader products that are as comfortable and natural to read as paper.

Core competencies, proximity and externalities

The core competency of Firm B is its expertise in producing flexible active-matrix display modules for electronic reader products. Locally embedded tacit knowledge and skills serve as a source of competence for the firm, and a source of enduring competitive advantage. There are at least two dimensions within which the firm develops strategically important local competencies. The first is that the firm acquires its unique disciplinary expertise from the local university as well as its local environment. The expertise of at least two of its founders builds on a foundation of experience at the local University, so much so that the firm still retains a very strong link with the university, as at least one of its founding professors is still based within the university's laboratory. Fundamental engineering knowledge plays a critical role in the electronics industry, and therefore the firm's proximity to the local university is important in acquiring knowledge of latest developments in engineering. For example, one of its founders, who is still based at the university, pioneered the study of organic polymers and revolutionized the understanding of the electronic properties of molecular semiconductors. Therefore when he was asked about the involvement of the university in developing the product, he answered that 'there is a formal relationship with the university'. Second, the firm engages with many other local firms for the development and commercialization of its products.

Critical success factors

As new technology-based start-ups are often resource constrained, the firm's success relies to a reasonable extent on its strategy of partnerships with other local and international firms to support volume production and marketing of its first product. As stated by the CEO of the company, 'If we do not, we are going to have customers and no factory.'

Strategy and competence building

The competitive strategy of the firm depends on using a destructive technology to enable the world's first 'take anywhere, read anywhere' electronic reader product. Thus, the firm employs an innovative differentiated strategy, which demands a lot of competence building in order to be the first to launch this destructive technology as other rival

Table 7.2 The competency framework for Firm B

Strategic goals	Managerial functions	Working situation	Areas of responsibility	Existing Competencies	Wished competencies
To be the first firm in the market with 'read anywhere, take anywhere' plastic electronics	Operations, product development, all divided	Collaborating with local university and firms to develop and bring plastic electronics to market	Different functionalities and divisions, owing to its rapid growth	Knowledge • plastic electronics Capability • process for printing electronic circuits on plastic substrates	Develop a range of front-plane technologies including next-generation colour and video-capable electronic paper

companies have already joined the race in launching the technology to market. Firm B collaborates actively with numerous businesses and a local university to build its competence in developing the innovative new product. In order to acquire both cognitive and socio-political legitimacy for its destructive product which is targeted at electronic news market, the firm has joined a network of more than 20 leading publishers in a collaborative electronic news project on mobile reading. The project is designed to look at the opportunities there are for content providers, such as publishers. Thus the CEO stated, 'We are delighted to be working with the newspaper community to ensure our plastic electronics technology meets their requirements for mobile e-readers.' Through this network, the firm is better positioned in gaining the knowledge and competence to launch its first product into the electronic news market in a way that better meets the needs of its customers and other stakeholders, thereby giving its products more socio-political legitimacy.

(Source: adapted from: (A) Mitra (2009) and (B) Mitra and Abubakar (2007))

Conclusion

Observing entrepreneurship as a learning process enables us to obtain fascinating insights into the conditions, mechanisms and different forms of entrepreneurial activity. Creating new firms to house innovative activity is also an organizational development process. In this sense entrepreneurship is a form of organizational learning process involving the acquisition and nurturing of certain types of competencies. These competencies are developed in multiple settings and through numerous pedagogic channels enabling knowledge creation and consolidation or altering existing know-how for new venture creation or innovative growth.

Knowing about learning provides a cognitive connection between the environments that can be conducive to entrepreneurship, the framework conditions and institutions relevant for these environments, the entrepreneur, the new venture that is created, and the continuing entrepreneurial activities of that venture. It also helps to provide a framework for understanding different types of new ventures and their formation and growth as part of the learning system. Understanding these learning systems and their evolution is a step towards appreciating the role of learning institutions such as universities and their role in fostering entrepreneurship.

Self-assessment questions

1. What constitutes a learning process?
2. What forms of organizational learning are conducive to entrepreneurship development, and why?
3. Is there a difference in the learning process in smaller firms? How do SMEs learn?
4. Explain the different forms of learning for and by SMEs. Do contexts matter?
5. What are entrepreneurship skills and how can they be acquired?

8 Entrepreneurship, internationalization and globalization

Learning, innovation and development in the international context

Learning outcomes

In this chapter the reader will:

- obtain a critical overview of the meaning and scope of entrepreneurship and innovation in an international context;
- obtain a critical appreciation of the role of learning in international business and entrepreneurship;
- examine critically the internationalization process in terms of traditional models and also in relation to new developments in venture creation and innovation;
- explain critically the differences between international business and international entrepreneurship, and between internationalization and globalization;
- gain critical insights into topical issues of innovation and entrepreneurship in a global context; and
- identify the conceptual tenets and practical issues associated with new venture creation, new product and service development and new forms of network-centric organizations in an international context.

Structure of the chapter

In earlier chapters we have argued that the growth of firms is predicated upon the ability of firms to learn from previous experience, to develop their stock of knowledge and technologies, and to establish an increasingly large foothold in markets. In this chapter the agenda of internationalization incorporates the learning experience. The chapter first explores the learning process that underpins entry, growth and the development of firms in the international market. The focus is on issues that have special implications for opportunity recognition and achievement, new venture creation, new product and service development, and the emergence of new types and modes of organization. Part II focuses on different models of learning that emerge from and also influence the internationalization process. Different modes and models of internationalization require specific sets of competencies relevant to the actions taken by firms in the process of internationalization. This issue is taken up in Part III. There are also spatial aspects to learning that enable us to understand why there are variations in the process of internationalization, and its effects for firms in different regions. The coverage of spatial aspects takes place in Part IV. Consideration of the spatial aspects provides insights into collective patterns of behaviour by firms as they are affected by globalization, which is discussed in Part V. This is followed in Part VI by an examination of the role of the Internet in the internationalization process of firms and how firms oscillate between their engagement in the internationalization process and their management of the currents of globalization, which can have an effect on the former process. This prompts a discussion in Part VII explaining the meaning of globalization and current trends in globalization and internationalization that bring together small and larger firms across geographical boundaries, opening up opportunities for new forms of ventures and entrepreneurial activities, before the chapter is concluded.

Introduction

A considerable amount of importance has been attached in recent years to the subject of globalization and internationalization as a stage for innovative growth, the emergence of 'born global' firms, and the 'connected' environment of network-based small and large firms developing new products and services collaboratively in a highly competitive market place. The global market place and the globalization process are the currency of our times. Successful business activity and entrepreneurship are assumed to be determined by global factors, where nation states and national boundaries appear to matter less than the larger global canvas (Ohmae, 1995; Cairncross, 1997). Technology, especially information and communications technology, is deemed to be largely responsible for such developments.

We need to distinguish between 'globalization' and 'internationalization', not least because interchangeable use of terminology can be confusing. They do not, of course, mean the same thing, and the processes involved, their influence, impact and scope all have different connotations. We shall come to that later.

More importantly, and long before the often emotionally charged debate of globalization acquired any prominence in both business meetings and dinner table conversation, the business of commerce and industry and the creation of new ventures have all had an international dimension to their modus operandi. What we do know is that businesses of all shapes and sizes operate in international markets and are affected by the internationalization process that brings foreign firms into competitive domestic markets. Intuitively, we tend to assume that larger firms are better equipped to operate in the international marketplace than smaller firms. Some of the literature tends to back that view because internationalization is a resource-intensive process requiring the experience and know-how that is acquired more easily by larger businesses. The reality can be somewhat different.

We have noted elsewhere (Chapter 5) that medium-sized firms, for example, are key operators in the global marketplace, earning huge export revenues for firms in countries such as Germany, some of the Scandinavian states and the USA. Network-based operations and global projects often involve small and large firms working together in the global marketplace. Size may be an issue, but there are other factors that need more serious consideration. In this chapter we focus mainly on SMEs and how they engage with the internationalization process in developing their new products and services, and how they organize themselves through new structures and channels in new markets.

The size conundrum

The size question is an unresolved issue. Whether small firms are better than medium-sized or larger firms in obtaining and generating better value for their firms, the industry and the economies in question continues to be debated widely. In an interesting thesis, Simon (2009) has argued that when we examine the export performance of countries such as Germany,

Switzerland or Sweden, we note that their strong performance results are not due to large corporations but to smaller and especially mid-size firms. The latter are world leaders (with global market shares of 70%–90%). They are regarded as the 'hidden champions'; they are generally twice the size of their competitors and only a few multinationals achieve their market positions (Simon, 2009). These firms are generally anonymous, highly innovative, have low-key managers and are driven by innovative growth. Similarly larger firms, as Schumpeter argued, can be better disposed towards innovation, especially when R&D and capital investment raises the threshold of participation in the innovation process.

PART I: INTERNATIONALIZATION, LEARNING AND SMES: A BASIC PROPOSITION

The successful internationalization of small and medium-sized firms (SMEs) is a function of their learning process and environments. Based on this assumption, this chapter examines a range of theoretical models and some empirical evidence to identify the modes, forms and methods of learning adopted by SMEs as they enter and grow in an international business environment.

Learning for internationalization operates at various levels. Individual entrepreneurs bring to bear their own knowledge and experience, growing firms accumulate knowledge and skills with which to interact with international partners, and the environment in which firms operate also opens up opportunities for learning. Various forms of learning (by 'imitating', by 'doing', by 'interacting', by 'clustering') enable identification of opportunities for innovation and their realization. In the international environment, firms take different routes to enter and operate in unfamiliar territory. How they reduce uncertainties in such territory is the basis of new product and service development, together with changes to organizational forms necessary for sustaining these developments.

The exploration of different forms of learning occurs at multiple levels of individual, organizational and pan-organizational effort. In considering each of these levels of learning, four sets of propositions are made. Taken together, these propositions offer a framework for analysing how firms internationalize and why they adopt different strategies for engaging in the international market. The chapter moves from identifying complex forms of learning, associated with the SME internationalization process, their strategies and actions, to more recent thinking centred around ideas for new communities of creation and cross-border innovation and venturing.

Proposition 1

The *basic proposition* (P1) here is that small firms exploring international markets evolve as members of different communities of international interest, working together to:

- create new forms of economic activity that meet their own economic needs together with those of their counterparts;
- generate distinctive forms of economic activity that transcend their separate needs;
- retain their own involvement in hubs of local activity which that are enriched by the experience of their exploration and the creation of new forms of economic activity; and
- generate innovative growth and promote entrepreneurship through individual and collective learning, and in an international context.

Testing this proposition requires critical investigation using different units of analysis. This is because inputs, processes, influences, innovations, outputs and outcomes are all realized at the level of the individual, the organization, the region and the global marketplace. Researchers using traditional epistemological paradigms may encounter some difficulty in exploring such a proposition, and it may require isolation of the various elements to investigate issues using different units of analysis. This can be done first by reviewing selected literature and some empirical data to explore the relationship between learning, entrepreneurship and internationalization in the context of innovative small firm growth.

The examination of the relationships referred to above spawns other propositions (see below), which when examined together could help to develop a framework for the better study of international entrepreneurship.

PART II: INTERNATIONALIZATION, LEARNING, THE INDIVIDUAL ENTREPRENEUR AND THE FIRM

Entrepreneurial characteristics and the decision to internationalize

If opportunity identification is the key to entrepreneurial endeavour then the scanning of markets looking for new opportunities and marshalling resources to exploit those opportunities can be considered to be a strong motivational factor at the individual level (Zacharakis, 1997; Oviatt and McDougall, 1994). Similarly, certain pull-push factors, such as external forces, drive the entrepreneur to search for opportunities in foreign markets, if only to survive (Westhead *et al.*, 1998). A population ecology approach (Ibrahim, 2004) attempts to link entrepreneurial traits with the entrepreneur's decision to internationalize, but this raises issues of relevant and measurable empirical evidence.

The belief that entrepreneurs are opportunity driven and are, therefore, 'built for internationalization', is tempered by the reality of barriers to entry brought about by financial market imperfections, differences in languages and culture, differences in legal systems, lack of intellectual property rights protection, and the risk factor of high levels of investment in uncertain conditions. A consideration of these external factors suggests that organizational factors probably have to be reckoned with more than entrepreneurial traits. If the survival of the firm is a motivating factor then that is different from the nature of existence of the individual entrepreneur. Moreover, if as is commonly believed the entrepreneur/owner-managers is the face, arms and limbs of the small firm then separate analysis of the individual(s) is almost irrelevant. The separate analysis of traits simply distinguishes entrepreneurs from non-entrepreneurs, and suggests that all members of the homogeneous first group pursue opportunities at local and international levels in an identical manner. This latter suggestion is reinforced by the overwhelming emphases on performance rather than the way in which objectives are realized.

Who makes decisions about internationalization?

Much has been argued in the name of the individual entrepreneur or the owner-manager, and the locus of control that resides in him/her. This applies equally to several decision-making processes, including the decision to internationalize. The Table 8.1 indicates that the locus of decision-making processes for all types of decisions is essentially in the hands of the owner-manager. It is only when firms acquire 'medium-sized' status that some of those tasks are delegated to other managers. The smaller the firm, the greater the possibility of such decisions being made at the level of the owner-manager.

Table 8.1 Internal and external factors affecting the internationalization process of small and medium sized firms

Internal factors			External factors		
Type of factors	Manufacturing n=2157	Services n =3683	Type of factors	Manufacturing n = 2157	Services n = 3683
Owner-manager knowledge/competencies	78.26	73.2	Global networks and contacts	48.27	48.87
Skills and human resources	67.13	66.41	Specific global and marketing information	44.14	45.72
Internal financial resources	53.87	55.99	Global distribution channels	41.49	42.87
Other	11.68	16.43	Economic conditions	36.72	31.25
			Availability of external agents	28.38	22.18

Table 8.2 The locus of decision-making processes in SMEs

Band code	No. of employees	Size Distrn.	Locus of Financial & Human Resource decisions		
			Owner – Manager (%)	Other Managers (%)	Other Personnel (%)
A	1–10	Micro	100	0	0
B	11–49	Small	88.68	11.32	0
C	50–250	Medium	14.95	85.05	0
D	251+	Large	0	100	0

Source: Mitra and Matlay (2004).

The evidence referred to here would also suggest that the decision to enter international markets is confined to the owner-manager, and the chances of the small firm entering the international market is severely constrained by size factors.

That small firms tend not to be international players is almost a tautology when we note that the internationalization process is a function of size. If small firms do not represent a significant proportion of the community of international players, two questions can be posed:

1)   Is the study of small firm internationalization relevant?
2)   Does internationalization make any difference to those small firms that do?

The relevance of small and medium-sized firms

The first question is easily answered. The study of the internationalization process of small firms is important because it is the Schumpeterian (Mark 1) small firms that are the standard bearers of innovation and it is their ability to innovate constantly that is critical to the prosperity of most economies (Acs *et al.*, 1996). Second, the fact that most small firms do not internationalize does not mean they cannot do so. If barriers to entry are removed, and various trajectories of small firm entry into the international market are considered, then small firms could find effective ways of playing a larger role in the global marketplace. Third, there is growing evidence of small firms playing critical roles in networks, and clusters of small and large firms in specific and related industries operating in different regions across the world. Their 'secondary' or linked status often hides the significance of the role just as much as the numbers do not reveal the nature and scope of their operations. Finally, there is also increasing evidence of small, innovative firms emerging as key players in high-technology-based producer services in networks of global cities (Sassen, 2002).

As regards the second question, Acs *et al.* (1996) argue that smaller firms that do expand abroad are more profitable than those that do not (profit to sales ratio of 7.9% in 1990 compared to 4.2%). They also refer to the UN Report (1993), which points out that 'in contrast to small and medium-sized firms in general, not only do transnational small and medium-sized firms conduct more R&D, but they produce more patented products' (UN Report, 1993; cited in Acs *et al.*, 1996). With reference to the points made in the previous paragraph, the specific role of small, innovative firms in industrial clusters or in urban agglomerations linked to international counterparts is indicative of the fact that firms that participate in such environments are likely to gain from such exposure compared to those that do not do so.

What small firms gain by entering international markets is dependent on whether the costs of entry barriers and protection of property rights, building up organizational support infrastructures, efficient operations in foreign markets, transactional elements including those of contracts, spending and monitoring, and rents payable to intermediaries are outweighed by the benefits derived from international business activity. The economic argument offers learning opportunities for the small business owner-manager especially when he/she is considering direct forms of entry as against using intermediaries. The owner-manager will be motivated to enter and operate in the international market as long as there is net gain from the activity.

Motivation for internationalization

The motivational-learning axis of small firm internationalization can also be understood when we examine empirical data showing us the different types of motivation for small firm owner-managers and the specific factors affecting their involvement. Figure 8.1 shows the motives for internationalization of small firms in the UK who had entered the market for at least three years.

Whatever the personal orientation or characteristics of the entrepreneur, the motivational issues referred to above suggest that it is the circumstances of the business that push or pull small firms to internationalize. Chance does feature to some extent, in that enquiries from foreign agents and personal contacts can open up opportunities when they are not expected. But how do the owner-managers translate their motivations into the realization of opportunities? How do we know whether the motivations can influence entrepreneurial outcomes?

To answer such questions we need to examine factors affecting the internationalization process. Such factors are both internal and external to the firm, indicating the level of control owner-managers can have over how these factors affect firm behaviour. Table 8.3 identifies these factors from the same data source that was used by Mitra and Matlay (2004) to examine motivations.

What the data here shows is the particular importance of the knowledge and skills base in the firm that is required to convert the motivation to internationalize to genuinely realizable opportunities. Of note, however, is the motivation for services to seek international opportunities, namely the decline in local markets which is almost as high as the availability

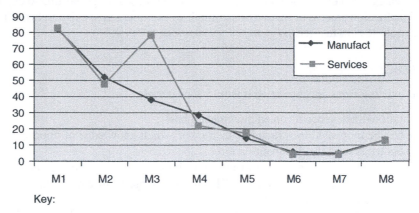

Key:

M1 = greater strategic opportunities in foreign markets
M2 = inquiries from foreign agents/firms
M3 = Stagnating/declining domestic markets
M4 = product/service saturation in domestic market
M5 = internationalisation drive of known competitors
M6 = personal/professional contacts abroad
M7 = competitive pressures from large firms
M8 = other

Figure 8.1 Motives and factors affecting small business internationalization

Source: adapted from Mitra and Matlay (2004).

of strategic opportunities. What the data also tends to suggest is that this learning process can be incremental insofar as it is based on the experience of existing firms. This incremental approach does not take into consideration the opportunities realized by so-called 'born global' firms, and to that extent our understanding of the learning process is limited to a

Table 8.3 Internal and external factors affecting the internationalization process of small and medium-sized firms

Internal factors			External factors		
Type of factors	Manufacturing n=2157	Services n =3683	Type of factors	Manufacturing n = 2157	Services n = 3683
Owner-manager knowledge/competencies	78.26	73.2	Global networks and contacts	48.27	48.87
Skills and human resources	67.13	66.41	Specific global and marketing information	44.14	45.72
Internal financial resources	53.87	55.99	Global distribution channels	41.49	42.87
Other	11.68	16.43	Economic conditions	36.72	31.25
			Availability of external agents	28.38	22.18

particular category of experience. In view of this limitation, studies purporting to explain the internationalization process of small firms through an examination of existing firms' motivations can only lead us to a *second group of propositions* (P2).

Proposition 2

As far as existing firms are concerned it would appear that:

a) internationalization occurs on an incremental basis;
b) they can be motivated by a range of factors, of which knowledge of opportunities and markets tends to be the dominant factor;
c) while manufacturing and service firms show similar patterns, there is a significant difference in some motivational factors. This in turn suggests different modes of learning for service and manufacturing firms;
d) the existence of a strong knowledge and skills base correlates positively to internationalization.

In taking the points made so far for the purpose of exploring the subject of internationalization, new questions emerge. If internationalization is consequent upon certain motivations then how do firms enter international markets? Do all firms enter such markets in the same way, following similar pathways? To what extent do possibilities of developing new products and services influence how they enter specific international markets? These questions are concerned with modes of entry and models of internationalization. As there are variations in these modes according to the circumstances of individual firms, they open up different pathways of learning for owner-managers and their employees.

PART III: DIFFERENT MODELS OF INTERNATIONALIZATION AND THE LEARNING PROCESS

Incremental models

The *stage* or *incremental* process of internationalization resulting from organizational learning is referred to by some authors (Coviello and McAuley, 1999) as being shaped over time. Owner-managers gain experience and knowledge of foreign markets in much the same way that the respondents to the survey carried out by Mitra and Matlay (2004) suggest. Specific models, such as the Uppsala model (Johanson and Vahlne, 1977) and the innovation model (Cavusgil, 1980) elaborate on the incremental or stage processes and tend to maintain an internal perspective, specific to the firm and managerial-related issues. Experiential knowledge of the international market and of business in general leads to resource commitments (Camino and Carzola, 1998; Oviatt and McDougal, 1997) and changes in the firm's 'global horizon' (Aharoni, 1966). These process models have also considered internal and external factors influencing managerial decisions, the role of tacit managerial knowledge (Johanson and Vahlne, 1977) or experience (Cavusgil, 1980) as the key determinants of internationalization.

Life cycle theory

The *life cycle (industry or product)* theory of internationalization is similar in concept to the stage process because the firm follows the various stages of the product or industry life cycle (O'Farrell and Hitchens, 1988; Robock and Simmonds, 1989). Essentially firms generate 'firm-specific assets' first and then use 'firm-addressable' assets available in the external environment to generate new business opportunities (Mitra, 2000), and to acquire, accumulate, and assimilate new market-based, entrepreneurial and technological knowledge (Autio *et al.*, 2000; Zahra *et al.*, 2000).

Resource-based view

The *resource-based* view of the firm suggests that the firm uses internal resources and explores international opportunities to build up existing, limited resources (Penrose, 1980; Autio *et al.*, 2000; Ibrahim and McGuire, 2001). It also reflects the gradual evolution of the firm's capacity and capability for internationalization.

The gradual process of development is evolutionary, and the learning processes that inform the development and help to identify new opportunities in the international arena also evolve as the firm seeks variation, selection, retention, and new modes of survival (see Figure 8.2). Each stage of its evolution is marked by different forms of learning appropriate to that stage, and it is through a combination of these forms that the firm gradually becomes an international player. The movement through each stage is also characterized by the accumulation of experiential knowledge. It is this critical mass of knowledge that acts as a foundation for the firm's ability to interact with others in the international arena, increase its capacity of production, and emerge as a global player.

Foreign direct investment

A variation of the process stage model is the theory related to *foreign direct investments* (FDIs). A firm will consider FDI only when it has a sufficient stock of knowledge and learning that outweighs any disadvantage that may accrue as a result of entering unknown territory. It is largely a prerogative of larger firms, and the theoretical contributions are dependent on economic considerations of levels of investment, transaction cost, locational factors and

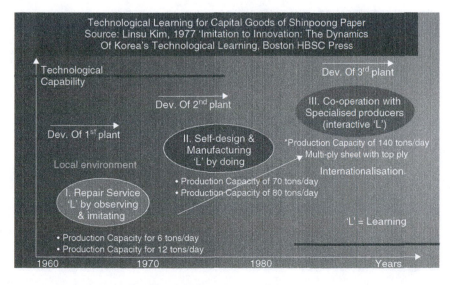

Figure 8.2 Technological learning for capital goods

Source: adapted from citation in Mitra (2001).

competitive advantage (Dunning, 1988; Zacharakis, 1997). The notion of competitive advantage that a foreign direct investor may enjoy over a local firm is based on the idea that competition creates imperfect markets, and that competitive advantage is a function of product differentiation, product innovation and technological superiority (Ibrahim, 1993).

It is unclear whether the larger firm with significantly more resources has more advantage even over the highly innovative smaller firm as far as FDIs are concerned. Setting up, transaction and management costs may be stacked up too high for the smaller firm, and it is only in situations where the latter can piggyback on the larger intermediary firm with an existing presence in another country that it can realize particular gains.

However, Manalova (2003) has suggested that SMEs are likely to undertake FDI in particular circumstances. Such circumstances include:

- lower economies of scale achieved through worldwide production volume;
- lower levels of technological intensity of a globally integrated industry;
- higher level of technological intensity of a globally fragmented industry;
- lower levels of capital cost intensity;
- higher growth rates of an industry;
- higher degrees of standardization of market demand in a globally fragmented industry; and
- higher degrees of localization of market demand in a globally integrated industry.

The gradual, incremental process, has, however, been challenged by Oviatt and McDougall (1994), Schrader *et al.* (2000) and *Autio et al.* (2000), who argue that the process theory is too limited and does not take into account the entrepreneurial motives for internationalization. Entrepreneurial small firms seek rapid growth and are not phased by 'quantum leaps' in different and unexplored markets because they act fast when they see a good prospect. In some cases, the search for resources is combined with the exploration of new opportunities, and the learning process is symbiotically tied in to this exploration. Figure 8.3, showing the rapid progress of a firm in Hong Kong, tends to support this argument.

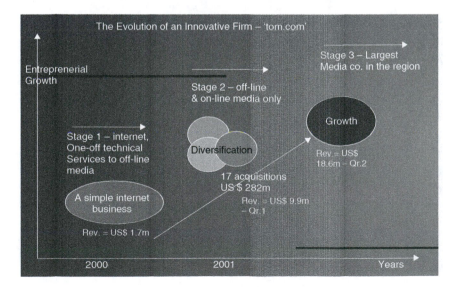

Figure 8.3 The evolution of an innovative firm

Source: adapted from citation in Mitra (2001).

The literature on internationalization is rich with theories and models that make interesting reading for all scholars of the subject. This chapter has a different objective. The purpose here is to take a selective approach to some of the traditional theoretical models on international business that appear to have a bearing on entrepreneurship and innovation in an international or global context. This selective approach allows us to explore how the internationalization process influences new venture creation and identify some of the modern variants of the process that extend or call into question some of these models. What follows is a brief exploration of the new modes and processes of internationalization.

Technology, modern variations and influences

The accelerated pace of internationalization may have something to do with the nature of the firm and the industry in question. High-technology firms, including information and communications technology (ICT) firms, source technologies and skills from diverse, international sources; the organization of the sourcing process takes various forms, from diversification through joint ventures through to FDIs, networks, strategic alliances, depending on the specific business proposition with which it is concerned. What is significant is the pace at which these variations to or transformations of the routine can take place.

A great deal of recent debate, mostly of the political kind, has taken place around the idea of 'outsourcing'. The internationalization of firms, large and small, has tended to focus around manufacturing industries. Large and small firm internationalization has subsumed outsourcing of goods, which are produced abroad, assembled in a second country, and shipped back to the original buyer of outsourced goods. However, the globalization agenda has witnessed a major change in the trajectory of outsourcing as it finds a range of services, especially those that were previously considered non-traded services, being produced abroad and then sent back via the Internet or telephone wires (outsourcing is discussed in Chapter 5). There is a suggestion that 'knowledge-based' and 'white-collar' economic activity is moving its production base from the 'advanced' West to developing countries such as China, India and Russia. In reality, however, just as manufacturing businesses have reorganized industrial production into intricate layers of designers, subcontractors, assemblers and logistics specialists but have continued to manufacture close to where the goods are consumed, so the service industry has started using cheap and abundant telecommunications, bandwidth, and excellent skills sets to hand over work to specialist suppliers but provide the actual services close to where they are required. Innovative SMEs are more likely to gain from this evolution in the service industry both at 'home' and 'abroad', with distinctive opportunities opening up where it was not economically feasible for this to occur or where high-value niche services are required (Bhagwati *et al.*, 2004; Edwards, 2004).

The brief review of some of the different models of internationalization leads to the *third set of propositions* (P3) in this chapter.

Proposition 3

It is proposed that:

a) firms use different methods for internationalization depending on the nature of the industry in which they operate;

b) the differences in the methods offer variable forms of learning, from linear models to more accelerated forms of speedy, interactive learning;

c) the nature, scope and type of learning process that entrepreneurs engage in in different locations and industries distinguish different types of entrepreneurs rather than any fixed model of entrepreneur using his/her traits to identify and seize opportunities for economic gain;

d) the internationalization process is a function of the innovative firm's connections to its industry, its location, its use of specific technologies and the use of a range of different organizational forms;

e) firms in manufacturing and service industries tend to follow similar routes to internationalization, with similar effects on the opportunity index of small firms.

PART IV: SPATIAL ASPECTS, COLLECTIVE LEARNING, AND THE INTERNATIONALIZATION PROCESS

One of the critical questions that the various models referred to above have not answered is whether the learning process is simply an organizational phenomenon, occurring either within individual firms or between different firms. There is no indication whether or not spatial aspects of the firms' activities have any significance. Do firms engage randomly in international business activity, using their particular resources irrespective of their location? Do they establish international links without any consideration of the location factors of their buyers, partners or suppliers? In a technologically connected global business environment, geographic proximity has tended to diminish in importance (Cairncross, 1997), especially as it offers contradictory points of view to scholars, making investigation and analysis more difficult. This is further complicated by the fact that the traditional unit of analysis (either the entrepreneur or the firm) is not well served by spatial considerations. Finally, spatial analysis tends to regard firm size issues as being less important than innovative organizational outcomes resulting from different levels of interactions among various players for multiple objectives.

There are a number of reasons why the ostensible neglect of the spatial aspect of and firm size related to the internationalization process need to be dealt with critically.

Firm structure

First, as Teece (1992) argues, the discussion of the link between 'firm size and innovation remains inconclusive since the boundaries of the firm can no longer be assessed independent of the co-operative relationships which particular innovating firms may have formed' (p. 381). Moreover, firm boundaries are difficult to delineate especially where there are complex alliances in place, as in Japan. Here legal contracts become less important than alliances and networks of relationships.

Industrial competencies

Second, global industrial competence has dispersed widely over a century of industrial production as a result of increased competition, the liberalization of trading and investment regimes, and the growth of venture capital. The resulting geographical and organizational dispersion of industrial competence is coupled with the generic nature of new technologies such as microelectronics and biotechnology. The organizational coordination necessary for such dispersed activity is not necessarily provided by the price mechanism, which tends to ignore the uncertainty attached to the inability of firms to predict future actions, preferences and states of technological imperfection. Strategic alliances and inter-firm networks across national boundaries provide for more effective coordination upstream, downstream, laterally and horizontally. This means that owner-managers of firms need to manage externalities evinced in the relationships and alliances with other firms.

Clusters and geographical proximity

Third, the new literature of economics and business studies has demonstrated the value of geographic proximity and of the processes occurring in localized clusters, especially the influence on the structure of firms and industries (Porter, 1990, 1994, 1998; Enright, 1998; Ohmae, 1995). The processes of knowledge creation and diffusion are also well served by the clustering of firms in geographically constrained areas and the geographic embeddedness of tacit knowledge and interactive learning processes. That these dynamics have positive implications for the competitiveness of multinationals, especially in terms of the diffusion of knowledge within such firms and between them and other, smaller firms when they operate in geographic clusters, has been well noted by Dunning (1997,1998), Cantwell and Iammarino (1998) and Patel and Vega (1998). The competitive advantage of firms in geographic clusters is derived from the concentration of specialized skills and knowledge, institutions, rivals, related businesses and customers (Porter, 1998), and the interaction between those firms. 'However, firms based in localized clusters often participate . . . in international competition, and the question thus arises as to the extent to which locally based processes can provide these firms with the necessary sources of knowledge and expertise . . . to compete successfully in international markets' (Nachum and Keeble, 1999, p. 2).

The economic advantages found in localized clusters also appear to exist in the interaction between broader spatial configurations, in particular global networks, and in the synergies between firms in different spatial scales. Amin and Thrift (1992) have emphasized the need to consider local clusters as the outgrowth of a world economy that is rapidly internationalizing, leading to the development of 'neo-Marshallian' nodes in global networks (p. 571). Storper (1997) and Scott (1998) have suggested that these clusters are shaped and configured by the growing integration and globalization of markets, innovation and production. This form of international integration does not disrespect differences in cultural values and attitudes across countries, indicating that there are multiple and diverse levels of spatial influences on and learning by firms. All of these levels and the ways in which they are managed affect the competitiveness of firms. Firms are managing not only 'externalities' in the local environment but also internal and external resources in the global environment.

What successful firms in geographical clusters, and especially those that are linked globally, tend to find is the concentration of specific assets such as skills, knowledge, institutions, suppliers, customers and collective learning is as much a function of local supply as it is of international sourcing. In examining the media cluster in Soho, London, Nachum and Keeble (1999, 2000) found that:

a)   in relation to labour supply, the availability of high quality and low cost skills eliminate any dependency on external division of labour, and that this availability attracts more firms and resources to the area. Furthermore the non-routinized and non-standard work of media production requiring close interaction encourages use of local labour;

b)   scale economies in distribution and technological advances allow for the growth in spatial linkages with customers, especially for post-production firms. But this does not hold for non-standard production processes involving small-scale designers and photographers who serve local markets almost exclusively;

c)   while film production firms enjoying horizontal investment patterns typical of larger, multinational firms, tend to collaborate across countries with suppliers and clients, this does not apply to those firms with vertical investment patterns, such as post-production firms or advertising agencies;

d)   global links have become as important for accessing intangible resources such as knowledge and learning, and larger firms tend to demonstrate a greater need than smaller firms because of their wider geographic scope; and

e)   the particular mix of local and global dynamics reduces the significance of interaction at the national level. The orientation of these clusters with their specialized characteristics is towards the global economy. Thus both the firms and the regions in which they are located, operate as linked communities of interest across borders, where the learning and business development processes are occurring both at the level of the region and across spatial concentrations, depending on the type of industry, the levels of investment and size relative to the functions that they carry out. This is what links London more closely to Munich and New York than Birmingham in the UK, and Bangalore with Silicon Valley. The urban focus of these linkages is well documented by Sassen (2002) who recognizes the anchoring of multiple cross-border dynamics in a network of places, prominent among which are cities, particularly global cities.

Global networks of innovative firms

One of the outcomes of networking among firms in global communities of varying interest is the distributed innovation process. If firms operate across borders directly or indirectly, and especially as part of a cluster of firms with mixed forms of organization, then collective forms of learning enable firms to manage the external relationships, albeit at various levels for different types of firms. In this scenario the locus of control for innovation and internationalization has shifted in part from the owner-manager to outside the boundaries of the firm. This poses a difficult problem for the typical owner-manager who is 'naturally' tuned into control structures that lend themselves to hierarchical governance systems that follow the growth of firms.

In isolation, growth through internationalization opens up opportunities for control of intellectual property rights, and the development of appropriate management systems to reduce transaction costs emanating from coordination. This in itself is a challenge for owner-managers of growing firms who find it hard to relinquish control to managers. That he/she may need to consider even other forms of management to enable him/her to benefit from the creativity, diversity and compatibility of partners complicates the learning process. There is a need for the socialization of knowledge, which can be afforded in 'communities of creation' (Sawhney and Prandelli, 2003) that requires their members to work with a social epistemology of knowledge.

In interactive, geographical clusters, firms forge different relationships in time and space to benefit from innovative outcomes of the socialization process. The dependency on multiple levels of skills, knowledge and financial resources across geographical space, coupled with the uncertainty surrounding the pace of change in product development or the extension of the value chain for both products and services, calls for a greater degree of reliance on the socialization process and the corollaries of sharing and trust-building. As part of a development of appropriate governance mechanisms for innovative firms:

> any process of knowledge socialization and collective learning is based on relationships of meaning building and sharing. Such relationships cannot be enacted in the absence

of a context of co-participation. It is important to create a 'cognitive minimum common denominator' for all the individuals and the groups participating in knowledge creation. This context promotes the development of shared values, reciprocity and mutual trust. (Sawhney and Prandelli, 2003)

PART V: THE ROLE OF THE INTERNET

The complex social structure of trust and collective learning acquires a new dimension of complexity with the emergence of the Internet, e-business and e-learning, and other variations of the 'e' word (not forgetting the 'm' word in mobile commerce!). The growth in the use of computers and the Internet has resulted in the mushrooming of a wide range of communities to serve customer needs for communication, information and entertainment. This has for some time resulted in the cult of hyperbole as numerous forays in 'journalese' have argued for the extraordinary possibilities of the Internet. The bursting of the dot com bubble may have calmed down the hype, as various authors have been critical of the strategies adopted by internet pioneers. Porter (2001) argued that nearly every precept of good strategy was violated. Christenson and Tedlow (2000) suggested that doing business on the Internet represented only a fourth major disruption in retailing, and some have argued that e-commerce is simply an extension of direct marketing.

The Internet's role in disintermediation, or the removal of the middleman, has been seen to be its main advantage. But as stated earlier, the Internet has also generated growing communities of interest leading to what Carr (2000) calls 'hypermediation', a situation in which content providers, affiliate sites, search engines, portals, internet service providers, software makers and others are positioned to capture most e-commerce profits. Interestingly, however, their individual search for the holy grail of profits is also a function of their interaction as they share technologies, information and, in the case of Linux or the Sun Microsystems' Jini project, open source models, based on the simple notion that it is difficult for a single company to house all the expertise it needs to succeed, especially when it intends to build infrastructure on which other businesses depend.

The learning outcomes from the use of the Internet, or e-learning, rest on the understanding of how knowledge is created. Unlike traditional goods and services where knowledge is embodied in the product or the service, digitization detaches information from tangible objects by allowing information to be transported freely and instantaneously (Sawhney and Prandelli, 2003). This is evident in the growth of internet trade from backroom services to business process outsourcing. Ideas can be separated from their physical expression (goods and services), thus dislocating the trajectories of traditional learning. Much learning and the economic rent that is derived from learning in business activities are a function of the security provided by intellectual property rights of goods and services which embody information and ideas. However, when information flows freely then a new community of learning needs to emerge to protect the rights of ideas.

For the owner-manager of a small firm, it is not enough to be simply a competitor; he/she must also consider being an 'adaptive innovator' or a 'good evolver'. This is because the competitive advantage derived by any one firm may only be temporary. Moreover, understanding and appreciating the complex factors involved in creating communities of practice and interest in different geographical regions, or in cyberspace, call for higher levels of interaction among knowledge creators and users, which can involve both the producer of goods and services and the customer, both within areas of geographical proximity and outside defined spaces. These ideas allow for the *fourth and final set of propositions* (P4).

Proposition 4

It can be argued that:

a)   SMEs are able to derive specific competitive advantages through internationalization by being part of different communities of interest represented by both similar and different firms in the same or different industries;
b)   SME internationalization is through participation in different communities of interest in geographical concentrations of firms, suppliers, customers, and institutions, or geographical clusters;
c)   firms in geographical clusters attract the interest of global competitors and multinationals, who provide the business case for being part of the cluster;
d)   operating in geographical clusters with an array of firms with complementary or different technologies, skills and other resources, and their international links, allows for the creation of different types of organizational forms based on principles of networking;
e)   forms and methods of learning need to adjust with the evolution of new forms of business activity, increasing levels of cooperation, and the availability of learning resources outside traditional, geographic or institutional spaces.

This fourth proposition offers the possibility of a synthesis of the earlier propositions, especially in the context of modern global scenarios of innovation. In these scenarios internationalization is not an incremental business process outcome. Internationalization is the only business process! Where internationalization is the very norm of business activity, we begin to enter the realms of globalization. Businesses are being increasingly directed to:

*   ensure that they can lead the industry in identifying market opportunities worldwide and in pursuing these opportunities, establishing a necessary presence in key markets;
*   work unremittingly to convert global presence into global competitive advantage;
*   cultivate a global mindset; and
*   take full account of the rapid growth of emerging markets, in particular the BRIC countries of Brazil, Russia, China and India, and within the BRIC family, the growth of China and India.

(Gupta *et al.*, 2008)

These are canny directions in an increasingly globalized world, where entrepreneurial opportunities abound as much as unproductive or even destructive forms of entrepreneurship find succour, through the same institutions and in the flows of unchecked or over-complex modes of business practice. So what does globalization mean?

PART VI: GLOBALIZATION

Gupta *et al.* (2008) put together an interesting scenario:

> At one extreme imagine a world that is a collection of economic islands connected . . . by highly unreliable and expensive bridges or ferries. At the other extreme, imagine a world as an integrated system where the fortunes of the various peoples inhabiting the planet are highly intertwined. The sneakers that you wear were manufactured in Indonesia. Your mutual fund company invests a part of your savings in companies listed on the Hong Kong Stock Exchange. The software that you just downloaded from the Web was developed in India. And the company that you work for routinely exchanges technology

and management ideas with its subsidiary operations in Japan and Germany. If you agree that over the last 50 years, the world around you has undergone a transformation from something like the first scenario to something like the second one, then we would say that the worldwide economy is indeed undergoing a process of globalisation . . . globalisation refers to the growing economic interdependence among countries as reflected in increasing cross-border flows of three types of entities: goods and services, capital and know-how.

A number of key points emerge from this explanation above. First, the scenario has shifted from 'travel overseas' for the purpose of buying and selling in foreign markets to integrated and connected operations for firms and even industries. Second, the cost of maintaining separate and physically oriented overseas operations is being replaced by different cost models based on connections and ICT-based activities. Third, the speed of business transactions has changed dramatically owing to ICT, covering multiple operations across many countries and many business units instead of bi-lateral exchange between two or three firms across a limited number of countries. Fourth, instead of the exchange of just goods and services, we observe the flow of money, know-how and talent alongside goods and services.

Taking a broader perspective on globalization, many writers have argued that globalization is not a new phenomenon, and that there are historical antecedents that help to explain the narrative of globalization better than many a narrow business case can do (Hopkins, 2002; Darwin, 2007; Maddison, 2007). These explanations indicate that globalization has a history and a trajectory of development. We are not going to debate the meaning and scope of globalization,[1] but it is worth capturing at least a sketch of the general features of the 'globalized world' as understood in its present stage of development. These features are summarized below:

- the appearance of a single global market – not for all but for most widely used products, and also for the supply of capital, credit and financial services;
- the intense interaction between states that may be geographically very distant but whose interests (even in the case of very small states) have become global, not regional;
- the deep penetration of most cultures by globally organised media, whose commercial and cultural messages (especially through the language of 'brands') have become almost inseparable;
- the huge scale of migrations and diasporas (forced and free), creating networks and connections that rival the impact of the great European out-migration of the nineteenth century or the Atlantic slave trade;
- the emergence from the wreck of the 'bi-polar age' (1945–1989) of a single 'hyper-power', whose economic and military strength, in relation to all other states, has had no parallel in modern world history;
- the dramatic resurgence of China and India as manufacturing powers. In hugely increasing world ouput and shifting the balance of the world economy, the economic mobilization of their vast populations (1.3bn and 1bn respectively) has been likened to the opening up of vast new lands in the nineteenth century.

(Darwin, 2007)

A simplistic view suggests that the resulting economic interdependence makes for a flat world of business commerce, research and development, and talent sharing. Some statistics tend to reinforce this view, implying that firms, industries, regions and countries are becoming fully integrated. This flattening process:

has happened faster and changed rules, roles and the relationships than we could have imagined . . . we are entering a phase where we are going to see the digitisation, virtualisation and automation of almost everything. The gains in productivity will be staggering for those countries, companies, and individuals who can absorb the new technological tools. And we are entering a phase where more people than ever before in the history of the world are going to have access to these tools – as innovators, as collaborators, and alas, even as terrorists.

(Friedman, 2005)

Friedman's richly anecdotal panegyric to flat-world globalization suggests a kind of integration that is not necessarily borne out by reality. Historical, cultural, political, social and technological factors are diverse across different countries, regions and firms. Moreover, it is this very diversity that informs the purpose of doing business, and sharing know-how and resources across borders. Additionally, different countries have adopted varied speeds to integrate globally.

Gupta *et al.* (2008) offer a critical explanation of what it means to globalize across different units of analysis – the country, and the industry. For a country, the extent of inter-linkages of its economy with those of the rest of world is what describes globalization. While countries such as Cuba remain isolated and others such as Iran are threatened with sanctions, others such as the BRIC countries have made rapid strides in globalization as measured by the share in their GDP of exports and imports, inward and outward flows of FDI, and portfolio investment and inward and outward flows of royalty payments associated with technology transfer.

At the industry level, globalization refers to the degree to which a firm's competitive position is interdependent with the competitive position of another firm in another country. This global interdependence allows it to leverage technology, manufacturing, prowess, brand names and capital across borders. This degree of interdependence tends to favour larger firms such as Nokia, Motorola, Samsung, Sony Ericsson, Coca-Cola, Pepsi-Cola and Cadbury Schweppes (Gupta *et al.*, 2008). However, this analysis ignores the role of small innovative firms on two counts:

- the role that many small firms play in subcontracting work with larger forms or in some cases licensing technologies to larger firms; and
- the opportunities for fairly small players to enter the global market independently through the Internet and through portals and platforms such as eBay or Amazon, and increasingly through the so-called 'apps' or applications world of web-based technologies and cloud computing.

Table 8.4 Trends in globalization

Trade in goods and services (% of GDP)	10 (1970)	23 (1999)	31 (2006)
FDI (% of GDP)	1 (1990)	2.2 (2005)	
Cross-border transactions for bonds and equities (% of GDP)	5 (1970) – for USA, Germany and Japan	200 (2005)	
Cross-border mergers and acquisitions	$22 bn (1990)	$58 bn (2000)	$135 bn (2005)

Source: (Gupta *et al.*, 2008).

This chapter will not pursue the intricate details of the wonders of cloud computing and the 'apps' world. That requires special attention. However, it is important to refer to the substance of the globalization phenomenon in terms of its ability to enable innovation and entrepreneurial behaviour and outcomes through networks of communities, technologies and ideas. The heart of globalization is in this network-centric formulation of new products, new ventures and new organizations that create the new landscapes of internationalization, innovation and growth, involving SMEs and large firms.

PART VII: THE NEW LANDSCAPES SCENARIOS OF INTERNATIONALIZATION, INNOVATION AND GROWTH

The changing landscape of business today, especially for high-technology and innovative firms, is characterized by how these businesses pursue entrepreneurial activities in the way that they:

- source, produce and develop ideas, skills, technologies, intermediary products and services as part of a collaborative ecosystem, often made up of networked centres of excellence, where access to resources requires a high level of computational and organizational skills (as in supply/demand chain management, IT-enabled logistics). It is argued that the 'confluence of connectivity, digitization and the convergence of industry and technology boundaries are creating new dynamics between consumers and the firm' (Prahalad and Krishnan, 2008; Nambisan and Sawhney, 2008), and between producers and end-users (Hippel, 2005);
- involve the development of global, network-centric, open innovation environments consisting of large and small firms, and a host of other organizations participating in 'free' mode to enhance technologies, services, the development of new products and, crucially, business models (as in Skype, Linux, Kazza, Rhapsody) for a wide variety of 'verticals' (industry sectors).

These activities are entrepreneurial in the sense that they seek to identify opportunities in previously unknown and highly uncertain environments, engage in different modes of production and exploitation of resources, and in the process generate economic value that is not necessarily associated with growth: for example, not in terms of market share, but in terms of better value propositions for users of such products and services (Mitra, 2009). A large part of these entrepreneurial activities takes place across borders, between firms that are networked with each other.

As the example of Apple's iPod shows, virtually the entire process of design, production and use is based on a form of diversity that acknowledges inputs of knowledge at various stages from multiple sources. Access to resources and know-how is global and multiple; the product is personalized to meet the individual customer's preferences and usage patterns; a range of technologies converge to create a high-specification product covering different uses; and co-creation with customers, suppliers and distributors is the other side of accessing resources. In Prahalad and Krishnan's (2008) conceptualization, N=1 where the sale of every iPod is a unique proposition based on the individual customer, and where R = G in the sense that all resources are more or less sourced globally.

This approach to value creation demands new configurations and business models based on ideas of network-centric models, including open innovation.

**Interconnectedness of Firms and Globalisation
Experience of Apple I-Pod**

Personalisation and multiple sourcing

- Original software based on 'PortalPlayer's' reference platform
- Design and user interface outsourced to Pixo (USA)
- ARM Ltd. (UK) developed CPU

  The N = 1 and R= G model
- Fraunhofer Institute for Integrated Circuits (Germany) licensed MP3 sound compression technology to Apple
- 1.8 inch hard drive came from Toshiba (iPod Mini 1 inch drive from Hitachi (Japan) and Seagate (USA)
- Flash memories in iPod nano from Toshiba (Japan) & Samsung (Korea)
- Audio codecsfrom Wolfson Electronics (Scotland)
- Music content = large & small firms & independent artists
- Podcast content = traditional media, individuals & firms
- Device:
  - Disk drives = Toshiba, Japan
  - SDRAM = Samsung, Korea
- Video Processors = Broadcom, USA
  - Assembly – Inventec, Taiwan
  - Design – California

Figure 8.4 The iPod and the new model of innovation

Source: adapted from Prahalad and Krishnan (2008); Bhide (2008).

Network-centric models

Nambisan and Sawhney (2008) argue that, with the advent of the Internet, various phenomena such as the 'Open Source Software movement, electronic R&D marketplaces, online communities and a whole new set of possibilities . . . reach out and connect with innovative ideas and talent beyond the boundaries of the corporation' (p. 11). Innovation itself is increasingly being described, in different ways, as 'open', 'democratic', 'distributed' and 'community-led'. There is a shift in the language, the processes and the construct of innovation. It tends to exist almost 'outside' the organization – a far cry from the methods used in the past to engineer growth, essentially through mergers and acquisitions (M&As). The legendary failure of M&A's (Nambisan and Sawhney (2008) refer to between 70 and 80% of M&A initiatives ending up in failures) does, thankfully, have an alternative in the new quest for growth based on new forms of innovation and connectivity.

The term 'network-centric' applies to a wide range of subjects, from computing through to warfare, operations, enterprise and advocacy of social movements. In applying the term to innovation, Nambisan and Sawhney (2008) define network-centric innovation (NCI) as being externally focused on innovation, relying on drawing on the resources and capabilities of external networks and communities to enhance reach, speed and quality of production of innovative products, services and organizations.

There are certain principles that apply to such network-centric approaches and formats. These range from shared goals and objectives to communities or specific architectures of participation of disparate groups of players. Table 8.5 provides a snapshot account of these principles.

To enable these principles to work effectively, innovators and businesses need to adopt different models and operational infrastructures to have control over issues such as intellectual

Table 8.5 Principles of network-centric innovation

Principles	Description	Examples
Shared goals and objectives	One or more goals that help bring the network members together and channel their diverse resources and activities	*Customer community*: identify product flaws and contribute to product enhancement (e.g. Ducati's separate web division to coordinate internet-based collaboration with customers in both front- and back-end innovations for its motorcycles)
Shared world view	Common assumptions and mental models related to the innovation and its external environments	*Open source community*: shared understanding about the software product's ties with other technologies and products
'Social' knowledge creation	Places the emphasis on interaction among network members as the basis of value creation and on the cumulative nature of knowledge creation	*Inventor networks*: interactions among individual inventor, intermediary and large firm for the development of new product concepts (e.g. Staples Inc., the office suppliers, and their 'Innovation Quest' contest, which sources innovative ideas from inventors)
Architecture of participation	Defines a set of systems, mechanisms and processes to facilitate participation in value creation and value appropriation	*Open source software community*: modular product architecture and GNU General Public License Scheme (e.g. IBM's decision to promote and align strategies to leverage power of these communities link with Apache Open Source solution for the design of the Olympic web site for the Atlanta Olympic games) in markets ranging from Web servers and operating systems.

Source: adapted from Nambisan and Sawhney (2008).

property and talent sourcing. These issues relating to business models, together with an overview of the tools of open and collective forms of innovation, are discussed in Chapter 5.

Conclusion

This chapter has focused on the evolution of the learning process associated with SME internationalization and innovation. Learning takes place at the level of the individual entrepreneur who brings his/her own knowledge base and motivations to bear on the decision to internationalize. Learning also occurs at the level of the firm, especially the existing firm, as it graduates to international working standards, using its experience, its influences and its collective skills and knowledge base to generate international business activity. It has also been noted that in some cases the learning process is more immediate, as with 'born global' firms, who tend to occupy high-technology sectors. Their learning in more uncertain environments suggests that the entrepreneur(s) has a higher starting threshold of knowledge with which to take advantage of new forms of learning. The spatial aspects of learning and small firm internationalization are best examined in the context of networks, and geographical clusters where learning is part of the process of managing distributed innovation in communities of creation. Finally, the Internet affords e-learning through e-business activity where shared and open-source information and ideas become part of the immediate exchange of ideas and information in communities of creation.

Communities of creation are the theatres of internationalization for small firms. They do not simply represent another community of interest or a community of practice. The creation of their community, where diverse interests are connected, sometimes without the explicit motivation to do so, is a product of the innovation process itself. The entrepreneurs in these communities are able to innovate both personally ad collectively, with disparate groups of people and organizations across different national, economic, social and political boundaries. The community of creation brings together the basic tenets of the internationalization process by considering the role of the individual entrepreneur, the organizational forms that are generated and that interact with each other, and the environment or the stage in which these entrepreneurs and organizations best manage the innovation process inherent in successful internationalization activities.

So far we have moved along in a journey that has taken us from theoretical insights that underscore our understanding of entrepreneurship, innovation and regional development through to an examination of critical factors, organizations, contexts and environments that impinge on the entrepreneurial process and its impact on regions and development. This chapter and the one preceding it have given some attention to the learning process and how that underpins entrepreneurship and innovation in both theory and practice. Firms learn in their own local habitats and extend this form of local learning through internationalization. Their ability to obtain better opportunities for learning, innovation and performance within locally networked environments, such as business clusters provides, paradoxically, better ammunition for their international adventures. Their international success reinforces their local standing and often the regions in which they are located. Much of this ebb and flow of innovative business practice tends to define the knowledge economy where universities can and often do play an important institutional role. It is to this subject of universities and their role in entrepreneurship and regional economic development that we turn to in Chapter 9.

Self-assessment questions

1. Explain the distinctive features of the internationalization process of SMEs.
2. How do local factors influence a firm's capacity and capabilities for internationalization?
3. In what way can the Internet make all firms engage in the internationalization process?
4. Explain the difference between the two concepts of globalization and internationalization.
5. How do the network-centric and open architecture models of innovation enhance the process of entrepreneurship?

9 Higher education, universities and entrepreneurship

Learning outcomes

In this chapter the reader will:

- obtain a critical overview of role and function of higher education in promoting entrepreneurship;
- understand and appreciate critically the context in which higher education institutions (HEIS) play a role in advancing entrepreneurship and innovation;
- identify and evaluate critically the main strategies and mechanisms adopted by HEIs to support entrepreneurship and economic development; and
- obtain a critical overview of the evolution of HEIs in terms of their engagement with entrepreneurship and economic development.

Structure of the chapter

This chapter examines the range and breadth of interactions that universities as major institutions have with the wider economy. It locates these relationships in the context of the region in which HEIs are based. The dynamics of the local region inform the relationship with entrepreneurship. There are three strands to these dynamics:

- the varied *contexts of learning*, its history and its various changing forms, and what that means for universities in terms of their contribution to entrepreneurship and economic development;
- the specific *local environment*, the resources and the assets that universities have at their disposal for developing entrepreneurial activities; and
- the *mechanisms and instruments* that HEIs use to encourage entrepreneurship and support economic development including science parks, incubation centres and entrepreneurship education and training.

These three strands are discussed in three separate sections of the chapter.

Part I provides an overview of higher education institutions (HEIs) and their relationship with entrepreneurship. Part II looks at the learning context and the historical antecedents of HEI involvement in direct and quasi entrepreneurial activities associated with economic change. The discussion of contexts continues in Part III but this time with a clear reference to the local context for HEI-related entrepreneurial activity. Part IV then focuses on the different forms, models and mechanisms of entrepreneurship pursued by HEIs, before the chapter is concluded.

Introduction

We have looked at the critical role of institutions and of learning in the promotion of entre-preneurship in terms of both policy and new venture creation activities across a range of economic and social spheres (see Chapters 6 and 8). We turn our attention in this chapter to one of the big institutional players, higher education, and especially universities,[1] which have been drawn into the hurly burly of entrepreneurship particularly since the early 1970s. Their ability to influence thought and action among young and old and across different domains through strategic direction, learning provision and exchange has now attracted much atten-tion in various economies around the world.

Entrepreneurship has entered the realm of 'higher' learning. As protectors of the 'higher learning realm', higher education institutions (HEIs) across the world have taken up the chal-lenge of entrepreneurship. HEIs support entrepreneurship education and training and indulge in a variety of knowledge transfer activities that promote entrepreneurship directly (as in aca-demic spin-offs) or indirectly through research, training and education. Increasingly, much of this 'indulgence' occurs at the regional level where HEIs enter into different relationships with other stakeholders pursuing economic growth and competitiveness.

The much vaunted and well-publicized roles of higher education institutions (HEIs) in new venture creation and the evolution of an entrepreneurial and learning environment, especially in the United States and then Europe, together with rapid developments across the world, suggest that certain antecedents are worth consideration. Since education, and especially universities, play a vital role in the transformation of economies and societies, the specific role of HEIs in fostering entrepreneurship is considered to be an appropriate topic of investigation, discourse and dissemination.

Universities are providers of research, teaching and knowledge transfer. They are the prin-cipal custodians of learning, and especially 'higher' forms of learning for their students and for their staff. Ideas of intellectual curiosity, in-depth enquiry and original findings are not circumscribed by either geography or narrow concerns of immediate or contingent relevance predicated upon purely economic considerations. What they create is a learning context that has global and local ramifications over the short, medium and longer terms. What obtains are the means and structures of economic, social, cultural and personal value creation, which help to identify opportunities for the growth and development of individuals, organizations and the wider environment.

Different countries and regions offer varied and interesting contexts for discussion on the topic of entrepreneurship, and especially the role of HEIs in encouraging entrepreneurship. For example, the transition to market economies from a variety of command structures present Central and South Eastern European (CESE) countries with specific problems and opportuni-ties. The economies and societies of these countries have witnessed variegated statist hegemony over economic activity, resulting in some states being in a better position to make the transi-tion than other economies (Formica *et al.*, 2005). Add to this complex set of circumstances the purpose and state of higher education and the role of universities in those countries. It is not difficult to infer from this description that any focus on entrepreneurship and higher education needs to pick up on the environment, the institutional factors that provide the necessary rules and constraints for entrepreneurial activity and higher education involvement, and the organi-zational capabilities of both firms and universities to be part of an entrepreneurial network.

HEIs do of course contribute to the national output and well-being of countries. They do so as a collective of learning institutions producing scientists, engineers, philosophers, busi-nessmen and businesswomen, and even politicians. They engage with national governments, advising on policy matters; and academic luminaries are often called upon to interact with other governments, industry and non-governmental agencies around the world. They attract students and researchers from across the globe. However, most institutions have a local base; their names represent the region they are located in – as, for example the University of Essex in the UK. Even if they take the responsibility of producing future leaders of the world, their measurable contribution to economic development is best understood in terms of their place and role in those regions in which they are located.

To what extent do universities play a role in their regions? What contributions do they make to entrepreneurship and economic development in those regions? What lessons could be learnt from good or best practice in different countries? To what extent do countries whose economies are characterized by entrepreneurial growth benefit from the contribution of HEIs? What forms of involvement by HEIs allow for optimal or maximum levels of impact on the economy? What are the driving factors for university involvement in entrepreneurial activity? While there may not be adequate space to answer all of these questions, this chapter will explore some of the issues raised by the questions.

PART I: HEIS AND ENTREPRENEURSHIP

To begin, let us assume that HEIs' role in entrepreneurship development is best understood in terms of the relationships universities develop with firms, especially SMEs in their region.

The locations of certain universities, and indeed of firms in particular regions, have a bearing on the nature, scope and outcome of such linkages. The nexus of relationships is often a function of the state of the economy, the propensity of firms to absorb knowledge from universities, and the capability of universities to meet the needs of firms in the region. Thus context is a key consideration. While universities may often engage, formally or informally, with firms in a variety of ways, the specific impact on new firm creation is a peculiar and difficult outcome to measure. New firm creation follows unstructured paths, and universities are often not well placed to work in such chaotic environments. Successful entrepreneurs who do interact with HEIs tend to make use of their local institutions, although this is difficult to achieve in locations where there is either an absence of suitable HEIs or the range of relevant expertise is limited (Storey, 2003).

The extent to which universities are actually responsible for firm creation, directly, is a contentious issue since other factors, from individual or team motivation to venture finance and public policy, also influence such phenomena. Finally, not all universities with similar capabilities have the same impact on their region, suggesting the varied culture of different regions and the strategic role and function of separate universities.

To help us explore the differences and the nuances we need to obtain:

- a critical understanding of the learning context and antecedents of HEIs, which inform both policies relating to higher education and the organization of HEIs, and how they influence their role in fostering entrepreneurship;
- an appreciation of the importance of the local or regional environment in which universities can help to foster entrepreneurship; and
- HEIs to promote entrepreneurship, with a particular focus on entrepreneurship education and training (including vocational training) and knowledge transfer (including technology transfer and academic spin-offs).

PART II: THE LEARNING CONTEXT AND ANTECEDENTS FOR THE PROMOTION OF ENTREPRENEURSHIP

At the heart of any attempt by HEIs to promote entrepreneurship is the question of universities and their relationship to the wider world outside the institutions. Cultivating these relationships focuses attention on the need to balance the three key elements of the mission of universities:

- the generation of new knowledge (research and intellectual capital);
- the passing of this knowledge to future generations (teaching and the generation of human capital);
- serving the needs of industry, commerce (Goddard *et al.*, 1994) and the wider social community (the triple helix network and the generation of social capital).

Research-intensive universities play an important role as a source of fundamental and blue-sky knowledge and, sometimes, relevant (for industry) technology in modern economies. The following table shows how specific subject areas appear to have made a contribution to relevant industrial benefits.

Since the early 1990s, universities and other HEIs have not been exonerated from the rapid technological and structural changes in most economies, with a range of factors (funding and resources, forms of learning, institutional relationships, etc.) influencing the way HEIs contribute to the production and dissemination of knowledge and their roles and responsibilities in the creation and sustainability of national systems of innovation (Gibbons *et al.*, 1994; Howells *et al.*, 1998). What emerges from a consideration of these influences are three crucial questions:

Table 9.1 The relevance of university science to industrial technology

Science	# of Industries with "relevance" scores		Selected industries for which the reported "relevance" of university research was large (≥ 6).
	≥ 5	≥ 6	
Biology	12	3	Animal feed, drigs, processed fruits/vegetables
Chemistry	19	3	Animal feed, meat products, drugs
Geology	0	0	None
Mathematics	5	1	Optical instruments
Physics	4	2	Optical instruments, electronics?
Agricultural science	17	7	Pesticides, animal feed, fertilizers, food products
Applied math/operations research	16	2	Meat products, logging/sawmills
Computer science	34	10	Optical instruments, logging/sawmills, paper machinery
Materials science	29	8	Synthetic rubber, nonferrous metals
Medical science	7	3	Surgical/medical instruments, drugs, coffee
Metallurgy	21	6	Nonferrous metals, fabricated metal products
Chemical engineering	19	6	Canned foods, fertilizers, malt beverages
Electrical engineering	22	2	Semiconductors, scientific instruments
Mechanical engineering	28	9	Hand tools, specialized industrial machinery

Source: Mowery and Sampat (2005).

- How do HEIs interact with the wider community of learning?
- How do they establish institutions of good practice that identify different forms of learning and knowledge production both within HEIs and in communication with other organizations, as part of a lifelong learning system?
- How do these interactions generate innovation and new enterprises?

The triple helix

These questions have invoked the idea of a 'triple helix' of relationships between HEIs, industry and government (Leydesdorff and Etzkowitz, 1996). All three aspects of the archetypal mission of an HEI – research, teaching and knowledge transfer – are enmeshed in these interactions, resulting in a variety of frameworks and mechanisms for HEI–industry relationships. These frameworks and mechanisms include research and consultancy links, commercialization of research, intellectual property management, spin-off activities, and property-led developments, such as science parks, links to teaching, and staff support and funding. Central to the measure of any effectiveness of the outcomes of these links is the generation of intellectual, human and social capital. How have these issues become part of the agenda of HEIs? What antecedents or historical patterns can we find in the formation of these issues over time, and how does any ensuing enquiry help us to obtain a better grasp of HEIs' contribution to entrepreneurship, innovation and economic development?

Antecedents

A cursory review of the antecedents of higher education–industry relationships indicates that industry–academic links go back a long way. The first independent, self-governing universities appeared during the Middle Ages in Bologna and Paris, and were recognized by both church and local governmental authorities right up to the period prior to the eighteenth century.

To obtain an understanding of the true value of HEI–industry links, we need to turn to Germany and the emergence of the Technische Hochschulen in the late nineteenth century. Education in Germany evolved from the classical humanist tradition of *Bildung* in the *Gymnasium* and the university to the accommodation of pragmatic/utilitarian curricula such as science, technology and modern languages in the *Realgymnasium*. The *Technische Hochschulen* recruited students from the latter, and together with the *Technische Mittelschulen* (small, local training institutes) they offered diverse, 'pliable, transverse structures' of technical education and learning, enabling industry to recruit new employees in response to changing technology and economic opportunities (Shinn, 1998). As Cahan (1989; cited in Shinn, 1998) also pointed out, indirect research contributions from the *Physikalisch-Technische Reichsanstalts* (specializing in technology) also helped to establish German-based technological standards and carry out significant work in the field of instrumentation.

The emergence of the relevance of universities to economic development

What is apparent in any consideration of the evolution of industry–academia links is, first, the development of human capital through the creation of qualities of motivation, loyalty, flexibility, training and skills. Second, it demonstrates the value of different forms of education (in this case technical education), and how diverse and flexible forms of learning have to be taken into account when assessing the value of education and its contribution to economic development.

What is not apparent is any direct link between academia–industry connections and entrepreneurship, *defined here as the identification and realization of opportunity for value creation through innovation and new enterprise development.* However, the interesting outcome of a journey back through history is the realization of the timing and the nature of the contributions of certain forms of education to economic development. The references to German industrial development are to a particular point in time and place, when innovation in terms of new product development, new technology standards, new supply side measures (as in education and training), and the creation of new forms of intellectual and human capital paved the way for German industrial growth. This outcome could be taken as a reasonable proxy for entrepreneurship development, with the use of the key instruments of diverse forms of technical education and applied research being critical to the process of innovation and entrepreneurship. What is distinctive here is the direct involvement of diverse forms of higher education in promoting industrial development and economic competitiveness.

The rise of the modern state corresponded with greater degrees of control over public university systems, especially in much of Continental Europe, notably France and Germany, as well as in Japan. This was not the case, however, in Britain and the USA. US universities, in particular, retained great autonomy in their administrative policies. Rosenberg (2000) and Ben-David (1968) have argued that this lack of central control probably compelled American universities to be more 'entrepreneurial' in their research and curricula to be more responsive to changing socio-economic demands than their European counterparts.

During the decades preceding and following the First World War, very few French firms possessed any research capacity. Neither was there any real scope for applied research within the educational system. Immediately after the Second World War the USSR boasted a significant fundamental and applied research community, bigger even than that of the USA. But while French industry made advances despite restrictive innovation acquisition practices during the First World War, post-war Soviet industry hardly grew at all (Shinn, 1998).

Much of this debate about the nature and value of university–industry interaction and universities' contribution to innovation has taken place in western economies, suggesting a natural correlation with their highly industrialized status. Increasingly, however, and with the rapid growth of emerging economies, science and policy development in countries such as Taiwan, Israel, China, India and Malaysia have all begun to address the received wisdom associated with this debate. A key policy outcome of such debates has been the creation of national innovation systems and the role of universities in the promotion of such systems.

National innovation systems and universities

Universities are widely cited as critical institutional actors in national innovation systems. Much of the literature on the topic defines such systems in terms of the institutions and actors that help to create, develop and diffuse innovations. A lot of emphasis is put on the importance of strong linkages among these various institutions for improving national innovative and competitive performance, with universities playing a key role. While national systems suggest a form of political, economic, social and cultural dynamic that is geographically inimitable, they have, over time, become interdependent, reflecting rapid growth during the post-1945 period in cross-border flows of capital, goods, people and knowledge. 'Yet the university systems of these economies retain strong "national" characteristics, reflecting significant contrasts among national university systems in structure and the influence of historical evolution on contemporary structure and policy' (Mowery and Sampat, 2005).

Table 9.2 University research models and national innovation systems

Models	Source	Scope	Critiques
The Linear Model	Vannevar Bush, (1945), *Science: The Endless Frontier*	Expanding public funding critical to innovation and economic growth; universities were most appropriate institutional locus for basic research; based on 'market failure' rationale for funding basic academic research developed by Nelson (1959) and Arrow (1962)	Critiques offered by Kline and Rosenberg (1999) pointing to curvilinear approach; reference to growth of industrial Japan and evidence of non-essential requirement of basic research; technology considered to be more useful than science for economic growth
Academic Research *v.* Industrial Research	Dasgupta and David (1987); David, Foray and Steinmueller (1999); Branscombe *et al.*	Cultural differences between academic and industrial research: academic research concerned with original insights, discoveries and critical methodologies plus prompt, refereed publication; industrial research dependent on sponsorship, secrecy, problem-solving issues	Differences can be overstated – pharmaceutical research relies heavily on publications, for example; many academic researchers combine 'pure' and 'applied' work, which support each other, especially in new technology areas
Mode 2 Science	Gibbons *et al.* (1994)	Holistic, interdisciplinary approach linked to networked institutions; different from past and associated with post-modern economic environment and scale and diversity of knowledge inputs required from various sources for modern forms of production	Does not imply decline in value of HEIs in producing knowledge and in the contribution of such knowledge to economic growth
Triple Helix	Leydesdorff and Etzkowitz (1996); Etzkowitz *et al.* (1998)	As in Mode 2 above, emphasizing increased interaction among institutions, and quite importantly each institution taking on some of the roles of others (universities creating firms; firms taking on more academic research, etc.)	Emphasis on 'industrial' component of academic research obscures limited scope of such an approach; lack of sufficient empirical evidence

We can trace the development of certain models of university research activity which impact on the development of national innovation systems, as shown in Table 9.2.

Diversity of systems and practises

It is the absence of diversity in education systems and provision that has thwarted effective and entrepreneurial partnerships being formed. Saddled by notions of high-minded science, and anti-utilitarian values, academics have long rebelled against connections with industry. Despite the existence of the third dimension to the mission of HEIs, collaboration with industry was considered to be inimical to the central ethos of universities. An early OECD report (1970) also noted the tensions that arise from the perception that staff may be distracted from their main academic functions by industry-directed work. However, as Howells *et al.* (1998)

have noted, the strongest and most productive relationships with industry are founded upon HEIs doing what they are best established to do, that is:

> pursuing excellence in research and teaching, rather than attempting to duplicate the functions of industry. The necessary cultural shift comes in terms of being able to understand the needs of industry and provide an interface which allows the swift and effective flow of knowledge and people to their most productive use. (Howells *et al.*, 1998, p. 7)

Cultural and structural shifts

Entrepreneurship is directly concerned with the flows of intellectual, human and social capital to their most productive use, especially in the form of new venture creation. But entrepreneurship goes beyond routine forms of industry–academia collaboration; it engages both parties, and indeed government, to derive competitive economic value from innovation and a cultural shift in the process of learning that results from innovation.

The cultural and structural shifts that have enabled both policy makers and HEIs to recognize this significant role of HEIs in fostering entrepreneurship has five components:

1) mass higher education and changes in the government's definition of the mission of HEIs;
2) related increase in the demand for skills and knowledge in all aspects of work . . . in response to increasing competition in the global economy;
3) increasing rates of technological change and new ways of organizing the production and distribution of goods and services, including changing relationships between large and small firms;
4) changes in the structure of government and a greater diversity of bodies having a stake in the governance of local territories; and
5) new patterns of urban and regional development arising from the greater mobility of capital and labour, the decline of old sectors and the emergence of new ones, as in the creative and cultural industries.

(Goddard *et al.*, 1994)

The five components also reflect the need for diverse approaches to education and learning. Not only is a response in different forms of education necessary to generate varied capabilities; it is also necessary to capture forms of learning both in traditional educational institutions and in other 'centres of learning' outside HEIs. The idea of 'learning organizations' stems from this notion of diversity. In part, this approach to diversity recognizes the need for accelerated learning and innovation that cuts across traditional disciplinary lines. Gibbons *et al.* (1994) refer to this form of learning as Mode 2 science, where scientists, engineers, technicians and managers seize on industrial and societal problems for their work. In this world, researchers include an intellectually and institutionally flexible group transferring from one problem domain to another as and when opportunities arise, independent of their organizations.

The Gibbons Mode 2 model does recognize the way entrepreneurship and innovation work, namely in a disorganized and non-linear fashion and across disciplines or profession-bound institutions. Current thinking on convergence of technologies and organizations also supports the idea of interactive, cross-institutional forms of learning.

Production and commercialization of knowledge

Since the recognition of the industrial and policy significance of HEI–industry links, especially in the USA in the 1970s, many universities have engaged not only in commercialization of knowledge but also in helping to foster entrepreneurial attitudes and skills in faculty, staff and students, identify different sources of funds for applied research and prototype development, bring together technology and business resources in incubators, and offer new degrees in entrepreneurship and innovation (McNaughton, 2005). The development of entrepreneurial attitudes in HEIs is symptomatic of the attitudes to entrepreneurship in wider society. While it may be argued that positive attitudes are higher in environments where total, entrepreneurial activity (the Total Entrepreneurial Activity Index, or TEA, of the Global Entrepreneurship Monitor) itself is high, the encouragement of clement attitudes may be more necessary in environments where the TEA is not strong.

Many countries and their universities have adopted many of the measures and tools that various OECD nations and their HEIs have used over the years with varying degrees of success (Varblane *et al.* 2005; Formica *et al.*, 2005). It is not clear whether the paths followed by these countries replicate the basis of knowledge production and dissemination process of most western economies since the Second World War, namely mass production, economies of scale, integration of existing technologies, and an industrial infrastructure dominated by large firms. Luczkiw (2005) refers to the report 'An Agenda for a Growing Europe', which states that economic globalization and strong external competition demand increased movement internally and externally among firms, increased flexibility of labour markets, increased investments in research and development, and education and diversity in the innovation process. Preparing the labour market of tomorrow to acquire more entrepreneurial skills and producing knowledge that can help to manage these demands is central to the policy agenda for HEIs, industry and government.

Adaptive, network-based and entrepreneurial learning

Much of the production of knowledge in the modern economy is decentralized and distributed widely across regions and countries. Much of the production and dissemination of knowledge is also distributed across different types of organizations. This spatial and organizational distribution of knowledge has complex outcomes for learning in both HEIs and industry. The emerging learning system mirrors this complexity in that the most relevant forms of learning and knowledge creation now call for:

- adaptive networks of HEIs and industry, where learning can take place in either environment, and in which duality can be accommodated by policies for education and research;
- adaptive networks that continually build and make use of intellectual, human and social capital for new products, services and organizations; and
- adaptive networks of knowledge production and dissemination that are global in operational terms.

Entrepreneurship provides for a context for learning, in that the continuous process of accelerated innovation and the creation of new forms compel us to explore learning from a variety of institutional perspectives. Possible chaos and disequilibrium are avoided through the recognition of the role of multiple agents in generating new knowledge. Similarly, learning itself takes on an entrepreneurial character in that there is a greater recognition of each agent's unique and related contributions, which can be aligned with activities that lead to a commitment from different players in a particular context.

The global character of entrepreneurship and the role of HEIs in fostering entrepreneurship can be observed in the demonstration of varied strengths of HEIs across the world. Excellence today is measured in global terms; *ipso facto*, knowledge is best shared among global players. However, much of the strength of HEIs in the global arena of knowledge production, dissemination and transfer is mediated at the local or regional level. It is this local/regional context of HEIs that enables them to direct intellectual, human and social capital towards entrepreneurial outcomes.

PART III: THE LOCAL CONTEXT OF HEIS AND THE PROMOTION OF ENTREPRENEURSHIP

A key element of government policy for entrepreneurship, innovation and economic regeneration has been the increased role of regional governments and decision-making at the local level. Part of this role is attributed to the notion that decisions about economic prosperity and quality of life are best made at the regional level. This has often resulted in a patchwork of institutions and arrangements for issues such as the enhanced role of business leaders in regional strategic and investment decision-making (as in the creation of the Regional Development agencies in the UK). Universities, which have always had a regional, physical presence (in the case of the best of them, an international research and student profile), have been drawn into this regional agenda because of:

- the historical roots of their regional presence;
- changes in policies for funding and the consequent need to seek money explicitly from varied sources;
- the perceived direct and indirect impact of their work on regional economic performance;
- the profile of university research strengths and the presence of regional agglomerations of industrialized specialisms; and
- strategic policy objectives for innovation and business development at the sub-national level.

(Adams and Smith, 2004)

As Malecki (2005) points out, HEIs bring long-term benefits to a region because they are seen as an 'important element in a region's knowledge infrastructure, and the knowledge infrastructure, to a large extent, decides the success of a region in today's knowledge-based economy' (Rutten *et al.*, 2003; cited in Malecki, 2005). Regions increasingly organize themselves as 'learning regions', and it is important to realize that, as part of this organization, HEIs are important drivers of economic growth only as one among other producers of knowledge. This role of HEIs in the web of knowledge-producing economic actors reinforces the point about HEIs working in conjunction with other learning organizations referred to earlier in this chapter.

Knowledge spillovers

In common with the problem of HEIs being a point in the linear mode of knowledge creation and transfer, the recognition of HEIs as drivers of economic growth suffers from the restrictive view that relies on their capacity to produce explicit and tangible forms of knowledge. What tends to get ignored is the unintended, informal spillovers of knowledge that occur from HEIs to SMEs. They do not carry the weight of prestige, money and contacts that alliances with larger firms bring. Their informal character poses problems for formal procedures-oriented institutions and their administrators. It is well recognized that much of the knowledge and the technologies are embedded in academics, other staff members and students. Among knowledge-intensive firms, much of the knowledge is embodied in their personnel. These forms of tacit knowledge combine with more explicit ones in a process of iterative exchange and relationship among academics and SME owner-managers and their employees. It is argued that such relationships generate larger benefits for both HEIs and the firms in a region (Benneworth, 2001). Furthermore, the fruitful cultivation of such relationships, and the appropriate valorization of tacit forms of knowledge and the use of social capital, distinguishes one region from another.

Tacit knowledge, spillovers and HEIs

The literature on spatial agglomeration ('geography and knowledge spillovers') has woven together concepts of tacit knowledge and localized spillovers (Agrawal, 2001) to explain why regions post different rates of technology-based entrepreneurship (Mitra and Abubakar, 2005) and how knowledge spillovers impact on innovative capacity and technology-based entrepreneurship in regions (Jaffe, 1989; Acs, 2002). Central to the argument about geographically mediated spillovers is the distinction between tacit and explicit knowledge, introduced by Polanyi (1962), which is considered to be of fundamental importance to the geographical concentration of technological activity (Jaffe, 1989; Acs, 2002). (See Chapter 6 for a short discussion on tacit knowledge, learning and entrepreneurship.)

In a seminal work, Jaffe (1989) explored the existence of geographically mediated 'knowledge spillovers' in the USA from university research to commercial innovation. Building on the tacit–explicit knowledge distinction, Jaffe agues that 'it is certainly plausible that the pool of talented graduates, the ideas generated by faculty, and the high quality libraries and other facilities of research universities facilitate the commercial process of innovation in their neighbourhood' (Jaffe, 1989, p. 957). As stated by Grossman and Helpman (1991), technological spillovers from R&D mean:

- firms can acquire information created by others without paying for that information in a market transaction; and
- the creators or current owners of the information have no recourse, under prevailing laws, if other firms utilize the information so acquired.

University knowledge spillover refers to the type of externality for firms which use such knowledge without necessarily compensating the source of that knowledge (Harris, 2001).

Jaffe's (1989) study highlighted the 'public good' nature of university research, as his analysis provided evidence that corporate patent responds positively to commercial spillovers from university research. Zucker *et al.* (1998) linked the increasing number of American biotechnology firms, which grew from a non-existent base to over 700 in less than two decades, with university research activities by arguing that the commercialization of biotechnology is actively intertwined with the development of underlying science in local research universities. Acs (2002) concluded that university spillover plays an important role in certain industries, such as electronics and instruments, and no significant role in others, such as drugs and chemicals.

Research on high-technology firms seems to support these findings. They suggest that research universities serve as important origins of regional technology-based firms through mechanisms of collective learning (Lindholm, 1999), university knowledge spillovers (Zucker *et al.*,1998) and university spin-offs (Shane and Stuart, 2002). These universities have also been identified as one of the two major sources of new technology firm entrepreneurs (Oakey, 1995).

Yet not all research-intensive HEIs have contributed to technology-intensive economic development (Feller, 1990; Feldman, 1994). What appears to underpin the successful generation of a local culture of innovation are critical notions of 'untraded interdependencies' between institutions and people (Storper, 1995), collective learning in innovative milieux (Keeble and Wilkinson, 1999; Capello, 1999) and networking (Saxenian, 1994). Others have argued that the mechanisms for the transfer of knowledge in spatial terms are socially embedded owing to the common technological and institutional routines in a region (Capello, 1999). This perspective of knowledge transfer is supported by sociological insights into new venture creation (Yli-Renko *et al.*, 2001) and the literature on 'firm characteristics' which argues that the main ingredient for the utilization of externally generated scientific knowledge such as that which is transferred from universities is 'connectedness' between universities and the firms (Lim, 2000; Mitra, 2000). Lim identified three different mechanisms for fostering connectedness:

1) cultivating university relationships by way of sponsoring research, collaborating with faculty and recruiting graduate students;
2) partnering with other companies that do related scientific research; and
3) participating in research consortia.

Despite the theories and the availability of some empirical observations, it is still problematic to demonstrate a clear connection between HEI activity (especially research) and the creation of technology-based ventures at an inter-regional level. As Zucker *et al.* (1998) have observed, 'Localised spillovers may play fundamental roles in both economic agglomeration and endogenous growth . . . However, our evidence, like the other literature cited here, specifically indicates localised effects without demonstrating that they can be characterised as spillovers (or externalities).'

Social capital, institutions and HEIs

The difficulty in finding causal relationships between HEI knowledge spillovers and new venture creation does not preclude an association between the two, which in turn informs a number of overlapping sets of interactions between different players in a local system. Causality notwithstanding, these relationships create institutions of learning that foster a culture of entrepreneurship in the region. Central to this culture is the creation and use of social capital, which includes structural and psychological elements in the networks of personal relationships and the sense of mutual understanding that enable people to live and work together effectively. Social capital can enhance the rapid diffusion of knowledge between individuals and communities as well as within and between firms (van Schaik, 2002). In essence, social capital helps to harness intellectual and human capital and generate synergistic returns for the network in regions. How effectively that is done is a matter for the custodians of regional innovation systems, with regions being able to demonstrate their competitive edge through that process. As Bartlett (2005), Audretsch and Keilbach (2005) and Morgan (1997) have noted, research on innovation systems suggests that differences in innovative capacities between countries and regions are linked to the institutions that promote learning and technology transfer, activities that in turn depend upon the existence of institutions and firms that permit exchange of knowledge and other resources.

HEIs, industry and government need to work towards establishing particular institutional structures that enable networks of relationships generating social capital to be safeguarded and nurtured. These structures also need to recognize that the most successful forms of relationships transcend local geographical boundaries, as knowledge, skills and financial capital are sourced globally. These flows of resources help to establish international networks. At the same time they reinforce regional capabilities, giving succour to the paradox of modern times that the more international the scope of economic activities in a region, the stronger is the region's own economic identity. HEIs, firms and policy makers in different countries tend to follow complementary areas of expertise, which helps units of explicit knowledge to be traded across geographical boundaries. This in turn strengthens local expertise. The greater the production of local expertise, the more there is an opportunity for spillovers, or 'untraded interdependencies', which attract investment, technologies and skills to the area.

Internationalization and local economic development

HEIs help to foster a culture of innovation by concentrating on mechanisms that facilitate personal interactions between firms and academics and create banks of social capital. This can be achieved both locally and globally by augmenting the ideas, materials and resources available in one region through effective use of international connections with other leading institutions in different countries. The culture of entrepreneurship is created by the fusion of ideas, resources, know-how and technologies leveraged by the universities The internationalization process is not entirely a new path for universities to tread in terms of the unknown and unwanted! Universities take particular pride in their international students and staff, global research projects, and participation in the plethora of training, development, knowledge transfer and research initiatives supported by public resources such as those from the European Commission. The difference that universities can make is in the application of this knowledge base to:

a) enable other organizations, especially businesses and industry to use it; and
b) obtain a 'knowledge return' on the knowledge capital invested in the process.

Typically, universities set up projects after obtaining resources from public or private sources. These projects connect universities in one region of one country with a 'compatible' region in another. Compatibility is secured by a common subject base of mutual expertise among the partner HEIs and the bringing together of industry partners, ideally from a local industry cluster, and supportive public support services. They establish an international network that allows for visits, exchange of information on potential markets, applied research and training opportunities, intelligence on technologies and possible sources of finance for new projects. The 'knowledge return' takes the form of new data, information, case studies, a base for research through a new body of potential respondents, resources and connections that can be reinvested in the main business of universities – research and teaching. There is a special 'knowledge exchange' premium on such activities in that the beneficiaries of projects are the participating firms (from the same regions as the universities) which establish real business connections with their overseas counterparts.

A good example is the 'Internationalization of Entrepreneurial Clusters' project at the University of Essex (at the Centre for Entrepreneurship Research, Essex Business School), which brings together complementary regions in China, India and the UK and their HEIs, SMEs, trade representative bodies and policy makers, to work together in generating new business opportunities in specific and connected industrial sectors). This is an interesting triple helix case study of a university using and leveraging its own international contacts (students, research collaborators, formal and informal HEI links, work with government agencies, corporate connections and small firm representative groups) in the countries stated above.

Mini case study 9.1: Universities and the internationalization of entrepreneurial clusters

The **'Internationalization of Entrepreneurial Clusters'** (IEC) project was developed by the School of Entrepreneurship and Business (SEB),[2] University of Essex, UK, as a forum for sharing experience and learning within selected growth clusters in the UK and partner countries. The focus of the pilot project was on partnerships with regions in India.

The project helped to establishing working links between a network of businesses and institutions in specific business clusters, selected jointly by the lead institutions in partner countries. The project was designed as a unique platform for business-to-business activity, and university–industry interaction for regional development within growing, international business clusters. Critical to the project and its international character was the involvement of all stakeholders connected to entrepreneurship and business development. The project evolved from the initial pilot scheme, 'Clustered Advantage', developed jointly by SEB with the support of the British Council in New Delhi, India, and UK Trade and Investment offices in the Eastern region of the UK.

Objectives

The main objectives of the project were:

a) *Competitiveness, Innovation and Internationalization:* to enable accelerated growth and competitiveness of UK and partner country businesses (especially SMEs) in appropriate and compatible clusters, through internationalization (from trade, imports and exports through to strategic alliances, joint ventures and other business-to-business links);

b) *Policy development:* to generate conducive internationalization policies, structures and strategies, and instruments to enable the above;

c) *Identifying and developing new markets:* to enable businesses and especially SMEs in manufacturing and manufacturing services sector in the UK and partner countries to explore international markets with a view to creating new market investment opportunities for both the UK and partner countries;

d) **Technology and knowledge-sharing:** to facilitate interactive technology and knowledge-sharing between businesses and institutions in regional clusters;

e) **Learning and research:** to promote better awareness and improved learning opportunities for all key stakeholders through an action research/learning programme supporting participating stakeholders;

f) **Regional innovation and entrepreneurship:** to enable a sustainable programme of activities at the regional level for innovation and entrepreneurship.

Rationale for the Project

The IEC project is unique in its representation of the joint interests of businesses, business support organizations, policy-making organizations and higher education Institutions in both the UK and partner countries. It took time, patience and a degree of ingenuity to bring together these disparate interests and start the process of working together across national boundaries. The phenomenon of 'clusters' makes this possible because of:

- the increasing recognition today of the importance of regions;
- the creation and dissemination of knowledge in geographical concentrations of firms and institutions;
- the paradoxical significance of their global content; and
- the call for greater links among innovators.

When the import of such developments is coupled with the economic and social advantages of connections between two (or more) regions in two (or more) different countries, the possibilities of economic gain abound.

The main assumptions include the following:

- Cluster-based economic and business development is a central policy plank in many countries in the world.
- Cluster-based business activity generates greater productivity, new technology development, employment opportunities and skills enhancement.
- Cooperation and interaction between SMEs and stakeholders leads to the realization of greater competitive advantage.
- Networking between regional clusters allows for an exchange of a critical mass of knowledge and resources necessary for sustainable economic growth.
- A global village environment is better supported through sustainable growth based on an optimal level of activities involving a critical mass of resources.
- Knowledge-sharing is best facilitated through stakeholders who have benefited from an international education, such as the UK alumni in China and India.

Activities

- **Profiling of compatible clusters and key stake holders:** Project managers led by experts in UK and their counterparts in higher education institutions (HEIs) in partner countries helped to identify the stakeholders on either side.
- **Initial orientation on clustering internationalization:** Project managers led by experts in UK and their counterparts in HEIs in partner countries carried out initial

orientation to the project and its objectives together with information about the regions and countries involved in a workshop.

- *Design of activity programme:* Project managers led by experts in UK and their counterparts in HEIs in partner countries carried out this activity through consultation among the stakeholders.
- *Design of monitoring and evaluating mechanisms:* Project managers led by experts in UK and their counterparts in HEIs in partner countries developed the instruments for monitoring and evaluation through consultation.
- *Implementation of the action learning programme:* Preparatory work: development of individual business plans for the SMEs.
- *Visit to partner countries:* Cluster-based site visits; business-to-business forum; management development programme; general reception.
- *In UK and partner countries:* Follow-up action-planning programme at the SMEs by the HEIs; support to SMEs by HEIs.
- *Feedback and actions taken:* Undertaken by HEIs by monitoring activities of the SMEs.
- *Evaluation – continuously throughout the project:* Project managers at each end.
- *Completion report – 1 month:* Project managers.

Stakeholders

- **Project leader:** School of Entrepreneurship and Business, University of Essex, United Kingdom.
- **Lead cluster partners in the UK and partner countries:**

  - businesses from clusters in selected regions;
  - trade bodies and business federations;
  - HEIs from the above regions;
  - regional and other development agencies.

Student involvement

The IEC Project was opened out to students in the UK and those from partner countries studying in the UK. Plans are now in place for graduate students to enrol on PG Certificate programmes in Entrepreneurial Management and in Global Project Management, which will link them to Chinese and Indian businesses operating or intending to locate in the UK and their British counterparts exploring opportunities in China and India. This programme is expected to be launched in 2011.

Evolution of the first successful pilot

The 'Internationalization of Clusters' project generated its first success story emerging from the activities linking the East and the West Midlands regions in the UK to Delhi, and its surrounds, in India. This bilateral linkage centred round the interests of the 'food and agro industry', advanced engineering and the ICT/multimedia clusters. Two visits by groups of firms and other stakeholders from the UK to India, and two visits from

Indian counterparts to the region, have tested successfully the possibilities and the objectives of the project. Success was evinced in

a) the identification of regional clusters which feature networks of firms and key demand and supply-side organizations (including public sector agencies), which demonstrate sufficient critical mass to have a 'cluster' status;
b) the identification of policies in both regions that support cluster-type business and economic development initiatives;
c) the identification of a pilot group of firms in both regions that could forge business links (joint ventures, strategic alliances, trade, other networks), supported by pubic and private agencies;
d) the identification of key issues, technologies and business opportunities on which to base international relationships;
e) the development of working links between higher education institutions;
f) the production of initial research reports analysing trends in clusters and in internationalization prospects;
g) the formulation and agreement of action plans with which to build on the initial advantages gained from this project; and
h) the contribution to the development of the international strategy for the eastern region.

Benefits for participating stakeholders

What do businesses gain from the project?

- direct contact and introductions to businesses in UK and partner countries in key growth clusters;
- visits to cluster-based sites in the UK and partner countries;
- business-to-business networking with fast-growing business counterparts;
- contact with key business support and development agencies in UK and partner countries in participating regions;
- direct knowledge of country- and region-specific business conditions;
- direct knowledge of new ways of working in changing economic environments and in the international context;
- access to R&D, information and training support provision from higher education institutions;
- high potential for innovation based on new product and service development in new markets, involving collaboration and competition;
- participation in management development programme (MDP);
- project reports and learning materials from MDP.

What do support agencies gain from the project?

- implementation of internationalization support programmes;
- realization and implementation of cluster-based internationalization of firms;
- access to cluster-based research reports on links between international clusters;

- access and use of learning materials for businesses;
- using outcomes of pilot programme to develop major international initiatives;
- supporting and developing international aspects of economic and business development strategy;
- developing a database for international technology transfer and business networking through direct links with regional agencies.

What do higher education institutions gain from the project?

- direct contact with and access to counterparts in leading institutions in both countries;
- development of cluster-based R&D projects;
- working directly with SMEs and business support agencies in both countries;
- developing new working links with counterparts;
- developing new learning materials for extended use and future accreditation of programmes;
- developing an international profile.

The pilot project involved eight SMEs from the UK and 20 from India, three HEIs from India and two universities from the UK; a British Regional Development Agency which sponsored part of the project, and a range of government agencies from the Delhi-NCR region. Five out of the eight businesses were able to register direct business contact and a working link, and the universities also developed new initiatives for research and education projects centred around the interests of their business partners.

Since the completion of the project, the Centre for Entrepreneurship Research at Essex Business School has:

- led another regional initiative involving nine UK representatives from the creative industries of ICT, new media, software development, film, graphic design and advertising in the western region of India in Mumbai and Pune; and
- established links with a university and one of the best-known information technology parks just outside Shanghai in the high-technology region of Wuxi in China to develop a new version of this successful project.

(Source: CER, 2005)

Regional variation and differentiation

Some distinction needs to be made between regions which have a well-established profile in entrepreneurship and those that do not. It is often argued that well-developed regions benefit mainly from high levels of innovation within the surrounding region and do not depend on HEI activities fostering entrepreneurship (e.g. academic spin-offs), while less developed regions benefit from a proactive role of HEIs (Clarysse *et al.*, 2005). This distinction provides an interesting analytical construct but does not necessarily reflect reality. It tends to ignore the self-reinforcing nature of successful regions, such as Cambridge in the UK, where existing social capital continues to feed higher levels of HEI-business activity. Second, the majority of academic spin-offs tend to establish themselves in new or novel sectors, such as life sciences and information technologies (Dahlstrand, 2005). In some of these sectors the knowledge production base is often found to be stronger in business than in the universities. The creation of academic spin-offs, therefore, is more a necessity (in the sense that it is through industry-oriented activity that new knowledge can be generated and commercialized faster).

While HEIs in successful regions can build on the richness of social capital in their patch, it may not be appropriate for government policy to continue to support development in those regions where no additionality may be secured.

Both Bartlett (2005) and Formica *et al.* (2005) identify myriad measures and policy instruments that suggest that current policy considerations support multiple levels of HEI activity aimed at entrepreneurship and innovation. Much of this activity takes place at the regional level and there is a clear appreciation of systems of innovation or clusters of economic activity that bring together HEIs, business and government.

It is, therefore, incumbent upon policy makers at the level of both HEIs and government to develop policies and strategies for encouraging entrepreneurship that can make best use of core, existing capabilities, while obtaining a better appreciation of mechanisms for new forms of learning.

PART IV: STRATEGIES, MECHANISMS AND INSTRUMENTS: FORMS AND PROVISION FOR ENTREPRENEURSHIP AND INNOVATION BY HEIs

Numerous studies on HEI–industry links have identified a variety of support measures that purport to create, develop and establish firmly the ways in which HEIs interact with industry and the local community in which they are located. Much of the direct impact can be measured by means of investigating the distribution of university employment, and local purchasing of goods and services. These direct but static measures do not help to obtain an understanding of the role of HEIs in fostering entrepreneurship. The promotion of entrepreneurship is better gauged by a consideration of some of the indirect relationships that provide us with a picture of the dynamic environment of change in different economies.

In common with the Mode 2 framework, the 'triple helix' emphasizes the increased interaction among these institutional actors in industrial economies' innovation systems. Etzkowitz *et al.* further assert that in addition to linkages among institutional spheres, each sphere takes the role of the other. Universities assume entrepreneurial tasks such as marketing knowledge and creating companies even as firms take on an academic dimension, sharing knowledge with one another and training at ever-higher skill levels. The triple helix literature devotes little attention to the 'transformations' in industry and government that are asserted to complement those in universities. The helix's emphasis on a more 'industrial' role for universities may be valid, although it overstates the extent to which these 'industrial' activities are occurring throughout universities, rather than in a few fields of academic research. The model has yet to yield major empirical or research advances, and its value as a guide for future empirical research appears to be limited.

As Goddard *et al.* (1994) and Howells *et al.* (1998) have illustrated in their studies, typical support measures include the transfer of technology based on research, the creation of new firms from university research activities or academic spin-offs, work-related training, business training, economic policy development support and certain non-educational services.

Technology and knowledge transfer and entrepreneurship

Technology transfer has taken a central role in the canon of any university work on external linkages with industry. Some of the reasons attributed to the increasing importance of technology transfer as the third mission (research and teaching being the other two) of universities, include:

- the transformation of the technology base of industry to complex and diverse forms requiring access to external sources of knowledge and technology;
- the growth in the importance of SMEs (since Birch's (1981) seminal study on SMEs), especially in high-technology industries as against the decline in employment in branch plants of large firms; and
- the increasing interest in seeing enhanced industrial appropriation of knowledge produced by universities using public funds.

(Goddard *et al.*, 1994)

To this list can be added the need for HEIs to seek revenues from diverse funding sources as public funding for both research and teaching has shrunk over the years.

The term 'technology transfer' has been overtaken by the notion of 'knowledge transfer' in the modern HEI-industry lexicography, because of the growing recognition of both explicit and tacit forms of knowledge. Technology's association with 'solid', codifiable processes or products implies that the transfer process is linear and that knowledge is produced first within HEIs before it is transferred to industry. Such an understanding does not allow for the recognition of dual forms of knowledge, its multiple sources, and the interactive model of the innovation process best articulated by Kline and Rosenberg (1986). Technology transfer also does not provide any room for the realization of opportunities for new business creation, either in the form of academic spin-offs or by providing appropriate knowledge-based resources for entrepreneurs outside the HEI.

Knowledge is transferred through fairly varied and complex processes including formal mechanisms, casual networks, or 'somewhere in between' (Malecki, 2008).

Indeed, the main processes by which scientific and technological knowledge is exchanged with knowledge from different agents (entrepreneurs, large firms and the government) – namely research collaboration, information and knowledge transfer (via information and expertise of people) and spin-outs – all contain ingredients critical to new venture creation in and the competitiveness of modern economies.

The best of HEIs are 'global players' in that their knowledge-producing functions are at the cutting edge of research, and are valued, respected and sought after by industry across the world. To that extent, a regional agenda may appear to circumscribe their activities. However, because of the very reasons for the importance of technology transfer cited above, and the capacity of local firms to retain their competitive advantage, it is crucial that regions boasting a presence of innovative firms take advantage of premier league research and training expertise available locally. This nexus of interactions is more likely to take place in modern industrial clusters where there is a presence of both innovative firms and industries. But there is no reason to believe that innovative firms in all regions will necessarily work in conjunction with local HEIs, especially where there is either a deficit of HEIs or a shortfall in the type of knowledge production demanded by industry. As Mitra and Abubakar (2005) show in their comparative study of two sub-regions in the UK, entrepreneurship is more likely to be sustainable, first, where there is a correlation between university research activity and local enterprise development, and second, where because of the first link, higher levels of social capital are generated to further boost effective linkages between firms and HEIs.

SMEs that are most likely to seek relationships do so through informal means, including direct contact with faculty, student internships and class assignments. These firms are referred to as extrovert firms (Fuelhart and Glasmeir, 2003; Kingsley and Malecki, 2004). It is difficult to find any clear documentation of these forms of interaction and, as Malecki (2008) observes, where efforts are made to catalogue such activity it is difficulty to track longitudinally the real effects of knowledge transfer on the performance of firms.

There is a lack of empirical evidence showing a causal link between knowledge transfer activities and entrepreneurship or small firm involvement. Perhaps it is difficult to demonstrate such links as there are other factors, not least the availability of suitable forms of new venture finance, influencing new business creation. However, there is some evidence to suggest that venture finance follows regions that provide fertile ground for high-technology ventures. As stated earlier, much of the knowledge necessary for creating and sustaining these ventures is generated at the intersections of HEI–industry links. What can be demonstrated is the kind of relationship that is based more on associations than on cause and effect, leading to the creation of associational economies (Cooke and Morgan, 1998).

Different forms of knowledge transfer in particular regions that promote entrepreneurship are socially embedded. This means that local institutions are themselves entrepreneurial in nature, and are able to respond flexibly to the specific needs of local environments (Gibb, 1993). They need to have absorptive capacity to take advantage of the opportunities for new venture creation that are on offer through knowledge transfer activities. In some cases, they need to set up training programmes to help their staff to acquire specialist skills with which to derive best value from knowledge transfer activities.

Intermediary institutions and processes

To enable knowledge transfer to take place effectively and systematically, several intermediary vehicles or institutions have been set up in various countries.

Science parks and incubators have enjoyed a degree of popularity, despite mixed success in numerous parts of the world. They are referred to as a property-based initiatives that:

- have formal and operational links with a university or HEI;
- are designed to encourage the formation and growth of knowledge-based businesses and other organizations, normally resident on site;
- have a management function which is actively engaged in the transfer of technology and business skills to the organizations on site.

Science parks

Devised originally to help meet the needs of entrepreneurially minded academics, science parks were an American phenomenon of the 1950s. The idea took a long time to transfer across the Atlantic, and it was not until the 1970s that the United Kingdom saw the first such park at Heriott-Watt University, Edinburgh. As the development of other parks took place, it brought into reckoning the roles of a whole range of stakeholders – from local authorities to banks, property developers and others, firmly embedding the parks in the economy – and through this process, the role of universities in regional development.

The International Association of Science Parks (IASP) boasts 400 members in 70 countries worldwide, connecting professionals from these parks from across the globe and providing a range of services for the growth and effectiveness of its tenant firms. As the charts from the United Kingdom Association of Science Parks (UKSPA) suggest, the rise in membership implies a growing trend towards formalization of these organizations, with individual single-site firms representing the largest block of tenants in the parks (Figures 9.1–9.4). SMEs are the main beneficiaries of the parks with small firms (in this case, with up to 15 employees) in particular being the largest representative group. Interestingly, the share of HEI spin-off firms in these parks has declined, suggesting that the firms have moved on from their original conceptualization of university-based agencies for small firm creation. The growth in the share of non-university firms also shows that the parks have probably generated a growing interest among other technology-based firms seeking a good address, high-quality facilities and various forms of dedicated support.

It has been argued that, as universities are a prime source of knowledge, linkages with such institutions should facilitate the transfer of knowledge through exchanges of people, contracts or sponsorship. Tenant firms are, therefore, expected to carry out their research in universities (Lofsten and Lindelof, 2002).

Westhead and Storey (1994) have also emphasized the importance of linkages with universities for new ventures. Their findings showed low incidences of linkages between off-park firms and universities, and higher incidences of linkages for on-park firms. This difference acquires a particular poignancy when a comparison is made between firms on and off parks in the same 'assisted' (special support by government) area, with small firms off-park showing a higher rate of closure than their park counterparts. Since there is not much of a difference in the closure rates of firms in science parks in either assisted areas or outside assisted areas, it could be argued that linkages with higher educational institutions (HEIs) increases new venture survival rates (Westhead and Storey, 1994). Fergusson and Olofsson (2004) also found that cooperation with universities showed significant differences in the growth patterns of on-park and off-park firms, with higher levels of growth being detected in firms associated with linkages to universities. There are question marks over the extent to which localized technology transfer benefits (as between the university and its science park firms)

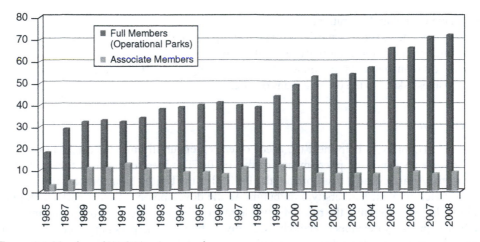

Figure 9.1 Number of UKSPA science parks

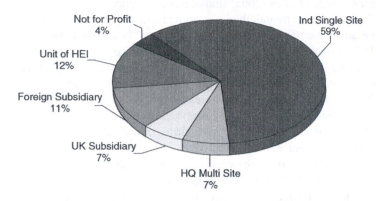

Figure 9.2 Status of tenant companies

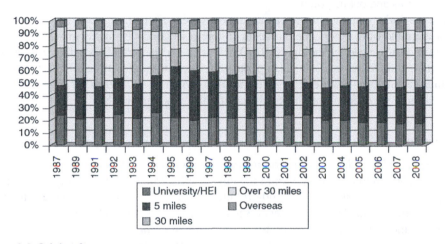

Figure 9.3 Origin of tenants

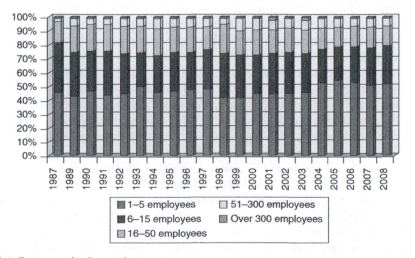

Figure 9.4 Company size by employment

accrue to tenant firms. Phillips (2005) finds cases of technology transfer but not necessarily with the universities, even though the ventures had a faculty member as a principal.

A prestige address close to a 'centre of excellence' is an inevitable attraction, at least in theory. But proximity is not a condition for linkage or interaction with such centres (Johannison, *et al.*, 1994), and it is doubtful whether parks enhance the prospect or propensity of new firm formation. It has also been argued that the establishment of a science park does not create the opportunities for new firm creation or economic regeneration by itself. What is needed is a an innovation or regional ecosystem that includes a constellation of highly specialized firms, support services for such firms, and mechanisms for connections with larger firms (Bahrami and Evans, 1995; Mitra, 2002). Whether planning specifically for a science park actually delivers the goods for entrepreneurship is a debatable matter. As Macdonald and Deng (2004) show, serendipity and social capital drawn from the benefits of agglomeration and spillovers, rather than deterministic planning, have helped to create fertile playing fields such as Silicon Valley (see also Chapters 6 and 10 for references to creative environments and public policy).

Science parks with incubators can attract entrepreneurs with higher levels of education, knowledge and work experience. These factors are associated with higher growth rates, easier adoption of advanced technologies, R&D activities and better collaborative arrangements (Colombo and Delmastro, 2002). Do parks with incubators offer more effective conditions for high-technology-based entrepreneurship and economic regeneration? To try to answer this question, we need to examine the incubator phenomenon briefly.

Incubators

The closure of the Massey Ferguson manufacturing plant in 1959 in Batavia, New York, left a large idle building in that part of the city. Charles Muncuso, who bought the building (Phipps, 2002; Hackett and Dilts, 2004b) failed to find a big tenant and this resulted in the building being available for entrepreneurs to rent in small sections . This event led to the birth of the first incubator, the Batavia Industrial Center (Aerts *et al.*, 2007; Phipps, 2002; Stevens, 2004). Others argue that the first incubator was developed as an organizational entity at the Rensselaer Polytechnic Institute (Etzkowitz, 2002).

The growth of the incubation industry was initially slow until the 1970s, when the business incubation concept was embraced as a global phenomenon (CSES and ECED-G, 2002). To date, the incubation industry is one of the fastest-growing global industries (Chandra, 2007; CSES and ECED-G, 2002) with well over 5,000 incubators spread around the world (Adkins, 2007). The emergence of the business incubation industry in the UK followed the collapse of the steel industry (Costa-David *et al.*, 2002). Early incubator initiatives in the UK started in 1972 as part of the development of science parks, especially the Cambridge and Herriot-Watt Science Parks (Colombo and Delmastro, 2002). The slow start has given way to fast growth rates recorded in the industry's late comers such as China, which according to Chandra (2007) has the second largest number of incubators after the United States, at more than 500. Brazil is ranked fourth in the list of lead incubator countries, with 400 incubators. In the UK, the number of incubators rose from 25 in 1997 to 250 in 2002 (Phan *et al.*, 2005). and to over 325 incubators as at 2007 (UK Trade and Investment, 2007). Figure 9.5 shows how incubators have evolved over time to create a varied family of different types, forms and shapes.

There is some dispute over the actual numbers of incubators. For example, Phan *et al.* (2005) noted that there were 850 incubators in the European Union in 2001, while Costa-David *et al.* (2002) records 911 for the same year. The lack of accurate and global statistical

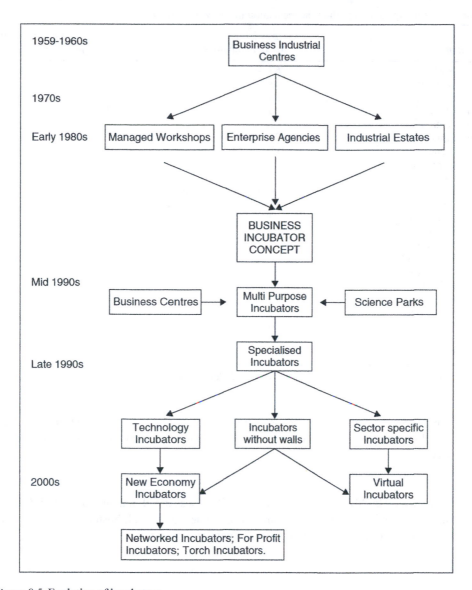

Figure 9.5 Evolution of incubators

Source: CSES-ECED-G (2002); Hannon (2004); Hughes *et al.* (2007); Aerts *et al.* (2007); Phipps (2002); Chandra (2007); Hackett and Dilts (2004b).

data is blamed on the newness of the industry (OECD, 1999). Table 9.3 gives an overview of the growth of the incubation industry in 22 countries, while Figure 9.6 shows the number of international incubators in different parts of the world.

Various definitions of incubators tend to both explain and confuse the picture. The National Business Incubation Association (NBIA) of the United States of America (USA) and the United Kingdom Incubation Association (UKB1) define incubation as follows:

Table 9.3 Examples of growth of the incubation industry in numbers

Country	Up to 2001 No. of incubators	Between 2001 and 2007 No. of incubators
1. Austria	63	
2. Belgium	13	
3. Brazil	160	400
4. China	200	500
5. Denmark	7	
6. Finland	26	
7. France	192	
8. Germany	300	
9. Greece	7	
10. Ireland	6	
11. Italy	45	
12. Luxembourg	2	
13. Macau	1	
14. Malaysia	1	
15. Netherlands	6	
16. North America	12	950
17. Poland	63	111
18. Portugal	23	
19. Singapore	1	
20. Spain	38	
21. Sweden	39	
22. United Kingdom	144	325

Source: Costa-David *et al.* (2002); Phan *et al.* (2005); Chandra (2007).

A business support process that accelerates the successful development of start-up and fledgling companies by providing entrepreneurs with an array of targeted resources and services.

(NBIA)

a unique and highly flexible combination of business development processes, infrastructure and people, designed to nurture and grow new and small businesses by supporting them through the early stages of development and change.

(UKBI)

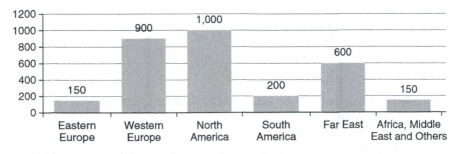

Figure 9.6 No of international Incubators in 2002

Source: CSES and ECED-G (2002).

The Centre for Strategy and Evaluation Services (CSES) defines a business incubator as:

> an organisation that accelerates and systematises the process of creating successful enterprises by providing them with a comprehensive and integrated range of support.
>
> (CSES and ECED-G, 2002, p9)

To these working definitions of incubators we can add a list of academic insights and explanations as listed in Table 9.4.

As with many academic pursuits, there is very little agreement over the definition of incubators. Some definitions tend to focus on the form and nature of incubators, viewing incubators as organizations (Phan *et al.*, 2005; Bollingtoft and Ulhoi, 2005; CSES and ECED-G, 2002; Soentano and Geenhuizen, 2005; Chandra, 2007). Not all incubators are property based; there are also virtual incubators, and definitions focusing on bricks and mortar do not take into account the processes carried out by the organization to ensure new venture creation. Incubators are also not limited to shared office space and administrative services. They also provide support in the form of mentoring, coaching and networking. Finally, incubators are also structured organizations with operational systems in place. Like other systems, the business incubation system has inputs such as finance, stakeholder objectives and management skills (CSES and ECED-G, 2002).

Seen as a 'process', the incubator is characterized by four areas of value creation which take the form of the main activities executed by business incubators, including business need

Table 9.4 Incubator definitions

Incubator definition	Contributors
Incubators are property-based organizations with identifiable administrative centres focused on the mission of business acceleration through knowledge agglomeration and resource sharing.	Phan *et al.* (2005), p. 167)
Business incubator is an umbrella term for any organization that provide access to affordable office space and shared administrative services.	Bollingtoft and Ulhoi (2005)
Facility with adaptable space that small businesses can lease on flexible terms and at reduced rents. Support services – financial, managerial, technical and administrative – are available and shared, depending on the nature of tenants' needs.	Kuratko and Hodgetts, (2007), p. 221
Dynamic tools for fostering new ventures	Chandra (2007)
Location in which entrepreneurs can receive pro-active, value-added support, and access to critical tools, information, education, contacts, resources and capital that may otherwise be unaffordable, inaccessible or unknown.	Bayhan, (2006), p. 3
An organization – private or public – which provides resources that enhance the founding of new small businesses.	Löfsten and Lindelöf (2002)
Facilities that houses young small firms to help them develop quickly into competitive businesses.	Hughes *et al.* (2007)
Shared office space facility that seeks to provide its incubatees with strategic value-adding intervention system of monitoring and business assistance.	Hackett and Dilts (2004a, 2004b)
Organizations dedicated to support of emerging new ventures.	Bergek and Norrman (2008)

diagnosis, selection and mentoring, provision of access to finance, and provision of access to incubator networks (Hackett and Dilts; 2004b). The outputs are available at three levels: the short-term level emphasizing survival and talent, the intermediate level concerned with viable firms and firm closure, and the long-term level which focuses on an increase in business churn (Hackett and Dilts, 2004b). A third view of incubation outputs is offered at the operational level and suggests that business incubation success could be determined by physical space, networking, types of services, and admission and exit criteria (CSES and ECED-G, 2002). In essence, the success of the incubation process is determined by elements of selection, monitoring, assistance and resource infusion (Bergek and Norrman, 2008; Hackett and Dilts, 2004a; Hackett and Dilts, 2004b; Hackett and Dilts, 2008) and incubator mediation (Bergek and Norrman, 2008). Figure 9.7 depicts incubation as a system with inputs, process and outputs.

Science parks and incubators have evolved over time to play varied roles in different economies with or without the involvement of HEIs and direct academic inputs. However, a key instigator of their development was the idea of academic venturing or academic spin-offs. We stop briefly to take stock of the phenomenon of academic spin-offs.

Academic spin-offs

Where HEIs are directly engaged in entrepreneurship knowledge transfer is through the mechanism of academic spin-offs. Shane (2004) defines a university spin-off as 'a new company founded to exploit a piece of intellectual property created in an academic institution' (p. 4). This definition includes all start-up firms created by the students and employees of universities. The creation and development of academic spin-offs is not recorded systematically across different countries, and this again creates problems for definition. Given this constraint, the actual number of recorded spin-offs is around 2 percent of all new firm creations in any OECD country (Callan, 2001; cited in Dahlstrand, 2005), with the USA leading with the highest rates of, on average, two new firms per research institution per year.

The low levels of such activity, the long gestation period and slow growth rates (Callan, 2001) suggest that spin-off activities may actually be quite marginal in the scheme of entrepreneurial activities. Furthermore, the close association between research-intensive HEIs and the formation of the spin-off firms in their backyard, especially in clusters, indicates

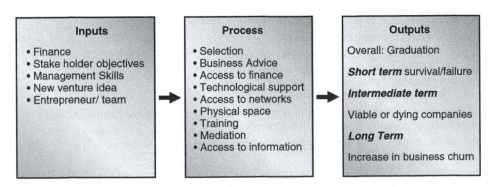

Figure 9.7 Business incubation as a system with inputs, process and outputs

Source: adapted from Lumpkin and Ireland (1988); CSES and ECED-G (2002); Hackett and Dilts (2004b); Bergek and Norrman (2008).

first that there is likely to be uneven spatial distribution of these activities, and second that any pronounced effort at supporting such activity can exacerbate economic disparity between regions. They do, however, reinforce the location-specific nature of entrepreneurship.

As Shane (2004) observes, even a casual observation of the academic spin-off phenomenon cannot disguise the fact that some of the most important technology firms ever created were academic spin-offs. An exemplary list includes, among many others:

- Digital Equipment Corporation (DEC), founded by Kenneth Olson to exploit intellectual property that he developed when working at Lincoln Laboratory at the Massachusetts Institute of Technology;
- Wang Computers, founded by An Wang to develop technology developed at Harvard University's computer laboratory; and
- TurboGenset, spun off from Imperial College in the UK.

Stanford University funded the research project of two of its PhD students – Larry Page and Sergey Brin – that resulted in the creation of the popular search engine Google in 1998. The university's initial investment translated into an equity stake of 1.8 million shares when Google Inc. went public in 2004. The university made $336 million by selling part of the stock in 2004–05. It also gets steady revenue from the patented technology of the search engine. To date, Stanford holds an equity stake in at least 80 companies, out of about 1,200 that got their start on campus.

Hewlett-Packard Co., Sun Microsystems Inc., Cisco Systems Inc., Yahoo Inc., EBay Inc., Logitech International SA and Dolby Laboratories Inc. also obtained start-up funding from Stanford funds. These firms have contributed to both life-changing technologies for the world and considerable revenues for Stanford University. The revenue from the sale of stocks is treated as a form of endowment (well over $15 billion) by Stanford University. Stanford is of course not the only university in the US to generate large additional revenues through such activities.

What is it that spin-offs do and achieve? Spin-offs are considered to be agents of change. They encourage economic value by:

- producing innovative products that satisfy customer needs and wants;
- generating jobs especially for highly educated people;
- attracting investment in development of university technology; and
- generating localized impact.

(Shane, 2004)

Table 9.5 provides an overview of some of the economic development benefits that spin-offs generate.

From a policy perspective, support for academic spin-off activities can be a costly exercise. In such scenarios, rather than direct forms of support for spin-offs, the value of spin-off activities can be realized indirectly by considering their role as intermediaries between industry and HEIs or as research boutiques (Dahlstrand, 2005. Countries that have gone down the route of encouraging spin-off activities will need to tread carefully when developing strategies for HEIs and local entrepreneurship development. A blanket policy decision is unlikely to have an impact on economic growth. Differentiated policies for regions are also unlikely to have any early impact unless a clear assessment is made of the nature and scope of such development in different territories. If academic spin-off activities have better prospects

Table 9.5 The value of academic spin-offs and economic development

Spin-off value and achievements	Description
Economic value generator and multiplier	American universities generated \$33.5 billion in economic value added (Cohen 2000); 40% of all high technology firms founded in France between 1987 and 1997 were university spin-offs (Mustar, 1997); 17% of new technology firms founded in the Cambridge area of the UK were university spin-offs (Wickstead, 1985); lesser dependence on old industries in region and economic diversification plus novel products and services
Job creation	280,000 jobs in 19 years between 1980 and 1999 (Cohen, 2000); 44 jobs on average per spin-off firm in the UK (Charles and Conway, 2001); 53 spin-off firms generated 650 full time jobs in University of Linkoping in Sweden up to 1992 (Blair and Hitchens, 1998); higher value than licensing of university technologies; knowledge-intensive jobs
Inducing investment in university technologies	

in playing intermediary or niche roles as part of an established set of policies and activities, such as those for clusters, then their promotion becomes secondary to the development of clusters and other primary activities.

Entrepreneurship education and training

Skills training and entrepreneurship

The fostering of entrepreneurship in a region is not necessarily a function of an HEI's direct intervention in new venture creation. It can also be a function of the training of people who could contribute to the development of entrepreneurial organizations through their employment. The focus on certain skills and competencies, especially those of problem-solving, creativity, and inter-personal and cognitive skills, can lead to the development of entrepreneurial capabilities and mind sets necessary for entrepreneurial activity.

There is, therefore, a need for both HEIs and business to articulate, recognize and promote the type of skills that enable and enhance such capabilities. This aspect of training to support entrepreneurship is often ignored by HEIs, industry and policy makers. Such training can be embedded in the provision of HEIs and needs to be distinguished from entrepreneurship education or training (see below for an exposition of the latter).

Skills training in HEIs is also concerned with the employability of students. HEI effort has thus been directed at offering a range of skills and competencies, embedding them in the curriculum. Employer involvement in training and mentoring, both in the HEIs' provision and in the workplace, also feature prominently in various programmes. The nature of employee/employer involvement and questions of employability are a function of both the subjects studied at HEIs and different sectoral interests. Certain subjects (for example, Business Studies or Computer Science) increasingly demand novel, innovative forms of or approaches to learning. These approaches involve the sharing of resources and differentiated pedagogic platforms. Entrepreneurship and business education, especially in the USA, make wide use of entrepreneurs and industry practitioners in the teaching of programmes (Zahra, 2005), thus adopting similar ideas to those related to work-based or workplace learning. These forms of entrepreneurial learning can better prepare employees and students for work in innovative organizations. They also contribute to independent forms of learning that allow for self-sufficiency in the acquisition of knowledge and skills and their deployment in employment, entrepreneurship within organizations, and new business creation.

New trends

Alongside the growth in indirect forms of promotion of entrepreneurship, HEIs in both OECD and non-OECD countries have started committing themselves to entrepreneurship education and training. The growing value of entrepreneurship as a subject of study is based on the following key factors (Mitra, 2002):

- the growing importance of SMEs and the evolution of large firms as distributed and semi-autonomous units of activity;
- the challenge to HEIs to meet the demands of economic and social change, and the consequent attention to entrepreneurship in business education (Porter and McKibbin, 1988);
- the large volume of academic research and empirical evidence differentiating start-up venture activity and that of mature organizations, enabling the legitimization of entrepreneurship as a field of study within academia (Hills and Morris, 1998);
- the need for graduates to acquire a wide array of entrepreneurial skills; and
- the growing attention to cross-disciplinary and cross-functional integration in both education and industrial activity, coupled with the idea that the qualitative, applied and subjective elements of study are as important as the quantitative, conceptual and analytical forms.

(Ivancevich, 1991)

The equation of entrepreneurship with SME development is in part attributable to the particular importance of SMEs in job creation and innovation, and their dispro-portionately larger presence among all firms in most economies. SMEs play a key role in new, pan-organizational forms of economic development, such as clusters, and derive competitive advantage through flexible specialization, economies of scale and scope, and agglomeration. Assessing this role of SMEs requires critical understanding of:

- the type of people who engage in these activities (*entrepreneurial people*);
- the types of organizations created by these people or ones in which they thrive (*entrepreneurial organizations*); and
- the wider environment in which enterprising people and entrepreneurial organizations evolve (*entrepreneurial environment*).

Firm-size-related issues do not necessarily act as constraints to a proper understanding of entrepreneurship. Entrepreneurship is a leaky concept (Mitra, 2002), and the notions of 'smallness', flexibility, innovation, new opportunity identification and realization can also be said to apply to other types of organizations. Larger entrepreneurial firms increasingly demand entrepreneurial people and seek to operate in small, autonomous and entrepreneurial units. Community-based organizations seek creative, entrepreneurial people to identify opportunities for self-sufficiency and innovative resolutions of problems in creative social environments, in their evolution as social enterprises. A wider application of the concept of entrepreneurship puts less emphasis on types and traits of entrepreneurs for particular forms of economic activity, and other static features. Rather, there is a growing recognition of defining entrepreneurship as the process of creating value by bringing together a unique package of resources to exploit an opportunity (Stevenson *et al.*, 1985). The people and organizations creating value are those whose behaviour and skills are applied individually, or collectively, to help individuals and organizations of various kinds to cope with uncertainty and complexity as a means of personal fulfilment (Gibb, 2000).

How do HEIs in both traditional OECD and other countries make provision for entrepreneurship education and training? Zahra (2005) refers to the extensive and varied forms of entrepreneurship in the USA, from high school through to doctoral training. In US HEIs, most entrepreneurship education takes place at the graduate level, quite often allowing for a combination of the skills of traditional academics with those of entrepreneurs to co-teach specialized courses, and a broad set of courses that exploit the intellectual capital within universities and the human capital in industry. Undergraduate training tends to focus on skills training and functional aspects of new business creation (see also Solomon (2005) for a detailed analysis of content, forms and methods of study in the USA, and Roman (2005) for details on entrepreneurship education and training in Hungary).

OECD countries tend to equate entrepreneurship more with the successful management of small business. Some of the newer EU countries, such as Poland and Slovenia, have developed initiatives that reflect the tradition of vocational education centred around small business creation and ownership (Zahra, 2005). Entrepreneurship education remains limited despite the creation of new Chairs of Entrepreneurship and Centres for Entrepreneurship Research. Unlike the USA, European OECD countries tend to give their programmes a distinctive academic flavour, grounding the study of entrepreneurship in some of the traditional disciplines of economics, sociology and psychology. There is a growing trend in science-based entrepreneurship, with science and technology subjects offering electives in entrepreneurship, and a gradual convergence of interest in the practical aspects of entrepreneurship among both US and European institutions.

Varied modes and methods

A variety of methods, ranging from hands-on training, creativity techniques, case studies, communication training, inter-personal skills development, team working, the use of entrepreneurs, role playing and business plan development, inform the experiential thrust of entrepreneurship programmes (Zahra, 2005; Mitra, 2002). The late entry of, for example, CESE countries, and in some cases the preoccupation with forms of governance and legal frameworks to facilitate greater risk taking (Roman, 2005; Zahra, 2005) have slowed down progress in these countries. Estonia is one of the few exceptions (Varblane *et al.*, 2005; Zahra, 2005) introducing entrepreneurship education in the 1990s. Donor-led initiatives, with a strong vocational underpinning, are sometimes the most important means of educating entrepreneurs in south-east European countries (OECD, 2003b). Multiple and diverse forms reflect the various stages of development of different economies, and it will take some time before a pattern of activities can be found in such provision.

Despite the differences in approach to entrepreneurship education and training between different OECD and other countries, it is unclear whether HEIs should adopt any templates of learning about and teaching entrepreneurship. Different approaches reflect the economic status of countries and their approach to education. The differences in approach are, to some extent, also due to the lack of a consensus on the value of entrepreneurship education and whether or how it can be taught. The absence of uniformity of content or pedagogy adds to the confusion (Solomon, 2005).

Entrepreneurship education and business education

The confusion also stems from the conflation of entrepreneurship education with business education. The equation of entrepreneurship with SME management is a good example of this conflation. The need for a quicker response to exploit business opportunity and the uncertain and equivocal nature of the business entry, require a focus on the integrated nature, specific skills and business life cycle issues inherent in new ventures (Solomon, 2005). Designing and developing education programmes that can meet these objectives is more appropriate for entrepreneurship education. It also helps to differentiate entrepreneurship education from business education or SME management training.

A movement towards a commonly accepted definition of entrepreneurship, the division of entrepreneurship into individual and corporate entrepreneurship, a move away from exploratory to causal research and the availability of sophisticated research designs, methods and techniques, also add to the differentiated value of entrepreneurship education and research (Solomon, 2005).

In reality, the design of the curriculum and the form of delivery of entrepreneurship education is influenced by its location within the field of management education. The prevailing view is that the form and content will help the learner – the start-up entrepreneur or the innovative manager – to find answers to problems, which they will then apply to practice: 'The locus of such thinking is the positivist epistemology of practice or the model of "technical rationality" (Schon, 1999) which states that professional activity consists of instrumental problem-solving made rigorous by the application of scientific theory and practice' (Mitra, 2002).

Differentiated content

In making concessions to 'practical pedagogy', entrepreneurship programmes only address part of the challenge of entrepreneurship education. The determinants of rigour and relevance prompt the avoidance of the messy bits that fall outside the scope of technical solutions to problems. Value creation and the study of behaviour to cope with issues of uncertainty and complexity in different new-venture-creating situations require locally mediated forms of learning that are characterized by 'reflection', 'reflecting in action', 'knowing in action' and 'reflecting in practice' (Schon, 1999). Entrepreneurship education offers management education a new lease of life. It goes beyond the limitations of management education, because unlike the latter it is concerned more with the cycle of discovery and the expansive horizons of opportunity identification and realization than with reductionist approaches to the management of organizational routines and structures. As Noteboom (2000) observes:

> There must be a relation between entrepreneurship and the cycle of discovery. There is a variety of notions of entrepreneurship . . . and different types of entrepreneurship may be seen as belonging to different stages in the cycles of discovery . . . different notions of entrepreneurship emphasize different things in different combinations . . .
>
> •   innovation (Bentham, Thuen, Schumpeter and perhaps Say);
> •   creative destruction through novel combinations (Schumpeter);

- the identification and utilization of possibilities for consumption and production (Cantillon, Smith, Menger, Mises, Hayek, Kirzner);
- the configuration and management of production factors for efficient production (Say, Marshall, Mises);
- the provision of capital.

Recognizing the diversity in entrepreneurship which reflects the above 'cycle of discovery' is the key to entrepreneurship education and training. Different cycles prevail in varied economic and social environments. It also provides for basic principles of entrepreneurship education and corresponds to the appropriateness of different forms of education provision in different locales of opportunity. Moreover, recognition of the diversity of entrepreneurship in education and training programmes allows for the greater appreciation of different forms of entrepreneurship, from new start-up ventures through to corporate and social entrepreneurship.

Another form of diversity can be introduced through international collaboration in entrepreneurship education programmes. New and emerging market economies can avoid reinventing the wheel by collaborating on certain programmes, adapting courses to meet local needs, making joint provision by different institutions possible, honouring the Bologna protocol for recognition of credits, staff and student exchange together with entrepreneurs, case study development and other means.

Measurement and evaluation

Finally, measuring the impact of entrepreneurship education and training is the natural outcome of any policy that provides support for its provision. What needs to be measured is of critical importance. Direct outcomes of entrepreneurship skills training (such as creating a new business venture) can be measured more effectively than indirect ones of attitudinal change and raising awareness. But even direct outcomes cannot simply be attributed to training and education. Policy makers typically look at job creation as an overriding measure for most programmes, together with other outputs such as the representation of women, or new product development. These measures can help to achieve some social and economic objectives, especially where there is under-representation or a need for economic regeneration. These 'performance indicators' can have both national and local dimensions, but their main limitation is that they only measure outputs.

What needs to be measured, especially at the regional level, are outcomes of practice exemplified by the nature and relevance of entrepreneurship education provision, the network-based approach to education and training, and shared pedagogic platforms among different providers. Of equal value is a measure of entrepreneurship education that helps to evaluate the generation of an entrepreneurial culture in institutions and in regions, as evinced in the attitudes of people towards entrepreneurship before and after training. HEIs should be able to track enrolment on entrepreneurship courses over time, the type and mix of students on these courses, the number of business created (perhaps more than the number of examinations passed!), the type of jobs created and the levels of sophistication of products created (Zahra, 2005). HEIs could also track the levels of involvement of staff, staff training in entrepreneurship, the development of institutional frameworks for entrepreneurship activity, and proportionate investment of resources in entrepreneurship education against income derived from entrepreneurial activities in HEIs.

The three key, intricate strands of HEI–industry interaction discussed above have led to overtures for the establishment of entrepreneurial universities. It is easier to find accommodation of new approaches to the provision of learning by HEIs incorporating entrepreneurial values among institutions blessed with a rich tradition of high-quality research and teaching and with significant contributions from donors. The richer the learning base, the greater the propensity for experimenting with new ideas. It is, therefore, not surprising that some of the world's best-known institutions such as Harvard, MIT, Stanford and the University of California (to name just a few) in the US, Cambridge, Warwick and London Business School in the UK, the Indian Institutes of Management and the Indian Institutes of Technology in India, Tsinghua, Peking and Fudan University in China, Nanyang University and the National University of Singapore are among the best providers of entrepreneurship research, education and training, along with their enviable track record in knowledge exchange activities with industry, government and community organizations across the world.

Conclusion

The development of an analytical framework for the proper study of HEIs and their role in fostering entrepreneurship has two purposes:

- it provides a guide to the thematic aspects of the subject; and
- it provides a basis for policy considerations relating to the role of both HEIs and governments in fostering entrepreneurship.

HEIs fostering entrepreneurship generate and use intellectual, human and social capital and various institutional norms and practices to engage with different stakeholders towards that end.

One of the key issues emerging from the analysis of HEI roles and functions in OECD and other countries is the varied and differentiated nature of activities that promote entrepreneurship. The attraction of resources and alterative sources of income are as significant as the strategies adopted by HEIs to better inform and educate people in an era of considerable change. Entrepreneurship is a well-recognized process for dealing with technological, structural, organizational and social change. As HEIs are not exempt from these changes and as they affect forms and methods of higher learning, involvement in entrepreneurial activities is a legitimate response of HEIs. Equally, the growth in the body of knowledge that addresses issues of change and the opportunities for new venture creation that arises from such change provide for serious and concentrated study and investigation.

A second key issue is one that emerges from the involvement in entrepreneurial activities and the provision of entrepreneurship education. The nature of such involvement highlights the regional character of HEIs. This regional character does not cancel the international aspirations of excellence of universities; the latter reinforces the former, together with the growing recognition of endogenous forms of economic growth. The concentration of global economic activity in regions is often supported by HEI research, education, training and knowledge-transfer activities. In this role HEIs are one among many different players in a web of knowledge-producing actors in a region. Their value and their particular contributions are often best realized when research and education provision is linked to the work of other organizations. In this network of organizations learning takes different forms, and the greater the involvement of HEIs in these networks, the greater is the wider impact of learning for economic growth. This network approach challenges traditional HEI orthodoxy and demands alternative policies for its realization.

The regional aspects of entrepreneurship and HEI involvement are best understood through an appreciation of the nature and effect of knowledge spillovers from both HEI research and business activities. The use of tacit forms of knowledge to derive appropriate benefits from spillovers creates opportunities for the better use of human, intellectual and social capital. Although they vary across environments, it is through the spillovers and the use of different forms of capital that HEIs and business promote entrepreneurship in specific regions.

A typical education development policy framework that embraces entrepreneurship could, therefore, benefit from a consideration of the following issues:

- the critical underpinning philosophies affecting the provision of higher education and in particular entrepreneurship education, and their evolution over time;
- the positioning and convergence of different instruments and mechanisms together with their integrated evaluation within different types of institutions;
- the wider learning contexts – local, regional, national and international – in which different HEIs operate.

HEIs have a considerable opportunity to move out of mechanistic and reactive approaches to education and entrepreneurship development and instead to foster entrepreneurship through education, research and knowledge-transfer activity. This involvement can help to change mindsets among both beneficiaries and providers, and generate opportunities for value creation.

Countries emerging from the shadows of a command economy to embrace the peculiarities of the marketplace need to both organize themselves and obtain support for their institutions to promote entrepreneurship. Their HEIs could play an important role in driving some of the change processes, enabling the adoption of policies for the early introduction of entrepreneurship in society, encouraging entrepreneurial attitudes among students, and guiding existing professionals to entrepreneurial careers. Much of this needs be done at both the regional level and in local institutions. Much more needs to be achieved through international collaboration with partners across Europe and elsewhere. Such partnerships should be less about emulation and more about the desire to carve out distinctive entrepreneurial futures for their economy and their institutions.

Self-assessment questions

1. Explain how universities can play a key role in promoting entrepreneurship in their local environments. Why is this role important?
2. Explain the relevance of universities and learning to economic development.
3. To what extent do local factors influence universities and the promotion of entrepreneurship?
4. Enumerate the different mechanisms that universities can use to foster entrepreneurship and innovation.
5. How does knowledge transfer promote and facilitate the innovation process?

Acknowledgements

Some parts of this chapter appeared in an earlier version of the OECD publication *Higher Education and Entrepreneurship*, ed. J. Potter (Paris: OECD, 2008), along with my two chapters 'Towards an Analytical Framework for Policy Development' and 'Higher Education's Role in Entrepreneurship and Economic Development'. I am grateful to Sergio Arzeni, Director of the Centre for Entrepreneurship and the Local Economic and Employment Development programme of the OECD, for permission for their use here.

For the section on science parks, and especially the information on incubators, I am indebted to one of my PhD students, Gaofostse Ntshadi, who allowed me to draw on some of the data, charts and tables she used as part of her PhD studies.

10 Entrepreneurship policy
Its emergence, scope and value

Learning outcomes

In this chapter the reader will:

- obtain a critical overview of the meaning, scope and purpose of entrepreneurship policy;
- distinguish critically between SME development policy and entrepreneurship policy;
- explore the evolution and emergence of entrepreneurship policy from a critical perspective; and
- gain a critical insight into the development of entrepreneurship policy in different environments.

Structure of the chapter

The chapter is constructed to blend theory relating to the meaning, purpose and scope of policy with its relevance for entrepreneurship and the practice of implementing policies in different environments. Following the introduction, the chapter provides the economic backdrop to entrepreneurship policy development, locating its development in terms of the need for a policy response to changing economic conditions today. Part II explores how and why governments become involved with entrepreneurship policy. It shows how the multidisciplinary character of entrepreneurship impacts on policy-making, the type of systems within which policy emerges, its objectives, its distinctiveness (especially with reference to small business policy), its features and the particular contexts that shape such policy-making. Part III considers various approaches to entrepreneurship policy, including different typologies and frameworks that help with our understanding of its value and significance. The final part then returns to the evolution question by elaborating how, when and why approximations of entrepreneurship policy have surfaced to change the direction of government initiatives for economic growth with specific reference to major theoretical models that have shaped our understanding of economic growth in recent times.

Introduction

The focus of this chapter is on public policy and entrepreneurship. Reference here is to policies developed by the governments of sovereign states. Government policy has considerable implications for business creation, growth and development and the ability of businesses to be innovative in particular circumstances. Creating suitable conditions for new businesses to start and thrive, enabling existing firms to grow by developing new products and services in new markets through appropriate tax policies, supportive physical infrastructure, provision for training and information, promoting incubation facilities, research and development facilities and entrepreneurship education are just some of the means by which governments can encourage entrepreneurship in a country and its regions. The chapter explores the scope and purpose of entrepreneurship policy, its principal features, how and why policy has evolved, the connection between economic development entrepreneurship, and some of the key questions that plague observers, analysts and decision makers. The approach is theoretical, with appropriate references to practical considerations and examples.

The types of policies governments create and implement will depend on the stage or circumstances of development of a country and its particular environment. There may well be differences within countries demanding focused and differentiated policy for different regions, each of which has its particular local environment. This chapter should be read in conjunction with Chapter 11 ('Entrepreneurship, Innovation and Economic Development') and Chapter 6 ('The Entrepreneurial Environment').

PART I: THE EMERGENCE OF GOVERNMENT POLICY FOR ENTREPRENEURSHIP

Policy for entrepreneurship and economic growth has enjoyed a rather fragmented and unplanned journey. It has slipped in and out of governmental reckoning as circumstances have changed with times. The bursting of the dot.com bubble and the more recent shenanigans of financiers experimenting with different forms of alleged financial innovations have made the public and policy makers both wary and curious about the positive role of entrepreneurship. What was the vogue of the 1990s, as evinced in books on 'daring visionaries', videos and movies on the ebb and flow of start-up ventures (Hart, 2003) in Silicon Valley, Bangalore, Munich, Guandong, London and Goteburg, and the apparently ready availability of venture capital, business angel money and private equity, seems to have evaporated and given way now to a mix of home-spun and informed scepticism. The large brand names and their larger-than-life Chief Executive Officers, regained momentum almost as if to corroborate Schumpeter's (1942) second phase view that innovation and entrepreneurship were better placed in the hands of larger corporations. In other words, 'entrepreneurship' has suddenly acquired a rather questionable status, if not a bad name! Additionally, the association of entrepreneurship with small businesses, a long-held assumption, has begun to be questioned. In some quarters the idea of the apparent security and capacity of larger firms to innovate and be entrepreneurial has gained renewed momentum.

The hankering for a stable, post-recession environment has both historical and current reasoning to justify it for policy purposes. They include for example:

- the rather fragile and fragmented environment of small businesses, their resource constraints and dependency on externalities that make it difficult to formulate policy that sticks, and can be easily hung on pegs of fiscal, monetary and industrial policy instruments;
- the overwhelming conflation of entrepreneurship and small businesses (despite Schumpeter!) and the associated difficulties of developing meaningful policy for this fragmented community of businesses;
- the undefined and uncalibrated environment of entrepreneurship, which could include business and social entrepreneurship, the creation of an entrepreneurial culture and

environment, and large and small businesses, making it difficult to develop a specific entrepreneurship policy; and

- a revival of the views of, for example, the great economist Galbraith that contemporary economic life was dominated by large corporations serving consumers in a highly competitive market place and dictating the terms of engagement with suppliers and buyers (Auerswald and Acs, 2009).[1]

The reality of entrepreneurship and policy awakening

Yet, the idea of this hesitant yearning for corporate-driven stability hides the realities of our day. Higher levels of international competition, a drop in productivity levels, lack of innovation, rising inflation, and a shortage of skills over the past two decades have seen a gradual shift to alternative organizational forms including the smaller enterprise. The push for innovation in inclement economic times, rising levels of unemployment, globalization and dispersed modes of production and service provision, the ascendancy of information and communications technologies, and the rise of the new industrial economies have called for varied pronouncements on policy that matter – policies that are shaped and formed by and for entrepreneurial people, entrepreneurial organizations and entrepreneurial environments.

In harsh times, economic policy-making has for long focused on rescuing the economy from 'free fall, boosting demand, however indiscriminately, and rescuing falling companies, however expensively (AIG received $180bn worth of government support). But policy makers are beginning to turn their minds to the potentially more rewarding question of tomorrow's jobs, rather than trying to save yesterday's. The buzzwords in government circles now are entrepreneurship, innovation and venture capital' (*Economist*, 2009).

New conditions, factors and reasons for supporting entrepreneurship

Jobs have always been the mainstay for economic policy in most countries. However, the shift in emphasis, if any, is the search now for new types of jobs and policies that resonate with questions of innovation, sustainability, a cleaner and more secure environment, effective use of new technologies, higher levels of connectivity between different parts of the world, its organizations and its people, democratic use of innovation processes such as open innovation, ethical investment, and of course the ubiquity of the Internet (OECD, 2009, 2010).

The unravelling of these new phenomena manifests itself in multiple forms across different parts of the globe. New opportunities abound in many guises in different countries, irrespective of the stages of their economic development. What is even more interesting is the mutual interdependency of these environments in realizing these opportunities. Countries, organizations, people do not innovate alone. They do so as networked nodes in webs of enterprise that connect them socially and for economic ends. These new questions help recreate the platform for fresh debate on policy centred round the very basis of entrepreneurship – opportunity identification, opportunity realization, value creation, and new types and forms of organization to enable such value creation. They could well offer the setting for new paradigms for policy-making.[2]

But what do we mean by public policy and what do we understand by the idea of entrepreneurship policy? How has such policy evolved? To try to answer these questions (and we should!), we turn to basic issues about public policy with specific reference to the promotion and development of entrepreneurship.

PART II: WHAT CONSTITUTES ENTREPRENEURSHIP POLICY?

We have explored the scope and meaning of entrepreneurship in earlier chapters. But as Hart (2003) acknowledges, the definition of entrepreneurship has become blurred with the use of different parts of speech, labels and neologisms, such as 'entrepreneur', 'entrepreneurial', 'entrepreneurialism' and the like to refer to different types of entrepreneurial activity, people and organizations. Most writers and observers of the subject would probably agree with Hart's meaning of entrepreneurship as the 'processes of starting and continuing to expand new businesses' (p. 5). Therefore, entrepreneurship policies are those measures that aim to foster a 'socially optimal level' of new business venturing, and their targets include new, existing and nascent entrepreneurs.

This new venture-focused view, therefore, considers that there is value in recognizing both the possibility and the probability of entrepreneurs, that is the lot of existing entrepreneurs together with the prospect of new entrepreneurs in the future. It underlines the judgement made by decision makers about the prospect of entrepreneurship in an economy and assumes that new ventures created today can be as important as those that may be created tomorrow. Analysts and critics also evaluate the effectiveness of policy along these lines, examining, for example, the way policy supports necessity-driven or opportunity-pulled entrepreneurs now and in the future, as the Global Entrepreneurship Monitor (GEM) project tends to do.

Predicting entrepreneurship can be fun, especially when models are at play to forecast trends and directions in an economy. There is, however, a serious side to the decision-making process which weighs up economic opportunities in the future, especially:

- when the level and nature of entrepreneurship can make a difference to the economic well-being of business, the wider economy, communities and society, through new products, services, organizations and jobs; and
- conversely, when restrictive circumstances in the present constrain entrepreneurial endeavour and outcomes.

Choices have to be made about how best to allocate resources to optimize gain for the economy in at least the near future.

But what about the possibilities of entrepreneurship in existing ventures, where spin-offs can occur or where other forms of corporate entrepreneurial activity can be maximized? What about the broader manifestations of entrepreneurship in terms of social or cultural value creation, which can embrace opportunity identification and realization in the social and community sphere or in terms of change processes that enhance the quality of life through, for example, new media or better systems of public governance where citizens actively contribute to local development using information and communications technologies (see Chapter 3)? How does policy address these questions, which represent different dimensions of the multidisciplinary culture of entrepreneurial activity?

Multidisciplinarity of entrepreneurship and its impact on policy

The implicit acknowledgement of the multidisciplinarity of entrepreneurship suggests that the very nature and scope of entrepreneurship policies is also multidisciplinary. Furthermore, entrepreneurship policy is essentially a mirage, and it is the real oasis of different economic and social policies that create opportunities for entrepreneurship. In other words, we find that the real scope of any entrepreneurship policy can be found in a range of other fiscal, industrial and monetary policies rather than in any clearly or separately defined entrepreneurship policy. Taxation and monetary policies, for example, can offer fiscal incentives for start-ups or capital allowances for the purchase of equipment by innovative firms, and help innovative firms through specific instruments such as the lowering of interest rates for borrowing for investment purposes or cash injection for research and development-oriented small firms. Industrial policy can help promote business clusters in regions attracting smart high-technology firms. The multidisciplinary nature of policy-making supporting entrepreneurship can be stated to reflect the multidisciplinary nature of entrepreneurship itself.

So what we do know is that there is a degree of confusion in our understanding of entrepreneurship, which in turn can lead to ineffective public policies. Karlsson and Andersson (2009) are even more scathing in their view, stating that there is a general 'lack in the literature of fundamental principles, problems and opportunities of entrepreneurship policies' (p. 112). On a more optimistic note, the literature on the subject does help us to either disentangle the differences between entrepreneurship and small business policies (Karlsson and Andersson, 2009; Audretsch *et al.*, 2006; Lundstrom and Stevenson; 2001 Reynolds *et al.* 1994) or accept the focus on small business (Storey, 1994, 1992, 1991).

Distinctiveness of entrepreneurship policy

What we also know is that most writing on entrepreneurship is concerned with small businesses. But are all small businesses entrepreneurial? While many entrepreneurial ventures are small, larger businesses, especially in pharmaceuticals, airlines, telecommunications and utilities industries, are also entrepreneurial in that many continue to expand, demonstrate an inexhaustible ability to spawn new products, reorganize the way to do business as they adapt to new opportunities, and generate new value through their activities. Consider Microsoft, GE, Google, Huwaei or SAP – all fine exponents of constant innovation. At the other end of the spectrum, many lifestyle businesses and others that tend to displace existing small businesses because of their narrow scope or markets do get started, but they can hardly be regarded as entrepreneurial ventures. They do not scale up, they do not necessarily add any new value through new products or services, and they are often vulnerable players in any economic environment. Consequently, small business policy may not be addressing those novel and dynamic factors that characterize entrepreneurship. Yet the conflation of small business and entrepreneurship (as defined above) subsists, making it difficult for a consensus on both the term 'entrepreneurship' and entrepreneurship policy.

The distinctiveness of entrepreneurship policy, as described by Lundstrom and Stevenson (2001) for the OECD, is based on the notion that such policy is made up of those measures intended to influence directly the level of entrepreneurial vitality in a region or a nation. This influence is evinced in policies which:

- encourage economic agents to conceptualize business ideas;
- facilitate the entry of new businesses (including indirect measures such as improvements in institutions and direct ones such as the targeting of economic agents that might start a business);
- facilitate the growth of existing businesses; and
- facilitate the exit of businesses.

(Reynolds *et al.*, 1994)

Inherent in what Lundstrom and Stevenson (2001) and Reynolds *et al.* (1994) observe is the emphasis on the 'change' process. It is in the breadth of policy direction and various instruments and in the multiple government department or agency location of entrepreneurship that we can find the distinctive features of entrepreneurship policy. By focusing on existing, new and nascent entrepreneurs, entrepreneurship policy focuses on the change process acknowledging the need to respect antecedents and consider future opportunities.

The focus on the process of change disregards the organizational unit, and deals more with the task or the facilitative environment in which opportunities are identified and realized. A proper study of entrepreneurship policy could, therefore, examine various conditions in alternative environments at different levels – the individual, the enterprise, the industrial sector, a cluster or network of firms, the region, the country and even across national geographical boundaries (Audretsch *et al.*, 2006). Within and across these units there are considerations of culture, institutions, education and training, among many other issues that constitute the range of instruments with which to implement policy. The units of analysis are rich and varied, leading to an inevitable breadth of orientation and instruments. Its varied form allows for the interest of different disciplines of economics, sociology, psychology and management in the exploration of its evolution.

SME policy and entrepreneurship policy

SMEs and SME policy are well integrated into entrepreneurship, and there may be two reasons why this link remains vital:

- SMEs make up the largest constituency of all businesses, so the change process is inevitably strongly manifest in these firms; and
- at the heart of all the different units of analysis lies the special significance of the presence of SMEs, and the dynamics of their interactions with other SMEs and with other organizations.

The distinctiveness of entrepreneurship is the focus on newness of ventures created to exploit and commercialize new knowledge.

While most countries have ministries, government departments, units or agencies charged with the responsibility of supporting SMEs through effective policies, entrepreneurship does not have a clearly identifiable public office dedicated to its promotion. A Ministry of Foreign Affairs could be as involved in encouraging entrepreneurial activity as the Ministry of Industry or its Home Affairs counterpart, either working together or vying with one another in silos of policy-making effort to do so.

Different government departments assist or hinder entrepreneurship directly or indirectly. A good and testing example for many governments is their policy on immigration. Immigration cuts across social, cultural and economic concerns. Demographic issues related to an ageing population, shrinking pension purses, the decline in skills levels and the erosion of the capital base often lead to conscious policy-making to attract foreign labour, money and technologies. Skills associated with labour are the province of the Industry or Labour ministries, while interest in the management of capital, foreign direct investment and technologies from abroad lies in the hands of Industry. Work permits, residency rights and security are generally overseen by the Home or Internal Affairs Ministry, while overarching relations with the country of origin of immigrants are within the jurisdiction of the Foreign Affairs department. How effectively these departments can work together is crucial for policies that encourage immigrant entrepreneurship or investment in entrepreneurial activity.[3]

Systems

Reference was made earlier to the systemic nature of entrepreneurship policy. Given the multifaceted nature of entrepreneurship policy, it is in the associations and connections between different parts of a system that provide a basis for such policy. Part of the development of effective policies is identification of the critical components within a system and examining how they link with one another as part of a robust system supporting innovation, new business creation and value creation in any society. The critical elements within each system provides its lifeblood.

The dynamic nature of entrepreneurship requires dynamic systems that evolve as different elements come together, get deselected, varied or retained as part of the process of change, a process marked by the creation, growth and death processes of enterprises (Wennekers *et al.*, 2001). This implies that both success and failure are part of the entrepreneurial dynamic and that the role of policy is to create conditions that augment success and reduce failure without adopting a directly interventionist stance, leaving such outcomes to chance or market forces and events. The conditions for different countries and regions are of course not the same, and there are variations even across nations with similar characteristics.

Germany and the United States of America are well recognized as highly industrialized, wealthy western economies. They have similar though not identical political and economic systems and ethical values (Grimm and Audretsch, 2005). The differences stem from the realities that face each country and the cultural fabric that is woven by the threads of these realities.

Failure is acceptable because it is a legitimate outcome of any entrepreneur's activity for testing ideas. Not all ideas can evolve successfully. However, not all cultures accommodate failure as a basis for future success, often resulting in highly interventionist policies that attempt to mitigate the effects of 'sickness' in industry or offer privileged access to public contracts through subsidies and other incentives, distorting market prices and offering unsustainable protection to targeted businesses.

Prior to 1991 and the deregulation of the Indian economy, government policy encouraged and provided subsidies for small firms in key sectors of the economy. There were pronounced policies to revitalize 'sick' small-scale industries which ate into the efficiency and growth of the economy. However, not all interventionist policies are inimical to growth and development. The much vilified state-sponsored entrepreneurship in public enterprise policies of the Chinese government has actually allowed for a range of opportunities for the state, its companies, local contractors, foreign firms, subcontractors and employment, and of course astronomical economic growth patterns since the 1990s and more, albeit at some cost to the economy and the social fabric of the country.

Systems and their effectiveness are dependent on the particular and prevailing circumstances of different countries and regions. The various contexts help to determine specific policy objectives, which lead to particular recommendations that are made to help implement those policies.

Objectives and recommendations

The different approaches to entrepreneurship policy-making in varied environments indicate that there are considerable variations in both attitudes towards and capacity for new venture creation and growth. These variations require identification of a relevant set of areas and political measures with which to act in those areas. This focus implies that policies are formulated on the basis of clear objectives. Thus Raposo (2009) shows how the strengthening of an entrepreneurial culture among any population can imply the creation of specific objectives and particular recommendations with which to achieve these objectives, as demonstrated in Table 10.1.

What we find from Table 10.1 is that government policies can provide a basis for:

- motivating and encouraging people directly and indirectly through education and training, the removal of barriers to business creation and growth, to help people start up new business ventures or to grow them successfully; and

Table 10.1 Policy objectives and recommendations

Policy objectives	Policy recommendations
• Creating measures to encourage individuals to become entrepreneurs and providing them with the necessary capacities in order to obtain success, as well as introducing reforms in the education and culture system and also removing the identified obstacles from the creation of enterprises	• Introduce teaching about entrepreneurship in the education curriculum • *Distinguishing between training and education initiatives* • *Distinguish between education and training for and about entrepreneurs*
• Developing a business-minded climate in the community, which promotes the rise of start-ups and the development of growth of already existing enterprises	• Encourage universities and investigation units to explore the results of research and development through the creation of enterprises; • *Encourage formation of different types of enterprises and enterprises with different sets of values, as in both business and social entrepreneurship* • Aim at specific groups, such as women and the unemployed, to increase their interest in the potential of entrepreneurship • *Work with both individuals and teams within target groups to enhance capacity and leverage resources* • Make the surrounding institutional environment of small and medium-sized enterprises more entrepreneurial and aware of the specific requirements of new enterprises • *Work to market-oriented (including the social market) needs of businesses and customers in regions where ventures might be set up* • Promote the accompaniment of newly created enterprises by already retired businessmen or by specialists • *Promote advocates of enterprise and value creation in the community* • Stimulate large enterprises to outsource certain functions in order to render opportunities for the appearance of small, new enterprises • *Encourage early the connection between local and global markets, resources and networks* • Involve the media, with the view of giving entrepreneurship due importance in society, in a positive manner • Adjust legislation in the area of bad debt credit and bankruptcies, in order to protect the rights of debtors and creditors

Source: Adapted from Raposa (2009). Recommendations in italics are those of this author.

- an environment that is conducive to innovative and successful business and venturing: creating a supportive business climate and generating appropriate framework conditions (see Chapter 6 for a fuller discussion on framework conditions).

Policies, therefore, can be effective if they are created to enable people to establish appropriate organizations with which to develop new products and services in environments that are conducive to the emergence of these organizations. In these environments effective policies help:

- people to be enthused and to acquire confidence in their ability to start or grow new ventures;
- people to make choices about starting or growing new ventures because they are economically and socially desirable and there are economically viable opportunities to do so;
- individuals and groups to realize that they can obtain financial, institutional and other forms of support to pursue their ideas for new ventures; and
- societies to derive economic and social value from the availability of new products and services, together with the opportunity to build on these successes.

Stevenson and Lundstrom (2002) and Lundstrom and Stevenson (2005) interpret the value and meaning of entrepreneurship along similar lines, encapsulating their argument in terms of three key areas of human and social interest: motivation, competencies and opportunities. This people-oriented approach is the basis of creating entrepreneurship policies which:

- relate to the three stages of conception, start-up and the post start-up initiation point of the entrepreneurial process;
- act to encourage motivation, enable competency development, and identify and realize opportunities; and
- have as their main objective the encouragement of more individuals to consider the possibility of becoming entrepreneurs.

(Raposa, 2009)

Contexts

Even where the orientation of policy is towards increasing the population of entrepreneurial people, this objective cannot be achieved without examining the context in which such people live, work and play. An examination of these contexts means the necessary identification of the interrelationships between individuals, the organizations that they create or work with, the wider, prevailing marketplace, and the economy and the society in which they operate. Entrepreneurship policy is, therefore, concerned with specific contexts in which support can be provided for:

- the role and motivation of individual or collective agents;
- the business or the organization that provides a structure for agency activity;
- the marketplace where new goods and services are exchanged, replacing or augmenting incumbent ones as part of the process of efficient allocation of resources or in the disruption of the means of such allocation; and

- the availability of opportunity across society to increase the supply of entrepreneurs and to generate innovation.

Features

We are now entering relatively complex territory where the orientation of policy referred to earlier is not simply predicated upon supporting potential and actual entrepreneurial people but on considering different units of analysis or levels of activity, namely the individual, the business or organization, the wider economy and society. Goals, targets and instruments are organized distinctively to operate at these levels. Effectively, policies help entrepreneurs to make occupational choices (between becoming an entrepreneur or an employee in a business), enable business to innovate continually, support economies to attain economic growth through proper forms of institutional engagement, and create social conditions for wider and equal opportunities for entrepreneurial activity. Table 10.2 captures these crucial features of entrepreneurship policy.

A variation of the above formulation of the scope and features of entrepreneurship policy can be found in Lundstrom and Stevenson (2005), where connections are made between motivation, opportunities and skills (or competencies), to identify appropriate policy measures, as Figure 10.1 shows.

So far the examination of the nature and scope of entrepreneurship policy has helped to determine:

- its broad scope and meaning;
- its distinctiveness;
- its multidisciplinary character demanding a multidisciplinary response in terms of the activities of different organizations and departments of government; and
- its systemic identity, which sets its objectives and plans for implementations in particular contexts.

Table 10.2 Features of entrepreneurship policy

Units of analysis/levels of activity	Goals	Targets	Instruments
Agent – occupational choice policies	More effective entrepreneurs	Individuals	Create awareness; entrepreneurship training; facilitate networks
Business – enabling policies	Continuous innovation	New firm formation	Finance; regulatory relief; SBIR; science parks; tech commercialization
Economy – supporting policies	Economic growth	Institutions – universities, governments, corporations, modes of conduct, social mores	R&D; higher education; venture capital
Society – social policies	Equal opportunity	Wealthy individuals; government programmes; social enterprises	Philanthropy; taxes; social pressure; legal structure

Source: adapted from Acs (2005).

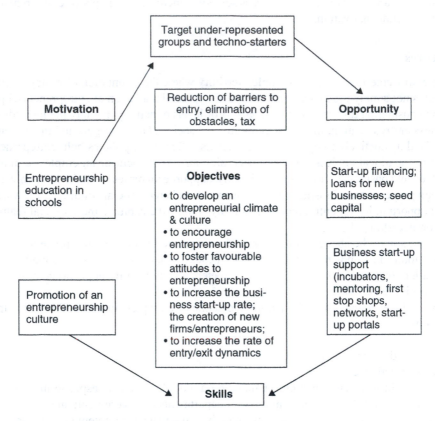

Figure 10.1 Typology of measures of entrepreneurship policy

Source: adapted from Lundstrom and Stevenson (2005, p.61; cited in Raposa 2009).

Consideration and analysis of the above issues require appropriate approaches that help us to better understand the purpose of entrepreneurship policy.

PART III: APPROACHES TO A FRAMEWORK FOR ENTREPRENEURSHIP POLICY

Inherent in the different formulations of public policy and the measures used to implement such policies is a mix of economic and sociological arguments. Policies are created to ensure effective allocation of scarce resources through the creation of new firms and the growth of innovative businesses. They are also centred around people, their needs and use of competencies that are woven into the fabric of social interactions and networks.

Contingent approach

Arguing that while an economic approach is useful in appreciating the entrepreneur's contribution to the economy, Mokry (1988) suggests that it may not be sufficient to explain what type of individuals act in entrepreneurial ways or indeed the surroundings in which they pursue entrepreneurial activities. Mokry (1988) proposes a contingency approach (combining economic, psychological and sociological perspectives) which supports the proposition that entrepreneurial activities emanate from the interaction of the characteristics of individual entrepreneurs (psychological make-up), specific turning points in the lives of individuals (precipitating events), their background, cultural factors and exposure to successful role models (role models). Entrepreneurship occurs when an organizational form uses the resources available to or developed by them to supply goods and services that others want to consume and pay for through mutually beneficial but not necessarily equal transactions. The three key variables of psychological make-up, role models and precipitating events lead to the perception and realization of opportunities, and the design of a suitable organization with which to manage venture creation and performance. A diagrammatic expression of this argument is shown in Figure 10.2.

Note that Figure 10.2 and the explanation above highlight the influence of external factors such as social networks and a supportive environment, which help to establish framework conditions that can be conducive to successful entrepreneurial outcomes. The role of policy is to facilitate these factors enabling worthwhile venture performance.

But why is policy justified? Why consider entrepreneurship policy when fiscal, monetary and industrial policies can suffice? Just because entrepreneurship matters or is seen as being a positive contributory force in the economy does not justify public intervention. Is it a question of approach rather than the creation of a distinctive set of policies? To answer such questions we have to explore the rationale and justification for entrepreneurship policy-making.

Rationale, justification and the mandate for entrepreneurship policy

The argument that entrepreneurship and innovation play a decisive role in economic and social development is discussed in detail in Chapter 11. We assume for now that entrepreneurship and innovation provide the basis for competiveness and welfare in all countries.

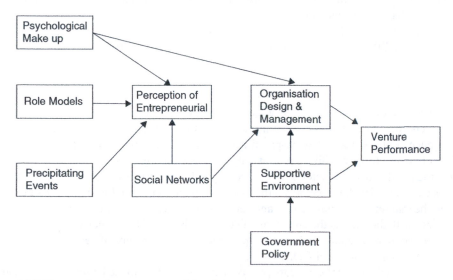

Figure 10.2 Factors shaping entrepreneurial activity

Source: CSES-ECED-G (2002); Hannon (2004); Hughes *et al.* (2007); Aerts *et al.* (2007); Phipps (2002); Chandra (2007); Hackett and Dilts (2004b).

The circumstances may be different for each country. Developed economies may need to steer away from the speculative economies driven by fancy and unsustainable financial innovations while developing countries may need to address wider agendas to support the poor and achieve the Millennium Development Goals (MDGs – see Chapter 11 for details). There are the overarching imperatives of the modern world as manifested in terms of climate change, the need for reduced carbon emissions, protection of biodiversity and the elimination of poverty, which affect all nations. For all countries technological improvements are necessary, and entrepreneurship and innovation are critical for achieving these improvements.

There are both proactive and reactive features of entrepreneurship policy. From a proactive sense, and in seeking to foster entrepreneurship and innovation, governments attempt to ensure the availability of competitive markets for goods and services, a fair, non-punitive and predictable taxation system, a propitious macroeconomic environment, and effective and efficient institutions, and enforceable rights to physical and intellectual property. These constitute what is referred to in the literature as framework conditions (see Chapter 6).

Reference was made earlier to variations in the make-up of different economies. These differences both account for variations in the operation of institutions and systems in different countries and have an effect on social outcomes. Attempts have been made by a new school of economists that collaborated for a period of time in the Wissenschaftzentrum in Berlin (Bronk, 2009)[4] to explain the divergence in economic and social outcomes through a systematic analysis of the role of distinct national institutional frameworks and framework conditions. The role of institutions matters considerably and their value is dependent on regulatory regimes. As these regimes differ from country to country, there are differences in economic performance at the national level (Hall and Soskice, 2001). The variations in the framework conditions allow for alternative ways of coordinating economic and social activities. Typically, the German, Swedish and Dutch national systems of capitalism provide firms with non-market institutional resources (including business associations and works councils) while the US and UK systems rely more on the market mechanisms of competition, price signals and legal contracts (Bronk, 2009).

Economic analysis of failures in the market helps us to understand the importance of the differences in different national framework conditions (OECD, 2003a).

Market failure

Market failure occurs when there is a gap or a 'systematic divergence' between private and social benefits and costs linked to transactions in the market place. This form of systemic divergence is at the heart of widespread acceptance of free competitive markets not being able to reach optimal equilibrium. But why do these divergences occur in the first place? Often the public good characteristics of certain goods and services, such as education or blue sky research and development, mean that there is not enough room for their trade or exploitation in the marketplace. These goods and services are provided rightfully for the benefit of all in society with the state as the custodian of such provision. Without such custodianship there might be too many inequalities in society preventing certain groups of people from accessing these goods and services (OECD, 2003a).

The heated debate over health care provision and legislation in the United States beginning in 2009 is a case in point, with a wealthy and strong lobby of private sector health care firms trying ferociously to protect their vested interests against the starkness of inaccessibility to many ordinary Americans, especially the working poor, of basic health care. In a different scenario we find the highly entrepreneurial poor of the Dharavi ghetto in Mumbai, India, struggling to access high-cost utilities, often forsaking basic provision, for the relative consumption-driven luxury of digitial TV sets or fancy mobile telephones because of the highly regulated utilities market in India. Information asymmetries, the domination of certain industrial sectors by a few firms, and overreliance on economies of scale limiting supplies of some goods and services to only a few firms are other examples of market failures.

Information asymmetries and high uncertainty

In essence, efficient outcomes and allocation of resources can be adversely affected by information deficiencies. High levels of uncertainty, because the future cannot be known and is made the subject of probability forecasts, create such information problems. Different people involved in market transactions (within a firm or between firms or among shareholders and creditors) hold different information, giving them an information advantage or disadvantage. The probability of opportunistic behaviour and mispricing can engender distrust and freeze up markets.

Exploitative or hold-up problems

One party to a transaction may take advantage of sunk costs from added value investment made by another in terms of their special expertise or a special relationship. Large firms contracting with smaller counterparts may hold up the latter in terms of their ability to contract freely with other customers. Firms providing long-term, in-house competency-based training may exploit their employees, who may not readily be able to transfer their skills and competencies elsewhere.

Spillovers

Firms in one region may benefit from the special knowledge and expertise from research and development activities of other firms or from high rates of specialist employee turnover. These spillovers and their value are not reflected in market prices and are often referred to as 'untraded dependencies' (Storper, 1997).

Table 10.3 shows how different areas of market failures are connected to various aspects of business creation and growth.

Not all market failures can be resolved by extending the activities of the market. For example, 'hold-up and exploitative problems' leading to opportunistic behaviour are often best resolved by business networks, associations and works councils. In other cases, such as knowledge spillovers, patents and other forms of intellectual property rights (IPR) can help firms to internalize the benefits from the protection offered by IPR. It should also be recognized that certain types of specialized economic activity are probably more inclined to generate market failures than others. Highly complex products using non-standard technologies (as, for example, customized software or specialist advanced manufacturing equipment) are more likely to be associated with specialist know-how and different levels of information and knowledge among firms and their customers. This specialist knowledge is often guarded zealously during outsourcing operations when outsourcing firms are required to maintain separate silos of services for individual clients. In these circumstances market failures are best avoided by non-market solutions such as having board membership in client firms or the other way round (Bronk, 2009).

Table 10.3 Market failure and opportunities for policy intervention

Areas of market failure	Type of market failure	Examples	Comments
Finance	The dysfunctional aspects of credit markets	Economic theory (especially neo-classical market-based theories) claims good projects should be funded regardless of resources of proprietor. In reality, collateral- and track-record-based lending predominate.	Theory suggests that there may not be sufficient cause for concern and that credit gaps may not be decisive. For example, a funding gap may be associated more with factors such as management skills, or specific economic conditions (recession or boom periods) may have their own effect on the availability of credit
		Supply of equity could be more problematic than debt because of high transaction costs associated with small amounts of lending	Venture capitalists and business angels typically rely on a minimum level of investment, but they vary considerably. The investment of the former represents a 'primary equity gap' (the smallest size investment required by VCs). The secondary equity gap is the minimum equity investment considered by business angels
		Absence or inadequacy of demand can limit equity investment	Lack of good projects is often cited as a good reason
Business development services	Imperfections in the market for and/or asymmetries of information between demand and supply of information; high costs of provision of services to large numbers of small firms	High cost of information search; unawareness of information needs, especially in uncertain or changing environments; over-reliance on psychology of self-help	Increased use of Internet and better educated entrepreneurs can mitigate some of these problems
Training	High cost, especially opportunity cost, of training against benefits of training; inappropriate or irrelevant training provision Generic training provision against specific problem-solving business-based needs	Benefits of training pitted against not only cost but also possible future loss – applies to both formal training external to firm and sometimes even to training on the job; entrepreneurs and small firms more concerned with problem-solving issues related to specific tasks	Short-termism militates against acquiring the benefits

Source: Adapted from OECD (2003).

Market failures and externalities

With reference to the knowledge-based economies of our times, Audretsch and Keilbach (2005) and Audretsch (2006) conceptualizes market failure in terms of four distinctive types or instances of such failure, or what he refers to as externalities. These specific types of market failure are (a) network externalities; (b) knowledge externalities; (c) failure externalities; and (d) demonstration externalities. These externalities are typical of conditions that prevail in knowledge-driven economies or where knowledge spillover results in new firm formation.

1) *network externalities* result from the value of a firm's capabilities as a function of its geographical proximity to complementary or related firms, individuals and institutions. In other words, the value of an entrepreneurial firm increases when it finds itself in the presence of other entrepreneurial firms and when it operates with similar partners in a dense network. These complementary resources are found best in business clusters where there is an overlapping and sharing of technologies, and easier access to financial and human capital. Such a concentration of clustered resources and firms is inevitably limited to some regions, and those areas that do not have a rich density of firms are inevitably burdened with considerable barriers to entrepreneurship. As Audretsch (2006) argues, the expected value of any recognized opportunity is correspondingly lower in regions where there is no such agglomeration of firms;

2) Audretsch (2005, 2006) draws his idea of *knowledge externalities* from Arrow (1962), who stated that knowledge that involves new ideas is essentially a public good with its production generating externalities in the sense that a public good can be shared by all concerned. In other words, there is a 'knowledge spillover' effect of public goods. However, the use of this public good can be appropriated by firms in close local proximity with one another (in clusters) where the individuals or firms that generate knowledge can be spatially bounded (that is, confined to a particular geographical area). Some analysts, such as Audretsch (2006), argue that in the absence of such cluster-based benefits in all regions, public policy intervention may be appropriate to induce entrepreneurial locations to create entrepreneurial clusters;

   The problem is that not all regions provide environments conducive to business clustering, and public resources are generally constrained or need to be shared among highly competitive, often more worthy, public services and causes. Not all firms can be relocated to clustered environments. The inevitable attraction for policy makers is to rely on 'winners' in, for example, 'clusters' at the expense of firms in isolated regions. But as Abubakar and Mitra (2009) have shown, innovative firms in isolated regions rely on different types of knowledge spillovers with an emphasis on international alliances and network. These regions can attract firms that are tied in one form or another (subsidiaries, associates, joint ventures, etc.) with global players relying on intra-firm and global inter-firm networks for their innovations. Rather than replicate cluster building, public policy could focus on harnessing and supporting higher levels of internationalization and global connectivity for firms in those regions. Such an approach calls for differentiated and distinctive locally focused policies instead of an all-embracing national template;

3) failure often leaves a legacy of opportunities for other, third parties. This phenomenon is known as *failure externalities* and is evinced in the economic value derived by third parties when firms, especially knowledge-intensive firms, fail. Indeed, the failure rates

of knowledge-based firms are especially high because of the higher levels of uncertainty (Bhide, 2006). Surviving firms often appropriate the value of the ideas, products and services of failed counterparts. In these circumstances, the private investor of the failed firm loses out to the appropriating survivor firm, especially as the value derived from the latter is often intangible. Even where such appropriation is tangible, as in the hiring of talent from the failed firm, there is no gain for the private investor from his/her original investment. Individual firms are, therefore, not incentivized to invest in clusters because they cannot gain from any returns from these clusters, and especially from the failure of investee firms. Can or should government intervene in such market failures? The answer is perhaps no because as long as some entrepreneurial firms succeed and secure prospects of growth there is not much left for the government to do;

4) when successful entrepreneurial activity inspires similar activity among others who spot the process of opportunity creation together with the results of pursuing such action, what emerges is a *demonstration externality*. Individuals other than the original entrepreneur and his/her business counterparts imitate the actions of the latter as they begin to consider entrepreneurship to be a viable alternative to, for example, jobs in the wage economy. This form of imitation tends to occur in non-market environments since those who are influenced by the demonstration of success are not necessarily in the same sphere of economic activity as the original entrepreneur. It is argued that those regions that have a strong entrepreneurial tradition are more likely to create conditions for such positive demonstration externality. Typically high-agglomeration regions are good examples of places where these externalities prevail, thus generating the kind of market failure similar to knowledge externalities.

Beyond market failures

Addressing market failures is crucial for effective policy-making. However, a broader view of entrepreneurship and innovation suggests that a proactive and holistic approach that supports the creation of a favourable environment, the establishment of appropriate institutions and the implications for the wider society is also important for policy makers. Table 10.4 illustrates the importance of entrepreneurship for policy from this broader perspective.

As Table 10.4 shows, entrepreneurship policy has meaning both because of what it means and because of its role in the currency of technological, environmental, structural and social change. Its meaning lies in its contribution to and what it stands for in society. It is probably the oldest form of economic activity in the world and in common with some aspects of the oldest profession attracts similar opprobrium! The creation of a firm precedes its management activities and, as Mises wrote many years ago, it is part of all our lives. The transformative nature of our world today has opened up considerable opportunities for productive and unproductive entrepreneurship, and it is the former, with the assistance of effective institutions and regulatory frameworks, that helps to answer the questions relating to the eternal verities of citizens and consumers.

Entrepreneurship policy-making has evolved over time to cope with our best understanding of our economic and social situations in different environments.

Audretsch *et al.* (2006) argues that the four externalities that define market failure create a gap in the value attributed to entrepreneurial activity by private parties and policy makers. Outside knowledge-driven environments that house a concentration of high added-value businesses, it may be difficult to, for example, attract finance and other resource necessary for starting or nurturing entrepreneurial activity. Consequently, it is incumbent upon policy

Table 10.4 The importance of entrepreneurship for policy

What is entrepreneurship?	What constitutes entrepreneurship today?	What do citizens and consumers want?
E = positive relationship with economic growth and building social capital	Growth in concentration of firms, networks and linkages	A safer society
		A clean green environment
	Convergence in technologies and resources	
Best form of job creation for yourself and others in times of 'jobless' growth		More spending on health and education
	Higher levels of education, skills and learning	
		Caring communities
Entrepreneurship lasts longer than any functional aspect of business	Growth in intermediary organizations to whom some tasks are delegated, and in	A well-performing economy and growth in business sectors
The way we live creatively with change	different forms of entrepreneurship – *new firms, social entrepreneurship, entrepreneurial culture*	Style, design, culture
	Direct influence of internationalization – technology, human resources, capital and information flows	
	New opportunities in addressing environmental, social and structural change	

makers to identify and support the specific and concentrated connections between firms and institutions in a region to promote economic growth through the generation of entrepreneurial opportunity. But as stated earlier, it may not be possible to engineer such environments and connections across all regions because of the enormity of spatial variations in culture, attitudes, traditions, values and institutions.

But how and why have these market failures occurred, and how have the conditions giving rise to the externalities referred to above emerged in the first place? To answer this question we need to obtain a brief overview of the changing economic environment and the evolution of policies and various theoretical models that have tried to explain the rationale for public policy in the past, especially since the Second World War.

PART IV: EVOLUTION OF ENTREPRENEURSHIP POLICY: CHANGING TIMES, AND POLICY PROBLEMS IN RECENT TIMES

Market failures have prevailed since the beginning of economic development and the recognition of the value of markets. Adam Smith's insights into both the significance and the limitations of the market have been referred to by historians, economists and other commentators. Our interest is in recent times, and this is because of the particular transformation in the recognition of the importance of entrepreneurship for economic growth and development over the past half-century or so. In dealing with those failures over time, little recognition has been given to either entrepreneurship or the particularities of small and especially new small firms. Various models developed by economists and policy makers did not recognize entrepreneurship as a vital force for growth and development.

After the Second World War, three distinctive views of the economy and its evolution, corresponding roughly to specific phases and conditions, provided the ingredients for the eventual emergence of an entrepreneurial economy. While the 'Capital Economy' prevailed over the early post-war era, the 'Knowledge Economy' reflects the ebb and flow of the economy in the 1980s. Both phases provided the early setting for the emergence of the 'Entrepreneurial Economy' which took off in the 1990s (Audretsch *et al.* 2006; Audretsch, 2007; Acs and Armington, 2006; Baumol *et al.*, 2007). The mandate for entrepreneurship policy emerged from these directions.

Previous theoretical models

Previous theoretical models, appropriate for their times, tended to call either for policy and instruments promoting investment in physical or for financial capital and labour. Expressed in simple mathematical terms, economic output ('Q') was a function of capital ('K') and labour ('L') and expressed as follows:

$$Q = f(K, L)$$

Technology or technological change was exogenous or given, and therefore not considered an important contributory or functional factor for economic growth.

The Solow model: capital economy

The Solow model of the economy, or the capital economy (named after Robert Solow's seminal work of 1956 on economic growth), had as its principal focus the idea of economic growth necessary to reignite economies and societies after the war. Growth could only be induced through investment in physical capital (plants, equipment, mills and factories). It was based on two key principles. The first principle demonstrated that increasing labour (instead of physical capital) could expand the level of economic output but that would not lead to any increase in the rate of economic growth. The second principle relied on the notion of scale economies realized from large capital investments necessary for productivity gains. The latter had its antecedents in the work of Adam Smith (1776), and its subsequent acceptance in all neo-classical economics and public policy in the 1920s and also after the Second World War (Acs, 2008a; Audretsch *et al.* 2006; Acs *et al.*, 1996).

For Solow, increases in capital and labour did not fully account for economic growth. There was another factor 'A', which represented 'technical change' and improved the productivity of labour and capital. The equation that sums up Solow's findings is as follows:

$$Q = Af(K, L)$$

Although technical change was considered to be beyond the reach of public policy because it was exogenous (something that was given and/or external to models under consideration), the policy mechanism of physical investment for economic growth was not disputed. What was at stake was the debate over the necessary instruments; with monetarists claiming that interest rates to help induce capital investment were more important than fiscal policy aficionados who promoted the idea of taxes and public expenditure being particularly important for enabling investments in physical capital and consequently economic growth. It is interesting to see how some of this debate and the flurry of ideas continue to inform recent economic arguments, especially after the economic crisis of the early twenty-first century.

Countries and regions that prospered after the war have found their industrial competiveness, especially in traditional sectors, take a battering with globalization. These economies had been characterized by the presence of automobiles, steel, ship building and related industries and the combination of large-scale capital and unskilled or semi-skilled labour. The West Midlands and the North East in the UK, and Detroit and Pittsburgh in the USA, carry the historical narrative of the decline and fall in economic performance (Audretsch *et al.* 2006, 2005). Not much was different in developing nations who espoused the same policy mechanism of physical investments for economic growth but with the different mechanisms of foreign direct investment (FDI). China's recent economic growth has been attributed, albeit partially controversially, to its ability to attract large quantities of FDI.

The upshot of such policy is the inevitable benefit that accrues to large firms, their alleged superior productive efficiency, and economies of scale. Both their hegemony and the threat of their unbridled growth became part of the agenda of three key economic stakeholders – the government, industry and trade unions – in the 1950s. These stakeholders formed what Auserwald and Acs (2009) describe as the 'Iron Triangle'. Small firms could not get a look-in because they were considered a drag on such efficiency with their limited resources and low-quality employment offer. Small firms were not seen as efficient survivors in the competitive economy. If the latter were to be worthy of public policy consideration then it was only for social and political reasons. They needed to be protected because so many people earned their livelihoods from running small firms. or because they could act as a control mechanism in the event of market disequilibrium occurring from gaps in the provision of goods and services. This guardianship of small firms lay at the root of what happened in capitalist economies, where firms got bigger and the share of small firms declined.[5]

We find similar strategies adopted perhaps in an even more pronounced fashion in developing economies such as India, which under a strong protectionist environment safeguarded small scale industries (SSIs) against competition from their larger counterparts, especially prior to the deregulation of the economy in 1991 (Thareja, 1998).

The Romer model: knowledge economy

Romer's (1986) emphasis on the importance of investment in knowledge capital emerged from a rather different approach to growth theory. He propounded the idea of endogenous change (change that came from within). Technology was no longer exogenous to economic growth but a central reason for it. Firms were still considered to be exogenous in terms of the knowledge-production function, but their performance was seen as generating technological change. Central to this performance was knowledge that could be included in the production function explicitly, as expressed in the following new equation where T (technology) is the outcome of R&D and HC (human capital):

$$A = f(R\&D, HC).$$

In addition, such knowledge spilled over from the producer to third-party firms. This knowledge capital augmented other investments in human capital, as well as research and development. Universities and other public research activities were considered to be a key contributor, alongside education at all levels, and for economic reasons too (as opposed to it being vital for social and moral purposes).

Further empirical work led to a modification of Romer's equation, with R&D and HC now substituted for technology, leading to the following equation:

$$Q = f(K, L, R\&D, HC)$$

Countries such as Germany and Sweden, along with the USA, paved the way for knowledge-induced economic growth. Over time this has captured the imagination of policy makers around the world as we see numerous instruments combining physical capital investment and knowledge capital spearheading economic development in countries as widely dispersed as China, India, the United Arab Emirates, Brazil and Mexico. Measures such as the ration of R&D investment to Gross Domestic Product and the filing of patents still remain at the core of statistical evidence of economic growth in most countries today. High investments in knowledge capital have featured across Europe and in Japan. China's recent leapfrogging of most western economies in terms of relative R&D spend as a percentage of GDP is seen as an example of profound change in the global economic order. Interestingly, in a country such as India, knowledge capital in the private sector, especially in the software industry, has been at the heart of that industry's phenomenal growth, resulting in a belated response by the government to capitalize on that change, establish a new Knowledge Commission, and deregulate the poor-performing higher education sector. The focus on knowledge capital and the role of different players has led to the creation of policies for National Innovation Systems (Nelson, 1993; Lundvall, 1992).

The realization of the value of knowledge capital has not yielded a corresponding interest in the role of small firms in generating such knowledge or indeed in terms of their contribution to economic growth. It is not at all clear whether policy makers in government, researchers, general commentators and trade unions have actually seen the value of small firms either in relation to knowledge production or in connection with the commercialization of knowledge. Audretsch *et al.* (2006) refer to a *Harvard Business Review* article by Ferguson (1988) which suggested that fragmentation, instability and entrepreneurialism caused by tax subsidies for the formation of small firms, as evinced in the infrastructure of small subcontractors in Silicon Valley, were not signs of well-being – this despite the findings of Acs and Audretsch (1990) and others of the higher correlation between R&D inputs and innovative output among small firms (0.84 for four-digit standard industry classification manufacturing industries compared to 0.40 for larger firms).

The entrepreneurial change-over

Both models and their consequent implementation in terms of policies did not stand the test of time as poor economic performance dogged leading industrial countries. While followers of the Solow model have found developed countries affected badly by globalization and the switch of both effective and efficient manufacturing activities to emerging nations, policies based on the Romer model of investment in knowledge capital (such as R&D and human capital) in countries such as Sweden, Japan and various regions in the USA have witnessed lack-lustre growth or even stagnant economic performance.

Accompanying the sluggishness of economic growth models referred to above were regulatory constraints which have acted as a break on the possession of large amounts of market power generally displayed by large firms. Similar constraints could also be found in policies sheltering small firms from market-based competition and protecting their role in the economy irrespective of their performance and capabilities. When these firms were turning to knowledge capital, the outcomes were not healthy. This made it difficult to accrue the economic benefits of such capital. The deficit could be met by turning to policy which gave an appropriately higher premium to entrepreneurship; to new opportunity creation, through new combinations of resources; and to organizational change which valued the creation of new ventures. These new ventures took the form of start-ups or of existing firms mutating to reshape their organizations to adopt new ways of working around global projects and rely more on outsourcing and globally networked activity. The mandate for entrepreneurship policy lies in the recognition for making sense of and utilizing the value of these new opportunities arising in the global market place.

The discussion so far suggests that there might be a linear trajectory to policy development, from capital-intensive production to knowledge capital investment through to the emergence of entrepreneurship policy. The issue is not so much about linearity as about the peculiarity of adoption of policies to suit particular environments. It would be impossible to conceive of uniform policy development across different countries when there are so many differences in the economic, geographic and human resource landscape of both countries and regions in those countries. The application of different approaches is, therefore, dependent on the stages assumed to be related to stages of economic development in an economy. This relationship between entrepreneurship and economic development is explored in more detail in Chapter 11.

Mini case study 10.1. Entrepreneurship and industrial policy in Israel

Israel's story of 50-fold economic growth within 60 years is a tale of 'Israeli character idiosyncrasies, battle-tested entrepreneurship . . . geopolitical happenstance' and adaptive government policies (Senor and Singer, 2009). Israel's economy can be described as one of two great periods with an interregnum of stagflation and hyper-inflation between these two stages. In the first period (1948 to 1970), GDP per capita nearly quadrupled while the population tripled in size despite the country's involvement in three major wars. The second period from 1990 to today has seen the transformation of the country from a 'sleepy backwater into a leading centre of global innovation'. An entrepreneurial government dominated over a relatively small private sector during the first period, while the second period saw the emergence and mushrooming of a thriving private sector created initially by government action.

The first period

The first period had its roots in the country's founding and early Jewish settlers living a fragile existence in Petach Tikva, a farming community a few miles from what is now Tel Aviv, till 1883 when the French-Jewish banker Edmond de Rothschild provided financial support. The first planting of eucalyptus trees in or near the swamps created by the river's overflow drained these swamps, ensuring a dramatic drop in the incidence of malaria, which had plagued the early settlers. Labour productivity in the 1920s in the Yishuv, the Jewish community of pre-state Palestine, increased by

80 per cent and even during the global depression of 1931–35 the average annual economic growth of Jews was 28 per cent. The small communities of early settlers were joined by large numbers of new immigrants, whose pioneering approach to life 'overturned a charity-based economy'.

Nation building

Ben Gurion, an immigrant from Poland, was considered to be the first national entrepreneur of Israel, organizing as he did a functioning nation state. His main achievement was centred around the 'operational management and logistics planning' of an extremely complex subject – the organization of the flows of immigrants. His first effort consisted of inspiring and organizing 18,000 Jews living in Palestine to return to Europe to join the British army in their fight against the Nazis while creating an underground agency to secretly transport Jewish refugees from Europe to Palestine in defiance of the UK's policy on immigration. The British were an ally in Europe but an 'enemy' in Palestine Despite being steeped in the socialism of his era, Ben Gurion was a classic 'bitzu'ist' (the Hebrew word for pragmatist, or more importantly a word that stands for someone who gets things done!), whose only objective was nation building. 'Bitzu'ism is at the heart of the pioneering ethos and Israel's entrepreneurial drive . . . The "bitzu'ist" is the builder, the irrigator, the pilot, the gunrunner, the settler . . .' (p. 106).

Ben Gurion's main task was to disperse the Jewish population widely over what would become Israel so that the future sovereignty of the country could be guaranteed. It was imperative that government took the lead in settlement arrangements and provided incentives to people who did not wish to move far away from urban centres. Private players were not willing to underwrite such efforts.

Social innovation

The great innovation of the first period was the social innovation of the 'kibbutz'. At less than 2 per cent of Israel's population, kibbutzniks (the members of the kibbutz) produce 12 per cent of the nation's exports. Created as agricultural settlements dedicated to equality and to abolishing private property, the kibbutz movement grew in 20 years to 80,000 people living in 250 communities (4% of Israel's population) from the original population of 16,000 people in 1944, four years before the founding of the state.

The kibbutzim (plural for kibbutz, which means 'gathering' or 'collective') were hyper-collective and hyperdemocratic societies where questions of self-governance were at the heart of their functioning. Agricultural and technological breakthroughs accounted for the growth of the kibbutz. A kibbutz such as Hatzerim was founded one night in 1946, when the pre-state Jewish militia decided to have a presence at key points in the southern Negev desert. Despite the initial hostility of a deserted environment and the ravages of the 1948 War of Independence, the community withstood the problems and flushed out the soil to grow crops. In 1965 a water engineer called Simcha Blass approached the members of the kibbutz with an idea for commercialization referred to as 'drip irrigation'. This event was the founding of the firm Netafim, the global drip irrigation company. Taking a major problem such as the lack of water and converting it to an asset by becoming experts in the field of desert agriculture, drip irrigation and desalination became a hallmark for Israel and its approach to national economic development.

Almost 95 per cent of the country is categorized as semi-arid, arid or hyperarid, and although the Negev is Israel's largest region, its encroachment has been reversed with its northern regions now being covered by agricultural fields and planted forests. Innovative water policies have led to Israel now leading the world in recycling waste, with over 70 per cent of the water being recycled – approximately three times the percentage that Spain (the second-ranked recycling country) recycles. Great stories of, for example, recycling water twice are part of the legend of innovation in Israel. For example, the Kibbutz Mashabe Sade in the Negev desert dug a well as deep as ten football pitches only to find water that was salty and warm. After consulting academics at the nearby Ben Gurion University, it was realized that this water would be perfect for raising warm-water fish – an unusual prospect in a desert! Ponds were filled with the 98 degrees water and stocked with barramundi, tilapia and sea bass for commercial production. The water from the fishponds now contained waste products that helped to produce fertilizer, and it was then used to irrigate olive and date trees.

The Yatir Forest survives only on rain water even though a meagre 11 inches of rain fall each year. However, trees in that forest grow faster than expected, soaking up as much of the carbon dioxide from the atmosphere as lush forests do in temperate climates. Planting forests on just 12 per cent of the world's semi-arid lands reduces the atmospheric carbon by one gigaton (or the annual CO_2 output of about one thousand 500 megawatt coal plants) per year.

From 1950 to 1955 Israel's economy grew by about 13 per cent each year, experiencing what some have described as a 'leapfrog', or the shrinking of the per capita wealth gap with rich first-world countries. Between 1950 and 1970 Israel's per capita income relative to the United States jumped from 25 per cent to 60 per cent, thereby doubling its living standard relative to that of the USA. During this period there was no encouragement of private entrepreneurship. High levels of investment in water systems, factories, ports, electrical grids and housing construction, together with the creation of industries as entrepreneurial projects within government, pre-dates the activities now taking place in China by several decades. This left the future open to private entrepreneurs and a breakdown in state economic management, which after the 1967 military victory and the 1973 Yom Kippur War left the country in crisis. Hyperinflation followed in the 1980s, with inflation rising from 13 per cent in 1971 to 111 per cent in 1979!

Preparations for the second period

Quite strikingly, Intel had set up shop in Israel in the 1970s. Immigration had started to fuel the economy. Between 1990 and 2000, 800,000 citizens of the ex-USSR immigrated to Israel, with the first 500,000 coming in over a period of only three years. These Jews had made up roughly 30 per cent of doctors and 20 per cent of engineers in the Soviet Union. They arrived just at a time when the technology boom was picking up in the 1990s and just as Israel's private technology sector became hungry for engineers. Immigration became the main spur for entrepreneurship, as it did in a different environment during the founding of Israel and as it has indeed been a catalyst on the East and West coasts of the USA. Israel may be the only country that seeks to increase immigration.

The Israeli government created 24 technology incubators, giving Russian scientists the resources and financing of up to $300,000 that they required to carry out R&D activities for their innovations. The main purpose was to explore the commercialization prospects of their technologies. But the Russian immigrants hardly had any experience of start-ups, and government financing was unable to break this barrier down. It was felt that private venture financing was the only solution to this problem of new venture creation.

Throughout the 1980s the absence of VC underscored the lack of entrepreneurial experience. While Israeli entrepreneurs had to think globally almost from the start, serious questions about how to make, market and distribute products undermined their efforts. Israeli start-ups could apply to the Office of the Chief Scientist for matching grants, but this source of money did not provide for sufficient start-up money. The alternative was to apply for grants for joint ventures from a fund set up by the US and Israeli governments called the Binational Industrial Research and Development (BIRD) Foundation. BIRD provided modest grants of $500,000 to $1 million over two to three years, recouping monies through royalties earned from the projects. BIRD provided a learning experience for both entrepreneurs and the government, especially, about how to do business in the United States, thus offering a kind of shortcut to American markets. By 1992 almost 605 of the Israeli firms that went public on the New York Stock Exchange and 75 per cent listed on NASDAQ were BIRD supported. Yet the benefits were not as dispersed as they could have been. Seventy four per cent of high technology exports came from only 4 per cent of high technology firms. Bootstrapping was the only other solution to funding problems of entrepreneurs.

The second period

With the gradual realization of the need for private VC funding, the Minsitry of Finance established a new programme called 'Yozma' (meaning 'initiative' in Hebrew). The government invested $100 million to create ten new venture funds and each fund had to have a tripartite structure made up of Israeli VCs in training, a foreign VC firm and an Israeli investment company or a bank. One Yozma fund of $20 million could invest directly in high-technology firms. The programme offered initially a kind of one and half to one match. The first Yozma fund was created in partnership with the Discount Israel corporation an investment bank, Advent Venture Partners, a VC firm from Boston, and the fund was led by the long-time director of the BIRD Foundation, Ed Mlavsky, and Yossi Sela. The ten Yozma funds created between 1992 and 1997 raised just over $200 million with the assistance of government funding, and they notched up high-profile successes. Currently there are just under 50 VC funds (45 according to the Israeli Venture Association), although Ed Mlavsky states that between 1992 and 2009 some 240 VCs were established in Israel by both foreign and domestic firms.

Immigration has been accompanied by the growth of the Israeli diaspora. The waves of talent that have become high-technology pioneers in the US and elsewhere are now very well documented. They have pioneered new technologies in firms such as CISCO and Intel, who have responded with operations in Israel through the assistance of these 'argonauts'. Israel has experienced investment and technology booms linked to expatriate leadership and what Annalee Saxenian refers to as the 'brain circulation' of talented people returning home after periods of settling down abroad, but without losing links with the latter. They travel back and forth between these places and have been instrumental in creating important global centres of innovation. However, these links have not come easily, with the passionate Jewish diaspora's links with their home country stemming from the activities of institutions such as the Israeli air force.

The story above captures only part of the story of the Israeli miracle. It shows the approach that the government of that country took right from the beginning to support entrepreneurship in all its forms. The evolution of entrepreneurship policy from a entrepreneurial nation-building project to a set of high-technology-focused programmes is a remarkable one of public ingenuity and purpose mixed with eventual private endeavour.

(Source: Adapted from Senor and Singer, 2009)

Conclusion

This chapter has explored the theoretical basis for entrepreneurship policy-making and implementation from a variety of perspectives. It has attempted to give the reader appropriate tools for understanding the scope of entrepreneurship policy given the numerous elements that make up such policy, outlining the relevant connections between and implications for entrepreneurs, policy makers and students of the topic. This has been achieved by taking a route of enquiry that follows a map showing:

- the meaning, nature and scope of entrepreneurship policy, its distinctiveness, its multidisciplinary character that calls for a multidisciplinary policy response, and its systemic identity which sets its objectives and plans for implementations in particular contexts, together with;
- a theoretical framework for understanding how and why policy is made and its evolution over time; and
- some insights into the practice of policy development.

We may conclude this chapter with a question mark about the importance of the environment in which policies are made and the framework conditions that pertain in those environments, especially when we attempt to measure their value. We should also recognize the significance of specific contexts in a globalized world and how that influences the practice of entrepreneurship and policy-making that supports or hinders such practice. An examination of how environments are conducive to entrepreneurship, innovation and economic development, and where policy can be constructed effectively, is the substance of Chapter 11.

Self-assessment questions

1. Does entrepreneurship policy matter? Why?
2. What is the difference between entrepreneurship policy and small business policy?
3. What are the different reasons and motivations for developing entrepreneurship policy?
4. Chart the emergence of entrepreneurship as a key plank for economic policy development.

11 Entrepreneurship, innovation and economic development

Learning outcomes

This chapter has two sections. In Section One the reader will:

- obtain a critical overview of relevant concepts and issues relating to economic development;
- examine critically the relationship between entrepreneurship and economic development;
- analyse and offer a critique of current thinking on entrepreneurship and economic development; and
- propose critical, alternative approaches to entrepreneurship and its role in economic development.

In Section Two the reader will:

- obtain a critical overview of concepts and issues relating to regional economic development and review critically the connection between entrepreneurship and regional economic development;
- gain critical insights into regional innovation and economic development systems and how entrepreneurship and innovation contribute to regional economic growth;
- review and analyse critically how new business formation impacts on regional economic development;
- obtain a critical overview of current paradoxical trends of globalization and regional development and how entrepreneurial opportunities are created in globally connected regions;
- propose policies for economic development based on entrepreneurship in a modern context and ideas for growing new businesses in regions.

Structure of the chapter

This chapter provides an overview of the vast subject of entrepreneurship, innovation and economic development. It constitutes the core of this book. For this reason it is longer than the other chapters as it weaves into the fabric of the book all the major threads and patterns of the trinity of critical components of the book.

The chapter is organized in two sections. In Section One we first explore the concept of economic development through a short journey through the literary canons of development studies. This journey opens up possibilities for the connection between economic development and entrepreneurship with an attempt to look at the role that the latter plays in achieving the goal of the former, drawing on the literature of, among other subjects, development economics and economic geography. This journey is global in scope as it examines the extent to which entrepreneurship can help to obtain a better understanding of the mechanics of and the social interrelationships underpinning economic development. In Parts II and III of this section an overview of extant theories and concepts, including the various stages of growth of countries and what drives such growth in specific conditions, is accompanied by a critique of key issues and their relevance in a modern global economy.

In Section Two the investigation switches to the specific characteristics of local and regional development and the function of entrepreneurship and innovation in such forms of development. Part I locates entrepreneurship within the boundaries of regional development. Part II then explores the meaning of regions in the context of economic development, and this exploration is followed by a specific examination of new firm formation and regional development in Part III and the relationship between entrepreneurship and unemployment in Part IV.

The unevenness in growth patterns across nations and, in particular, within countries, suggests that the importance of local or regional factors may have more to offer by way of accounting for different levels of economic development. Included in these factors is the 'local' nature of entrepreneurship, regional memory and path dependency that both creates and locks in regional capabilities. These issues are discussed in Parts V and VI. In Part VII the reader returns to the idea of stages of development but this time in a regional context. Entrepreneurs start their ventures locally; they draw from local resources, experience and institutions to start and grow their enterprises. Entrepreneurship can, therefore, be seen as a central part of a system, especially a local one, where the different elements combine to create new opportunities for growth. Growth, however, brings with it other attractions, namely the resources, markets and technologies that flow between regions and across country borders. This phenomenon is not simply about the internationalization process of growing firms but rather the emergence of global production networks enabled and enhanced by technologies, and human and social capital.

Development has become less about different countries going through linear stages of growth and more about regions and bounded environments connected to each other by new technologies, talent, knowledge and capital as part of global production networks. Regional growth fractures countries as there are greater disparities between regions within countries. These disparities then call for new policy interventions, which to be effective need to harness entrepreneurial opportunities. The opportunities that arise and the innovations that follow are not limited to particular organizations. Product, process, technological and organizational innovations occur in multiple, large, small and medium-sized organizations in networked space. More importantly, the connectivity of these organizations in those networks creates entrepreneurial opportunities for the region. The region is, therefore, the seedbed for global entrepreneurship. These key issues form part of the discussion in Parts VII, VIII and IX before the chapter is concluded.

The contents in the two sections of the chapter highlight the critical links between the three main learning blocks of this book – entrepreneurship, innovation and regional development. In elaborating on the issues of development and entrepreneurship, what holds is the tension between problems and opportunities. This tension could well be a characteristic of the 'creative destruction' process of Schumpeter and the environment of dramatic economic and social change that occurs with each wave of technological evolution together with its impact on people, social norms and practices, institutions, growth and development.

Introduction

Entrepreneurship's theoretical nurture in the hands of Schumpeter was directly concerned with its relationship with economic development. Traditional factors of production, land, labour and capital did not appear to account for all the changes and the major transformations in economies around the world. Schumpeter (1934) argued that it was entrepreneurship that played the key role in such transformations. In more recent times, the limits of mass production (Agiletta, 1976; Piore and Sabel, 1984) and the apparent transition from a managed to an entrepreneurial economy (Audretsch and Thurik, 1997) have also drawn attention to entrepreneurship as an alternative tool for economic development. The gradual recognition of the value of new products and services, technological change (critical components of innovation) and new firm creation (the signature of the process of entrepreneurship) to economic growth gave entrepreneurship its proper place as a new quadrant in the circle of production and economic development.

The early recognition of entrepreneurship as a critical contributor to positive economic growth and dynamism (Schumpeter, 1934; Hayek, 1937/1949; Cassson 1982) and the diffusion of a start-up culture and its importance (Mastakar and Bowonder, 2005; Audrestch, 2002; Birch 1981; Armington and Odle, 1982) led to the identification of small and medium-sized firms as the principal vehicles for job creation. Since then entrepreneurship's role as an economic value creator has steadily entered the consciousness of policy makers and researchers. The availability of risk capital being conducive to new venture creation (Lockett and Wright, 2002), the global mobility of entrepreneurs (Saxenian, 2006) and the hybridization of different business models (Tushman *et al.*, 2001, have added to the significance of the role of entrepreneurship for economic growth.

A central question occupying the minds of policy makers today is how to promote economic development when typical and separate policy measures such as infrastructure development, job creation and foreign direct investment, together with a range of other fiscal, monetary and industrial policies, have generated only partial and often unsustainable economic development in nations, and regions across the world. The problem of inadequate knowledge about economic development, and the absence of the necessary tools with which to identify and evaluate such development, came to a head with the recent economic crisis that has engulfed the first decade of the twenty-first century. As the financial system collapsed and governments around the world, but especially in developed economies, struggled to find suitable economic measures with which to combat the crisis, a surge in interest about the trajectories, measures and objectives of growth has generated a new momentum for the search for a better understanding of and new opportunities and approaches to economic growth.

Consider the following data:

- 139 financial crises between 1973 and 1997 (44 in high-income countries); 38 between 1945 and 1971; Twice as common as before 1914;
- 40 house price bubbles across OECD countries in past 50 years;
- foreign credits for investment– USA ($5.7 trillion or 405 of 2007 GDP; Britain (20%); Spain (50%) – leading to cheaper credits;
- 2007 – big financial corporations showed profits > $70 bn in Britain alone;
- 2009 – huge losses + public bailouts = $15 trn (equal to one quarter of the world's annual income (i.e. $2,200 for each of 6.7 bn people) as against the average annual income of $1.3 bn people in poorest countries = $573);

- governments incurred unlimited liabilities by offering guarantees on bank deposits and bank loans (Iceland – pop. 311,000, per capita income $34,000 and borrowings of $33,000 per head is bankrupt).

Couple this with complicated financial instruments, such as collateralized-debt obligations to aid and abet, individual, corporate and state borrowing. The story continues!
(Source: *New Internationalist*, April, 2009; *World Development Report*, 2009; P. Lunn, *RSA Journal*, Spring, 2009)

Multiple, and the highest number of, economic recessions in the second half of the twentieth century, culminating in the remarkable failure of major banking institutions, critical levels of budget deficits in countries around the world and institutional paralysis in the very first decade of this century, have laid bare the effectiveness of economic policy and indeed some of the research evidence used to make such policy. When problems of such magnitude engulf large parts of the so-called developed world and indeed some developing nations, there is inevitably a high degree of 'soul-searching' among decision makers and researchers. The extraordinary new power of emerging economies saved the day for the 'developed' nations. Curiously, the fastest-growing countries, especially China, in whose reserves ailing nations could find comfort, all boast the power of the state and state-led economic activity as the main conduit for their economic progress and wealth. Did this suggest an end to organizations, modes and norms of behaviour associated with private sector enterprise? Or did it open up possibilities for a more serious look at development through the active pursuit of entrepreneurship and innovation?

The scale of the problem is compounded by other structural, economic and social problems, including the changing nature of industrial organization in the wake of globalization and technological change, the severity of climate and environmental degradation, related population and demographic issues, migration, and the growing gap between the rich and poor between and within nations.

Could it be that policy development and deployment at the national level is limited, especially when it has difficulty adopting linked and shared instruments across nations? Is it possible that policy development at the level of the region has more purchase for economic growth across nations given the uneven levels of distribution of wealth across regions and greater economic connections between regions of the world? Could it be that a fixation on growth and development without any serious consideration of the mediating process or mechanisms for opportunity creation through entrepreneurship is in itself the problem? Could it that the game is up, especially in European countries, as *The Economist* (July 2010) suggests provocatively? These questions make it difficult to find easy answers.

Problems aside, we find significant developments taking place across regions of the world that are often linked with one another through flows of financial capital, technologies, and human capital and talent (Yeung, 2010; OECD, 2010), with the Internet offering a new language of connected development. Much of this development is accompanied by new forms of innovation, new firm formation, new product development, collaborative work, the increasing phenomenon of service-sector-led growth, and socially conscious economic activity. These developments capture the essence of new opportunities in an uncertain world. These are not equal opportunities in a flat world, as Thomas Friedman (2005) would have us believe, but rather uneven ones in a spiky world of the kind that Florida (2002, 2007) refers to in his writings. Many of these developments are concentrated in specific regions and often in cities.

   Problems and opportunities are the drivers of entrepreneurship. But how does entrepreneurship contribute to economic development? What enables innovation to emerge unevenly across space in different countries? What is the nature of the development process in different economies, and how do regions provide a more fertile ground for economic development through entrepreneurship? This chapter attempts to answer these important questions by exploring the subject of development through the lenses of entrepreneurship.

Section One

PART I: ENTREPRENEURSHIP AND ECONOMIC DEVELOPMENT

Discussion on the role of entrepreneurship and economic development takes us back to Schumpeter, who was particularly interested in explaining the importance of the connection between the two.[1] The extent to which entrepreneurship does actually contribute to economic development and growth varies from country to country and even from region to region. It depends on:

- the stage of economic development of a particular nation or a region;
- the level of entrepreneurial activity (as in new firm formation) in a country or a region;
- the nature of the entrepreneurial activity (productive, unproductive or destructive, as per Baumol, 1990);
- the institutional structures, forms of governance and incentives in the economies under question; and
- the cultural and social factors of the economies being studied.

It follows that the study of the role of entrepreneurship in economic development has to take the above issues into consideration. Furthermore, any detailed examination of the function and role of entrepreneurship and its contribution to economic development has also to take into account the connections between these variables. Some of these issues have been discussed at length in other chapters (institutions in Chapter 6; cultural and social factors in Chapter 4; and productive and unproductive entrepreneurship in Chapters 6 and 10). The focus of this chapter is on how these elements come together to have an impact on economic development.

Stages of development and the role of entrepreneurship

Received wisdom and many theories on the value of entrepreneurship have tended to focus on advanced economy contexts in which entrepreneurs operate. In these contexts once entrepreneurs have demonstrated alertness to opportunities there are no other barriers to their realization of those opportunities. This is because in these situations there are few or no institutional constraints (Kirzner, 1997; Von Mises, 1949). Institutions are fully developed, and if there are any barriers such as information asymmetry then the entrepreneurs show their real mettle in overcoming them by exploiting them. Institutions, however, are never fully developed. In developed economies they break down quite often, as recent experience of both banking organizations and government regulations in the USA and in Europe have shown. In developing and especially poor economies, the typical institutional structures that are necessary for opportunity creation and realization, such as capital markets, are weak or even non-existent. Countries, therefore, go through various stages of development that create possibilities for new and robust institutions to be created and managed.

Classical economists, including Smith, Malthus and Ricardo, pointed out the key role of physical, financial and human capital factor accumulation for increases in productivity and structural economic change and development. From a developmental perspective, Lewis (1954) argued that as the economy develops higher levels of productivity and technological change are facilitated by capital accumulation. This does not take place in economies at the early stage of development when agricultural activity dominates the economic landscape. In that scenario we find low levels of productivity, a high level of subsistence activity and the eventual availability of surplus labour. However, with the advent of the manufacturing sector surplus labour is attracted from other traditional (mainly agricultural) sectors. Capital accumulation and institution building (regulatory framework, capital market and financial institutions, governance) make possible higher marginal productivity and, therefore, promise and offer higher wages. Developing economies are caught in a dual mode of functioning that finds a generally stagnating agricultural sector operating alongside a progressive manufacturing sector. This duality disappears as all surplus labour shifts to the manufacturing sector and workers are paid according to their marginal productivity. In developed economies a similar duality occurs with all the concomitants of structural change when the economy hosts a growing service sector alongside its declining manufacturing counterpart.

It was Rostow (1960) who observed that countries go through five stages of economic growth:

- stage 1: a traditional society specializing in agricultural production and small-scale manufacturing run by sole proprietors;
- stage 2: situations where there are preconditions for take-off, with gradual decreases in manufacturing;
- stage 3: the take-off stage, with higher levels of manufacturing;
- stage 4: the drive to maturity; and
- stage 5: the age of high mass consumption.

The interesting point to note is that these theories do not really address what happens between these changes and how entrepreneurship either propels or takes advantage of structural changes in a productive way by creating new organizations with which to manage new technologies that effect change.

Gris and Naude (2008) have called into question the Lewis model, which has been a major influence on development economics, by referring to the absence of the role of entrepreneurship in the literature on structural change and development. In expanding the Lewis model they consider specifically the emergence of financial institutions and the need for access to finance by entrepreneurs, together with the distinction between large firms, referred to as incumbents, and small entrepreneurs. Mature firms offer goods for final consumption while start-up entrepreneurs innovate with unique, intermediate goods and services. Structural changes that move economies from dependence on traditional to modern sectors are generally accompanied by the transformation of production methods, made possible by entrepreneurs who spot the opportunities and pull together the resources to create new firms, attract surplus labour from traditional sectors, produce innovative products (including intermediate ones for the end producer), and raise productivity and employment in both new and incumbent sectors (Gris and Naude, 2008).

A more recent version of Rostow's model is the one developed by Porter (2002), who collapsed the five stages to three, and most importantly identified the role that innovation plays in stimulating and advancing growth. The three stages include:

- a factor-driven stage;
- an efficiency-driven stage; and
- an innovation-driven stage and two transitions.

The high-mass consumption idea of Rostow gave away to Porter's topical emphasis on the innovation-driven economy. We note that the first factor-driven stage is characterized by high rates of agricultural self-employment linked to low-cost efficiencies in the production of commodities and/or low-value products. Sole proprietorship is the main organizational form of the day for small manufacturing and service firms. The nature of knowledge creation and innovation where it occurs is essentially localized. Quite often, both the produce and the knowledge are appropriated by colonizing states (as in history) or large, multinational organizations (in recent times) that appear to use their financial and technological muscle to either seize, occupy or exploit the land and its produce (Storr, 2002; Massey, 1997; Prebisch, 1959). It is not the case that all use of land or other resources is necessarily exploitative, and there is ample evidence of genuine engagement with poorer countries through both overseas state aid and new business models that create and redistribute wealth, solve seemingly entrenched problems, and offer new opportunities for productive development. Public policy in these environments has to make careful choices to ensure that opportunities for new business creation and participation are not thwarted by instruments that preclude their emergence.

Increases in production efficiency, education and training make it possible to enter the so-called efficiency-driven stage with suitable technological adaptations. The pre-conditions are those of increases in efficiency, education and training and technological change driven mainly by the presence of relevant institutions. The type of efficiencies in play enable firms to consider operations in large markets and ensuing economies of scale. We also see a fall in self-employment because managers find it easier to earn more money by being employed. Entrepreneurial activity diminishes also because of improvements in the economic and physical infrastructure, including transportation and credit markets, and an increase in capital stock with resulting higher returns from employment, especially in larger firms. The capital stock of private enterprise, foreign direct investment and government ownership helps to increase returns to employment relative to self-employment.

Increases in entrepreneurial activity tend to take place in Porter's third stage, the innovation stage. There are probably four reasons for this phenomenon:

- there has been a decline in manufacturing, which now occupies a lower share of the economy than before. Over the past 30 years almost all industrialized countries have experienced such a decline together with a reduction in the average size of the firm. Instead the professional service sector has expanded relative to manufacturing, and firms in services sector are generally smaller in size than their manufacturing counterparts;
- a second reason for this change of direction towards increased entrepreneurial activity can be attributed to the nature of technological change in the post-war period. A range of technologies and services built around these technologies, including telecommunications, the Internet, and web-based and mobile services, have enabled speedier communication, and easier and cheaper access to and use of information, especially over long distances;

- increases in per capita capital make it easier for someone to become an entrepreneur;[2]
- increases in knowledge flow as a result of globalization and technological advance open up new opportunities for local knowledge to be exploited overseas and for tapping into knowledge created abroad. This phenomenon drives entrepreneurial organizations to take advantage of the new opportunities and generate even greater prospects for the creation of new enterprises. The knowledge that flows may be assisted by technology but is not necessarily dependent on technological know-how. Opportunities are also found in new business models resulting from open innovation activities, increased end-user engagement, and the attraction of talent and human and social capital from different countries and from connected project management activities.

(OECD, 2010)

Figure 11.1 shows the nature of the S-shaped relationship between entrepreneurship and economic development as it evolves over the three-stage Porterian-type model, connecting modes of production with modes of development.

The account so far helps us to obtain an overview of the points in the curve and within each stage where entrepreneurial activity contributes to development. We begin to note that very small firm activity is not necessarily entrepreneurial in the sense that it contributes to economic growth. This could be one reason why in some poor countries you can find high levels of artisan-type entrepreneurial activities (generally self-employment) that are not making any impact on economic development in those places. Acs (2007) points to Peru, Ecuador and Uganda as examples of such countries. Almost paradoxically, high income countries such as Germany, France, Belgium, Italy and Finland have low levels of entrepreneurial

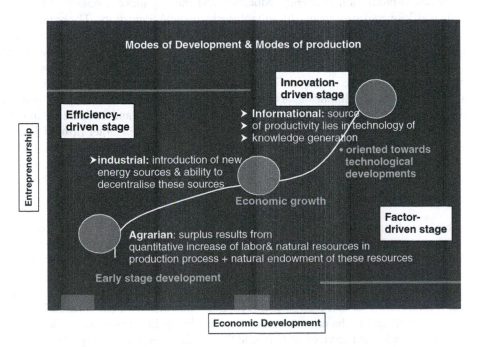

Figure 11.1 The S-shaped relationship between entrepreneurship and economic development and the corresponding stages of development and production (à la Porter)

Source: adapted from Acs and Szerb (2007).

activity because the trade off between wage employment and self-employment favours the former as growing firms take advantage of economies of scale to offer more employment opportunities.

We also note the difference between self-employment driven by necessity mainly in low-income countries, and opportunity-driven entrepreneurial activity in high-income countries especially those where the structural transformation of manufacturing to services open up new opportunities for new firm creation. Finally, we obtain almost a moving image of the relationship between the respective roles of large and small firms in the process of development. Low levels of national income associated with a low amount of per capita income opportunities for self-employment and market creation are more prevalent than scalable new firm formation in the early stages. As the economy improves, increased manufacturing activity and growth prospects of larger firms offer better prospects of employment in larger firms over time. As economies undergo further changes, entrepreneurial framework conditions at a time of rapid technological change and lower costs allow for more people and firms to consider options for new enterprise development.

What drives people and countries to consider entrepreneurship varies according to the challenges, both economic and social, that different regions of the world face at any given time. In the very first issue of the *World Review of Entrepreneurship, Management and Sustainable Development* (2005, vol.1, no.1), Ahmed and McQuaid attempted to identify the different entrepreneurial and management challenges facing the world. Using a e-forum of their editorial board, they explored the regional and geographical differences in these challenges from North America through to Europe, sub-Saharan Africa, East Asia and the Pacific, the Middle East, North Africa, and the Indian Ocean Commission. The Table 11.1 outlines these differences.

The contribution that entrepreneurship can make to economic development in different countries will depend on how the former is able to address some if not all the multiple layers of issues affecting different parts of the world with a view to enabling change for the better.

The relatively complex picture of change prompts us to examine the account against some of the key theoretical tenets of Schumpeter, Kirzner, Baumol, Romer and others.

PART II: RECALLING THE SCHUMPETERIAN AND THE AUSTRIAN HYPOTHESES AND THE ROLE OF ENTREPRENEURSHIP IN DEVELOPMENT

Disequlibrium and the firm

Schumpeter's entrepreneurs upset the circular flow in economic systems and create disequilibrium, giving rise to a process of constant change. As catalysts and agents of this disequlibrium,, entrepreneurs earn profits by technological and organizational innovations and by creating, temporarily, monopolistic firms. Incumbents are, therefore, compelled to change or adapt to technological and organizational developments. The economy in turbulence sees entrepreneurial innovators who create both new firms and manage adaptive, entrepreneurial firms. Some incumbents are more concerned with protecting their established market positioning; they refrain from radical innovations which are taken up by the smaller firm. David and Goliath operate in a symbiotic relationship (Baumol, 2002). However, it is only a small proportion of small, new firms that are innovative and entrepreneurial in highly uncertain environments. It is these firms that contribute to economic development. The higher the

Table 11.1 Regional entrepreneurial and managerial challenges for sustainable development

East Asia and Pacific	European Union	Indian Ocean Commission	Middle East and North Africa	North America	Sub-Saharan Africa
Corporate governance; corruption; financial volatility; capacity development for good-quality human resources; enhance self-reliance and sustaining competitiveness resources	Environmental protection; corporate social responsibility; corporate governance and information transparency; improvement of the quality of life; economic growth; ageing population	Hurricanes and climate change; fragile ecosystems; more market access and better terms of trade; renewable energy; sustainable tourism; information technology; HIV/AIDS and malaria; security and vulnerability; poor human and institutional capacity; lack of technology transfer; poverty reduction, human rights and cultural diversity; gender equality; democracy; access to education for children	Unemployment; gender equality; weak institutional and legal framework; urban and industrial pollution; land and coastal degradation; desertification, and water scarcity and quality, etc.	Rapid move of the Chinese and Indian economies into high tech; recent scandals at Worldcom, Enron and Global Crossing have raised concerns about failing corporate governance mechanisms; failure of higher education to achieve long-term strategy and corporate social responsibility against profit and financial manoeuvring; sustaining higher fuel prices, etc.	Poverty; conflict prevention; peace and security; brain drain; political, economic and corporate governance; macro-economic stability; education and technical training; HIV/AIDS, malaria and health services; cross cultural and diversity management; role of women in social and economic development; development of infrastructure; agriculture and diversification into agro industries and manufacturing; promoting public-private partnerships; encouraging an entrepreneurial mind set; bridging the digital divide; promoting tourism and sustainable utilization of natural resources

Source: adapted and developed from different editorial notes (2005) by Amoateng and Rhoades (North America), Louw (Sub-Saharan Africa) de Pablos (European Union), Foong (East Asia and Pacific), Sohail (Middle East and North Africa) and Juwaheer (Indian Ocean Commission).

number of these groups of 'genuine innovating entrepreneurs', the greater the likelihood of economic growth.

The proposition that higher numbers of entrepreneurs contribute to economic growth does not, however, explain the role of innovative, adaptive larger firms, and the internationally oriented mid-size firms in the process of change. They too adapt and introduce incremental changes, develop new business models, and occasionally create new products (see Chapter 5), and from an overall economic perspective it is their products and services that account for the largest share of innovations across a range of categories, from product and process innovations to non-technological and new-to market innovations, including collaborative effort with other firms (OECD, 2010). In fact Schumpeter went on to his second phase to highlight the unique and dominant capability of larger firms to innovate and, therefore, contribute more directly to economic development.

Opportunity and resource utilization

The Kirznerian idea of market discovery of previously unknown market arbitrage and profit-oriented activities allows for entrepreneurs to capitalize on their particular insight, acquire relevant resources and use them productively. By doing so they help to remove slack from the economy and make effective use of undervalued or under-utilized assets. In the process they earn profits and enable higher productivity yields. Who makes such market discoveries? Is it only the early stage entrepreneur, or could adaptive, incumbent firms pushed to the edge by new players also spot similar opportunities? More importantly, perhaps, what form of capital (or their combinations) do they use most effectively to exploit the opportunities?

Resources utilized by entrepreneurs include physical, financial and human capital. It was Paul Romer (1986, 1990, 1994) and Robert Lucas (1988) who came up with the idea of knowledge being the main driver of economic growth. Technological progress is dependent on the search and generation of new ideas by researchers who wish to profit from their inventions and R&D activities. Both firms and research produce knowledge, and if such knowledge is protected by Intellectual Property Rights (IPR) then the inventors and the firms have an incentive to make new products and take advantage of their temporary monopolies resulting from knowledge of technological progress. Knowledge helps to improve and enhance efficiency levels of firms. Knowledge also spills over from firms to other firms and from one location to another. The outcome is increases in productivity. Romer's innovators and researchers are entrepreneurs. For him, the organization necessary for making such innovation happen was of secondary importance, and to that extent a new firm could be as productive as a larger firm.

Romer and Schumpeter come together in the 'knowledge spill-over' model developed, argued and refined by Audretsch *et al.* (2008); Acs and Szerb (2007); Acs (2006) and Acs *et al.* (2005). Romer's theory misses out on the intermediary and microeconomic mechanisms that transform knowledge into economic progress. Not all knowledge is useful; neither can all knowledge be commercialized. Not all leading innovations lead to market success. These deficits in knowledge as an asset can hinder productivity and economic growth. What converts knowledge to economic and social value is the organization behind the useful knowledge production, namely the firm. This firm could be a large incumbent or a new, dynamic, entrepreneurial firm. Acs *et al.* (2008b) suggest that sometimes incumbent firms invest in new knowledge but do not necessarily commercialize them. There are, therefore, opportunities from such knowledge spilling over to new firms. Similarly knowledge spilling over from university research provides opportunities for new product and service development by new firms.

In considering the role of entrepreneurship and economic development, Baumol (1990) noted that all societies have similar amounts of entrepreneurship but that activity is distributed between productive, unproductive and destructive entrepreneurship. If we are to agree with the S-curve and the evolutionary approach suggested by Figure 11.1, a nation's ability to move through the different stages will be dependent on the type of entrepreneurial activity being pursued in the country or its regions. We can also build in specific features of entrepreneurship policy discussed Chapter 10, especially those concerned with supporting the motivations, the conditions for opportunity creation and the specific role of institutions for each stage of development. A mix of these applications allows for consideration of the implications of both the role of institutions and the environment together with individual attitudes to entrepreneurship. Their application will of course vary from stage to stage. The Global Entrepreneurship Index (GEI) developed by Acs and Szerb (2009) shows a highly sophisticated approach in constructing a single index of entrepreneurship based on a broader definition of entrepreneurship (which is in part advocated in this book – see Chapter 1)[3] and an amalgam of three sub-indices, indicators, variables and weights to create a super-index, the GEI.

All of the models examine the relationship between entrepreneurship and economic development at the level of a country, comparing different countries through a set of indicators and parameters concerned with different stages of growth. But can we compare one country with another and rely on benchmarking policy based on such comparisons? Is such comparison valid when we find remarkable levels of unevenness within countries? How do we compare entrepreneurial ingenuity in Hyderabad, Bangalore and Noida in India with the eight states that harbour levels of poverty higher than those found in 26 sub-Saharan countries combined to provide us with a clear picture of entrepreneurship that can guide policy? What are the motivations for starting up business activity in the North East of England, with its high levels of economic and social deprivation, compared to prosperous London and the South East of England? How do we square the developments of the economic powerhouse that is the Asia-Pacific region, containing some of the most dynamic economies, with the deficiencies in rural sanitation, access to clean water and environmental sustainability (UN-ESCAP, 2008). There are problems with considering the role of entrepreneurship in the economic development of countries.

PART III: LOOKING AT DEVELOPMENT AND ENTREPRENEURSHIP CRITICALLY

Growth as the 'big' issue

There is a particular problem with approach to growth studies that tends to deal with broad-brush macro evidence of growth in terms of specific structures and stages. As Banerjee (2009) suggests, there is the 'illusion of commensurability' in such an approach. Since growth is a 'big' question for most economists, the response must be to provide evidence of 'big things'! The idea of structural transformation is a 'big thing', and the architects of such transformation need to be big players enabling big changes. The problem is exacerbated by the use of homogenous, or standard, principles and instruments of growth. Do all countries move uniformly from one stage to another if they use the right set of policies, tools and devices? Is there a defined 'right set' mechanism or formula, and can entrepreneurship rely only on these mechanisms for enhancing development? If the USA transformed itself from a country dependent on agriculture and extractive industries through to manufacturing and innovation-driven, knowledge-based industries, do the policies, strategies, conditions, and cultural and social dimensions hold for all countries aspiring to US heights? How does the US account for the wasted landscape of Detroit, its soup kitchens and its recalcitrant recovery post-Katarina alongside the extraordinary capacity for creativity, drive for technological change, opportunity generation and wealth creation in California, Richmond, North Carolina and Boston? Is such unevenness a necessary condition for entrepreneurship and economic development?

Writers using S-curve models of growth have suggested that the creative corpus of new firms can be found in advanced economies (the phenomenon being referred to as the 'Schumpeter effect'), while low-income countries are more likely to see a preponderance of the 'refugee effect'. Van Stel *et al.* (2005) found a degree of confirmation of a positive effect of total entrepreneurial activity (the old GEM index called TEA) on GDP growth in highly developed countries but not for poorer countries. This type of generalization and abstract explanation (even when supported empirically) does not explain how a low-income country such as India has regional pockets of highly creative new technology businesses generating the Schumpeter effect while other parts of the country serve as oases for 'refugee' firms. It also does not explain how firms in different regions from both high- and low-income economies do business with one another, creating regional 'hot-spots' that have more in common with one another than their national counterparts. Statistics at the aggregate level tend to hide such variations. The unfortunate use of terms such as 'refugee' to describe the emergence of new firms in developing or low-income countries masks an epistemological bias in the research process differentiating almost in a neocolonial fashion between notions of entrepreneurship in poor and rich countries. Should firms in high-income countries be referred to as 'landlord' firms, generating connotations of rapaciousness associated with the word? These distinctions preclude analysis of the value of different kinds of entrepreneurship according to their contexts.

Identifying specifically employment creation, innovation and economic growth as the key variables Thurik and Wennekers (1999, 2004) and Carree and Thurik (2003) in their extensive surveys of the literature suggest that entrepreneurship contributes to economic growth through the introduction of innovation, change, enhanced competition and, most importantly, start-ups and entry into new markets. They highlight the role that entrepreneurship and new venture creation play as a mechanism for achieving these outcomes. Others, however, have questioned the contribution of new ventures and growing firms, suggesting that the subject remains shrouded in controversy and that the contributory impact varies across time and nations (Henrekson and Johanssen, 2008; Acs *et al.*, 2008b). Various authors (Fritsch and Falck, 2007; Audrestsch and Keilbach, 2004; Acs and Armington, 2004; Van Stel and Storey, 2004; Nijkamp, 2003) have examined the function of agglomeration in entrepreneurship, investigating its impact on knowledge spillovers as measured against start-up rates and new venture formation.

If, as Baumol (1990) also argues, the nature of growth is linked to the type of entrepreneurial activity that is being pursued then is the reduction of unproductive or destructive entrepreneurship in the form of corruption, for example, necessarily a worthwhile institutional pursuit? What form of corruption is worst? In the absence of suitable data, relevant action may be difficult to consider. Moreover, what causes greater degrees of unhappiness or difficulty for the victim of corruption? Is it coercion or is it bureaucratic delays? And how do we account for other variables such as rent-seeking lobbying activities and biased decision-making, the costs of which are outside the scope of the individual entrepreneur? The need to investigate smaller issues at the micro level is perhaps more appropriate for the study of impacts and influences that matter for development because contexts are different.

Culture and development

There is the significant variable of culture and history of a nation. Culture, as Nijkamp (2003) suggests, is one of the three related factors for entrepreneurship, the other two being personal motivation and the social environment. Aoyama (2010) notes that 'culture is the most deeply embedded and resilient aspect of informal institutions, and they are closely tied to the regional trajectory, production system, and business opportunities' (p. 171). In common with Hayek (1937, 1949) and Casson (1982), he argues that culture shapes individual motivations, economic objectives and socially accepted behaviour.

Zapalska and Edwards (2001) refer to the dynamic factor of culture in regional development in the context of reforms in the Chinese economy. They suggest that some aspects of Chinese culture that may be conducive to entrepreneurship jostle with others that are trying to adapt to a market economy environment. Trial and error and a mix of ideas might be driving their approach to economic development. To give one example, the propensity for experimentation in China, which Deng Xiaoping described as 'feeling our way across the river', is at the core of public policy and action. As Ravallion (2008) indicates, the 'evidence from local experiments in alternatives to collectivized farming (using contracts with individual farmers) was eventually instrumental in persuading even the old guard of the Party's leadership that rural reforms could yield higher food output'. This form of experimentation in policy is seen in what Heilmann (2008) highlights as three forms of experimentation in China:

- regulations identified explicitly as experimental (that is, provisional rules for trial implementation);
- 'experimental points' (that is, model demonstrations and pilot projects in a specific policy area); and
- 'experimental zones' (that is, specially delineated local jurisdictions with broad discretionary powers to undertake experimentation).

Nearly half of all national regulations in China in the early to mid 1980s had explicitly experimental status, operating side by side with much grander national schemes. The idea of adaptability to change and gradual progression has implications for how any form of policy is developed. The results of the experiment may lead to either the take-up or the abandonment of particular policies in particular regions. Chinese reforms have been highly entrepreneurial in nature, and the outcome of that experimentation was initially private ownership and financial liberalization (Huang 2008). As early as 1985, of the 12 million businesses registered as township and village enterprises (TVEs), 10 million were private. He argues that policies before 1991 were perhaps more favourable to individual enterprise, especially in non-farm sectors which developed vigorously in the 1980s. Huang (2008) also points to the difficulty in making glib comparisons between firms in China and most western countries on the basis of ownership. For example, the TVEs are defined by their locations of establishment and registration (i.e. businesses located in rural areas) and not their ownership. Since the 1990s Chinese policy has changed to better provision for the cities and the state-led and urban-based boom. Culture in China, variations to the Chinese cultural theme in different regions of that country and the vagaries or exigencies of time in those contexts reveal the importance of cultural influences on development at particular points in time.

Goals and objectives

A critical issue relating to economic development and the direction of public policy is the need for appropriate and relevant goals. Alongside culture, we can consider the differential impact of the implementation of key technologies and the relatively simple local schemes meeting local needs on the economy of especially developing nations. Policies for both actions have significant impact. The use of mobile phones and an increase of 10 per cent in the number of mobile users results in approximately 1.2 per cent of economic growth, according to Waverman et al. (2007). At the other end of the spectrum, and as Jeffrey Sachs observes, social entrepreneurship in the form of free access to and distribution of nearly 200 million insecticide-treated nets to reduce malaria transmission together with community-based drug treatments have led to a plummeting of malaria deaths in Africa. Developed as part of the Millennium Development Goal (MDG) initiative of the United Nations, community groups worked closely to ensure scaling up, coverage and access to bed nets. The model for malaria control is being extended to smallholder farming as Malawi and other African countries have shown. Technical experts review and approve national action plans prepared by countries, and a global fund disburses money for bed nets, malaria medication, high-yield seeds and fertilizer, all part of a pledge made by Barack Obama to set up a global plan to make MDGs a reality. These policies generate economic and social value for a premium variety of entrepreneurship that overreaches limited attempts to measure the value of policy and economic growth in terms of the 'big' picture and major change. Clear and specific goals that are context-driven and apply to targeted, local economic and social needs offer productive outcomes for local development.

Causality

The question about causal links between key variables raises doubts about applications of macro growth models for policy measures. This question is essentially about what comes first. Does entrepreneurship lead to economic development or is economic development a necessary condition for entrepreneurship? Is entrepreneurship a 'necessity' in some countries because there is no other economic option? It is driven by opportunity where people can make choices, as in developed countries? The GEM reports categorization of 'necessity' and 'opportunity' entrepreneurship does not help us to understand prevailing factors and causes affecting new form creation and innovative growth in different countries. Even developed economies have large pockets of necessity-driven entrepreneurship in, for example, inner cities or when there is an economic downturn.

Does entrepreneurship skew allocation of resources because it disturbs the economic equilibrium, or does it reallocate resources effectively to help the economy attain equilibrium? How can we connect entrepreneurship with growth when certain writers, especially development economists such as Roland Benabou (1996), have shown that countries that redistribute grow faster! The identification of a growth curve and the neat categorization of different types of economies along that curve does not always help us to ascertain the causes of growth or causal relationships between growth and entrepreneurship.

Regions or nations?

Certain writers have argued that specific regions within countries not only buck the national trend in terms of growth and development but their technological, human, networking, cultural and infrastructure resources together with their interconnectedness with other parts of the world make them more important for the study of economic development (Ohmae, 1990; Florida, 2005, 2007; Sassen, 2007). In other words, regions are growing at a pace that far outshines growth levels in a country, and part of this growth is attributable to localized opportunities that also draw from global sources of talent, technologies and finance. Some of these regions do not follow an S-curve of development but rather their rapid progress often gives them an I-curve growth trajectory (Prahalad and Krishnan, 2008)! This is especially the case in countries that may be at the bottom to the upper middle of the S-curve. Examples include Bangalore, Shanghai, Taipei, Seoul, São Paulo and others. In these places a mix of private and state-sponsored entrepreneurship together with high levels of human capital is the contributory factor for growth.

Cities in particular, and the global networks of specific cities, are the nodal points of flows of capital, technologies, talent, culture and ideas between multiple nodes and hubs across vast networks, featuring especially the power of information and communication technologies, in particular the Internet, and finance, including corporate and venture finance (plus sovereign funds). These are the 'projective' cities of Boltanski and Chiapello (2007) that 'fly' outside the orbit of nations and are founded on the 'mediating activity employed in the creation of networks making it valuable in their own right'. The connections between, for example, London, New York, Frankfurt, Shanghai and Mumbai with specific reference to the financial services, information and communications technologies, new media, film and related creative industries has a greater significance for the growth of these industries and entrepreneurial opportunity than the links that these cities have with their in-country counterparts. This is because the flow of money, technologies and talent between these cities is constant and of immense magnitude, contributing to a new geography of centrality and marginality. As Sassen states:

> The most powerful of the new geographies of centrality at the global level bind the major international financial and business centres: New York, London, Tokyo, Paris, Frankfurt, Zurich, Amsterdam, Los Angeles, Toronto, Sydney and Hong Kong, among others. But this geography now also includes cities such as Bangkok, Taipei, São Paulo and Mexico City. The intensity of transactions among these cities, particularly in the financial markets, trade in services, and investment, has increased sharply and so have the orders of magnitude involved. (Sassen, 2007)

Where regions are connected globally and share common or synergistic features of production, technologies and skills, it is possible to consider the significance of mutual dependency between these global regions as being more important than the value of their country-bound geographical proximities. Broad-based development policies in a country may not have any bearing in certain regions of the same country unless policy makers choose to offer difficult, multi-level and differentiated solutions to complex region or sector-specific problems.

What the above discussion suggests is that different levels of data, and especially micro data about entrepreneurs, cultural conditions and specific contexts, may be required alongside the need to carry out localized evaluation to judge whether entrepreneurship has any effect on economic development. The other major issue is that about measurement and the use of a valid barometer of development. Should outcomes and outputs be mainly concerned with GDP (the standard measure), job creation (a central public objective), about 'happiness' as the Bhutanese and the French President, Nikolas Sarkozy, would prefer, or should they be about new products and services? Or is it the case that different types of entrepreneurial activity, as evinced in the motivations and actions of necessity-based (the push factor where entrepreneurship is the best or only option) or opportunity-based (voluntary participation in entrepreneurial activity) entrepreneurs (GEM), call for different measures for their proper evaluation?

While development is generally measured in terms of GDP, the value of entrepreneurship in policy circles lies in its ability to create new jobs and in some cases the retention of existing jobs, or both. Since, probably the second industrial revolution, and certainly the late nineteenth and early twentieth centuries, all industrialized or industrializing countries have seen the larger organizations, Moss Kanter's 'giants' and Chandler's custodians of 'scale and scope' dominate economic activity. Curiously, from the 1970s a new trend emerged as a number of studies showed that the dominant position of large firms had begun to reverse and that entrepreneurial activities were increasingly the domain of smaller firms.

There are differences across regions; there are differences in time and space, and within and between countries. There are cultural factors that constrain or facilitate entrepreneurship. Small firms and large firms engage with innovation in different ways and create better value at different points in the development curve. There are limitations in the general application of policies for development. In short, there is no universal panacea of entrepreneurship that can and should be used to promote entrepreneurship. Consequently, ranking countries using a composite index of development terms of 'best practices' may provide policy guidance but at worst could be dangerously misleading (Henrekson and Stenkula, 2009). Countries and regions need, therefore, to orient their entrepreneurial strategies and approaches to their particular environments. These environments are not necessarily points or stages in a single growth continuum, but a mix of cultural, social and economic trajectories informed by an incommensurable set of values, institutions and knowledge.

Mini case study 11.1: Haiti, development and entrepreneurship

Take the case of Haiti and its earthquake-ravaged economy. Six months after the disaster the cost is estimated at 120 per cent of Haitiain GDP. The international community has pledged almost US$10 billion to help re-build the country, and the International Committee for the Reconstruction of Haiti co-chaired by Bill Clinton, the former US President, and Jean-Max Bellerive, the prime minister of Haiti, are going to decide how the money will be spent. What are the choices they have for entrepreneurial activity in this region that could make a difference in the lives of the people through scalable and innovative activities, and contribute to economic development?

Job creation is a top priority. Only 120,000 people out of a population of 9 million people work in the formal economy. According to the prime minister, the agro-industry is one of the biggest pillars for growth. The Haitian Chamber of Commerce hopes that 1 million jobs can be created in the next ten years; that is, approximately 11 per cent of the population or roughly 1 per cent on average of the population obtaining jobs every year. But these jobs could help to generate growth of 10 per cent per year, possibly putting Haiti on track to becoming a developing nation.

Paid work is hard to come by. People employed on cash-for-work programmes run by aid agencies clear rubble in Port-au-Prince, the capital city, or help to prevent flash floods by digging canals. The fragility of their lives is underscored by the tented settlements dotted around the capital for people rendered homeless by the devastating earthquake.

Enterprising Haitians have turned some of these tents into beauty salons or cinemas, while others use portable generators to charge mobile phones at a price. These, generally short-term, opportunistic activities of necessity reinforce or complement the fragility of wage sector jobs described above. Their Kirznerian efforts reveal their alertness to opportunity and arbitrage, but they can hardly sustain or scale up these operations. Against this background is the country's massive dependence on imports, particularly agricultural imports accounting for approximately 80 per cent of food consumption.

Weaning itself off the costly imports by focusing attention on agriculture, and on niche products such as mangos, could help Haiti create new jobs and new business opportunities and grow its exports. Farmers who gather under the shade of a candelabra tree, listening to plans for the building of a mango collection centre in the small village of Kamo, north of Port-au-Prince, believe such a centre would 'revolutionize' their work by reducing waste and transport costs. The collection centre is a US-backed project supporting a key pillar of the economy – agriculture – by harnessing the capabilities of entrepreneurs to assist with plans for economic development. Although, according to one of Haiti's biggest mango exporters, a mango goes to waste for each mango that is exported, farmers could help grow exports five-fold if they were given the right tools, taught proper techniques and promised markets.

Alongside agriculture construction is another potential generator of employment. Together with the rebuilding of more than 250,000 homes, there is a need for new infrastructure. The textiles sector exports about $400 million of goods per year, which is approximately 70 per cent of Haiti's annual total. Thanks to a US Congressional bill giving Haiti preferential access to US markets, Haiti's textiles sector enjoys a promised or guaranteed market.

The prime minister does not believe in US tax exemptions as a panacea; his aim is to use the fund to motor real and long-term growth. Despite its ostensibly chaotic thrust, the extensive interest of business in the Haitian economy is high. Will these investors create new opportunities by buying out Haitians and their assets?

Between the search for local opportunities by local people, and the interventionist plans for international funds to guide the opportunity drive, there is the manoeuvring of private investors from abroad. Among many stories of private investment is an exceptional one of Digicel, a phone company founded by an Irish man, Denis O'Brien, long before the 12 January earthquake. O'Brien, who accumulated his capital from the sale of his Irish mobile-phone network, Esat, for an estimated $3.5 billion, has a 60 per cent market share in Haiti.

Before 2006, when Digicel arrived in Haiti, only 5 per cent of the local population used cell phones. Digicel has contributed to a rise to about 30 per cent of the population using these phones in a space of only four years. Digicel's engagement with the underprivileged in a market context was central to its success, enabling local people to find new opportunities for work and enterprise based on effective communications technologies. This development has echoes of Grameen Bank's use of mobile phones to boost productivity and enterprise among village women in Bangladesh or ITC's efforts in promoting farmers' auction markets with the effective use of computers and mobile phones.

After the earthquake Digicel donated free phone time worth $10 million, together with cargo planes and boats and relief supplies. The company has also donated $5 million to local non-governmental organizations and is also constructing 50 schools and distributing family-size tents to more than 100,000 Haitians. Alongside the commercial gains from the mobile phone business and the philanthropy following the earthquake, the new entrepreneurial opportunity that O'Brien is pursuing is better and more effective institution-building for supporting grass roots business generally ignored by large corporations. O'Brien is actively backing the construction of the Iron Market in Port-au-Prince – an important commercial nexus to better facilitate trade locally – and coordinating Bill Clinton's 'Clinton Global Initiative' (CGI), which has committed more than $100 million to education, infrastructure and business development projects.

The mix of philanthropy and business is not restricted to O'Brien. The Soul of Haiti Foundation, established by a group of Irish business leaders, is also working with local Haitians to help redevelop the economy. This approach is enabling fishermen to obtain solar panels to make ice, helping them to establish small seafood transport firms, and helping farmers with their biodiesel start-ups using jatropha plants.

Haiti has probably been forced back to the factor-driven stage by natural disasters. Underdevelopment was not of Haiti's making. It now finds a presence of small-scale entrepreneurs, some pushed to finding opportunities wherever there is information and other asymmetries and others identifying opportunities for change and growth using relevant technologies with a little backing from international donors and private investment. At another level, institution-building and reinvestment are making possible the rescaling of key components of its economy – the agricultural, textiles and construction sectors. Institutional support for these three sectors could help promote Haiti along the growth trajectory. To achieve such an outcome Haiti would probably have to combine the development of entrepreneurial framework conditions of skills development, incentives and encouragement of start-ups with broader national policies for education and training, FDI and infrastructure development for the agricultural, construction and textiles industries. This might help Haiti not only to wean off its overdependence on imports and reduce the number of necessity-driven self-employed. To some extent, it is irrelevant whether Haiti eventually leaves its 'factor-driven' stage and adopts an 'innovation-driven' model. Perhaps what matters more is Haiti's ability to fuse strategies for innovation-driven economic activities to drive and change its factor-driven industries, such as agriculture, alongside some of the efficiency-driven sectors of textiles. Entrepreneurship enables economic development where policy-making is multifaceted and is in itself entrepreneurial in facilitating the nexus of public sector intervention, international collaboration, including donations and private investment, and the harnessing of local absorptive capacity.

(Source: adapted from 'Haiti sets out on road to sustainable future'; reconstruction, by Benedict Mander, *Financial Times*, 13 July 2010, and 'Corporate Conscience: Answering the Call' by Tim Padgett (with reporting by Jessica Desvarieux), *Time*, 9 August 2010)

Section Two

PART I: REGIONAL DEVELOPMENT AND ENTREPRENEURSHIP

A way out of the maze of questions and answers relating to a variety of issues is to examine entrepreneurship and development at the spatially disaggregated level of the region. Such an approach might help us to focus on specific and containable issues and variables that affect growth in the region even if we know that there are various other external factors, including national policy, that affect outcomes at the local level. An examination of the relationship between entrepreneurship and regional economic development might better allow for a sharper focus of the interplay between different factors that impact on or influence new firm formation in specific regions. It also helps us to address the variations in the outcomes of entrepreneurship and economic development in terms of differences in firms being created or lost, jobs created and retained, and the roles of institutions and policies to support local economic development in those regions.

The European Union and the OECD have been promoting the particular role of entrepreneurship in benchmarking and catching-up for under-performing regions in Europe (OECD, 1998, 2010; EU, 2003; HM Treasury and BERR, 2008). In academic circles there has been growing interest in 'regional innovation systems', and 'regional competitiveness' and 'regional systems', both before and with the dawning of the era of globalization. They argue that regions compete globally for the location of foreign direct investment (FDI), innovation, skills and business opportunities (Martin and Tyler, 2000). Others have provided theoretical insights and empirical observations of connected regions such California (Silicon Valley) with Bangalore, Mumbai, Shanghai, Beijing, Tel Aviv and Taipei, with their flows of capital and technologies and circulation of brain and talent (Saxenian, 2006; Florida, 2007).

Regions and the role of entrepreneurship in the economic development of regions is what we turn to next in Part II.

PART II: THE MEANING AND STRUCTURE OF REGIONS

Origins

The origin of the word 'region' is to be found in the Latin regio, which has its roots in regere, meaning 'to govern'. The word 'region' is, therefore, associated with governance of policies of institutions facilitating economic development, social cohesion and environmental upkeep. In this sense of governance, the administrative aspect of a region and its institutions is particularly important. A region such as the West Midlands in the United Kingdo, is an administrative region with its constituent administrative institutions, including local authorities. Various countries have borrowed the term as the formal name for a type of entity at the level of a sub-national administrative unit, as for example the Administrative Region of Quebec in Canada or the 'Autonomous community of Murcia' (Region de Murcia) in Spain. The Brazilians group their 'estados'. the primary administrative divisions, into 'grandes regioes' or greater regions for statistical purposes.

Administration, politics and geography

The administrative unit is both political and geographical in scope, giving the regions their distinctiveness drawn from their unique historical, cultural and political backgrounds. The statistics division of the United Nations Division has classified regions according to whole continents, or macro-geographic regions, sub-regions and selected socioeconomic groupings. A purely spatial or geographical definition of a region is also possible. Regions can be defined by physical characteristics, human characteristics and functional characteristics. As a way of describing spatial areas, the concept of regions is important and widely used among the many branches of geography, each of which can describe areas in regional terms. For example, 'eco-region' is a term used in environmental geography. Political geographers focus on political units such as towns, counties (as in the UK), townships (as in South Africa) territories at the sub-national level and sovereign states at the national level, or in terms of wider multinational networks such as the Association of Southeast Asian Nations (ASEAN) or Middle Eastern and North Africa (MENA) countries. In an abstract sense, regions could be war zones, such as Helmand in Iraq, or functional, social and cultural spaces, characterized by the concentration of specific social, cultural, military or other activities.

Functionality

When a region has a defined core with a special characteristic that diminishes with distance from it, it is often referred to as a nodal or a functional region. The node is the focal point, which is linked functionally to its surrounding areas by various types of economic activity, transportation and communication systems. There is a specific and tangible geographical function for these nodes. Travel-to-work distances, commuting habits and patterns, the flow of goods and services, and personal consumption behaviour as expressed in the use of shopping malls between these nodes are typical measures of their nodal value or the area within which specific economic and social activities take place. This helps with data collection for the national and regional census and for research purposes.

Other measures and policy-oriented economic classifications

Economic indicators in Europe tend be classified by what are called NUTS (Nomenclature of Units for Territorial Statistics) regions. NUTS provide a uniform breakdown for the production of regional statistics for the European Union (EU). There are three levels of NUTS in the UK:

- NUTS 1: the developed administrations of Scotland, Wales and Northern Ireland and the 9 Government Office Regions (GORs) of England;
- NUTS 2: 37 areas, often referred to as sub-regions;
- NUTS 3: 133 areas, groups of unitary authorities or districts, sometimes referred to as local areas.

(ONS, 2009)

There is a fuzziness about these 'abstract' regions that stems from critical and analytical reconfigurations of beliefs, values and cultural perceptions of groups of people. Quite often these regions are difficult to define in terms of size, and confused with smaller 'districts' or 'quarters' such as the cultural quarters of Hoxton or Soho in London or the creative district of Xu-hui or Tianzifang in Shanghai, so called because of the natural or engineered concentration of specific creative industries in those sub-regions. What is important to note is that the typology of regions offers insights into their different economic and social compositions, the involvement of different stakeholders, and the creation and availability of different sets of opportunities mediated by entrepreneurs and by institutions. The effective combination of the functionality of regions, and the administrative and institutional arrangements, together with the optimal mix of relevant institutions, contribute to regional economic growth. Our concern here is first with the mechanisms and processes that contribute to the achievement of this optimal mix for economic development in regions. More specifically, our focus is on entrepreneurship and in particular on new firm formation.

This argument suggests that the regional milieu can affect an individual's propensity to engage in entrepreneurial activity. We therefore turn our attention to the specific question of new business formation (as a proxy for entrepreneurship) and regional economic development.

PART III: NEW VENTURE FORMATION AND REGIONAL ECONOMIC DEVELOPMENT

Kirzner (1973) wrote about entrepreneurship consisting of competitive behaviours driving the market process. According to this view, any new economic activity in the market can be regarded as an instance of entrepreneurship. Therefore new innovative and imitative forms entering the market are all part of the entrepreneurship process. Early writings by Cipolla (1981) and Lazonick (1991) show that the reallocation of resources to new opportunities, adoption of new techniques, diversity of outputs and the discovery of new markets confirm the positive connection between entrepreneurship and economic growth. New firm formation is based on rational decision-making by individuals who choose between becoming entrepreneurs and being employeess. Increasing levels of new firm creation generate additional inputs to the economy. The additional inputs create value through a market selection mechanism, resulting in business churn or the absorption of new businesses in the market and the elimination of incumbents from that market. The formation of new businesses has a range of supply-side effects including accelerated structural change, amplified innovation and higher levels of efficiency, all leading to growth and employment opportunities. This process of entrepreneurship leading to growth is clearly explained in Figure 11.2.

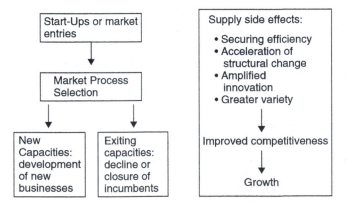

Figure 11.2 New business formation and the market process

Source: Fritsch and Mueller (2004).

Studies in the USA (Birch, 1979, 1987), Sweden (Davidsson *et al.*, 1998) and Canada (Baldwi and Picot, 1995) have attempted to show empirically the job creation capabilities of small and new firms. Similarly, Reynolds (1999) also found that job creation as a proxy for economic growth was dependent on new firms being established in 382 labour markets in the USA. Start-up firms can help to create employment opportunities both in themselves and in incumbent firms, as the latter are compelled to explore growth opportunities arising from new competition (Fritsch and Muller, 2004).

Fritsch (2008) suggests several ways in which competition created by the entry of new firms can encourage employment growth on the supply side of the market (see Figure 11.2). These include:

- securing efficiency and stimulating productivity increase: occurring as a result of challenges to established market positions of incumbents who are forced to perform efficiently (Baumol *et al.*, 1988);
- acceleration of structural change: the business churn effect (entry of new firms and the exit of established ones) arising from the 'creative destruction' process', with Marshall's (1920) old trees falling to make way for the new ones;
- amplified innovation: through the creation of new markets from radical innovations by new firms that take advantage of the insecurity or lock-in factor affecting incumbent firms who are more interested in exploiting opportunities for profit from existing goods and services, especially if the new firms threaten their old portfolio (Geroski, 1995);
- greater variety of products and problem-solving: variations in products introduced by the new firm or significant process innovations.

The advantages listed above may come from a variety of sources both within and outside any particular industry in which the new firms belong. The introduction of a product for use by an intermediary organization in another industry as an input is a case in point (for example, mirrors for cars). The sources of these changes and innovations could also emanate in different regions.

Mixed results

Is there a causal relationship between high business birth rates and economic progress, or is it essentially a by-product of the factors driving the growth process? For some authors the regional context for new venture creation and its effect on job creation (as a proxy for economic development) does matter (Plummer and Acs, 2004; Fritsch and Mueller, 2004; van Stel and Storey, 2004). However, Acs and Storey (2004) have argued in their review of a number of recent studies on new firm formation and regional economic growth that the evidence on the subject remains inconclusive. In many respects what we known about entrepreneurial activity at the regional level is limited (Audretsch and Keilbach, 2004). Regional distribution of entrepreneurial activity is uneven (Reynolds *et al.*, 1995), but the impact of regional location, or spatial factors, on an individual's decision to become an entrepreneur is still unclear (Anyadike-Danes *et al.*, 2005). Mueller *et al.* (2008) have suggested that quality of entrepreneurship may be more important than quantity when the long-term employment benefits and costs of start-ups are taken into account. But what does quality depend upon, and how do we square this point with another observation which suggests that new ventures are more likely to grow in regions where there is good stock of firms already?

Fritsch (2008) suggests that the reason for the mixed results of various studies is that the impact of new firms being created could increase the levels of productivity, compensating for the employment effect. Not all the effects of new firm formation on employment may occur immediately. There are likely to be time lags. Van Stel and Storey (2004) found that there are considerable time lags between new firms being created and their effect on regional development, which they found to be positive. They discovered an inverse U-shaped curve for the magnitude of the effects over time, indicating the peak for a start-up activity that occurred five years earlier. The impact then becomes weaker, with virtually no effect on regional employment for start-up rates with a time lag of more than ten years. Fritsch and Mueller (2004) found a 'wave' pattern in new business formation in West Germany. For years 1–5, the effect is negative, with a minimum in year 3. In years 6–9, a positive relationship could be found between the seventh and eight years. This positive effect then disappears after years 9–10.

The arguments referred to above have familiar echoes with questions of firm entry and the contexts of entry. A fuller discussion of contexts takes place in Chapter 6, but what we can note here is that, contrary to Gibrat's Law, contexts do matter, and the type of firm entry is dependent on the sectors, the life cycle of industry and indeed the geographical factors that impinge.

Take the case of the United Kingdom. Using a range of explanatory variables such as unemployment, inward investment, population growth and GDP per head at regional and sub-regional levels, researchers have concluded that variations in start-up rates are dependent on a set of inherited and historic supply-side characteristics combined with recent demographic and market demand trends (e.g. Ashcroft and Love, 1996).

This pattern gives rise to various forms of regional economic inequality over many decades at region, sub-region and city economy levels.

PART IV: ENTREPRENEURSHIP AND UNEMPLOYMENT REDUCTION

If growth through employment creation is possible through entrepreneurship, can the latter have an impact on unemployment? In other words, does growth in terms of employment created by new firms help to reduce unemployment? Both Storey (1991) and Audretsch and Keilbach (2004) found the causal relationship between new firms and reduction in the levels of unemployment to be ambivalent, despite what Evans and Leighton (1989) referred to as the 'refugee effect' or the push factor leading to individuals seeking self-employment because of unemployment. Moreover, as van Stel and Storey (2004) note, such push factors together with low entry barriers may lead to start-ups that guarantee self-employment of the owners of the new business but not necessarily any new jobs or economic growth because of displacement activities (fierce competition among small businesses leading to the closure of existing businesses because they are displaced by the newcomers).

Interpretations and data deficiencies

Research completed in the late 1970s indicated that new and smaller firms – not large established firms – were a major source of job creation. But this raises other questions of about what constitutes a start-up. It is difficult to identify an autonomous new firm unless the enterprises that make up a single firm can be identified. Otherwise an autonomous start-up can be confused with a branch or subsidiary created by an existing firm. Similarly, the closure of a listed firm could mean either the dissolution of an active firm or the outcome of a multi-location firm closing one particular unit. Changes in ownership of the same business need to be separated from new ventures started by an owner. Businesses that have been dormant for less than two years are not considered a death and birth but a productive unit in continuous operation.

Also, when is a firm born? A 'birth' is defined as 'the date at which the business first become active' (Eurostat/OECD, 2007, p. 2), raising questions about what is meant by 'active'. To try to minimize these data count problems, attempts have been made to harmonize national data sets. The OECD, for example, focuses only on employer firm data (only firms with employees), thus excluding the self-employed who, by definition, employ themselves only. Some new firms may also, however, start with one owner as the employee of the firm, and if such new firms are not counted then it may be difficult to track the emergence of new firms. Additionally, different types of firms attract employment at different stages of their business life cycle, and ignoring firms with no employees may raise issues about the appropriateness of measuring firm births, survival and growth.

A further issue is about the invisibility of many new births. In both developing and developed economies a good proportion of firms are not registered formally, because of problems associated with property rights in developing economies (De Soto, 1989) or because of underground work in the hidden economy due to social inequalities across regions or because people are marginalized from formal employment (Williams, 2006). Their invisibility often calls into question research evidence on firm creation in developing countries and deficiencies in policy-making that fail to 'legitimize' their worth. They do not appear in formal registers acknowledging their existence. Incentives and conditions for firm creation are, therefore, discounted, or at worst meaningless if a significant population of new firms are 'invisible'.

Regional factors and effects are likely to have varied connections with different types of start-ups. Population density and educational attainment levels, for example, may affect the degree to which employment-related scale economies can be organized or the extent to which high-quality teams can be assembled. Start-up rates at the regional level may also be affected by the availability of good schools and amenities (Florida, 2005) or by house prices (Ashcroft and Love, 1996). It could be argued that the level of human capital is more important than financial capital in a region, and that low levels of human capital tend to impede the creation and growth of financial capital.

The relationship between technological progress, entrepreneurship and social capital on the one hand and economic growth on the other creates problems for economists in that they find a difficulty in identifying the independent variable which is not adequately captured by the different growth models on offer.

The economic rationale for the role of entrepreneurship and economic development provided above by various researchers and discussed in the previous section does not, however, provide a clear explanation as to why various factors are important and how the process of development actually occurs. Entrepreneurship can be an individualized or a social process, where individual or group actions are influenced and shaped by social expectations, beliefs, obligations, norms of behaviour, ethics and institutions (Casson 1995; Davidsson, 1995), and myths, dogmas, ideologies and half-baked theories (Denzau and North, 1994). Uncertainty creates opportunities for interactions between individual mental models and collective institutions (both formal and informal) as part of a co-evolutionary process.

Entrepreneurial behaviour and action can correlate positively with familiarity and knowledge of other entrepreneurs, institutions and practices, or what Minniti and Bygrave (1999) referred to as 'regional institutional memory'. Such memory forms part of the legacy of a region, a concept that helps us to understand the distinctiveness of a region, the continuation and evolution of its regional culture, and what generates 'path dependency' for entrepreneurs, or a reliance on local practices and norms, even when they are acting as agents of change.

PART V: PATH DEPENDENCY, REGIONAL LEGACY AND REGIONAL INSTITUTIONAL MEMORY

In carving out new directions for the economy through new firms and the production of new goods and services, entrepreneurs draw from and sustain regionally prevalent skills, business customs and institutional norms. Their sustenance, supply and widespread use represents the economic equilibrium point which Schumpeter (1934) recognized as the starting point for all entrepreneurial, creative destroyers of equilibrium. Alertness to their deficiencies and asymmetries generated by uneven information flows among agents spurs the Kirznerian (or indeed Casson's) entrepreneur to harness opportunities for obtaining eventual equilibrium in the economy.

Mini case study 11.2 Path dependency and regional legacy: two Japanese stories

In an interesting study of Japan, a country that has consistently scored low among high-income economies in terms of business start-up rates, high-growth expectations, international orientation, new product-market combination and social acceptance of entrepreneurs (Bosma *et al.*, 2007), Aoyama (2010) examines two contrasting regions to evaluate the influence of regional legacies. He selects Hamamatsu and Tokyo because of their reputation for successful entrepreneurship in the knowledge industry of information technologies. Both regions are also unique in the sense that they are located outside the Tokyo Metropolitan Areas which monopolizes much of Japan's talent. Additionally, neither of them boasts the presence of a dominant parent company that organizes the region as a company town in the way Toyota does with 'Toyota City'. So both regions are different from the 'Tokyo-centred vision of Japan's entrepreneurship' and 'reveal dramatically different regional contexts shaping entrepreneurship behaviour' (p. 173).

Kyoto's industrial strength is based on a unique mix of the traditional and the modern. Its traditional handicraft industries include silk colouring, textile weaving (known as Nishijin), kimono accessories, Buddhist ceremonial cabinets, ceramics and dolls. It protected these industries tightly to maintain superior quality and beat other regional competitors in the same game. Family enterprises are the essence of the landscape of Kyoto's business organizations, partly because Kyoto was one of the few metropolitan regions that escaped the air raids of the Second World War. The small, family-run businesses are among the oldest in the country, and right up to 1970 some 500 firms could trace their ancestry back at least a century. Sole proprietorship in Kyoto is higher than in other urban areas in Japan.

Kyoto's industrial duality is represented by the new industries of silicon transistors and optical analytical, dental and scientific equipment. These industries draw on the tradition of craftsmanship that characterized older industries in the region. Small, high-quality batch manufacturing and the filling of niche markets characterize the operations of these new industries. As the Kyoto Prefecture Survey (2002) notes, the epithets 'high-class' and 'high-value-added' are the features of its products, not their 'affordability' according to the respondents of the survey.

In keeping with the tradition of dominant family-based industries, Kyoto's regional culture is supposed to be secretive, aloof and indirect.

Hamamatsu tells a different story. It is a manufacturing centre, an initial location of Japan's Technopolis programme and know for its unique regional culture referred to as the 'yaramika' spirit. Both its position as a regional capital and transport hub and special political circumstances played a role in the openness of its regional culture. Its industrial antecedents can be traced back to lumber and shipbuilding in the eighteenth century, the two industries being mutually dependent because of the latter's reliance on both wood and sophisticated carpentry skills. These skills were transferred subsequently to textiles, piano manufacturing, opto-electronics, motor cycles and automobiles. It was also the central region of innovation for automated looming machines, the most prominent among the key players being the founders of Toyota and Suzuki Motors.

Honda motors sold one of its first machine tools to the national railroad industry and produced the first 50cc engine mini-bike from its origins as an automobile repairs shop and parts manufacturer. Suzuki and Yamaha followed the motor cycle trail soon afterwards. The three firms established a large subcontractors' base drawn from the makers of looming machines and musical instruments. The region's electronics industry emerged from local innovation in broadcasting after a faculty member at a local technical college produced the first electronics-based television broadcasting in 1927. The market for electronics systems was augmented by demand from the region's motorcycle and automobile industries. The emergence of a substantial manufacturing base can be seen in the statistics produced by the Hamamatsu Chamber of Commerce (2000). One hundred per cent of pianos, 62 per cent of motorcycles and 34 per cent of subcompact cars were produced in Hamamatsu by the end of the last century. Successful large-scale manufacturers engaged in mass production helped to create a wide range of small manufacturers, generating new business opportunities all along the value and supply chains for entrepreneurs from both within and outside Hamamatsu. A huge bank of local skills which collected its human capital deposits over two centuries in the region also evolved through a process of migration of skills, shared learning and socialization.

The two regions are fine examples of path dependency and regional legacy at work. While paradigms have shifted over time and different industries have evolved, they have done so on the back of selection, variation, and adaptation. There are two dominant models in the two regions of Kyoto and Hamamatsu. Kyoto boasts an industrial tradition of 'heritage' craftsmanship, and the power and sustainability of the family enterprise, all of which has evolved over time to niche, high-quality, new industries. While knowledge has flowed with adaptation and learning from one niche industry tributary to another, much of this flow has been directed by the family enterprise and the small organizational make-up. Although there are a larger number of registered foreigners (mainly long-term resident Chinese and Koreans) than in Hamamatsu, their percentage is lower than in the latter region. Hamamatsu's dominant business tradition is based on large industry competencies and capabilities centred around mass production and innovation in automation. The overall, national start-up rates may be low, but new business ideas, the development of new products and services, and the formation of new organizations in specific regions remains buoyant. Both regions have lead firms, but while one large firm, Yamaha, had a huge impact in generating the regional IT industries through sub-contracting and the outsourcing of product development, entrepreneurs in Kyoto avoided employment in firms often because of family obligations and expectations. What is common to them is the region-specific resources they have used in to emerge as exemplars of different traditions of entrepreneurship and economic development.

(Source: *Aoyama*, 2010)

As the above case study of the two Japanese regions demonstrates, regions carve out a distinctive memory through the acts of entrepreneurs, the legacy of organizations and the arrangements of institutions over time. They create region-specific resources that entrepreneurs adapt to and use to develop new products and services. In some cases they disturb the circular flow of these goods, services and resources through the introduction of new ideas. What makes regions accept these new ideas is dependent on their absorptive capacity created out of the resources in the region. We proceed to a short review of some of the theoretical work on region-specific resources.

PART VI: REGION-SPECIFIC LEARNING RESOURCES AND SOCIALIZATION

What would have been regarded as the 'invisible hand' factor supporting the success of specific regions in the past can now be attributed to 'softer' issues. Such issues include competitive technical and managerial expertise, explicit and tacit knowledge, the synergies derived from strong interaction in input–output linkages, collective learning, and what Capello (1998) describes as the 'dynamic socialization' process based on trust, openness, reciprocity and voluntarism (Miles and Snow, 1992). These 'softer' issues have a tangible force only if they are embedded in regional economic activity (Granovetter, 1985; Becattini, 1989) and are almost impossible to duplicate.

The pressures, incentives, capabilities and competencies inherent in the socialization process work through collective learning, inter-firm linkages and the play of region-specific resources that support region-specific activities. Enright (1998), building on Barney (1991), argues that just as a firm's resource position can lead it to a position of sustainable competitive advantage if the resources are valuable, rare, imperfectly imitated and not subject to substitution, so the region's specific resources can help to lead to sustained competitive advantage for the region: 'As with firms, the region's resources will be difficult to imitate if they depend on unique historical conditions, the link between resources and competitive advantage is causally ambiguous or the resources are socially complex' (p. 322).

The learning and innovative milieu

Region-specific resources are generated by the close linkages among flexible and specialized SMEs, often in the same industry, contributing to the production of the same product group (Braczyk *et al.*, 1998), as in industrial districts. The Gremi group's idea of the 'innovative milieu' posits a dynamic model in which the milieu is a complex network of informal relationships in a limited geographical area enhancing local innovative capability through 'synergetic and collective learning processes' (Camagni, 1991). The 'territorial ecosystem' of innovation model developed by Mitra and Formica (1997b) highlights the spatial dimension to networking and learning among regional firms and institutions. They use the idea of a region as a 'territory' bound by inimitable behaviour, actions, institutions and forms of direct and tacit learning that are shared together with cultural and social values, skills sets and resources. It is this 'territorial' nexus of factors that generates path-dependency, allowing regions to evolve as spaces of change and industrial metamorphosis. They cite the case of the evolution of the packaging machinery industry from the early 1900s and the evolutionary path that took the region from early straw-hat making, to the invention of a powder that makes the water effervesce, through to the development of the automatic machine for packaging before the Second World War, and then on to large-scale packaging machinery for mass consumption and finally to modular machinery for the global packaging industry. Some parallels can be drawn with the evolution of Hamamatsu and Kyoto in the case study above.

Regional learning

The resources and activities of SMEs are often embedded in the region (Granovetter, 1985; Becattini, 1989), and innovative outcomes can sometimes be seen to be the result of a symbiotic relationship between the strategies of individual SMEs and other firms, small and large, in a region. Regional embeddedness takes both social and economic forms and is often an important determinant of learning. In this sense firms, wider communities and the region act collectively as 'learning organizations' or 'learning networks'. Firms cooperate and network to reduce uncertainty and maintain stability, for 'sensemaking' within a spatial setting. This helps to form a common set of meanings and agendas which constitute the building blocks for 'organizational learning' (Cullen and Matlay, 1999). Such learning is facilitated by what Storper (1997) referred to 'untraded interdependencies' between trust, tacit knowledge, and local norms and customs.

Regional learning and social capital

Central to this collective learning agenda is social capital (see Chapter 3 for a detailed account of the meaning of social capital and how it is related to entrepreneurship). Defined as the 'networks, norms, relationships, values and informed sanctions that shape the quantity and co-operative quality of a society's social interactions' (Performance and Innovation Unit, 2002), this includes shared rules for social conduct encompassing trust and civic responsibility. Networks, norms and sanctions facilitate the coordination and cooperation for mutual benefit of two or more members of a group, whether these groups are characterized by vertical (hierarchical) or horizontal (equal) relationships between the members (Puttnam, 1995; Coleman; 1988). As Iyer *et al.* (2005) suggest, there is an interesting parallel between the components of social capital and their place in an economy and the importance of 'informal institutions' in developing countries where these institutions are often the main building blocks of growth and development.

The contribution of social capital to economic development is predicated upon the distinction between the words 'social' and 'capital' and the eventual confluence of their meaning and values. The word 'social' connotes social interactions, and the extent to which these interactions might have some effect on economic performance; it can be construed as a form of 'capital'. Economic output is a function of labour or human capital, land or physical capital, technology and social capital in accordance with the Solow-Swan model of growth and its various versions (Solow, 1956). The availability of social capital may influence early adoption of technology facilitating growth or hindering such absorption and use, depending on the cultural and social norms, practices and institutions of different regions. This suggests that social capital can be positive or negative, the latter being a function of 'lock-in' where communities are locked into ways of doing and thinking that do not embrace change. Social capital influences group behaviour and/or group formations positively or negatively in economic terms. In influencing social behaviour, social capital can generate externalities where the costs or benefits associated with such behaviour go beyond the individual's benefit to benefit a wider group.

Social capital and networks

Given the level of private and social dependencies, social capital could be described as a system of interpersonal networks (Dasgupta, 2000) creating network effects (result of group membership) and externalities (behaviour of others affecting individual member). The informal institutions in developing countries (or for that matter in developed economies when the state's support systems are rolled back, as in a time of recession), for example, often overcome information asymmetries and contribute to growth, through trust leading to cooperative behaviour among those who use those institutions. Such trust can prevail in networks of destructive economic activity, as in criminal gangs, leading to a subversion of the economy. This negative effect can be countered by greater focus and promotion of social capital for civic cooperation backed by resources. In productive environments, cooperative behaviour can lead to positive externalities as they spill over from one network to another, especially with goods and services that are 'non-rival' or 'non-excludable', meaning that they do not affect any direct competition between the groups.

Much of the above discussion is centred round the macro- and microeconomic functions of social capital. Macroeconomic issues are compromised by the special characteristics of a region; and in relation to microeconomic considerations, a region is not a simple aggregation of many firms. The reference earlier to regions and the embeddedness of trust, learning, culture, norms and institutions is better explained by Marshall's explanation of regional competitiveness being driven by 'something in the air', which Iyer *et al.* (2005) argue was possibly an early recognition of the value of social capital. Entrepreneurial firms are dependent on such capital and spillovers, as Garnsey and Heffernan (2005) and Abubakar and Mitra (2007) have shown with respect to technology-based firms in the Cambridge area. However, as the economy expands, bonding social capital can decline and this can have a negative impact on collaboration and participation in networks. A growing technology-based local economy carries specialized labour as part of a supply chain connected with other parts of the world. Under these circumstances, local networks can be upstaged by global ones as a local economy grows and reaches critical mass. Rookie firms in new industries cannot penetrate these specialized networks.

How, then, to connect social capital with entrepreneurship and economic growth? The multiple variables and the levels of interaction that contribute to first identify entrepreneurial opportunities and achieve economic development are probably best organized within systems both organic and artificially created to stimulate innovation and entrepreneurship through these forms of connections and interactions at the regional level.

Systems of innovation and entrepreneurship

The idea of innovation as a 'system' with spatial and social/cultural dimensions involves the study of national and regional systems of innovation, including industrial districts, spatial networks, clusters and other 'focused environments'. A fundamental point of the 'systemic view' is that it allows for a connection between 'technological' innovation and 'organizational' innovation. This connection also suggests that the factors that foster or frustrate technological innovation are not limited to the internal jurisdiction of the firm (Cooke, 1998). When it occurs, innovation is 'new' to the firm and/or the market, and even when it is absorbed within the firm it has introduced a 'new' dimension. Competitive factors of cost reduction, value added and new market opportunities may be the spur for innovation, but in essence it has enhanced the firm's activities or capabilities. In this sense the firm has made an extra connection with the market and the wider environment, sometimes beyond the routine interactions of daily business. Additionally, the innovation process combines, inter alia, different activities of design, research, market investigation, process development, organization restructuring and employee development. The innovation process is, therefore, not complete without connections being made at the level of skills, functions, technologies, commercial production, markets and other organizations (Mitra, 1999).

The other critical element in innovation systems is what Jacobs (1969) referred to as the 'competition of new ideas' as opposed to the competition for new products. Jacobs's idea of competition is more likely to take place where there is a greater diversity of industries because of possibilities of new knowledge creation through interactive learning processes. This in turn facilitates new firm creation, specializing in niche services or products.

Lundvall (1992), Nelson (1997) and others, following the work of Freeman (1987), have focused on *national innovation systems*, while Saxenian (1994), Braczyk *et al.* (1998) and Cooke and Morgan (1998) have concentrated their attention on *regional systems*. Still others (Carlsson and Stankiewicz, 1991; Freeman and Soete, 1997) have studied *technological systems*. The basic proposition of this literature is that the study of the institutional context of the firm and its relations with other firms is as important as the study of the innovation process in a single firm.

The 'systemic' view has as it antecedents in the Marshallian (1920, 1923) notion of externalities where knowledge and its transfer to other economic stakeholders is a factor favouring spatial concentration of industries. The Marshallian idea of 'knowledge spillovers' plays an important role in the regionalization of innovation and is significant within both federal states (Audretsch and Feldman, 1994) and urban areas. Manifesting itself within supply chain relationships, horizontally related firms, transfer of people and their skills, shared pools of knowledge of markets, research, and so on, these spillovers are considered to benefit regions disproportionately. The economic rationale offered for the existence of such localization from Marshall (1920) onwards to Weber (1930), Enright (1990) and Krugman (1991) is to be found in this idea of special benefits coupled with that of the unique presence of natural resources that accrue in industrial or regional clusters. The cluster-based benefits help to reduce uncertainties and risks associated with innovation. Systems of innovation can, therefore, be located in regional clusters.

Regional clusters

Knowledge spillovers, inter-firm relationships, utilization of shared resources, a well-developed local skills base and the evolution of the region through tacit and explicit knowledge exchange are typical features of regional clusters. These features also provide the basis for social and economic 'connectivity' that underlines the operation of firms in clusters. Reference is made to 'clusters' as one of the most attractive phenomena in the evolution of economic activity engendering growth.

Enright (1998) defines a cluster as 'groups of firms in the same industry, or in closely related industries that are in close geographic proximity to each other' (p. 337). This view corroborates the findings of Glaeser *et al.* (1992), which in turn are attributable to the Marshall-Arrow-Romer model of externalities (Audretsch, 2002). The geographic concentration of interconnected firms is supported by interconnected suppliers, downstream channels, customers and manufacturers of complementary products, and can also extend to companies with complementary skills (Porter, 1998). Clusters also include public institutions, such as government education institutions, and support services, with cluster boundaries being defined by linkages and complementarities across institutions and industries (Porter, 1998).

Clusters represent the advantages of the agglomeration process. Firms agglomerate because of specific locational advantages. A Marshallian explanation, as provided by Ellison *et al.* (2010), suggests that agglomeration occurs for the following reasons:

- *Proximity to customers and suppliers* – firms locate near one another because they are inclined to reduce costs of procuring inputs or transporting goods to downstream customers. As Marshall (1920) argued, firms will trade off the distance between suppliers and customers based on the costs of inputs and finished goods. Ellison (2010) *et al.* offer the example of sugar refining, which was one of New York's largest industries in the nineteenth century. The advantage lay in transport costs and scale economies. Sugar was refined in New York instead of on the tropical plantations because the heat of a ship's hull coalesces refined sugar crystals during a long voyage.
- *Labour market pooling* – firms co-locate because they wish to take advantage of scale economies associated with a large supply of labour in a region. A large labour market offers risk-sharing properties. As the fortunes of firms wax and wane, employees can move across employers, potentially maximizing productivity and reducing the variance in wages. Agglomeration also enables better matches between the skills of workers and the expectations of firms and, interestingly, these workers may invest more in developing their own skills in a cluster because they do not face what Ellison *et al.* (2010) refer to as 'ex post appropriation', or the lack of opportunity to deploy new skills.
- *Intellectual or technology spillovers* – the third reason that firms are attracted to clusters is the relative speed of the flow of ideas and knowledge. This includes higher levels of information exchange (Saxeninan, 1996), the urban focus of high human-capital industries (Glaser and Kahn, 2001), networking benefits (Arzaghi and Henderson, 2008 – see others below), supplier–customer relationships because of co-existence (Scherer, 1984) and employee churn across firms.
- *Natural advantages* – various natural resource advantages attract firms in specific industries. Areas with cheap electricity from hydroelectric power will draw aluminium producers; timber merchants in the Baltic countries of Latvia, Estonia and Finland converge because of the abundance of forests; and disparate industries such as oil and

shipbuilding might co-exist because of a preference for coastal regions (deep sea oil extraction and a natural home for shipbuilding, respectively).

The connection between the idea of regional innovation and clusters lies in the understanding of the successful evolution of clusters whereby their formation, organization and structure are themselves features of an innovation process. Various clusters have evolved from having *comparative competitive advantage* (based on physical resources) to demonstrating *sustainable competitive advantage* (based on interactive relationships, learning and knowledge) – the way in which old clusters have overcome the loss of original locational advantage. Thus the replacement of water power by electricity, wood by coal, and the easy availability of steel, did not prevent Solingen from continuing as a successful base for the cutlery industry. It achieved this through its reliance on the particular expertise of its workforce (Enright, 1998). At another point on the spectrum, the disadvantages of a poorer regional economy has not prevented Sialkot in Pakistan from being the second largest exporter (after Germany) of surgical instruments in the world (Nadhvi, 1998). In essence, therefore, the ability to identify, accumulate, utilize and recycle learning resources embedded in the region has proven to be the major source of 'competitive advantage' for many regions.

The consequence of innovative evolution has been that clusters attract public and private finance, chambers of commerce and trade associations generating commercial market research, regional government providing industry-specific infrastructure, and local educational institutions doing industry-specific training and research. This combination of integrated and leveraged activity is often at the heart of innovation and collective learning, as the literature on innovation highlights (Rosenberg, 1982; Malecki, 1991).

Evidence from a variety of studies (Mitra *et al.*, 1999; Carbonara and Mitra, 2001; Mitra, 2002) shows that critical factors such as local partnership, collective learning, internationalization, availability of skilled workforce, proximity to market, an entrepreneurial culture, supporting services and the presence of local venture capitalist networks all contribute to successful cluster development.

It is noted that many clusters have developed in an organic manner. However, clusters do not emerge without considerable endeavour from the parties involved. On the one hand, as Birley *et al.* (1991) pointed out, entrepreneurs have to work hard to develop relationships: they have to persuade, socialize, bargain and reciprocate with others to create a relationship and maintain it. By and large, entrepreneurs' commitment to clustering will be dependent on their attitudes towards networking and their perception of clustering benefits. On the other hand, the emergence of a so-called knowledge economy allows for increased spillovers of knowledge within regions as the latter harness specialist technologies, related expertise and a knowledge base that contributes to global economic development.

Most small firms face the problem of resource constraint in the creation and growth stage. Yet small firms demonstrate an ability to generate a disproportionate share of innovations, especially in regional contexts where there is a presence of larger firms (Acs and Audretsch, 1990). Also, small firms, especially high-technology firms in conventional industries as in the UK, have a greater R&D intensity than their counterparts in high-technology industries (Hughes and Wood, 1999). There also appears to be a greater reliance on flows of information through collaboration and networking among firms, including R&D and information systems at the local level (Cosh and Hughes, 2000). The higher the stock of firms in a region, the greater is the propensity for growth, especially in niche areas of supply. Similarly, diversity of the industry base allows for greater collaboration, new firm creation and innovations (Feldman and Audrestsch, 1999; Audretsch, 2002).

As clusters grow, various problems emerge. Physical congestion often leads to space constraints, problems with power supply (as in contrasting places such as Silicon Valley and Bangalore), concentration of skills and expertise in a selected range of areas, the 'lock-in' factor which impedes new knowledge flows and absorption, and a gradual decline in relative expertise and competitive advantage as a result of the lock-in problem. Policy makers need to explore different strategies, as do firms seeking new opportunities for growth in the same, related or new industry areas.

Mini case study 11.3: Spatial factors, clusters and regions of IT growth

The emergence of second-tier locations is a factor determining the growth of the ICT industry in India. Locations such as Pune, Kolkata, Bhubaneswar, Amritsar, Cochin and Vizag have also grown both as 'out-location' initiatives of firms such as Wipro, and as centres for home-spun software firms that cannot find a place in the more expensive first-tier cities of Bangalore and Hyderabad. This combination of large firm involvement coupled with the smaller firm's birth and growth in these cities has generated a clustering of firms in particular regions as part of a process of agglomeration.

Software firms in India are highly concentrated in geographical terms. Ever since local entrepreneurs and the technology giant Texas Instruments discovered its potential as a high-tech city in 1986, Bangalore has seen a major technology boom, and is home to all the major home-grown giants suc as Wipro, Infosys, TCS and Cognizant I-Flex. Apart from being the hub for IT, Bangalore is also famous for some of the best education centres in India. It is home to some premier institutes such as the Indian Institute of Management – Bangalore (IIM–B), Indian Institute of Science (IIS) and Indian Institute of Information Technology – Bangalore (IIIT–B). Bangalore can boast some other research organizations such as Defence Research and Development Organization (DRDO), ISRO Satellite Centre, ISRO Telemetry Tracking and Command Network (ISTRAC) – organizations that have taken India into the space age.

But Bangalore now represents all the characteristics of a successful, probably overheating cluster, racked in the inside by congestion and other infrastructure problems, and on the outside by the growing strength of an abundance of other industrial clusters, as Figure 11.3 shows.

The growth potential of other regions is possible because of the knowledge spillover process. First, physical congestion prompts firms, especially lead global firms, to seek alternative or additional regions to carry out research, production and service development activities. Second, migration to other centres is made possible by the availability of talent in those regions. Third, there is the imitation effect as sharp levels of differences in regions resulting from the growth of these clusters creates possibilities of institutional support for new opportunities for growing and lead firms, including incentives and tax benefits. Fourth, diaspora communities look for alternative spaces in which to establish new ventures. Fifth and finally, different levels of expertise allow for differentiation in activities, especially in a large country such as India.

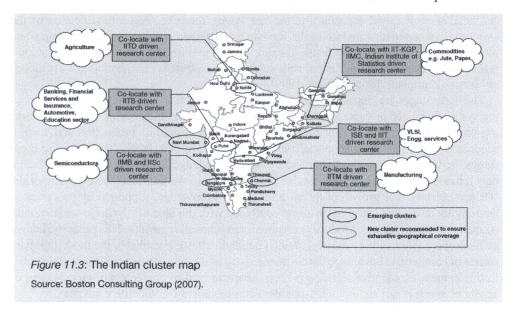

Figure 11.3: The Indian cluster map

Source: Boston Consulting Group (2007).

The extent to which local governments and policy makers are taking advantage of these new trajectories of development is open to debate. What is noticeable is a shift in policy-making priorities from the national to the regional/local stage (devolution) and the increase in the number of intermediary organizations managing delegated social and economic functions previously the domain of the state. Whether such induced forms of entrepreneurial activity can also embrace the organic developments referred to earlier depends on the realization that the former is perhaps a by-product of the latter, and that the latter can reinforce overall entrepreneurial growth through a plurality of entrepreneurial organizations in both economic and social spheres, as in a clustered environment.

PART VII: STAGES OF REGIONAL DEVELOPMENT AND ENTREPRENEURSHIP: INNOVATION AND THE LEARNING CURVE

The region-specific resources model does not necessarily explain how relationships between firms and regions work. What needs to be taken into consideration is the evolution of the innovation process through different stages of development of the firm in particular regions in association with other players in the network or cluster. Development through these stages is closely linked to learning as firms move from one form of organizational practice to another to create new portfolios of products and services.

In recent years, theoretical and empirical studies have identified significant changes in the distinctive characteristics of clusters and industrial districts (IDs). The evolutionary process of most IDs manifests itself in three stages:

1   the start-up stage of 'formation';
2   the 'development' stage; and
3   the growth stage of 'maturity'.

(Carbonara and Mitra, 2001)

As the IDs evolve (and especially in the last stage), there is often a modification of the structural characteristics including the innovation management processes. The stages and their evolution (including modification) would appear to reflect the processes of 'variation', 'selection', 'retention and diffusion' and 'struggle for resources' that distinguish evolutionary forms (Campbell, 1965; Aldrich, 1999).

The early stages are characterized by the reinforcement of a 'craftsman-like' manufacturing system localized in a specific geographic area, and then by the development of networking processes among firms that carry out an integrated system of production activities in accordance with the 'flexible specialization' model (Piore and Sabel, 1984). During these stages the technical-operative, tacit and informal knowledge, widespread in the local area, play a fundamental role in the innovative processes and in the industrial development of the IDs and clusters. The growth of technical-operative knowledge, supported by processes of learning by doing and learning by using, combined with the idea of 'dynamic socialization' (Capello, 1999) processes, produces very important innovative results. This property, known as 'widespread innovative capacity' (WIC) (Bellandi, 1989), is probably the most important source of competitive advantage for clusters, as long as the competitive environment is static. In this context an adaptive learning process, characterized by incremental improvement of products, services and technologies, enables firms to generate competitive advantage.

The description of the different stages of evolution is complicated by factors associated with both the density of inter-firm links and rapid change linked to technological developments, namely uncertainty, complexity and the constant need to assess relevant competencies with which to sustain the learning process.

PART VIII: FORMS OF CAPITAL, CREATIVITY AND ENTREPRENEURSHIP IN REGIONS

The discussion on clusters reinforces the point about the interplay between the different forms of capital – physical, financial, institutional, social and human. The pendulum swings gently from one end to another and often rests on specific points in the capital continuum as different writers emphasize the value of different forms of capital, the entrepreneurial use of such capital and the economic outcomes that flow from such use.

Richard Florida (2002, 2005) indicates that the source of the new competitiveness of nations lies in the movement of human capital. The passage of the most creative and talented people from nation to nation is fundamentally important to understanding a nation's future success or failure in global competition. At the centre of this thesis is the concept of the 'creative class'. Florida (2005) defines the 'creative class' as those employed in the fields ranging from science and engineering to architecture and design, and from arts, music and entertainment to the creative professions of law, business and finance, health care, and related fields (p. 7). The ability of regions to attract the creative class is a function of their talent, the use of critical technologies by such talent (hence their availability in a region) and the tolerance of the diversity of such talent. These three dimensions are converted to three separate but interrelated sets of indices and the formation of the 'Global Creativity Index' (GCI). The GCI is the weighted average of three indices:

- talent index, measured by creative class, human capital and scientific talent;
- technology index, measured by R&D index and innovation index (patents); and
- tolerance index, measured by values index and self-expression index.

Florida's arguments are based on the following assumptions:

a   we are witnessing the rise of the creative economy in which the primary drivers of eco-
    nomic growth for both regions and nations are technology, talent and tolerance (3 Ts);
b   creative talent and the knowledge and technology creative people bring with them are
    mobile factors, and an area's ability to hold these critical factors lies in its openness,
    diversity, and tolerance;
c   firms, instead of bringing talent to their existing locations, set up facilities where the
    talent already exists;
d   more urbanized and denser areas gain productivity advantage owing to their ability to
    bring together and argument creative talent;
e   the creative economy will aggravate economic inequality and increase social and politi-
    cal tension.

According to Florida (2002), creative centres across regions are those places where 'all forms
of creativity – artistic and cultural, technological and economic – can take root and flourish'.
In those creative centres, the agents of production are small firms with the entrepreneurial
drive; spatial proximity fosters social interaction and trust, and dense local networks create
a dynamic atmosphere that spurs innovation, lures talent, attracts investment and generates
growth through a self-reinforcing, endogenous process. This has led to the emphasis on the
importance of creative networks in cities. Cities are said to be privileged locations in the
new information-rich economy as nodes of intense business interaction and sharing of ideas
and insights, leading to rapid learning and innovation (Leadbeater, 1999). Florida seems to
imply that the creative sector, in his definition, tends to thrive in a small number of places
where both the infrastructure and the tolerant environment exist, and that the rise of the creative economy will therefore reinforce the pattern of regional disparity or the core–periphery
relationship.

Florida's work explicitly recognizes the nature of global connectivity, relationships and
dependencies between firms, regions and nations, based on the flows of capital, talent and
other resources in a spiky or uneven (as opposed to 'flat') world. He accords the movement
of human capital a particular premium given the advent of creative enterprises in all industries and in connected regions. While there are distortions in human capital development
across the world, talent appears to overcome such distortions because of the concentration of
innovation in regions, and especially cities. Either talent is concentrated in particular cities as
evinced in the majority of patents taken out by resident investors from only a small number of
countries; or there is migration of talent among those who are able to create new inventions
or start high-flying enterprises in a selected number of ecosystems. In both cases we find
innovative ecosystems, and these ecosystems matter (Florida, 2007).[4] Talented people form
part of a transnational elite community who contribute to international knowledge formation
from the old brain drain (one-way flow of talent from poor country to developed nation) to a
two-way process of 'brain circulation' as they crisscross continents to raise capital, transfer
and diffuse technologies, know-how, process information and become linked into global production systems. As Saxenian (2002) argues, they coordinate between the network flagships
and suppliers, often leveraging on their knowledge of local languages and cultures, and help
identify original equipment manufacturer (OEM) suppliers and inter-firm communication.
The connection of human talent from different regions across the world together with the
flows of knowledge and resources that accompany them points to a trend that has become a
feature of the so-called knowledge economy – the globalization of regional development.

PART IX: REGIONAL ECONOMIC DEVELOPMENT, GLOBALIZATION AND ENTREPRENEURSHIP

Studies on the impact of globalization on regional development have their theoretical antecedents in considerations of the different influences and factors that shape the direction and nature of regional economic development. External or exogenous factors or their internal and endogenous counterparts have caught the imagination of researchers. Research conducted in particular environments where the idea of the 'region' is clearly defined in terms of the path-dependent and evolving historical institutions tends to emphasize endogeneous factors. However, dramatic changes in the wake of the global economy have turned the dynamics of countries and regions on their head, setting up different relationships between organizations in different countries. Much of this interest in the new regional dynamics and transnational business activity stems from enquiries into the activities of multinational firms. Massey (1979, 1984), for example, refers to the spatial division of labour that occurred as a consequence of the dynamic relationship between foreign direct investment by large firms, the organization of their production through transnational firms and multi-plant operations, and the social relations between regions. The analysis of the role of multinationals in regions is seen primarily in terms of corporate control of business activities and the unevenness of different power relations between the core metropolitan regions in the West and the periphery in the developing countries. The ability of local firms to mediate and in some situations to develop their entrepreneurial agenda is ignored.

Regional studies including various attempts to construct regional innovation systems (see above) have focused on regional learning, innovation, networks and associations (Braczyk *et al.*, 1997; Morgan, 1997; 2004; Cooke *et al.*, 2007; Amin and Roberts, 2008; Fritsch, 2008). But the majority of these studies have paid limited attention to the linkages between global and local firms. Furthermore, the glorification of the region has resulted in some degree of myopia about the influence of both historical and recent global currents and interrelationships. Bialasiewicz (2006; quoted by Yeung, 2010) writes this about Veneto, a region much praised for its unique regional clusters:

> the fortunes [of Veneto] could not have been made without the global market and its hypermodern thirst for innovation, a thirst that Veneto entrepreneurs have been masterful in exploiting. (p. 46)

Bialasiewicz questions the much-vaunted assertion that all there is to the Vento model and its self-organizing system is hard work and local creativity. The idea that some regions, because of their unique internal factors, social embeddedness and tacit knowledge, were successful innovators and producers suggests that other parts of the country and the rest of the world are passive consumers.

The critique of an excessive focus on regional virtues allows us to consider other possibilities and avenues for enquiry. A 'relational' view of regional development (Sunley, 2008; Allen and Cochrane, 2007; Massey, 2007; Amin 2004) examines regions as self-sustaining territories. However, these authors also indicate that these regions are not closed systems and their networked environment is open to global exposure. Newer studies in regional development (Coe *et al.*, 2008; Harrison, 2007; Pike; 2007; Yeung, 2005, 2010) have begun to analyse the intricate relationship between regional change and globalization and the particular arrangements created by global production networks (GPNs), emphasizing the specific and varied nature of relationships between key actors that distinguish these GPNs.

The East Asian canvas provides for the detailed hues, pigments, shades, portraits and land-scapes of structural, institutional and organizational change in the context of globalization, nation states and regions. While many economists and management scholars have tended to examine the mechanics of the state or the large organization in driving development in East Asia, there is, as Yeung (2010) argues, a need to study the 'strategic coupling' of various economic actors, including small, medium and large firms together with their lead firms which 'orchestrate trans-regional networks on a global scale'. The firms (both regional and lead) and the institutions are part of the GPNs. In these networks both firms and institutions play major roles. Firms are truly entrepreneurial in that they not only produce new goods and provide new services, but more importantly they actively shape the regional economic landscape, enabling cluster formation, promoting inter-regional competition for investment and technologies, and the creation of what McKendrick *et al.* refer to as 'economic space' (McKendrick *et al.*, 2000). Figure 11.4 provides a picture of a GPN and the levels of inter-regional competition for investments.

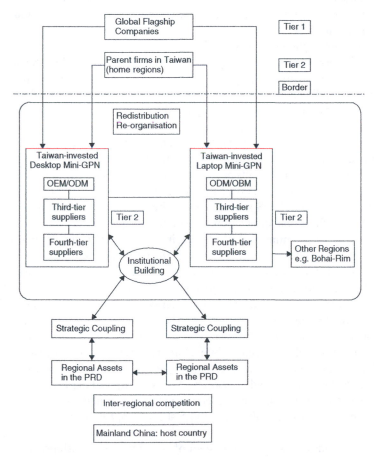

Figure 11.4 Inter-regional competition for Taiwan investment in the Pearl River Delta (PRD) and the Yangste River Delta (YRD) in the global production networks: a trans-local analytical framework

Source: Yang (2010).

Both history and local contexts provide insights into the varied forms of strategic coupling in East Asia. As Yang (2010), contrasting Taiwan and China, suggests, the nature of the relationships in this 'coupling' change over time and are dependent on different geographical contexts. He paints a fascinating picture showing that the difference between strategic coupling of regional development in China and other East Asian regions is explained by the fact that China lacks large local business firms, while in other parts of East Asia such firms actively cooperate with lead firms. The state and local initiatives also play a big role in China. Various tiers of Taiwanese computer firms drive the strategic coupling of regional development in the Pearl River and Yangste River deltas. More specifically, Yang notes that the desktop cluster in Dongguan has been driven by the bottom-up dynamics of Taiwanese third-tier firms without the need for local initiatives, while the notebook cluster in Suzhou has to a great extent been initiated by top-down local government actions. In both scenarios we find a region evolving as an entrepreneurial entity based on different forms of strategic coupling between global lead firms, regional large firms, local firms and institutions. Firms are the main engines for driving production, but it is in the interplay between different types of firms, their constant re-organization to adjust to different market imperatives and technological changes, and clever use of relational assets with institutions that we find the manifestations of growth and development.

Crucial to an appreciation of the dynamics of change in manufacturing and regional landscapes are the factors of speed and flexibility. Important as it is in the East Asian context, the cost dimension continues to be overplayed. There is always someone who produces something cheaper, and reliance on cost for competitive advantage does not help to explain the dynamics. Mathews (2005, 2006) and Kenny and Florida (2004) have shown that flexibility and speed are probably more important considerations. The organization of production in a fast-changing and highly competitive world with rapid changes in technology requires greater levels of innovative organizational arrangements. Reorganizing production in the past would have required the relocation of plants and production somewhere else. Innovations currently in vogue and that help firms to improve the flexibility of their operations include outsourcing, OEM, ODM, CM and EMS arrangements. These arrangements help to foster various forms of GPNs and the global orientation of manufacturing.

Enabling and supplementing organizational innovation are technological changes and usage capabilities. Electronic data interchange (EDI) with customers and suppliers, internet-based integration of manufacturing and service sectors, end-user platforms bringing users of products and services upstream with producers, enterprise resource planning systems, third-party logistics, and global tracking and information systems are critical technologies at work today. The upshot of the use of such technological capabilities is the increasing specialization of production and manufacturing together with connections with different parts of the value chain across different regions in automobile, clothing, electronics logistics and retailing sectors. New business models accommodate such specialization and connectivity with global lead firms engaged in research and development (upstream), and marketing, distribution and post-sale services (downstream), and international strategic and supply chain partners in charge of the rest of the value chain. Figure 11.5 shows scope of the changing organizational form in GPNs.

Figure 11.5 provides an alternative system of functions, relationships, flows of tangible and intangible resources and the processes of production and innovation that is different from the more contained models of regional systems discussed earlier. In doing so Ernst (2005), unveils a complex picture of the detailed levels of linkages and interactions and the opportunities they present at the level of both the firm and the region. Knowledge is diffused both as

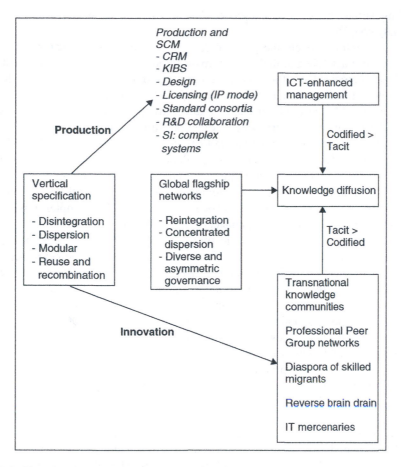

Figure 11.5 Changing industrial organisation and global production networks and their impact on knowledge diffusion

Source: Ernst (2005; cited in Yeung, 2010).

a result of the interactions of different agents and because of the complementary capabilities exchanged between firms and the regions. It is not always the case that there is an equal quantum of expertise in connected regions; rather, there is a complementary resource capability that is capable of being developed through those connections. In some cases the connectivity is made possible only between institutions in one region and firms in another, and in other cases it is simply a process of transferring know-how from partner firms of lead organizations through OEMs sand ODMS, coupled with local firms in the region.

Emerging from this model is a form of 'vertical specialization' which is different from vertical disintegration in that the latter is not associated with multiple specializations (Yeung, 2010). It also results in two forms of innovation – technological and organizational – shaping spatial arrangements and the regional contours of production. This form of strategic coupling is an organizational response to market disequilibrium which opens up opportunities for Kirznerian arbitrage. Equally, the strategy development process may be regarded as a form of Schumpeterian new combination between different types of organizations, skills and technologies, creating a form of permanent disequilibrium in a climate of constant change of coupling partners across time and space. The locale of this entrepreneurship process is the strategically coupled region.

Strategic coupling reflects the positive role of institutions (see Chapter 3), especially governments in East Asia and their active involvement in developing fiscal industrial strategies. These strategies have followed different trajectories. Taiwan and South Korea rely mainly on domestic firms collaborating with high-technology firms from the US and Japan for their role in GPNs, through for example direct investment in infrastructure, such as the Hscinchu Science-based industry park and the Industrial Technology Research Institute in Taiwan, and the development of the Korea Institute of Science and Technology (KIST), the Korea Institute of Electronics Technology and the business conglomerates or 'chaebols' of Hyundai, Samsung and LG. Industrial districts and selected growth regions have also been part of institutional involvement in development strategies. Taking these together, we can observe a remarkable outcome for regional development with, for example, chip design work moving from Silicon Valley to Asian clusters (Yeung, 2010).

The partnerships between firms and institutions as part of a global-local nexus has also spawned a community of transnational professionals who have used their experience in leading technology firms to start their own enterprises. Miin Wu, who worked for Siliconix and Intel, founded VSLI Technology; the founders of 'Microtek' were US-educated engineers who worked together in the 1970s on document engineering at Xerox; and a host of other entrepreneurs and professionals are fine products of what Saxenian (2006) calls brain circulation moving from the US to Taiwan to China and back with technologies, capita, knowledge and ideas as part of this new circuitry of entrepreneurship. The change process does not provide a one-way ticket of enterprise to East Asia. It enables connected regions to develop their changing entrepreneurial and innovative capacity. Front-running this change in the region are talented people with 'creative destruction' energy. As Saxenian notes:

> The overseas Chinese technical community has . . . altered the geography and structure of the semiconductor industry – first when engineers returned from Silicon Valley to Hsinchu in the 1980s and 1990s, and more recently when they moved to China, from across the Taiwan Straits and from Silicon Valley. Taiwan's semiconductor industry originated with talent and technology transferred from the United States, but when TSMC pioneered the IC foundry, it transformed the structure of the industry and accelerated the pace of innovation in both regions. The United States became home to the world's most sophisticated IC design firms, and Hsinchu to its leading foundries. (pp. 199–200)

Talent, technologies, institutions remain the key drivers of regional development in a globalized world. What appears to have changed is the new embeddness of globalized resources in regions and the networks of production systems connecting these regions. Enabling much of this change process is organizational and technological innovation harnessed and activated by the search and realization of new opportunities by entrepreneurs.

Conclusion

This expansive chapter has dealt with only some of the key elements of entrepreneurship, innovation and economic development. Each of these three themes deserves copious canons in its own right, as indeed they have done over time quite independently of one another, with perhaps entrepreneurship and innovation enjoying varied forms of courtship in the literature. Yet questions about development have always been at the forefront of thought and enquiry about entrepreneurship among the pioneers. Schumpeter's main concern was with the nature of economic development and of the unique role of entrepreneurship in making it happen. Where neo-classical economists failed to see the light, the Austrians and now growing numbers of modern writers from the evolutionary and other schools have opened up new vistas of knowledge on the subject. Surprisingly, development theory and empirical studies have only begun to acknowledge the possible value of considering the role of entrepreneurship in economic development.

In considering the scope of economic development (seen essentially in terms of economic growth in the literature), this chapter has explored how and where entrepreneurship features in the different stages of development. Development is a complex phenomenon, engaging different sets of actors and institutions. Entrepreneurship makes a contribution by generating new ideas and creating new ventures from the engagement of these disparate groups of actors and institutions. It does so by identifying opportunities in the very process of engagement with one another, reinforcing the point about the links between them. The entrepreneur provides the mechanism that makes possible the generation of economic, social, cultural and personal value from these connections. By considering the different stages of economic development, the reader can try to identify what specific actions and types of new venture creation can help countries to achieve higher levels of growth. Each stage offers different opportunities and varied conditions that influence entrepreneurial activity.

The conditions, the cultural make-up of the nation, the 'rules of the game', and the level of institutional sophistication affect how nations navigate their way through the stages of growth. However, simply by examining different stages of development on a country-by-country basis it is difficult to explain the unevenness of growth patterns within each country, the leaps that regions within different countries have made in terms of wealth creation, and the intense nature of connectivities that have been made possible through the globalized flow of technologies, talent and capital. Many of these regions have left their countries behind in terms of economic progress. They have become key stakeholders in global production networks. Many of the regions have been part of conscious public sector experiments while others have crafted their fortune through constructive use of their institutional memory and traditions. Such craft has been made possible by forms of collective learning, socialization, the use of social capital and networks, systems of innovation and increasingly these days through strategic global alliances of actors (firms, people and governments) located in regions. At least at the regional level there is a degree of control over the various factors that energize or hinder development. There is, therefore, a better opportunity to explain the directions that the region and its actors take to shape their development paths and environments.

12 Conclusion

Future directions and the romance of entrepreneurship

The book began with a voyage. In that voyage human vision and scientific discovery combined with technology, institutions and commerce to overcome the limitations of current knowledge about the human body. Today robot pills offer medical science new understanding of some aspects of our bodies, the economy opportunities for new ventures in the field of medical devices and health care, and the wider society possibilities for a healthier life. As with all journeys, there is movement upwards and forwards, and occasionally in the wrong direction. For some time now in economic terms, such movement in the allocation of goods and services, of upward mobility of people, of improved human capital and better and robust business activity, and of increases in the gross domestic product of a nation, has been associated with growth.

Entrepreneurship or the creation of new ventures through the identification and realization of opportunities can contribute to economic growth. However, it is this association with growth and especially the need to appropriate entrepreneurship and innovation within equilibrium models to explain in part the Solow residual for growth, that has, paradoxically, led to a neglect of the significant role and value of entrepreneurship. Growth, as Auserwald and Acs (2009) have argued, is not an end in itself, and the beginning and end of growth is opportunity. Identifying and realizing opportunity are dependent on the variegated dynamics of different social and economic conditions that allow for the emergence of different types of entrepreneurs who create new Schumpeterian combinations of economic and social activity. Their work leads to economic development, which by definition has different trajectories in countries and regions depending on the stages of their own development (see Porter and Schwab's three-stage model which identifies factor, efficiency and innovation stages (Porter and Schwab, 2008)). These arguments are overlaid with theoretical contentions of opportunities as exogenous in the entrepreneurship literature and as endogenous in the literature on innovation (Acs and Audrtesch, 2005).

The association with innovation seen in terms of the Schumpeterian view of new combinations or Kirznerian alertness to opportunity, and even in terms of value generation through the exploitation of information asymmetry, as proposed by Casson (1982), offers some sense of distinctiveness for entrepreneurship. Shane and Venkataraman's (2000) proposition that entrepreneurship is defined by the study of 'how and by whom and with what consequences opportunities to produce future goods ands services are discovered, evaluated and exploited' allows for a latitude of expression about the value of entrepreneurship suggesting a confluence of entrepreneurship with innovation. However, the absence of any contextual reference for such a process, and especially an organizational context (Acs and Audretsch, 2005), reflects an inherent weakness in the argument.

Acs and Audretsch (2005), in line with Gartner and Carter (2003), identify the context as those of new ventures, and the former, in particular, have referred to the specific significance of new ventures and small firms. Small businesses and entrepreneurship have enjoyed an inviolable relationship for several decades, and certainly among researchers and policy makers, ever since they latched on to Birch's (1979) seminal work on the value of small firms in creating jobs in the economy. Defined variously as new business creation and essentially concerned with a personalized unit of analysis – the individual entrepreneur – or the formation of a specific type of new venture – entrepreneurship has been closely associated with the early stages of a new, small business, and the trials and tribulations of the entrepreneur (or at best teams of entrepreneurs) in different contexts providing goods and services based on opportunities in the marketplace.

Extending the scope of entrepreneurship beyond the small firm

While there might be some definitional value in the organizational context of the small business, an uncritical concentration on the small firm as the unit of analysis for entrepreneurship confuses the relationship between entrepreneurship and innovation, and between these two concepts and economic development. The idea of the new venture can be taken out of the limited context of the small firm (Bhide, 2008) by focusing instead on the process of venturing in different organizational contexts. A conceptual framework that allows for the investigation of entrepreneurship only through the construct of a new small businesses does not provide for a proper appreciation of terms such as an 'entrepreneurial society'. If only a minority of people in any society start a new business then the socio-psychological impact of such activity on society will always remain marginal, even if the economic impact is strong.

Yet the creation of such a society lies at the heart of public policy considerations as governments across the world struggle to find solutions to the problems of the economy. What this book has attempted to do is to commence the examination of processes that cut across economic, social and cultural contexts of creativity, opportunity creation and realization, and not to restrict this examination to any obsession with size. Rather, the experiment here is to equate entrepreneurship with forms of value creation – economic, social and cultural – in different organizations, regions and contexts. This experiment could offer new directions and lay the foundations for an enhanced role for the project of entrepreneurship.

New directions, variables and connections

This examination across boundaries (of organizations, disciplines and forms) could help to allay some of the anecdotal (but well-informed) public antipathy for entrepreneurship and innovation in today's environment. Much debate on the current economic crisis has been attributed to the 'innovations' in the financial markets, especially in the form of sub-prime and securitized mortgages, and a raft of other instruments. Trivial as it may appear to the small community of academic researchers in entrepreneurship, there is a real danger of entrepreneurship taking a back seat in policy-making (if not in reality) as a result of an essential intellectual failure to take the debate where it matters. The distinctions made by Baumol *et al* (2007) between productive, unproductive and destructive entrepreneurship need urgent attention and elaboration.

Elaboration also needs to resonate with the critical, underlying concerns of our times, whether they are those of climate control/environmental degradation or growing income disparities between the rich and poor within western countries and between developed and poorer countries. The subliminal association with wealth creation for the few does not sit well with those who want to see economic and social change across nations, and at any level of debate the latter outcome is not negotiable. Entrepreneurship needs to be both prescient through its research insights and able to resonate to the needs and interests of society.

Underlying assumptions

Imagination and entrepreneurship

To consider new directions along the lines proposed above is to make certain assumptions about the main tenets of the discussion of the subject. First, any response to the issues of our times needs a critical examination of the present, and the past in the present, if only to track the value of the project and to point to possibilities for the future. This examination is not simply based on rational prediction but on what Hazlitt (1805) refers to as the imaginative anticipation of our future pleasure of the imaginatively projected future self of citizens, consumers, producers and entrepreneurs. Much of what policy makers and researchers are concerned with is the understanding of conditions and resources that make it possible to create new ventures in the future. This understanding of the future possibilities of the combination of resources is as dependent on precise forecasting as it is on imagination.

The reliance on imagination, or Webb's (1883) 'analytical imagination', helps to deal with what Schumpeter (1934) referred to as the ill-coordinated and overlapping fields of research and the constantly shifting frontiers. Schumpeter's reference to the study of economics may well apply to the field of entrepreneurship, not least because of the beacon he held out for entrepreneurship as an economist.

Overlapping ideas, concepts and fields of research

Second, the idea of overlapping fields of research is redolent of the concepts of convergence in technology and of externalities and knowledge spillovers in economics and in economic geography. Technological convergence, as in information, communications and biotechnologies, is commonplace in most industries (whether they are new high-growth technology firms or traditional manufacturing firms that rely on embedded technologies). Externalities and knowledge spillovers assume a social impact arising out of a cost-free, abstract form of exchange of know-how that is spilled over because of the leaky nature of new technologies and the geographical proximity of firms and research institutes (Jaffe, 1986; Griliches, 1990; Jaffe *et al.*, 1993), or even across wider territories and countries (Krugman, 1995) through the 'brain circulation' of talent across nations (Saxenian, 2006) and the cross-fertilization of R&D and production activities across borders. The idea of externalities and spillovers is manifest in the involvement of multiple players with varying levels and units of competencies, sometimes even involving consumers as co-producers, to make a product or provide a service. Prahalad and Krishnan (2008) argue that the 'confluence of connectivity, digitization and the convergence of industry and technology boundaries are creating a new dynamic between consumers and the firm' (p. 3). A consideration of the first assumption of discourse based on imagination leads us to this second assumption of confluence of different stakeholders as a form of new Schumpeterian combinations.

Social well-being

from the point of view of this author, the externalities argument can be stretched further to cover issues of social well-being and self-sufficiency – areas where economic, social and cultural values merge in the action of different communities of interest. Acting either in the interest of a specific community or conjointly with others to overcome social barriers and enable change, new combinations are forged to 'do things differently'. Evidence of such value creation can be seen in the growing role of social enterprises and in community-based activities such as those in the USA leading to the election of a new President, and now through to the 'Tea Party', a questioning of that President's policies and actions. There is much in such collective action that contributes to social change as it does to disrupting such change if vested interests prevail.

It is this approach to entrepreneurship – a multilayered examination of its significance in different walks of life – that can make a difference to our understanding of its contribution to economic development.

Incommensurable value

For imagination and knowledge-sharing to be grounded in reality, and for us to acknowledge the value of an extended definition of entrepreneurship, there is a need to assume what Kuhn (1996) described as 'incommensurable value'. All paradigms are limited in the sense that they cannot be combined into one all-encompassing perspective that provides a grand explanation of everything (Bronck, 2009). Entrepreneurship seen primarily in terms of new, innovative venture creation cannot make any real impact on economic development if its explanations are constrained by commensurable ideas of growth. Measuring the value of new venture creation according to some form of Pareto-efficient equilibrium model of growth, maximizing utility, limits the discussion of entrepreneurship to numerical value considerations in the form of market transactions. Commensurability leads to the type of narrow focus on entrepreneurship which, for example, streamlines the debate on social entrepreneurship by using one overarching index of entrepreneurial activity, namely that of economic growth.

Social enterprises are distinguished from voluntary or charitable organizations, for example, mainly in terms of the prospects and reality of growth (in turnover, assets and returns) (Social Entrepreneurship Coalition, 2009). While the former show an ability to grow by these measures, the latter struggle to achieve such targets. There is less 'value' in the nature of social service provision when the commensurability of economic value creation overrides the use of other measures of value. Commensurability and its attractions can lead the researcher to a trap of epistemological and moral absolutism (Bronck, 2009). This danger manifests itself when researchers of entrepreneurship examine business and social organizations within the confines of a singular definition of entrepreneurship (as in GEM or the UK government's definition of social entrepreneurship) or in loose equations of networking with the creation of a quasi factor of production, namely social capital. Consequently, social and community organizations are seen as another type of business enterprise with rather amorphous social objectives as their goal.

Commensurability is also evinced in approaches that adopt disequilibrium models to explain entrepreneurship. Shane and Venkataraman (2000) disentangle entrepreneurship from specific organizational constructs but limit their valuable conceptual framework for the study of the existence, discovery, decision to exploit and modes of exploitation of entrepreneurial opportunities to the examination of the creation of future goods and services for economic gain.

Value pluralism: economic, economic social and cultural value creation and entrepreneurship

What we should be looking at instead is a kind of 'value pluralism' (Gray, 1998) that allows for a recognition of the realization of different values of entrepreneurship in different contexts, and the incorporation of these sets of values (and their manifestation) as independent indicators of entrepreneurship in the business/economic, social and cultural arenas of society.

A consideration of the different values of entrepreneurship enables the creation of a new framework for the study of entrepreneurship in terms of economic, social and cultural value creation.

Economic value considerations, especially in today's context, are referred to in this book in terms of developments in the world of business where technologies, and user–producer relationships, are generating new configurations that challenge our understanding of both where, how and why opportunities are found and exploited, and how new forms of organization are generated to accommodate these configurations. This description may not, however, reflect the reality of all businesses. The purpose here is to identify change processes today and how these processes enhance value creation.

Social value creation is evinced in social embeddedness, social networks, strong and weak ties and cultural backdrops that form part of or influence new venture creation and growth. But they do not necessarily address the specific dimensions of entrepreneurial activity in the so-called creative or cultural industries or in various community arts events designed to enhance the cultural value of particular environments and influence social behaviour. Social value creation is understood to take place when individuals, communities, institutions and other agents of change network, interact and mobilize resources to create social capital and effect change in the lives of communities, in the political environment and, critically, in terms of the values they create for themselves to live by as individuals and in society.

Entrepreneurship as social movement

As Bridge *et al.* (2009) have shown, the social enterprise or even the wider concept of the social economy is not new. However, the real test of social value creation lies in the articulation of processes that engender social change and the measures used to evaluate social change. Such value creation is not the prerogative of so-called social enterprises, however defined, but is often in the hands of disparate and previously dysfunctional groups of individuals and community organizations. They come together to create 'movements' that either lead to short-term activities to effect a specific change process, as in the anti-war movements that change governmental policy, or achieve a longer-term objective, as in the amelioration of environmental degradation. The outcomes and the changes that they bring about are often small or localized, as in access to clean drinking water in a poor village, or they act as a catalyst for wider economic change through, for example, micro financing as found in the Grameen Bank movement in Bangladesh, the M-Pesa banking scheme in Kenya or the e-choupal marketing programme in India. Social dignity, access to individual property rights, the break-up of artificially structured asymmetries of information established by intermediaries, independent economic livelihood and a better quality of life are often the outcomes. Relevant technologies (whether they be a mosquito net or a mobile telephone) play a part but they do not define the project of entrepreneurship in society.

The coalition of social value creators is not confined to people in the community or community organizations. Social value change is often made possible by the mobilization of corporate, trade union, community and other interest groups forming a broad-based alliance and intending to articulate a different vision of society. Thus Barack Obama's election as President marked a historical, social and cultural shift in the United States not simply because he was the first Black President but also as a consequence of positive socio-economic externalities. These externalities were multi-layered in scope, character and activities. First, there was commonality of vision which contained the possibility of a generational shift in political orientation, and this included a 'new bloc of neo-Keynesian globalists attempting to redefine liberalism for the twenty-first century in both ideology and policy . . . The centre has shifted left, creating new dialogue and new debates . . . A New Deal has become the common expectation of millions' (Harris and Davidson, 2009, p. 4). The progressive base of minorities, trade union activists and anti-war youth appears to have found an ideological common ground with old corporate liberals and neo-liberals traumatized by the economic crisis, and a form of consensus with institutions at different points in the political spectrum such as the Peterson Institute for International Economics which argued for 'real' innovation' by moving resources from financial services to manufacturing and technology, and the Institute of Policy Studies which promotes investments in renewable energies, the refinancing of mortgages and support for state and local governments. Crucially, each sector organized their own networks and approaches, remaining both independent from one another and as broad coalitions at the same time. The Obama youth team of 'twenty somethings' formed neighbourhood teams and used blogs, e-mails and text messaging to communicate with voters and themselves. The Black community campaigned along traditional, working-class lines using the social communities of Black churches, tenant groups and civic organizations, and made common cause with Latino, Asian and Native American communities against efforts at anti-Black racism. Organized labour used its substantial resources for meeting halls, phone banks and other traditional campaign tools. This collective action was made possible because of the progressive agenda of new jobs and new industries, practical plans for green jobs and alternative energy sources, infrastructure repair, immigration reform and withdrawal from Iraq, to name a few (Harris and Davidson, 2009).

The social value creation that marks the opening-up of a new agenda for social, political and cultural action is entrepreneurial in terms of new combinations of resources (people, capital, institutions and technologies) and the identification of new opportunities in new social asymmetries. Business is still divided into those who wish to make hay with speculative capital and those who intend to pursue an industrial policy based on innovation and green technologies through the use of productive capital. The shift in foreign policy, which is more accepting of a multi-polar world as opposed to American hegemony, also offers possibilities for harvesting the gains made by innovative businesses that are more interested in accessing global resources than in owning them. The institutional, economic and social anomalies still abound, but the resulting tension provides opportunities for change in both social and economic terms.

Entrepreneurship and global change

Mixing the social with the economic, the cultural with the personal, in enabling the development of new formulations for social and economic well-being is perhaps one of the greatest challenges of our times. Social and institutionalized philanthropy is an example of active social intervention where even efficient markets are not equitable (Aursweld and Acs, 2009). A coalescence of interests generates what Nicholas Stern (2009) refers to as the 'power of the example' in drawing up a blueprint for a safer planet. These interests vary from individual action (at the level of reduced car travel, maintaining energy efficient homes) to political pressure through NGOs and the taking of risks and leadership (reduction of carbon footprint, Vinod Khosla's clean energy investments) and community action (the Dongtan or the Masdar eco-city projects in China and Abu Dhabi or the C40 project working in partnership with the Clinton Foundation). These conjoined activities raise public awareness and the possibilities for the provision of the right incentives for entrepreneurial activity in terms of both business and social action.

Drayton and Budinich (2010) notice a sea change in the way society's problems are being solved, in the way work is being performed and in how businesses are growing. They claim that collaboration between corporations and social entrepreneurs can help to create and expand markets, especially as these markets will help to reach the 4 billion people who are not yet part of the global economy. By developing collaborative strategies to reach these people, new products and services in areas as diverse as education, transportation and finance can be revolutionized. This view is based on the simple realization that, despite rapid economic progress and waves of innovation with per capita income rising by an average of 20 per cent in the 1700s, 200 per cent in the 1800s and 740 per cent in the past century (Drayton and Budinich, 2010), extraordinary imbalances between the rich and the poor, between needs and wants, and between the consumer and the citizen have been exacerbated over time. Rather than wait, the social or citizen sector has taken direct responsibility and has been creating jobs three times as fast other employers, especially in the OECD countries.

The apparent asymmetry in both the information gathered and used by and in the functions of social value creators (the social or citizen organizations) and economic value generators (business) provides an opportunity for collaboration. If both parties are creating values that affect the lives of people then there is opportunity in creating greater value through synergy. This synergy can be achieved by forming 'hybrid value chains' (HVCs). HVCs rely on collaboration between the two sides, with each side understanding and being willing to accept the risks and rewards to reach what Prahalad (2005) referred to as the fortune at the 'bottom of the pyramid' (BOP).

Mini case study 12.1: The Hindustan Lever case study

Prahalad's (2005) story of Hindustan Lever Ltd (HLL), the largest soap producer in the world, helping to create a unique approach to public-private partnership to address a major public health issues is a good example of a solution to a major social problem in India. Diarrhoea is one category of infectious disease that accounts for 2.2. million deaths annually around the world (Curtis, 2002). India's share of this miserable statistic is 30 per cent. Yet the solution is both known and inexpensive. Despite the efforts of NGOs and the government, the problem of enabling access to safe water, better sanitation facilities and hygiene practices has eluded them and the victims for decades. HLL is the largest soap and detergent manufacturer in India and its efforts in differentiating products based on a health platform have pushed the company to explore in depth consumer needs and behaviour with a view to making their products imperative to family health and safety. One way of exploring new opportunities was to make the connection between diarrhoeal disease prevention and the firm's soap products.

HLL's has immense market reach. It works with a dense network of autonomous agents, distributors, suppliers and end users to create and define a local presence. In doing so, it spawns or helps to grow numerous new small ventures (see Figure 12.1) as part of an ecosystem of wealth creation through entrepreneurship and innovation. Its global connections with Unilever Ltd allow it to extend its reach in other markets. Its corporate mission was to improve the health of a nation. Its ability to transform the nature of use in a country where subliminal and real beauty messages are associated with soap, to one of a combined beauty and health platform, makes it possible for the company to address public health issues beyond the use of soap. Finally, HLL's interest in leveraging sources of knowledge and expertise enables it build on its own research in handwashing. Using the experience of the successful public-private partnership (PPP) programme, the Central American Handwashing Initiative, which brought together four private sector corporations, HLL entered into a partnership centred around a World Bank and Water Sanitation programme supported by the Bank-Netherlands Water Partnership. The group obtained the assistance of the London School of Hygiene and Tropical Medicine, UNICEF, USAID and the Environmental Health Project. The initiative was called the Global PPP for Handwashing with Soap (which became 'Health in your Hands – a Public Private Partnership'). The idea was to reach 29 million people in the southern state of Kerala in three years. To make this happen, HLL leveraged all its interest as stated above to put together a viable model for making 'Lifebuoy Soap', involving communities, the private sector, academic and research institutions, and the government.

The HLL case study provides real insights into how products (soap, for example) can derive competitive advantage by:

- using specific platforms (in this case health);
- providing an affordable consumer and health product for the poor;
- achieving product differentiation by focusing on an untapped market enabling business growth;
- changing consumer behaviour through innovative campaigns;
- enhancing the perception of value for money through identifying the benefits for health;
- developing a hybrid value chain that accounts for both traditional suppliers and distributors, as well as community groups and organizations;
- achieving scalability in a large market and in leveraging international connections at corporate, governmental and institutional levels;
- developing new expertise in selling health through product, service and organizational innovation, and helping to support the creation and growth of new firms who act as suppliers, distributors and agents.

The HLL case study is one about the ecosystem of entrepreneurship in innovation, where the local dimension is as important as the global connections, where continuous innovation is manifest in developing new products and obtaining scalability in business activity and in addressing social missions, where government and institutions interact with the firm directly, and where independent, small-scale entrepreneurship is encouraged alongside innovations in the larger organization. Experimenting as it did in the state of Kerala, it augmented the scope of social and economic development through better health education and services coupled with business activity.

(Source: adapted from Prahalad (2005) 'The Fortune at the
Bottom of the Pyramid: Eradicating Poverty through Profits'
(Indian Subcontinent edition), Singapore, Pearson)

- Fast moving consumer goods & Hindustan Lever Ltd.

- Value = $ 2.3 bn

- 80 manufacturing facilities

- Supplier base of 150 SME factories

- Over 7,000 stockists, 12,000 wholesalers, 300,000 small retail shop owners (SMEs or micro firms)

- Rural direct distribution system = Shakti (> 1m individual entrepreneurs in urban & remote villages

- Advisory relationship with state govt. to help brand local produce from village & tribal areas

- No legal control over ecosystem

- HLL = nodal firm

- Shakti firms are independent

- Underpinning factor = education (about being responsible entrepreneur)

- Social collateral of open & honest entrepreneurship

- Connectivity of the poorest to rest of the world & market system

Figure 12.1 Ecosystem of wealth creation

Source: adapted from Prahalad (2005).

End note

The economic crisis that continues to unravel in different parts of the world has pointed to the failure of untrammelled, uncritical and homogenized beliefs in growth based on notions of factor accumulation, an assumption of convergence in growth patterns, a strange reliance on a notion of permanency and the continued concentration of resources among the few who have the most (Easterly and Levine, 2001). The relative bankruptcy of ideas suggests that there needs to be a new approach to change in social, economic and cultural systems and institutions that make up our society. The realization of such change constitutes the project of entrepreneurship.

In enabling the identification of opportunity, in supporting the realization of such opportunity through the generation of economic, social and cultural value, and in making possible the organizational arrangements through evolving business models in different contexts, entrepreneurship can and should play a key role in economic development. This book attempts to provide a conceptual framework for understanding and evaluating entrepreneurship in these different contexts and in terms of complementary sets of values. Economic value (new products, new processes, and new businesses) is enhanced by the creation of social and cultural value. Value creation opens up new ways of organizing self-sufficiency in the community, new organizations for changes to social systems, new forms of expression in the arts, and developing new portfolios of products and services in new markets that highlight the local zeitgeist of a nation or a region in the world community.

Notes

1 Entrepreneurship, innovation and regional development: an introduction

1 This story about 'Robot Pills: Doctor in a Capsule' is drawn from the article with the same title in *Scientific American* (August 2010).
2 Economic commentators and policy makers suggest that countries are coming out of a recession but there is only limited evidence of economic models that to some extent were responsible for the fall being changed to accommodate new directions. The looming threats of currency wars and the facile attempts to implicate those countries that have not experienced the downturn as badly as others are discussed in the same, unchanged context of growth models, with passing concessions to, for example, environmental impact.
3 Often dismissed as the underworld of fake products, the Shanzhai phenomenon involves the production of imitation electronics and other goods (but mainly mobile telephones) in China. High levels of imitation of standard global product models provide cheaper versions of those products in the borderline of illegality and acceptable copy products. However, this simplistic view masks the significant amount of user-friendly technological and organisational innovation that lies behind the making of these products (see *Wired* magazine and Si and Mitra (2010) for more details about this phenomenon).

3 Entrepreneurship theories: the economic arguments

1 Jean Baptiste Say's work in *Traité d'économie politique* (1803) and *Cours complet d'économie politique practique* (1828) provided an empirical analysis of entrepreneurship.

5 The entrepreneurial organization

1 For a comprehensive text on the management of innovation, see Tidd and Bessant (2009).
2 An odd juxtaposition of venture funding and larger firms with critical mass engaging in new organisational structures especially through management buyouts explains why venture capital is more suited for larger firms or organizations seeking significant capital investment.

8 Entrepreneurship, internationalization and globalization: learning, innovation and development in the international context

1 Globalization has its own detractors and a considerable number of critics. Since 2007 there has been rich fodder for such a constituency, who have argued forcefully and convincingly about the crisis being a function of globalization, that the poor have become poorer since the advent of modern forms of globalization, and of the need for localized economic horizons.

9 Higher education, universities and entrepreneurship

1 Higher education is more than the sum total of provision of learning by universities. There are private and public providers that do not enjoy the status of 'universities' and their contributions are recognized. However, the main focus in this chapter is on universities.

2 The School of Entrepreneurship and Business is now part of Essex Business School after merging with the School of Accounting, Finance and Management to form the county's first Business School.

10 Entrepreneurship policy: its emergence, scope and value

1 Galbraith, as Auersrwald and Acs (2009) argue, was considering a rather monochromatic view of the world in which big business, labour and government (the 'iron triangle') held the balance of power, especially in the USA. Against this we can examine the monolithic authority of the state in command economies making it impossible to even acknowledge private entrepreneurship in those environments. The emphatic denial of the value of small-scale or individual entrepreneurial effort in both capitalist and command economy havens suggests almost a curious conspiracy in keeping with the spirit of détente of the Cold War days.

2 One can draw an analogy between the way the history of world has been written in the past from a purely Anglo- or Eurocentric point of view till approximately the Second World War and the subsequent emergence of subaltern studies and the writing of local history by local historians in different parts of the world. The new studies unleashed information and discoveries about people and suggested that their economic lives that were rather different and more productive from the dominant picture portrayed in the past (Darwin, 2006). The story of large firms has similarly dominated the preoccupation of decision makers in developed economies till, first, the discovery of dense industrial clusters of small, highly innovative firms in Italy and the emergence of the new, globally connected economies.

3 What is stated in this text is one aspect of hypothetical immigration policy-related activity, which is often not discussed or adumbrated in policy or research circles. The common preoccupation is with resident immigrants in host countries, and especially that segment of the immigrant population that is disadvantaged either economically or by virtue of their class, race, gender and habitat.

4 Research papers of the Wissenschaftzzentrum in Berlin can be found at www.wzb.eu/default.en.asp (Bronk, 2009).

5 Acs (2008), referring to Brock and Evans (1986) and Joel Popkin and Co. (1988), states that while the real number of businesses grew from 10.7 million to 16.8 million between 1958 and 1980, the relative overall economic performance of small businesses declined. Firms with fewer than 500 employees saw their share of employment drop from 55.55 per cent to 52.5 per cent between 1958 and 1977. The same group of firms also saw the share of their added value contribution drop from 57 per cent to 52 per cent.

11 Entrepreneurship, innovation and economic development

1 For a fuller explanation of entrepreneurship theories, see Chapter 2.

2 These findings run contrary to Lucas, who worked on an economic model that showed higher levels of development leading to higher average firm size. Lucas identified a negative relationship between the elasticity of factor substitution and firm size, while studies by Acs (2007) and Aqulina *et al.* (2007 have shown that the high value of the elasticity of factor substitution leads to increases in per capita capital and makes it easier for someone to become an entrepreneur because of the negative aggregate elasticity of factor substitution.

3 Acs and Szerb define entrepreneurship as a dynamic interaction of entrepreneurial attitudes, entrepreneurial activity and entrepreneurial aspiration that varies across stages of economic development. For a fuller explanation of the Global Entrepreneurship Index see Acs and Szerb (2009).

4 Florida refers to Tokyo, Seoul, New York, San Francisco, Boston, Seattle, Austin, Toronto, Vancouver, Stockholm, Helsinki, London, Osaka, Taipei and Sydney as examples of cities that stand out in terms of patents taken out (based on data from the World Intellectual Property Organisation). Scientific advance is even more concentrated in the USA and Europe.

Bibliography

Abramovitz, M. (1956) 'Resource and Output Trends in the United States since 1870', *American Economic Review* 46: 5–23.

Ackerloff, G. A. and R. J. Schiller (2009) *Animal Spirits: How Human Psychology Drives the Economy and Why It Matters for Global Capitalism*, Princeton: Princeton University Press.

Acs, Z. J. (2002) *Innovation and the Growth of Cities*, Cheltenham: Edward Elgar.

Acs, Z. J. (2005) 'A Formulation of Entrepreneurship Policy', paper published in the Tenth Year Anniversary Series of the Swedish Foundation for Small Business Research and the Business Development Agency – the FSEF NUTEK Award.

Acs, Z. J. (2006) 'How is Entrepreneurship Good for Economic Growth?' The 25th Economic Conference of Progress Foundation, 'The Beauty of Entrepreneurship', Zurich, Switzerland, 31 Oct.

Acs, Z. J. (2008a) *Entrepreneurship, Growth and Public Policy: Prelude to a Knowledge Spillover Theory of Entrepreneurship*, Cheltenham: Edward Elgar.

Acs, Z. J. (2008b) *Foundations of High Impact Entrepreneurship*, Hanover, MA: Now Publishers.

Acs, Z. J. and C. Armington (2004) 'Employment Growth and Entrepreneurial Activity in Cities', *Regional Studies* 39: 911–27.

Acs, Z. J. and C. Armington (2006) *Entrepreneurship, Geography and American Economic Growth*, New York: Cambridge University Press.

Acs, Z. J. and D. B. Audretsch (1990; 1994) *Innovation and Small Firms*, Cambridge, MA: MIT Press.

Acs, Z. J. and D. B. Audretsch (eds) (1991) *Innovation and Technological Change: An International Comparison*, Ann Arbor: University of Michigan Press.

Acs, Z. J. and D. B. Audretsch (2005) *Entrepreneurship, Innovation and Technological Change*, Hanover, MA: Now Publishers.

Acs, Z. J. and P. Mueller (2008) 'Employment Effects of Business Dynamics: Mice, Gazelles', *Small Business Economics*.

Acs, Z. J. and D. J. Storey (2004) 'Introduction: Entrepreneurship and Economic Development', *Regional Studies* 38: 871–7.

Acs, Z. J. and L. Szerb (2007) 'Entrepreneurship, Economic Growth and Public Policy', *Small Business Economics* 28(2–3): 109–22.

Acs, Z. J. and L. Szerb (2009) 'The Global Entrepreneurship Index (GEINDEX), Apr., 2009'.

Acs, Z. J. and N. Virgil (2009) *Entrepreneurship in Developing Countries, Foundations and Trends in Entrepreneurship*, Hanover, MA: Now Publishers.

Acs, Z. J., D. B. Audretsch and M. P. Feldman (1994) 'Real Effects of Academic Research', *American Economic Review* 82(1): 363–7, 1994.

Acs, Z. J., B. Carlsson and R. Thurik (1996) *Small Business in the Modern Economy*, Oxford: Blackwell.

Acs, Z. J., R. Morck, J. Myles Shaver and B. Yeung (1997) 'The Internationalisation of Small and Medium Sized Enterprises: A Policy Perspective', *Small Business Economics* 9(1): 21–31; in J. E.

Oxley and B. Yeung (eds), *Structural Change, Industrial Location and Competitiveness*, Globalisation of the World Economy Series, Cheltenham: Edward Elgar.

Acs, Z. J., D. B. Audretsch, P. Braunerhjelm and B. Carlsson (2005; 2008b) *The Knowledge Spillover Theory of Entrepreneurship*, London: Centre for Economic Policy Research.

Acs, Z. J., W. Parsons and S. Tracy (2008a) 'High-Impact Firms: Gazelles Revisited', USA: SBA Office of Advocacy.

Adams, J. and D. Smith (2004) 'Research and Regions: An Overview of the Distribution of Research in UK Regions, Regional Research Capacity and Links between Strategic Research Partners', Higher Education Policy Institute, Oxford.

Adiga, A. (2008) *The White Tiger*, London: Atlantic Books.

Adkins, D. (2007) 'Five "Musts" for Incubation Success', *Economic Development America*.

Aerts, K., P. Matthyssen and K. Vandenbempt (2007) 'Critical Role and Screening Practices of European Business Incubators', *Technovation* 27(5): 254–67.

Agarwal, A. (2001) 'University-to-Industry Knowledge Transfer: Literature Review and Unanswered Questions', *International Journal of Management Reviews* 3(4): 285–302.

Agarwal, R. (1997) 'Survival of Firms over the Product Life Cycle', *Southern Economic Journal* 63(3): 571–84.

Aglietta, M. (1974) *The Theory of Capitalist Regulation: The U.S. Experience*, London: Verso.

Aglietta, Michel (1976) *Régulations et crises du capitalisme*, Calmann-Lévy; repr. Odile Jacob, 1997.

Aharoni, M. (1966) 'The Foreign Investment Decision Process', Boston Graduate School of Business Administration, Harvard University.

Ahmed, A. and McQuaidm, R.W. (2005) 'Entrepreneurship, Management, and Sustainable Development', *World Review of Entrepreneurship, Management and Sustainable Development*, 1(1).

Alampay, E. A. (2006) 'Beyond Access to ICTs: Measuring Capabilities in the Information Society', *International Journal of Education and Development Using ICT* 2(3): 1–17.

Albino, V., A. C. Garavelli and G. Schiuma (1999) 'Knowledge Transfer and Inter-Firm Relationships in Industrial Districts: The Role of the Leader Firm', *Technovation* 19: 53–63.

Aldrich, H. E. and M. A. Martinez (2001) 'Many Are Called But Few Are Chosen: An Evolutionary Perspective for the Study of Entrepreneurship,' Entrepreneurship: Theory & Practice 25(4): 41–56.

Aldrich, H. E. and T. Baker (1990; 2001) 'Learning and Legitimacy: Entrepreneurial Responses to Constraints on the Emergence of New Populations and Organisations', in C. B. Schoonhoven and E. Romanelli (eds) (2001), *The Entrepreneurship Dynamic: Origins of Entrepreneurship and the Evolution of Industries*, Stanford: Stanford University Press.

Aldrich, H. E. and C. Zimmer (1986) 'Entrepreneurship through social networks', in D. L. Sexton and R. W. Wilson (eds), *The Art and Science of Entrepreneurship*, Cambridge, MA: Ballinger.

Aldrich, H. E. (1990) 'Using an Ecological Perspective to Study Organisational Founding Rates', *Entrepreneurship Theory and Practice* 14(3): 7–24.

Aldrich, H. E. (1999) *Organisations Evolving*, London: Sage.

Aldrich, H. E. and C. M. Fiol (1994) 'Fools Rush In? The Institutional Context of Industry Creation', *Academy of Management Review* 19(4): 645–70.

Aldrich, H. E. and G. Widenmayer (1993) 'From Traits to Rates: An Ecological Perspective on Organisational Foundings', in J. Katz and R. H. Brockhaus (eds), *Advances in Entrepreneurship, Firm Emergence and Growth*, vol. 1, Greenwich, CT: JAI Press, pp. 145–95.

Aldrich, H. E. and C. Zimmer (1986) 'Entrepreneurship through Social Networks', in D. L. Sexton and R. W. Smilor (eds), *The Art and Science of Entrepreneurship*, Cambridge, MA: Ballinger, pp. 3–23.

Allen, J. and A. Cochrane (2007) 'Beyond the Territorial Fix: Regional Assemblages, Politics and Power', *Regional Studies* 41: 1161–75.

Almus, M. and E. Nerlinger (1999) 'Growth of New Technology-Based Firms: Which Factors Matter?' *Business and Economics* 13(2): 141–54.

Amin, A. (2004) 'Regions Abound: Towards a New Politics of Place', *Geografiska Annaler* B86: 33–4.

Amin, A. and J. Roberts (eds) (2008) *Community, Economic Creativity and Organization*, Oxford: Oxford University Press.

Amin, A. and N. Thrift (1992) 'Neo-Marshallian Nodes in Global Networks', *International Journal of Urban and Regional Research* 16(4): 571–87.

Anderson, C. (2010) *Wired*, March.

Ante, S. E. (2009) 'Fertile Ground for Startups', *Business Week* (23 Nov.), 46–54.

Aoyama, Y. (2010) 'Entrepreneurship and Regional Culture: The Case of Hamamatsu and Kyoto, Japan', in H. W.-C. Yeung (ed.), *Globalizing Regional Development in East Asia: Production Networks, Clusters and Entrepreneurship*. Abingdon: Routledge.

Argyris, C. (1990) *Overcoming Organizational Defenses*, Boston: Allyn & Bacon.

Argyris, C. (1996) *On Organizational Learning*, Oxford: Blackwell.

Argyris, C. and D. Schon (1978) *Organizational Learning: A Theory of Action Perspective*, Reading, MA: Addison-Wesley.

Armington, C. and M. Odle (1982) 'Small Business: How Many Jobs?' *Brookings Review* 1(2): 14–17.

Arrow, K. (1962) 'Economic Welfare and the Allocation of Resources for Invention', in R. R. Nelson (ed.), *The Rate and Direction of Inventive Activity*, Princeton: Princeton University Press, pp. 609–26.

Arthur, W. B. (1990) 'Positive Feedbacks in the Economy', *Scientific American* 262: 92–9.

Arzaghi, M. and J. V. Henderson (2008) 'Networking off Madison Avenue', *Review of Economic Studies* 75: 1011–38.

Arzeni, S. and J. Mitra (2008) 'From Unemployment to Entrepreneurship: Creating Conditions for Change for Young People in Central and Eastern European Countries', in P. Blokker and B. Dallago (eds), *Youth Entrepreneurship and Local Development in Central and Eastern Europe*, Aldershot: Ashgate, pp. 31–60.

Ashcroft, B. and J. H. Love (1996) 'Firm Birth and Employment Change in the British Counties: 1981–89', *Papers in Regional Science* 75: 483–500.

Attwell, G. (2003) Report on Brussels Seminar: Exploring Models and Partnerships for Elearning in SMEs. Developing New Pedagogies and Elearning in SMEs. Stirling, Scotland, Nov. 2002, and Brussels, Belgium, Feb. 2003.

Audretsch, D. B. (1995) *Innovation and Industry Evolution*, Cambridge, MA: MIT Press.

Audretsch, D. B. (1998) 'Agglomeration and the Location of Innovative Activity', *Oxford Review of Economic Policy* 14(2): 18–29.

Audretsch, D. B. (2002) 'Knowledge, Globalization and Regions: An Economist's Perspective', in J. Dunning (ed.), *Regions, Globalization and the Knowledge-Based Economy*, Oxford: Oxford University Press.

Audretsch, D. B. (2007a) *The Entrepreneurial Society*, Oxford: Oxford University Press.

Audrestsch, D. B. (2007b) 'Entrepreneurship Capital and Economic Growth', *Oxford Review of Economic Policy* 23(1): 63–78.

Audretsch, D. B. and M. P. Feldman (1994) *Knowledge Spillovers and the Geography of Innovation and Production*, Schumpeter Society Conference, Munster.

Audretsch, D. B. and M. Keilbach (2004) 'Entrepreneurship Capital and Economic Performance', *Regional Studies* 38: 949–59.

Audretsch, D. and M. Keilbach (2005) 'Entrepreneurship Capital and Regional Growth', *Annals of Regional Science* 39(3): 150–67.

Audretsch, D. and R. Thurik (1997) 'Sources of Growth: The Entrepreneurial vs the Managed Economy', *Tinbergen Institute Discussion Papers*, no. 97–109/3; Amsterdam, Tinbergen Institute.

Audretsch, D. B., M. C. Keilbach and E. E. Lehmann (2006) *Entrepreneurship and Economic Growth*, Oxford: Oxford University Press.

Auerswald, P. E. and Z. J. Acs (2009) 'Defining Prosperity: Why Opportunities Matters More than Growth', *American Interest* 4(5).

Autio, E. and H. Sapienza (2000) 'Comparing Process and Born Global Perspectives in the International

Growth of Technology-Based New Firms', in *Frontiers of Entrepreneurship Research*, Center for Entrepreneurial Studies, Babson College, pp. 413–24.

Autio, E., H. J. Sapienza and J. G. Almeida (2000) 'Effects of Age at Entry, Knowledge Intensity, and Imitability on International Growth', *Academy of Management Journal* 43: 909–24.

Averill, S. and T. Hall (2005) 'An Observatory of eLearning in Small Medium Enterprises (SMEs) in Europe – The Promise versus the Reality', in G. Richards (ed.), *Proceedings of World Conference on E-Learning in Corporate, Government, Healthcare and Higher Education*, Chesapeake, VA: AACE, pp. 220–25.

Ayer, A. J. (1965) 'Chance', *Scientific American* 213 (Oct).

Baets, W. R. J. (2006) *Complexity, Learning and Organizations: A Quantum Interpretation of Business*, Abingdon: Routledge.

Bahrami, H. and S. Evans (1995) 'Flexible Re-cycling and High-Technology Entrepreneurship', *California Management Review* 37: 62–89.

Bailey, Robert G. (1996) *Ecosystem Geography*, New York: Springer.

Baldwin, J. and G. Picot (1995) 'Employment Generation by Small Producers in the Canadian Manufacturing Sector', *Small Business Economics* 7: 317–31.

Banerjee, A. V. (2009) 'Big Answers for Big Questions: Presumptions in Growth Policy', in J. Cohen and W. Easterley (eds), *What Works in Development? Thinking Big and Thinking Small*, Washington, DC: Brookings Institution Press.

Bannock, G. (2005) *The Economics and Management of Small Business: An International Perspective*, London: Routledge.

Barney, J. (1991) 'Firm Resources and Sustained Competitive Advantage', *Journal of Management* 17: 99–120.

Barreto, H. (1989). *The Entrepreneur in Microeconomic Theory*. London: Routledge.

Bartlett, W. and V. Bukvic (2005) 'The Promotion of Innovation in Slovenia through Knowledge Transfer from Higher Education Institutions to SMEs', background paper, OECD Conference on 'Fostering Entrepreneurship: The Role of Higher Education', Trento, 23–24 June.

Basu, A. and A. Goswami (1999) 'Determinants of South Asian Entrepreneurial Growth in Britain: A Multivariate Analysis', *Small Business Economics* 13(1): 57–70.

Bateson, G. (1972) *Steps to an Ecology of Mind*, New York: Ballantine Books.

Baumol, W. J. (1990) 'Entrepreneurship: Productive, Unproductive and Destructive', *Journal of Political Economy* 98: 893–921.

Baumol, W. J. (2002) *The Free Market Innovation Machine: Analyzing the Growth Miracle of Capitalism*, Princeton: Princeton University Press.

Baumol, W. J., J. C. Panzar and R. D. Willig (1988) *Contestable Markets and the Theory of Industry Structure*, rev. edn, San Diego: Harcourt Brace Jovanovich.

Baumol, W. J., R. E. Litan and C. J. Schramm (2007) *Good Capitalism, Bad Capitalism and the Economics of Growth and Prosperity*, New Haven: Yale University Press.

Bayhan, A. (2006) *Business Incubator Process: A Policy Tool for Entrepreneurship and Enterprise Development in a Knowledge Based Economy*, Competitiveness Support Fund.

Beaugrand, P. (2004) 'And Schumpeter Said: This is How Thou Shalt Grow: The Further Quest for Economic Growth in Poor Countries', IMF Working Paper WP/04/40.

Becattini, G. (1989) 'Sectors and/or Districts: Some Remarks on the Conceptual Foundations of Industrial Economics', in E. Goodman and J. Bamford, with P. Saynor, *Small Firms and Industrial Districts in Italy*. London: Routledge.

Becattini, G. (ed.), *Modelli locali di sviluppo*, Bologna: Il Mulino.

Becker, G. (1975) *Human Capital*, 2nd edn, New York: Columbia University Press.

Bellandi, M. (1989) 'Capacità innovativa diffusa e sistemi locali di imprese', in G. Becattini (ed.), *Modelli locali di sviluppo*, Bologna: Il Mulino.

Bellini, E., G. Capaldo, M. Raffa and G. Zollo (1997) 'Universities as Resources for Entrepreneurship', Working paper, Fredrico II University of Naples, Italy.

Benabou, Roland (1996) 'Inequality and Growth', *NBER Macroeconomics Annual 1996* 11: 11–92.

Ben-David, Joseph (1968) *Fundamental Research and the Universities*. Paris: OECD.

Benneworth, P. S. (2001) 'Long-Term Academic Relationships and High-Technology Small Firms', *Enterprise and Innovation Management Studies* 2(2): 1–13.

Bergek, A. and C. Norman (2008) 'Incubator Best Practise: A Framework', *Technovation* 28: 20–8.

BERR (2008) *Simple Support, Better Business: Business Support in 2010*, London: BERR.

BERR/DIUS (2008) *Supporting Innovation in Services*, London: BERR/DIUS.

Bhagwati, J., A. Panagriya and T. Srinivasan (2004) 'The Muddles over Outsourcing', *Journal of Economic Perspectives* 18(4): 93–114.

Bhide, A. (2008) *The Venturesome Economy: How Innovation Sustains Prosperity in a More Connected World*, Princeton: Princeton University Press.

Bialasiewicz, L. (2006) 'Geographies of Production and the Contexts of Politics: Dislocation and New Ecologies of Fear in the Veneto Città Diffusa', *Environment and Planning* D: *Society and Space* 24: 41–67; cited in H.W.-C. Yeung (ed.), *Globalizing Regional Development in East Asia: Production Networks, Clusters and Entrepreneurship*, Abingdon: Routledge.

Birch, D. L. (1979) 'The Job Generation Process', in *MIT Program on Neighborhood and Regional Change*, Cambridge, MA: MIT Press.

Birch, D. L. (1981) 'Who Creates Jobs?' *Public Interest* 65: 3–14.

Birch, D. L. (1987) *Job Creation in America: How our Smallest Companies Put the Most People to Work*, New York: Free Press.

Birch, D. L. and J. Medoff (1994) 'Gazelles', in Lewis C. Solmon and Alec R. Levenson (eds), *Labor Markets, Employment Policy, and Job Creation*. Boulder, CO: Westview Press.

Birley, S. (1985) 'The Role of Networks in the Entrepreneurial Process', *Journal of Business Venturing* 1: 107–17.

Birley, S. *et al.* (1991) 'Entrepreneurial Networks: Their Emergence in Ireland and Overseas', *International Small Business Journal* 9(4): 56–74.

Blair, D. M. and D. M. W. N. Hitchens (1998) *Campus Companies: UK and Ireland*, Aldershot: Ashgate.

Blanchflower, D. G. and B. Meyer (1994) 'A Longitudinal Analysis of Young Self-Employment in Australia and the United States', *Small Business Economics* 6: 1–20.

Blaug, M. (2000) 'Entrepreneurship before and after Schumpeter', in R. Swedberg (ed.), *Entrepreneurship: The Social Science View*, Oxford: Oxford University Press.

Blomstrom, M. and R. Lipsey (1991) 'Firm Size and Foreign Operations of Multi-Nationals', *Scandinavian Journal of Economics* 93: 101–7.

Bollingtoft, A. and J. P. Ulhoi (2005) 'The Networked Business Incubator: Leveraging Entrepreneurial Agency?' *Journal of Business Venturing* 20: 265–90.

Boltanski, L. and E. Chiapello (2007) *The New Spirit of Capitalism*, London: Verso.

Bomers, G. B. J. (1989) *De lerende organisatie* [The Learning Organisation]. Nijenrode: Universiteit voor bedrijfskunde.

Bosma, N. and J. Levie (2009a) *The Global Entrepreneurship Monitor*, Babson College, USA, Univesidad Del Desarrollo, Santiago, Chile; Reykjavík University, Háskólinn Reykjavík, Iceland; London Business School, UK.

Bosma, N. and J. Levie (2009b) 'Global Entrepreneurship Monitor Report: 2009 Global Report', Babson College, Universidad del Desarrollo and Reykjavik University.

Bosma, N., K. Jones, E. Autio and J. Levie (2007) 'Global Entrepreneurship Monitor: 2007 Global Executive Report', Babson College and London Business School, London.

Bosma, N. E., Z. J. Acs, E. Autio, A. Coduras and J. Levie (2008) *The Global Entrepreneurship Monitor*, Babson College, Universidad Del Desarrollo, London Business School.

Bourdieu, P. (1980) 'Le Capital Social: Notes Provisoires', *Acts de la Recherche en Sciences Sociales* 3: 203.

Braczyk, H.-J., P. Cooke and M. Heidenreich (eds) (1997; 1998) *Regional Innovation Systems: The Role of Governance in a Globalised World*, London: UCL Press.

Brafman, O. and Beckstorm R.A. (2006) *TheStrafish and The Spider. The Unstoppable Power of Leaderless Organization*, New York: Portfolio Penguin Group.

Braudel, F. (1984) *Civilisation and Capitalism*. New York: Harper & Row.

Bridge, S., B. Murtagh and K. O'Neill (2009) *Understanding the Social Economy and the Third Sector*, Basingstoke: Palgrave Macmillan.

Brock, W. and D. Evans (1989) *Small Business Economics* 191: 7–20.

Brock, W. A. and D. S. Evans (1986) *The Economics of Small Firms*, New York: Holmes & Meir.

Brockhaus, R. H. (1980) 'Risk-Taking Propensity of Entrepreneurs', *Academy of Management Journal* 23: 509–20.

Bronck, R. (2009) *The Romantic Economist: Imagination in Economics*, Cambridge: Cambridge University Press.

Brown, C., J. Hamilton and J. Medoff (1990) *Employers Large and Small*. Cambridge, MA: Harvard University Press.

Brown, J. S. and P. Duguid (1991) 'Organizational Learning and Communities-of-Practice: Toward a Unified View of Working, Learning and Innovation', *Organizational Science* 2: 40–57.

Bruno, A. V. and T. T. Tyebjee (1982) 'The Environment for Entrepreneurship', in C. Kent, D. L. Sexton and K. H. Vesper (eds), *Encyclopedia of Entrepreneurship*, Englewood Cliffs, NJ: Prentice Hall, pp. 288–307.

Burt, R. (1992) *Structural Holes*, Cambridge, MA: Harvard University Press.

Burt, R. (2009) 'Indian Software Industry', in S. A. Mian (ed.), *Science and Technology Based Regional Entrepreneurship: Global Experience in Policy and Program Development*, Cheltenham: Edward Elgar.

Brusco, S. (1982) 'TheEmilian Model: Productive Decentralisation and Social Integration', *Cambridge Journal of Economics* 6: 167–84.

Brusco, S. (1990) 'The idea of the industrial district: its genesis', in F. Pyke, G. Becattini and W. Sengenberger (eds), *Industrial Districts and Inter-Firm Cooperation in Italy*, Geneva: International Institute for Labor Studies, pp. 11–19.

Busenitz, L. and J. Barney (1997) 'Biases and Heuristics in Strategic Decision Making: Differences between Entrepreneurs and Managers in Large Organizations', *Journal of Business Venturing* 12: 9–30.

Cahan, David (1989) *An Institute for an Empire: The Physikalisch-Technische Reichsanstalt, 1871–1918*. Cambridge: Cambridge University Press.

Cairncross, F. (1997) *The Death of Distance: How the Communication Revolution will Change our Lives*, Boston: Harvard Business School Press.

Callan, B. (2001) 'Generating Spin-Offs: Evidence from across OECD', *STI Review* 26: 14–54.

Camagni, R. (1991) 'Introduction: From the Local Milieu to Innovation through Co-operation Networks', in R. Camagni (ed.), *Innovation Networks: Spatial Perspectives*, London: Bellhaven Press.

Camino, D. and L. Carzola (1998) 'Foreign Market Entry Decisions by Small and Medium Sized Enterprises: An Evolutionary Approach', *International Journal of Management* 15(1): 123–9.

Campbell, D. T. (1965) 'Variation and Selective Retention in Socio-Cultural Evolution', in H. R. Barringer, C. I. Blanksten and R. W. Mack (eds), *Social Change in Developing Areas: A Reinterpretation of Evolutionary Theory*, Cambridge, MA: Schenkman; repr. in *General Systems: Yearbook of the Society for General Systems Research* 16 (1969): 69–85.

Caniels, M. (2000) *Knowledge Spillovers and Economic Growth*, Cheltenham: Edward Elgar.

Cantwell, R. and S. Iammarino (1999) 'Multinational Corporations and the Location of Technological Innovation in the UK Regions', Reading University Department of Economics, Working Paper no. 262.

Capello, R. (1998) 'The Role of Inter-SMEs Networking and Links in Innovative High-Tech Milieux', *Proceeding of the International Conference Networks, Collective Learning and Knowledge Development in Regionally Clustered High-Technology Small and Medium Sized Enterprises in Europe*, 7 Dec., Cambridge.

Capello, R. (1999) 'Spatial Transfer of Knowledge in High Technology Milieux: Learning versus Collective Learning Processes', *Regional Studies* 33: 353–65.

Carbonara, N. and J. Mitra (2001) 'New Actors for the Competitiveness of Local Clusters and Industrial Districts: A Cognitive Approach to Learning and Innovation in Clusters and Industrial Districts', *Proceedings of the ISBA Small Firms Research and Policy Conference*, Leicester, Nov.

Caree, M. A. and R. Thurik (2003) 'The Impact of Entrepreneurship on Economic Growth', in D. B. Audretsch and Z. J. Acs (eds), *Handbook of Entrepreneurship Research*, Boston and Dordrecht: Kluwer Academic Publishers, pp. 437–71.

Carlsson, B. and R. Stankiewicz (1991) 'On the Nature, Function, and Composition of Technological Systems', *Journal of Evolutionary Economics* 1(2): 93–118.

Carr, N. (2000) 'Hypermediation: Commerce as Clickstream', *Harvard Business Review* 78(1): 46–7.

Casper, S. and H. Kettler (2001) 'National Institutional Frameworks and the Hybridisation of Entrepreneurial Business Models: The German and UK Biotechnology Sectors', *Industry and Innovation* 8: 5–30.

Casson, M. (1982) *The Entrepreneur: An Economic Theory*. Oxford: Martin Robertson.

Casson, M. (1995) *Entrepreneurship and Business Culture: Studies in the Economics of Trust*, Cheltenham: Edward Elgar.

Caves, R. and M. E. Porter (1977) 'From Entry Barriers to Mobility Barriers', *Quarterly Journal of Economics* 91: 241–61.

Caves, R. E. (1996) *Multinational Enterprise and Economic Analysis*, 2nd edn, Cambridge: Cambridge University Press.

Caves, R. E. (1998) 'Industrial Organisation and New Findings on the Turnover and Mobility of Firms', *Journal of Economic Literature* 36(4): 1947–82.

Cavusgil, S. T. (1980) 'On the Internationalisation Process of Firms', *European Research* 8(6): 273–81.

CER (2005) 'Internationalising Entrepreneurial Clusters' Final Report, J. Mitra, Centre for Entrepreneurship Research, School of Entrepreneurship and Business, University of Essex.

Chan, K. F. and T. Lau (2005) 'Assessing Technology Incubator Programs in the Science Park: The Good, the Bad and the Ugly', *Technovation* 25: 1215–28.

Chandra, A. (2007) *Approaches to Incubation: A Comparative Study of the United States, China and Brazil*. Networks Financial Institute at Indiana State University.

Charles, D. and C. Conway (2001) *Higher Education – Business Interaction Survey*, London: HEFCE.

Chaudhury, S. (2005) 'Trading Networks in a Traditional Diaspora: Armenians in India, c.1600–1800', in I. B. McCabe, G. Harlafatis and I. P. Minoglou (eds), *Diaspora Entrepreneurial Networks: Four Centuries of History*, Oxford: Berg, pp. 51–70.

Chesbrough, Henry W. (2003) 'The Era of Open Innovation', *Sloan Management Review*, Spring: 35–41.

Chesbrough, H. W., Vanhaverbeke W. and Van de Vrande, V. (2008) 'Understanding the Advantages of Open Innovation Practices in Corporate Venturing in Terms of Real Options', *Creativity and Innovation Management*, 17(4): 251-258.

Child, J. (1980) *Organisations*, London: Harper & Row.

Christensen, C. and M. Overdorf (2000) 'Meeting the Challenge of Disruptive Change', *Harvard Business Review* 78(2).

Christensen, C. and R. Tedlow (2000) 'Patterns of Disruption in Retailing', *Harvard Business Review* 78(1): 42–5.

Cipolla, C. M. (1981) *Before the Industrial Revolution: European Society and Economy, 1000–1700*, 2nd edn, Cambridge: Cambridge University Press.

Clarysse, B., M. Wright, A. Lockett, E. Vande Velde and A. Vohora (2005) 'Spinning Out New Ventures: A Typology of Incubation Strategies from European Research Institutions', *Journal of Business Venturing* 20: 183–216.

Clemence, R. V. and F. S. Doody (1950) *The Schumpeterian System*, Cambridge: Addison-Wesley.

Clydesdale, G. (2010) *Entrepreneurial Opportunity: The Right Place at the Right Time*, New York: Routledge.

Coase, R. H. (1937) 'The Nature of the Firm', *Economica* 4: 386–405.

Coe, N., P. Dicken and M. Hess (2008) 'Global Production Networks: Realising the Potential', *Journal of Economic Geography* 8: 271–95.

Cohen, W. and R. Levinthal (1989) 'Innovation and Learning: The Two Faces of R&D', *Economic Journal* 99: 569–96.

Cohen, W. M. and S. Klepper (1992) 'The Anatomy of Industry R&D Intensity Distributions', *American Economic Review* 82: 773–99.

Cohen, W. M., R. R. Nelson and J. P. Walsh (2000) 'Protecting their Intellectual Assets: Appropriability Conditions and Why U.S. Manufacturing Firms Patent or Not', NBER Working Paper no. 7552.

Coleman, J. S. (1988) 'Social Capital in the Creation of Human Capital', *American Journal of Sociology* 94: S95–S121.

Colombo, M. and M. Delmastro (2002) 'How Effective are Technology Incubators? Evidence from Italy', *Research Policy* 31(7): 1103–122.

Cooke, P. and K. Morgan (1998) *The Associational Economy: Firms, Regions and Innovation*, Oxford: Oxford University Press.

Cooke P., C. De Laurentis, F. Tödtling and M. Trippl (2007) *Regional Knowledge Economies*. Cheltenham: Edward Elgar.

Coombs, P. H. and M. Ahmed (1974) *Attacking Rural Poverty: How Non-Formal Education Can Help*, Baltimore: Johns Hopkins University Press.

Cosh, A. and A. Hughes (2000) *British Enterprise in Transition*, Cambridge: ESRC Centre for Business Research.

Costa-David, J., J. Malan and R. Lalkaka (2002) 'Improving Business Incubator through Benchmarking and Evaluation: Lessons Learned from Europe', 16th International Conference on Business Incubation: National Business Incubation Association, Toronto, Canada.

Covielo, N. and A. McAuley (1999) 'Internationalisation and the Smaller Firm: A Review of Contemporary Empirical Research', *Management International Review* 39(3): 223–56.

CSES and ECED-G (2002) Benchmarking of Business Incubators, *Final Report,* Center for Strategy and Evaluation Services. European Commission, Luxembourg.

Cullen, J. and H. Matlay (1999) 'Collaborative Learning in Small Firms: Why Skill Standards Don't Work', paper presented at the 22nd Institute of Small Business Affairs Small Firms Policy and Research Conference, 'European Strategies, Growth and Development', Leeds, 17–19 Nov.

Cullum, P., L. Padmore and M. Purdy (2002) 'Entrepreneurship around the Globe: Adapting to Different Natural Environments', *Outlook: Point of View* (May).

Cunningham, I. (1994) *The Wisdom of Strategic Learning*, Maidenhead: McGraw-Hill.

Curtis, V. (Oct. 2002) 'Health in your Hands: Lessons from Building Private–Public Partnerships for Washing Hands with Soap', http://globalhandwashing.org/Publications/Lessons_learntPart1.htm, in C. K. Prahalad (2005) (Indian Subcontinent edition) *The Fortune at the Bottom of the Pyramid: Eradicating Poverty through Profits*, Singapore, Pearson.

Dale, M. and J. Bell (1999) *Informal Learning in the Workplace*. DfEE Research Report 134, London: DfEE.

Dario, P. and A. Menciassi (2010) 'Robot Pills: Doctor in a Capsule', *Scientific American* 303(2): 48–51.

Darwin, J. (2007) *After Tamerlane: The Rise and Fall of Global Empires, 1400–2000*, London: Penguin Books.

Dasgupta, P. (2000) 'Economic Progress and the Idea of Social Capital', in P. Dasgupta and I. Serageldin (eds), *Social Capital: A Multifaceted Perspective*, Washington, DC: World Bank.

Davidsson, P., L. Lindmark and C. Olofsson (1995) 'Small Firms, Business Dynamics and Differential Development of Economic Well-Being', *Small Business Economics* 7: 301–15.

Davidsson, P., L. Lindmark and C. Olofsson (1998) 'Smallness, Newness and Regional Development', *Swedish Journal of Agricultural Research* 28: 57–71.

Davidsson, P. and B. Honig (2003) 'The Role of Social and Human Capital Among Nascent Entrepreneurs', *Journal of Business Venturing* 18: 301–331.

De Geus, A. (1998) 'Planning as Learning', *Harvard Business Review* (Mar.–Apr.), 70–74.

De Soto, H. (1989) *The Other Path: The Economic Answer to Terrorism*, New York: Basic Books.

Denzau, A. T. and D. C. North (1994) 'Shared Mental Models: Ideologies and Institutions', *Kyklos* 47: 3–31.

Desai, M., P. Gompers and J. Lerner (2003) 'Institutions, Capital Constraints and Entrepreneurial Firm Dynamics: Evidence from Europe', NBER Working Papers no. 10165, Cambridge, MA: NBER.

Desai, S., Z. J. Acs and U. Weitzel (forthcoming) 'A Theory of Destructive Entrepreneurship', *Journal of Economic Literature*.

Dixon, N. (1994) *The Organizational Learning Cycle: How We Can Learn Collectively*, Maidenhead: McGraw-Hill.

Dodgson, M. (1993) 'Organizational Learning: A Review of Some Literatures', *Organization Studies* 14(3): 375–94.

Doms, M., T. Dunne and M. J. Roberts (1995) 'The Role of Technology Use in the Survival and Growth of Manufacturing Plants', *International Journal of Industrial Organisation* 13(4): 523–54.

Drayton, B. and V. Budinich (2010) 'A New Alliance for Global Change', *Harvard Business Review* 88(9): 56–65.

Drucker, P. F. (1985) *Innovation and Entrepreneurship: Practice and Principles*, New York: Harper & Row.

Dumaine, B. (2010) 'Lighting Up Africa', *Fortune* 9 (5 July): 14.

Dunning, J. (1988) 'The Eclectic Paradigm of International Production: A Restatement and Some Possible Extensions', *Journal of International Business Studies* (spring), 1–31.

Dunning, J. (1997) *Alliance Capitalism and Global Business*. London: Routledge.

Dunning, J. (1998) 'Location and the Multinational Enterprise: Neglected Factor?' *Journal of International Business Studies* 29(1): 45–66.

Easterby-Smith, M. and M. A. Lyles (2005) *Handbook of Organizational Learning and Knowledge Management*, Oxford: Blackwell.

Easterby-Smith, M. and I. M. Prieto (2008) 'Dynamic Capabilities and Knowledge Management: An Integrative Role for Learning?' *British Journal of Management* 3: 235–49.

Easterby-Smith, M., J. Burgoyne and L. Arujo (eds) (1999) *Organizational Learning and the Learning Organization: Developments in Theory and Practice*, London: Sage.

Easterly, W. (2001) *The Elusive Quest for Growth: Economists, Adventures and Misadventures in the Tropics*, Cambridge, MA: MIT Press.

Easterly, W. and R. Levine (2001) 'It's Not Factor Accumulation: Stylised Facts and Growth Models', www.worldbank.org.

Easterly, W. and R. Levine (2003) 'Tropics, Germs and Crops: How Endowments Influence Economic Development', *Journal of Monetary Economics* 50: 3–39.

Echecopar, G. (2004) 'Incubating Innovative Start Ups: Some Lessons from Chile'. In S. E. Tiffin (ed.), *Entrepreneurship in Latin America: Perspectives on Education*.

The Economist (2009) 'Global Heroes A Special Report on Entrepreneurship', by Adrian Woolridge, *The Economist* 390(8622).

The Economist (2010) 'Can Anything Perk Up in Europe?' and 'The Future of Europe and Staring into the Abyss', *The Economist* (8 July).

Edwards, B. (2004) 'A World of Work', *The Economist* (13 Nov.).

Elliott, J. E. (2008) 'Introduction to the Transaction Edition', in J. A. Schumpeter, *The Theory of Economic Development*, New Brunswick: Transaction Publishers.

Ellison, G., E. L. Glaser and W. R. Kerr (2010) 'What Causes Industry Agglomeration? Evidence from Coagglomeration Patterns', *American Economic Review* 100: 1195–213.

El-Namaki, M. S. S. (1988) 'Encouraging Entrepreneurship in Developing Countries', *Long Range Planning* 21(4): 98–106.

Enright, M. (1990) 'Geographical Concentration and Industrial Organization', Ph.D. dissertation, Harvard Business School.

Enright, M. (2001). 'Regional Clusters: What We Know and What We Should Know', paper prepared for the Kiel Institute International Workshop on 'Innovative Clusters and Interregional Competition', 12–13 Nov.

Enright, M. J. (1998) 'Regional Clusters and Firm Strategy', in A. D. Chandler, P. Hagstrom and O. Solvell (eds), *The Dynamic Firm*, Oxford: Oxford University Press.

Eraut, M. (2000) 'Non-Formal Learning, Implicit Learning and Tacit Knowledge in Professional Work', in F. Coffield, *The Necessity of Informal Learning*, Bristol: Policy Press.

Ernst, D. (2004) 'Global Production Networks in East Asia's Electronics Industry and Upgrading Prospects in Malaysia', in S. Yusuf, M. Ataf and K. Nabeshima (eds), *Global Production Networking and Technological Change in East Asia*. Washington, DC: World Bank/Oxford: Oxford University Press, pp. 89–157; cited in H. W.-C. Yeung (ed.), *Globalizing Regional Development in East Asia: Production Networks, Clusters and Entrepreneurship*. Abingdon: Routledge.

Ernst, D. (2005) 'Pathways to Innovation in Asia's Leading Electronics-Exporting Countries – A Framework for Exploring Drivers and Policy Implications', *International Journal of Technology Management* 29: 6–20.

Etzkowitz, H. (2002) 'Incubation of Incubtors: Innovation as a Triple Helix of University–Industry–Government Networks', *Science and Public Policy* 29: 115–28.

Etzkowitz, H., A. Webster and P. Healey (eds) (1998) *Capitalizing Knowledge: University Intersections of Industry and Academia*. Albany: State University of New York Press.

European Commission (1998) *Universities, Technology Transfer and Spin-Off Activities: Academic*.

European Commission (2003) 'Green Paper Entrepreneurship in Europe, Brussels, 21.01.2003, COM(2003) .

Eurostat/OECD (2007) *Eurostat/OECD Manual on Business Demography Statistics*, Paris: OECD.

Evans, D. S. and L. S. Leighton (1989) 'The Determinants of Changes in U.S. Self-Employment', *Small Business Economics* 1(2): 111–20.

Evans, D. S. and L. S. Leighton (1990) 'Small Business Formation by Unemployed and Employed Workers', *Small Business Economics* 2(4): 319–30.

Faris, S. (2010) in 'Global Business (Corporate Strategy): Rebuilding Lego', *Time* 175(22).

Feldman, M. P. (1994) 'The University and High Technology Start-Ups: The Case of Johns Hopkins University and Baltimore', *Economic Development Quarterly* 8: 67–77.

Feldman, M. P. and D. Audretsch (1999) 'Innovation in Cities: Science-Based Diversity, Specialization and Localized Competition', *European Economic Review* 43: 409–29.

Feller, I. (1990) 'Universities as Engines of R&D Based Economic Growth: They Think They Can', *Research Policy* 19: 335–48.

Fergusson, C. (1988) 'From the People who Brought You Vodoo Economics', *Harvard Business Review* 66(3): 55–62.

Fergusson, R. and C. Olofsson (2004) 'Science Parks and the Development of NTBFs – Location, Survival and Growth', *Journal of Technology Transfer* 29: 5–17.

Financial Times (2010) 'Haiti Sets Out on Road to Sustainable Future: Reconstruction', by Benedict Mander, *Financial Times* (10 July).

Fisher, D. and W. Torbert (1995) *Personal and Organizational Transformations: The True Challenge of Continual Quality Improvement*, New York: McGraw-Hill.

Flap, H. D. (1991) 'Social Capital in the Reproduction of Inequality', *Comparative Sociology of Family, Health and Education* 20: 6179–202.

Florida, R. (2002) *The Rise of the Creative Class*, New York: Basic Books.

Florida, R. (2003) 'Entrepreneurship, Creativity and Regional Economic Growth', in D. M. Hart (ed.), *The Emergence of Entrepreneurship Policy: Governance, Start-Ups, and Growth in the U.S. Knowledge Economy*, Cambridge: Cambridge University Press.

Florida, R. (2005) *Cities and the Creative Class*, New York: Routledge.

Florida, R. (2007) *The Flight of the Creative Class: The New Global Competition for Talent*, New York: Collins.

Florida, R. (2008) *Who's Your City: How the Creative Economy is Making Where to Live the Most Important Decision of Your Life*, New York: Basic Books.

Formica, P. and J. Mitra (1996) *Regional Innovation and Technology Transfer Strategies: The London Technopole Initiative, Stages 1 to 3*, London: European Commission, RITTS Initiative report.

Formica, P., T. Mets and U. Varblane (2005) 'Knowledge Transfer Mechanisms from Universities and other HEIs to the SME Sector', background paper, OECD Conference on 'Fostering Entrepreneurship: The Role of Higher Education', Trento, 23–24 June.

Freel, M. (2003) 'Sectoral Patterns of Small Firm Innovation, Networking and Proximity', *Research Policy* 32: 751–70.

Freeman, C. and L. Soete (1997) *The Economics of Industrial Innovation*, 3rd edn, London: Pinter.

Friedman, T. (2005) *The World is Flat: A Brief History of the Globalised World in the 21st Century*, London: Allen Lane.

Fritsch, M. (2008) 'How Does New Business Formation Affect Regional Development? Introduction to the Special Issue', *Small Business Economics* 30: 1–14.

Fritsch, M. and O. Falck (2007) 'New Business Formation by Industry over Space and Time: A Multi-Dimensional Analysis', *Regional Studies* 41: 157–72.

Fritsch, M. and P. Mueller (2004) 'Effects of New Business Formation on Regional Development over Time', *Regional Studies* 38: 961–75.

Fuellhart, K. G. and A. K. Glasmeier (2003) 'Acquisition, Assessment and Use of Business Information by Small and Medium-Sized Businesses: A Demand Perspective', *Entrepreneurship and Regional Development* 15(3): 229–52.

Galbraith, J. (1956) *American Capitalism*, Boston: Houghton Mifflin.

Galbraith, J. (1967) *The New Industrial State*, Harmondsworth: Penguin Books.

Galbraith, J. R. (2004) 'Designing the Innovating Organisation', in K. Starkey, S. Tempest and A. McKinlay, *How Organisations Learn: Managing the Search for Knowledge*, 2nd edn, London: Thomson Learning.

Garnsey, E. and P. Heffernan (2005) 'High-Technology Clustering through Spin-Out and Attraction: The Cambridge Case', *Regional Studies* 39: 1127–44.

Gartner, W. B. (1985) 'A Conceptual Framework for Describing the Phenomenon of New Venture Creation', *Academy of Management Review* 10(4): 696–706.

Gartner, W. B. and N. M. Carter (2003) 'Entrepreneurial Behaviour and Firm Organising Processes', in Z. J. Acs and D. B. Audretsch (eds), *Handbook of Entrepreneurship Research*, Boston: Kluwer Academic Publishers, pp. 195–222.

George, G. and A. S. Zahra (2002) 'Being Independent is a Great Thing: Subjective Evaluations of Self-Employment and Hierarchy', CESifo Working Paper no. 959.

Geroski, P. A. (1995) 'What do We Know about Entry?' *International Journal of Industrial Organisation* 13(4).

Gibb, A. (1996) 'Entrepreneurship and Small Business Management: Can We Afford to Neglect Them in the Twenty First Century Business School?' *British Journal of Management* 7: 309–21.

Gibb, A. (2000) 'SME Policy, Academic Research and the Growth of Ignorance, Mythical Concepts, Myths, Assumptions, Rituals and Confusions', *International Small Business Journal* 18(3), 13–35.

Gibb, A. (2009) 'The Small Business and Entrepreneurship Challenge to Vocational Education: Revolution or Evolution?' Paper presented at the OECD Conference on 'SMEs, Entrepreneurship and Innovation', Udine, 22–23 Oct., OECD LEED.

Gibb, A. and J. Ritchie (1982) 'Understanding the Process of Starting Small Businesses', *European Small Business Journal* 1: 26–45.

Gibb, A. A. (1993) 'The Enterprise Culture and Education: Understanding Enterprise Education and its Links with Small Business, Entrepreneurship and Wider Educational Goals', *International Small Business Journal* 11(3): 11–34.

Gibbons, M., C. Limoges, H. Nowotny, S. Schwartzman, P. Scott and M. Trow (1994) *The New Production of Knowledge*, London: Sage.

Gilson, S. C. (1999) 'Managing Default: Some Evidence on How Firms Choose between Workouts and Chapter 11', in T. M. Barnhill, W. F. Maxwell and M. R. Shenkman (eds), *High Yield Bonds: Market Structure, Valuation, and Portfolio Strategies*, New York: McGraw Hill.

Glaeser, E., H. Kallal, J. Scheinkman and A. Shelfer (1992) 'Growth in Cities', *Journal of Political Economy* 100: 1126–52.

Glaeser, E. L. and M. E. Kahn (2001) 'Decentralized Employment and the Transformation of the American City', *Brookings-Wharton Papers on Urban Affairs*, 1–47.

Glaser, E. L. (2005) Inequality, Harvard Institute of Economic Research, Discussion Paper Number 2078, July 2005, Harvard University, Cambridge, Massachusetts, http://post.economics.harvard. edu/hier/2005papers/2005list.html
The Social Science Research Network Electronic Paper Collection:
http://ssrn.com/abstract=756889.

Glancey, K. S. and R. W. McQuaid (2000) *Entrepreneurial Economics*, Basingstoke: Macmillan Press.

Gnyawali, D. R. and D. S. Fogel (1994) 'Environments for Entrepreneurship Development: Key Dimensions and Research Implications', *Entrepreneurship Theory and Practice* 18(4): 43–62.

Goddard, J., D. Charles, A. Pike, G. Potts and D. Bradley (1994) 'Universities and Communities', Committee of Vice Chancellors and Principals, London.

Goh, S. C. and G. Richards (1997) 'Benchmarking the Learning Capability of Organisations', *European Management Journal* 15(5): 575–83.

Grandi, A. and R. Grimaldi (n.d.) 'Business Incubators and New Venture Creation: Assessing Different Incubating Programmes', International Conference on 'Entrepreneurship and Learning', Naples.

Granovetter, M. (1973) 'The Strength of Weak Ties', *American Journal of Sociology* 78: 1360–80.

Granovetter, M. (1985) 'Economic Action and Social Structure: The Problem of Embeddedness', *American Journal of Sociology* 91: 349–64.

Grant, R. (1999) 'Toward a Knowledge Based Theory of the Firm', *International Journal of Innovation Management* 19(2): 121–39.

Gray, J. (1998) *False Dawn: The Delusions of Global Capitalism*, London: Granta.

Green, L., B. Jones and I. Miles (2007) *Global Review of Innovation Intelligence and Policy Studies: Skills for Innovation*, Brussels: EC DG Enterprise and Industry.

Griliches, Z. (1990) 'Patent Statistics as Economic Indicators: A Survey', *Journal of Economic Literature* 28(4): 1661–707.

Grimaldi, R. and A. Grandi (2005) 'Business Incubators and New Venture Creation: An Assessment of Incubating Models', *Technovation* 25: 111–21.

Grimm, H. and D. B. Audretsch (2005) 'Entrepreneurship Policy in Comparative-Historical Perspectives', in D. B. Audretsch, H. Grimm and C. W. Wesner (eds), *Local Heroes in the Global Village: Globalization and New Entrepreneurship Policies*, New York: Springer.

Gris, T. and W. Naude (2008) 'Entrepreneurship and Structural Economic Transformation', *UNU-Wider Research Papers*, Helsinki.

Grossman, G. and E. Helpman (1994) 'Endogenous Innovation in the Theory of Growth', *Journal of Economic Perspectives* 8: 23–44.

Grossman, G. M. and E. Helpman (1991) 'Trade, Knowledge Spillovers and Growth', Working Paper no. 3485, National Bureau of Economic Research, Cambridge, MA.

Gulati, R. (2007) *Managing Network Resources: Alliances, Affiliations and Other Relational Assets*, Oxford: Oxford University Press.

Gupta, A. K., V. Govindarajan and H. Wang (2008) *The Quest for Global Dominance: Transforming Global Presence into Global Competitive Advantage*, 2nd edn, San Francisco: Jossey-Bass.

Hackett, S. M. and D. M. Dilts (2004a) 'A Systematic Review of Business Incubation Research', *Journal of Technology Transfer* 29: 55–82.

Hackett, S. M. and D. M. Dilts (2004b) 'A Real Options-Driven Theory of Business Incubation', *Journal of Technology Transfer* 29: 41–54.

Hackett, S. M. and D. M. Dilts (2008) 'Inside the Black Box of Business Incubation: Study B – Scale Assessment, Model Refinement, and Incubation Outcomes', *Journal of Technology Transfer* 33: 439–71.

Hagedoorn, J. (1993) 'Understanding the Rationale of Strategic Technology Partnering: Interorganisational Modes of Co-operation and Sectoral Differences', *Strategic Management Journal* 14: 371–85.

Hahn, F. (1984) *Equilibrium and Macroeconomics*, Cambridge, MA: MIT Press.

Hakansson, H. and J. Johanson (1993) 'The Network as a Governance Structure –Interfirm Cooperation beyond Markets and Hierarchies,' in G. Grabher (ed.), *The Embedded Firm: The Socio-Economics of Industrial Networks*, London: Routledge, pp. 35–51.

Hall, P. A. and D. Soskice (2001) *Varieties of Capitalism*, Oxford: Oxford University Press.

Hamamatsu Chamber of Commerce (2000) '*Hamamatsu no sangyo gaiyo*', Hamamatsu, Hamamatsu Chamber of Commerce; cited in Y. Aoyama (2010) 'Entrepreneurship and Regional Culture: The Case of Hamamatsu and Kyoto, Japan', in H. W.-C. Yeung (ed.), *Globalizing Regional Development in East Asia: Production Networks, Clusters and Entrepreneurship*. Abingdon: Routledge.

Hamburg, I. and T. Hall (2008) 'Informal Learning and the Use of Web 2.0 within SME Training Strategies', *Summary Elearning Papers*, www.elearningpapers.eu, 2(11), November.

Hannon, P. D. (2004) 'A Qualitative Sense-Making Classification of Business Incubation Environments', *Qualitative Market Research: An International Journal* 7(4): 274–83.

Harris, J. and C. Davidson (2009) 'Obama: The New Contours of Power', *Race and Class* 50(4): 1–19.

Harris, R. G. (2001) 'The Knowledge-Based Economy: Intellectual Origins and New Economic Perspectives', *International Journal of Management Review* 3: 21–41.

Harrison, C. (1993) *Teaching and Learning: A Strategy for Anglia*, Cambridge: Anglia Polytechnic University.

Harrison, J. (2007) 'From Competitive Regions to Competitive City-Regions: A New Orthodoxy, but Some Old Mistakes', *Journal of Economic Geography* 7(3): 311–32.

Hart, D. M. (ed.) (2003) 'Entrepreneurship Policy: What It is and Where It Came From', in *The Emergence of Entrepreneurship Policy: Governance, Start-Ups and Growth in the US Knowledge Economy*, Cambridge: Cambridge University Press.

Hayek, F. (1937) 'Economics and Knowledge', *Economica* 33–54; repr. in *Individualism and Economic Order*, Chicago: University of Chicago Press, 1948, pp. 33–56.

Hayek, F. A. (1949) *Individualism and Economic Order*, London: Routledge & Kegan Paul.

Hayton, J. C., George, G. and Zahra S. A. (2002) 'National Culture and Entrepreneurship: Domains of Behavioral Research and Possible Extensions, http://www.ncl.ac.uk/nubs/research/publication/85897, '*Entrepreneurship: Theory and Practice*26(4): 33–62.

Hazlitt, W. (1825; 2004) 'The Spirit of the Age', *Essay on Jeremy* Bentham, 2nd edn, Wordsworth Trust.

Heilman, S. (2008) 'Policy Experimentation in China's Economic Rise', *Studies in Comparative International Development* 43: 1–26.

Henrekson, Magnus and Dan Johansson (2008) 'Gazelles as Job Creators – A Survey and Interpretation of the Evidence', IFN Working Paper no. 733, Research Institute of Industrial Economics.

Henreksula, M. and M. Stenkula (2009) 'Entrepreneurship and Public Policy', in Z. J. Acs and D. B. Audretsch (eds), *Handbook of Entrepreneurship Research*, New York: Springer.

Hills, G. and M. H. Morris (1998) 'Entrepreneurship Education: A Conceptual Model and Review', in M. G. Scott, P. Rosa and H. Klandt (eds), *Educating Entrepreneurs for Wealth Creation*, Aldershot: Ashgate.

Hippel, E. von (1976) 'The Dominant Role of the User in the Scientific Instrument Innovation Process', *Research Policy* 5: 212–39.

Hippel, E. von (1977) 'The Dominant Role of the User in Semiconductor and Electronic Subassembly Process in Innovation', *IEEE Transactions on Engineering Management* EM 24: 60–71.

Hippel, E. von (2005) *Democratizing Innovation*, Cambridge, MA: MIT Press.

Hitt, M. A., R. E. Hoskisson, R. A. Johnson and D. D. Moesel (1996) 'The Market for Corporate Control and Firm Innovation', *Academy of Management Journal* 39: 1084–119.

HM Treasury (2003) *Lambert Review of Business–Industry Collaboration: Final Report*.

HM Treasury (2008) *Social Bridges II: The Importance of Human Capital for Growth and Social Inclusion*, London: HM Treasury.

Hofstede, G. (1980) *Culture's Consequences: International Differences in Work-Related Values*, Thousand Oaks, CA: Sage.

Hofstede, G. (2001) *Culture's Consequences: Comparing Values, Behaviours, Institutions and Organisations across Nations*, 2nd edn, Thousand Oaks, CA: Sage.

Hopkins, A. G. (2002) 'The History of Globalisation – and the Globalisation of History?' in A. G. Hopkins, (ed.), *Globalisation in World History*, London: Pimlico, pp. 11–46.

Howells, J., M. Nedeva and L. Georghiou (1998) 'Industry–Academic Links in the UK', Higher Education Funding Council for England.

Huang, Y. (2008) *Capitalism with Chinese Characteristics: Entrepreneurship and the State*, Cambridge: Cambridge University Press.

Huang, Y. and T. Khanna (2003) 'Can India Overtake China?' *Foreign Policy* (July–Aug.), 74–81.

Huber, G. (1996) 'Organizational Learning', in M. D. Cohen and L. S. Sproull (eds), *Organizational Learning*, Thousand Oaks, CA: Sage, pp. 124–61.

Huber, G. P. (1991) 'Organizational Learning: The Contributing Processes and the Literatures', *Organization Science* 2: 88–115.

Hughes, A. (2007) 'University Industry Links and UK Science and Innovation Policy', in S. Yusuf and K. Nabeshima (eds), *How Universities Promote Economic Growth*, Washington, DC: World Bank.

Hughes, A. and E. Wood (1999) 'Rethinking Innovation Comparisons between Manufacturing and Services: The Experience of the CBR SME Surveys in the UK', Working Paper no. 140, ESRC Centre for Business Research, University of Cambridge.

Hughes, M., R. D. Ireland and R. E. Morgan (2007) 'Stimulating Dynamic Value: Social Capital and Business Incubation as a Pathway to Competitive Success', *Long Range Planning* 40: 154–77.

Hyland, T. and H. Matlay (1997) 'Small Businesses, Training Needs and VET Provision', *Journal of Education and Work* 10(2): 129–39.

Ibrahim, A. B. (1993) 'Strategy Type and Small Firms' Performance: An Empirical Investigation', *Journal of Small Business Strategy* 4(1): 13–22.

Ibrahim, A. B. (2004) 'Internationalisation: Motive and Process', in L.-P. Dana (ed.), *Handbook of Research on International Entrepreneurship*, Cheltenham: Edward Elgar, pp. 129–36.

Ibrahim, A. B. and J. McGuire (2001) 'Technology Transfer Strategies for International Entrepreneurs', *International Management* 6(1): 75–83.

Ivancevich, J. M. (1991) 'A Traditional Faculty Member's Perspective on Entrepreneurship', *Journal of Business Venturing* 6: 1–7.

Iyer, S., M. Kitson and B. Toh (2005) 'Social Capital, Economic Growth and Regional Development', *Regional Studies* 39: 1015–40.

Jacobs, J. (1969) *The Economy of Cities*, New York: Random House.

Jaffe, A. B. (1986) 'Technological Oportunity and Spillovers of R&D: Evidence from Firms' Patents, Profits and Market Value', *American Economic Review* 76: 984–1001.

Jaffe, A. B. (1989) 'Real Effects of Academic Research', *American Economic Review* 79(5): 957–70.

Jaffe, A. B., M. Trajtenberg and R. Henderson (1993) 'Geographic Localization of Knowledge Spillovers as Evidenced by Patent Citations', *Quarterly Journal of Economics* 108(3): 577–98.

Jo, H. and J. Lee (1996) 'The Relationship between an Entrepreneur's Background and Performance in a New Venture', *Technovation* 16(4): 161–71.

Joel Popkin and Co. (1988) 'Small Business Gross Product Originating: 1958–1982', prepared under contract for the US Small Business Administration Office of Advocacy, SBA-1040-OA-86, Apr.

Johanson, B., C. Karlsson and L. Westin (eds) (1994) *Patterns of a Network Economy*. London: Springer.

Johanson, J. and J.-E. Vahlne (1977) 'The Internationalisation Process of the Firm: A Model of Knowledge Development and Increasing Foreign Commitments', *Journal of International Business Studies* 8(3): 23–32.

Johnson, S., D. Kaufmann, J. McMillan and C. Woodruff (2000) 'Why Do Firms Hide? Bribes and Unofficial Activity after Communism', *Journal of Public Economics* 76: 495–520.

Jovanovic, B. (1982) 'Selection and the Evolution of Industry', *Econometrica* 50: 649–70.

Kanter, R. M. (1989) *When Giants Learn to Dance*, New York: Touchstone.

Karlsson, C. and M. Andersson (2009) 'Entrepreneurship Policies: Principles, Problems and Opportunities', in J. Leitao and R. Baptista (eds), *Public Policies for Fostering Entrepreneurship*, New York: Springer.

Keeble, D. and F. Wilkinson (1999) 'Collective Learning and Knowledge Development in the Evolution of Regional Clusters of High Technology SMEs in Europe', *Regional Studies* 33: 295–303.

Keeble, D., C. Lawson, H. Lawton-Smith, B. Moore and F. Wilkinson (1997) 'Internationalisation Processes, Networking and Local Embeddedness', in *Technology Intensive Small Firms*, ESRC Centre for Business Research Working Papers 53, University of Cambridge, Cambridge.

Keeble, D., C. Lawson, B. Moore and F. Wilkinson (1999) 'Collective Learning Processes, Networking and "Institutional Thickness", in the Cambridge Region', *Regional Studies* 33: 319–32.

Kenny, M. and R. Florida (2004) *Locating Global Advantage: Industry Dynamics in the International Economy*, Stanford: Stanford University Press.

Keynes, J. M. (1936) *The General Theory of Employment, Interest and Money*, New York: Macmillan.

Khanna, T. (2007) *Billions of Entrepreneurs: How China and India are Reshaping their Futures and Yours*, Boston: Harvard Business School Press.

Kim, D. H. (1993) 'The Link between Individual and Organizational Learning', *Sloan Management Review* 35(1): 37–50.

Kim, W. C. and R. Mauborgne (2005) *Blue Ocean Strategy: How to Create Uncontested Market Space and Make the Competition Irrelevant*, Boston: Harvard Business School Press.

Kingsley, G. and E. J. Malecki (2004) 'Networking for Competitiveness', *Small Business Economics* 23: 71–84.

Kirzner, I. M. (1973) *Competition and Entrepreneurship*. Chicago: University of Chicago Press.

Kirzner, I. M. (1997) 'Entrepreneurial Discovery and the Competitive Market Process: An Austrian Approach', *Journal of Economic Literature* 35: 60–85.

Klevorick, A. K., R. C. Levin, R. R. Nelson and S. O. Winter (1995) 'On the Sources and Significance of Interindustry Differences in Technological Opportunity', *Research Policy* 24: 185–205.

Kline, G. J. and N. Rosenberg (1986) 'An Overview of Innovation', in R. Landau and N. Rosenberg (eds), *The Positive Sum Strategy: Harnessing Technology for Economic Growth*, Washington, DC: National Academy Press, pp. 275–306.

Kline, S. and N. Rosenberg (1986) 'An Overview of Innovation', in R. Landau and N. Rosenberg (eds), *The Positive Sum Strategy*. Washington, DC: National Academy Press, pp. 275–305.

Kloosterman, R., J. P. Van der Leun and J. Rath (1999) 'Mixed Embeddedness, Migrant Entrepreneurs and Informal Economic Activities', *International Journal of Urban and Regional Research* 14(5): 659–76.

Knight, F. H. (1921) *Risk, Uncertainty and Profit*, Boston: Houghton Mifflin.

Knudsen, B., R. Florida, G. Gates and K. Stolarick (2007) 'Urban Density, Creativity and Innovation', Working paper, The Martin Prosperity Institute, University of Toronto.

Korten, D. (1995) *When Corporations Rule the World*, Hartford, CT: Kumarian Press.

Krugman, P. (1991) *Geography and Trade*, Cambridge, MA: MIT Press.

Krugman, P. (1995) 'Growing World Trade: Causes and Consequences', *Brookings Papers on Economic Activity*, 323–77.

Kuhn, T. (1996) *The Structure of Scientific Revolutions*, 3rd edn, Chicago: University of Chicago Press.

Kuratko, D. F. and R. M. Hodgetts (2007) *Entrepreneurship: Theory, Process, Practice*, 7th edn, Mason, OH: Thompson Southwestern.

Kyoto Prefecture (2002) *Kyoto Sangyo no Tembo*, Kyoto: M&T.

Landström, H. (1996) 'Award Winner David L. Birch's Contributions to Entrepreneurship and Small Business Research', Global Award for Entrepreneurship Research.

Langlois, R. N. (1998) 'Personal Capitalism as Charismatic Authority: The Organisational Economics of a Weberian Concept', *Industrial and Corporate Change* 7(1): 195–214.

Lank, A. G. and E. G. Lank (1995) 'Legitimising the Gut Feel: The Role of Intuition in Business', *Journal of Managerial Psychology* 10(5): 18–23.

Lave, J. and E. Wenger (1991) *Situated Learning: Legitimate Peripheral Participation*, Cambridge: Cambridge University Press.

Lazonick, W. (1991) *Business Organisation and the Myth of the Market Economy*, Cambridge: Cambridge University Press.

Leadbeater, C. (1999) *The Independents: Britain's New Cultural Entrepreneurs*. London: Demos.

Lee, S. Y., R. Florida and Z. J. Acs (2004) 'Creativity and Entrepreneurship: A Regional Analysis of New Firm Formation', *Regional Studies* 38(8): 879–91.

Levinthal, D. A. and J. G. March (1993) 'The Myopia of Learning', *Strategic Management Journal* 14: 95–112.

Lewis, W. A. (1954) 'Economic Development with Unlimited Supplies of Labour', *Manchester School* 28(2): 139–91.

Leydesdorff, L. and H. Etzkowitz (1996) 'Emergence of a Triple Helix of University–Government Relations', *Science and Public Policy* 23151: 279–86.

Licht, A. N. and Siegel, J. I. (2008) 'The Social Dimensions of Entrepreneurship' in Casson,M. B. Yeung, A. Basu and N. S. Wadeson , *The Oxford Handbook of Entrepreneurship*, Oxford, Oxford University Press.

Liebenau, U. (1993) 'Higher Education, Industry and the Two Souls of the British System', in U. Lindner, R. Coldstream, P. Levy, J. Nicholls and P. Rayer-Dyson (eds), *Interaction between Industry and Higher Education in the British Experience*, Milan: Franco Angeli, pp. 35–77.

Lim, K. (2000) *The Many Faces of Absorptive Capacity: Spillovers of Copper Interconnect Technology for Semi Conductor Chips*. Boston, MA: MIT Press.

Lin, N. (1982) 'Social Resources and Instrumental Action', in P. V. Marsden and N. Lin (eds), *Social Structure and Network Analysis*, Beverly Hills, CA: Sage, pp. 131–45.

Lin, N. (2001) *Social Capital: A Theory of Social Structure and Action*, Cambridge: Cambridge University Press.

Lindholm, D. (1999) 'Technology-Based SMEs in the Göteborg Region: Their Origin and Interaction with Universities and Large Firms', *Regional Studies* 33(4): 379–89.

Lindohlm, D. A. (2005) 'University Knowledge Transfer and the Role of Academic Spin-offs', background paper, OECD Conference on 'Fostering Entrepreneurship: The Role of Higher Education', Trento, 23–24 June.

Link, Albert N. and Siegel, Donald S. (2005) 'University-based Technology Initiatives: Quantitative and Qualitative Evidence http://ideas.repec.org/a/eee/respol/v34y2005i3p253-257.html'http://ideas.repec.org/s/eee/respol.html, Elsevier 34(3): 253–257.

Lipsett, B. (2000) 'The Impact of the Knowledge-based Economy of Women's Participation' in K. Rubenson andB.Schuetze (Eds.), *Transition to the Knowledge Society: Policies and Strategies for Individual Participation and Learning,* Institute for European Studies, University of British Columbia, Vancouver, Canada, pp. 322-340.

Lockett, A. and M. Wright (2002) 'The Structure and Management of Syndicated Venture Capital Investments', *Journal of Private Equity* 5(4): 72–83.

Löfsten, H. and P. Lindelöf (2002) 'Science Parks and the Growth of New Technology-Based Firms – Academic–Industry Links, Innovation and Markets', *Research Policy* 31: 859–76.

Low, M. B. and E. Abrahamson (1997) 'Movements, Bandwagons and Clones: Industry Evolution and the Entrepreneurial Process', *Journal of Business Venturing* 12(6): 435–57.

Lucas, R. (1988) 'On the Mechanisms of Economic Development', *Journal of Monetary Economics* 22: 3–39.

Luczkiw, E. (2005) 'Jazzin' in the Vineyard: Entrepreneurship Education in an Age of Chaos, Complexity and Disruptive Change', background paper, OECD Conference on 'Fostering Entrepreneurship: The Role of Higher Education', Trento, 23–24 June.

Lumpkin, G. T. and B. Lichtenstein (2005) 'The Role of Organisational Learning in the Opportunity-Recognition Process', *Entrepreneurship Theory and Practice* 29(4): 451–72.

Lumpkin, J. R. and R. D. Ireland (1988) 'Screening Practices of New Business Incubators: The Evaluation of Critical Success Factors', *American Journal of Small Business* (Spring), 59–81.

Lundberg, C. C. (1995) 'Learning in and by Organizations: Three Conceptual Issues', *International Journal of Organizational Analysis* 3: 10–23.

Lundstrom, A. and L. Stevenson (2001) *Entrepreneurship Policy for the Future*, Stockholm Swedish Foundation for Small Business Research.

Lundstrom, A. and L. Stevenson (2005) *Entrepreneurship Policy: Theory and Practice*, New York: Springer.

Lundvall, B. A. (ed.) (1992) *National Systems of Innovation: Towards a Theory of Innovation and Active Learning*, London: Pinter.

Lunn, P. (2009) 'The Descent of Rational Man', *Royal Society for the Arts Journal* (Spring), 14–21.

Macdonald, S. and Y. Deng (2004) 'Science Parks in China: A Cautionary Exploration', *International Journal of Technology Intelligence and Planning* 1(1): 1–14.

Maddison, A. (2007) *Contours of the World Economy, 1–2030 AD: Essays in Macro-Economic History*, Oxford: Oxford University Press.

Malecki, E. J. (1991) *Technology and Economic Development: The Dynamics of Local, Regional and National Change*, New York: Longman.

Malecki, E. J. (2005) 'Higher Education and the Promotion of SME Innovation: What We Know and What We Don't Know about Knowledge Transfer Mechanisms', background paper, OECD Conference on 'Fostering Entrepreneurship: The Role of Higher Education', Trento, 23–24 June.

Malecki, E. J. (2008) 'Higher Education, Knowledge Transfer Mechanisms and the Promotion of SME Innovation', in J. Potter (ed.), *Entrepreneurship and Higher Education*, Paris: OECD, pp. 213–34.

Manalova, T. (2003) 'Small Multinationals in Global Competition: An Industry Perspective', in H. Etmad and R. Wright (eds), *Globalisation and Entrepreneurship: Policy and Strategic Perspectives*, McGill International Entrepreneurship Series, Cheltenham: Edward Elgar.

Manimala, M. J. (2009) 'Sustainable Development through ICT: The Need for Entrepreneurial Action', in M. J. Manimala, J. Mitra and V. Singh, *Enterprise Support Systems: An International Perspective*, New Delhi: Response-Sage.

Marshall, A. (1920) *Principles of Economics*, 8th edn, London: Macmillan.

Marshall, A. (1923) *Industry and Trade*, 3rd edn, London: Macmillan.

Marshall, A. (1961) *Principles of Economics*, 9th edn, London: Macmillan, reprint of 8th edn of 1920.

Martin, R. and P. Tyler (2000) 'Regional Employment Evolutions in the European Union: A Preliminary Analysis', *Regional Studies* 34: 601–16.

Martinelli, A. (2005) 'The Social and Institutional Context of Entrepreneurship', in G. Corbetta, M. Huse and D. Ravasi (eds), *Crossroads of Entrepreneurship*, International Studies in Entrepreneurship, New York: Springer.

Massey, D. (1979) 'In What Sense a Regional Problem?' *Regional Studies* 13: 233–43.

Massey, D. (1984) *Spatial Divisions of Labour: Social Structures and the Geography of Production*, London: Macmillan.

Massey, D. (1997) *World Cities*, Cambridge: Polity Press.

Massey, D. (2007) *World City*, Cambridge: Polity Press.

Mastakar, N. and B. B. Bowonder (2005) 'Transformation of an Entrepreneurial Firm to a Global Service Provider: The Case Study of Infosys', *International Journal of Technology Management* 32: 34–56.

Mathews, J. A. (2005) 'Strategy and the Crystal Cycle', *California Management Review* 47: 6–32.

Mathews, J. A. (2006) 'Electronics in Taiwan – A Case of Technological Learning', in V. Chandra (ed.), *Technology, Adaptation and Exports: How Some Developing Countries Got It Right*, Washington, DC: World Bank, pp. 83–126.

Mathews, J. A. (2007) 'How Taiwan Built an Electronics Industry: Lessons for Developing Countries Today', in H. W.-C. Yeung (ed.), *Handbook of Research on Asian Business*, Cheltenham: Edward Elgar, pp. 307–32.

Matlay, H. (1997) 'Reflections upon the Enterprise Culture in Britain: Some Research Implications', SME Centre Research Seminar, University of Warwick.

Matlay, H. (1999) 'Vocational Education, Training and Organizational Change: A Small Business Perspective', *Strategic Change* 8(5): 277–86.

Matlay, H. (2000) 'Organisational Learning in Small Learning Organisations: An Empirical Overview', *Education + Training* 42(4–5): 202–10.

McCabe, I. B. (2005) 'Global Trading Ambitions in Diaspora: The Armenians and their Eurasian Silk Trade, 1530–1750', in I. B. McCabe, G. Harlafatis and I. P. Minoglou (eds), *Diaspora Entrepreneurial Networks: Four Centuries of History*, Oxford: Berg, pp. 27–50.

McClelland, D. C. (1961) *The Achieving Society*, Princeton: N. J. Van Nostrand.

McClelland, D. C. and D. G. Winter (1969) *Motivating Economic Achievement*, New York: Free Press.

McDougall, P. and B. Oviatt (2000) 'International Entrepreneurship: The Intersection of Two Research Paths', *Academy of Management Journal* 43(5): 902–6.

McGrath, R. (1999) 'Falling Forward: Real Options Reasoning and Entrepreneurial Failure', *Academy of Management Review* 24: 13–30.

McGrath, R. G. and I. C. Macmillan (2000) *The Entrepreneurial Mindset*, Cambridge, MA: Harvard Business School Press.

McKendrick, D. G., Doner, R. F. and Haggard, S. (2000) *From Silicon Valley to Singapore: Location and Competitive Advantage in the Hard Disk Drive Industry*, Stanford, C. A: Stanford University Press.

McNaughton, R. B. (2005) 'Technology Commercialisation and Universities in Canada', background paper, OECD Conference on 'Fostering Entrepreneurship: The Role of Higher Education', Trento, 23–24 June.

Meinig, D. W. (1986) *The Shaping of America: A Geographical Perspective on 500 Years of History*, vol. 1: *Atlantic America, 1492–1800*. New Haven: Yale University Press.

Merton, R. K. (1957) *Social Theory and Social Structure*, Glencoe, IL: Free Press.

Miles, R. E. and C. C. Snow (1992) 'Causes of Failure in Network Organizations', *California Management Review* 28(3): 62–73.

Mills, C. W. (1956) *The Power Elite*, New York: Oxford University Press.

Mills, D. Q. and B. Friesen (1992) 'The Learning Organisation', *European Management Journal* 10(2): 46–156.

Mitchell, J. (1973) 'Networks, Norms and Institutions', in J. Boissevain *et al.* (eds), *Network Analysis: Studies in Human Interaction*, London: Mouton.

Mises, L. von (1949) *Human Action*, New Haven: Yale University Press.

Mitra, J. (1999) 'Managing Externalities: Integrating Technological and Organizational Change for Innovation', keynote paper presented at the 9th *International Technology Forum, Minneapolis, Minnesota, USA*, University of Minnesota, 4–8 Oct., 1999.

Mitra, J. (2000) 'Making Connections: Innovation and Collective Learning in Small Businesses', *Education and Training* 42(4–5): 228–36.

Mitra, J. (2002) 'Consider Velasquez: Reflections on the Development of Entrepreneurship Programmes', *Industry and Higher Education Journal* 191.

Mitra, J. (2009) 'Learning to Grow: How New, Small, High Technology Firms Acquire Cognitive and Socio-Political Legitimacy in their Regions', *International Journal of Technology Management* 46(3–4): 344–70.

Mitra, J. and Y. A. Abubakar (2005) 'Fostering Entrepreneurship and the Role of Higher Education: Spatial Perspectives on Human and Social Networks and High Technology Firms', paper presented at Institute of Small Business and Entrepreneurship, 2005 Small Firms Policy and Research Conference, Blackpool.

Mitra, J. and Y. A. Abubakar (2007) 'Seeking Legitimacy: New Technology Firm Behaviour in Nascent and Established Environment', paper presented at the 30th Institute for Small Business and Entrepreneurship Conference, 'International Entrepreneurship', Glasgow, Scotland, 7–9 Nov.

Mitra, J. and Y. A. Abubakar (2009) 'Sources of Small Firm Innovation in Low Agglomeration: Comparing High and Low Agglomeration Regions', paper presented at the 2009 International Council for Small Business (ICSB) World Conference, Seoul, Korea, 21–24 June.

Mitra, J. and P. Formica (eds) (1997a) *Innovation and Economic Development: University–Enterprise Partnerships in Action*, Dublin: Oak Tree Press.

Mitra, J. and P. Formica (1997b) 'Innovative Players in Economic Development in Europe: Learning Companies and Entrepreneurial Universities', in J. Mitra and P. Formica (eds), *Innovation and Economic Development: University–Industry Partnerships in Action*, Dublin: Oak Tree Press.

Mitra, J. and J. Li (2003) 'Context Analysis and 'Competency Analysis' Reports, prepared for the LEONARDO. SOLCO project, ERDC, UCE Business School, UK.

Mitra, J. and M. Manimala (2005) 'Fostering Entrepreneurship: The University as an Innovative Stakeholder', background paper, OECD Conference on 'Fostering Entrepreneurship: The Role of Higher Education', Trento, 23–24 June.

Mitra, J. and H. Matlay (2004) 'The Internationalisation Efforts of Growth Oriented Entrepreneurs: Lessons from Britain', in H. Etmad (ed.), *International Entrepreneurship: The Globalisation of SMEs: Orientation, Environment and Strategy*, Cheltenham: Edward Elgar.

Mitra, J. and J. Murray (1999) 'Building Knowledge-Driven Clusters: Shifting Patterns in UK Competitiveness Policy and Practice', workshop paper presented at the 44th ICSB World Conference, Naples, Italy, 20–23 June.

Mitra, J. and Natarajan, G. (forthcoming) 'Technology, Entrepreneurship and the Indian Software Industry', in S. A. Mian (ed.), *Science and Technology Based Regional Entrepreneurship: Global Experience in Policy and Program Development,* Cheltenham: Edward Elgar.

Mitra, J., J. Murray, E. Corti, C. Storto and P. Formica (1999) 'Cluster-Muster: Cluster-Based Innovation and Growth Strategies for European SMEs', in *Proceedings of the 22nd Institute of Small Business Affairs Small Firms Policy and Research Conference*, 'European Strategies, Growth and Development', Leeds, 17–19 Nov.

Mizruchi, M. S. (1992) *The Structure of Corporate Political Action: Interfirm Relations and their Consequences*, Cambridge, MA: Harvard University Press.

Moingeon, B. and A. Edmondson (eds) (1996) *Organizational Learning and Competitive Advantage*, London: Sage.

Mokry, B. (1988) *Entrepreneurship and Public Policy: Can Government Stimulate Business Start-Ups*, Connecticut: Quorum Books.

Morgan, K. (1997) 'The Learning Region: Institutions, Innovation and Regional Renewal', *Regional Studies* 31: 491–503.

Morgan, K. (2004) 'The Exaggerated Death of Geography: Learning, Proximity and Territorial Innovation Systems', *Journal of Economic Geography* 4: 3–21.

Mowery, D. and B. Sampat (2005) 'The Bah-Doyle Act of 1980 and University Industry Technology Transfer: A Model for Other OECD Countries?' *Journal of Technology Transfer* 30(1–2): 115–27.

Mueller, P., A. Van Stel and D. J. Storey (2008) 'The Effects of New Firm Formation on Regional Development over Time: The Case of Great Britain', *Small Business Economics* 30(1): 59–71.

Mumford, A. (1995) 'Learning Styles and Mentoring', *Industrial and Commercial Training* 8: 4–7.

Murmann, J. P. and M. L. Tushman (2001) 'From the Technology Cycle to the Entrpreneurship Dynamic: The Social Context of Entrepreneurial Innovation', in C. B. Schoonhoven and E. Romanelli (eds), *The Entrepreneurship Dynamic: Origins of Entrepreneurship and the Evolution of Industries*, Stanford: Stanford University Press.

Murphy, K. M., A. Shleifer and R. W. Vishny (1993) 'Why is Rent Seeking So Costly to Growth', *American Economic Review* 83: 409–14.

Mustar, P. (1997) 'Spin-Off Enterprises: How French Academics Create High-Tech Companies: The Conditions for Success or Failure', *Science and Public Policy* 24(1): 37–43.

Muzyka, D. (1999) *Mobilising for Growth: Entrepreneurship within Companies*, Brussels: Video Management.

Nachum, L. and D. Keeble (1999) 'Neo-Marshallian Nodes, Global Competiveness and Firm Competitiveness: The Media Cluster of Central London', Working Paper 138, ESRC Centre for Business Research, University of Cambridge.

Nachum, L. and D. Keeble (2000) 'Foreign and Indigeneous Firms in the Media Cluster of Central London', Working Paper 154, ESRC Centre for Business Research, University of Cambridge.

Nadhvi, K. (1998) 'International Competitiveness and Small Firm Clusters: Evidence from Pakistan', *Small Enterprise Development Journal* 9(1): 12–24.

Nambisan, S. and M. Sawhney (2008) *The Global Brain: Your Roadmap for Innovating Faster and Smarter in a Networked World*, Upper Saddle River, NJ: Pearson and Wharton School Publishing.

NASSCOM-BCG (2007) *Nasscom-BCG Innovation Report, 2007: Unleashing the Innovative Power of Indian-ITES Industry*, New Delhi: Boston Consulting Group.

Nelson, R. R. (1959) 'The Simple Economics of Basic Scientific Research', *Journal of Political Economy* 67: 297–306.

Nelson, R. R. (ed.) (1993) *National Innovation Systems: A Comparative Analysis*, New York: Oxford University Press.

Nelson, R. R. (1997) *The Sources of Economic Growth*, Cambridge, MA: Harvard University Press.

Nelson, R. R. and S. G. Winter (1982) *An Evolutionary Theory of Economic Change*, Cambridge, MA: Harvard University Press.

New Internationalist (2009) 'Put People First' (main feature), 421: 13–29.

Nijkamp, P. (2003) 'Entrepreneurship in a Modern Network Economy', *Regional Studies* 37: 395–405.

Nohria, N. and R. G. Eccles (1992) *Networks and Organisations: Structure, Form and Action*, Boston: Harvard Business School Press.

Nonaka, I. and Takeuchi, H. (1995) *The Knowledge-Creating Company: How Japanese Companies Create the Dynamics of Innovation*, Oxford, Oxford University Press.

North, D. (1990) *Institutions, Institutional Change and Economic Performance*, Cambridge: Cambridge University Press.

Noteboom, B. (1994) 'Innovation and Diffusion in Small firms: Theory and Evidence', *Small Business Economics* 6: 327–47.

Noteboom, B. (1999) *Inter-Firm Alliances: Analysis and Design*, London: Routledge.

Noteboom, B. (2000) *Learning and Innovation in Organizations and Economies*, Oxford: Oxford University Press.

Oakey, R. (1993) 'Predatory Networking: The Role of Small Firms in the Development of the British Biotechnology Industry', *International Small Firms Journal* 11(3): 3–22.

Oakey, R. (1995) *High-Technology New Firms: Variable Barriers to Growth*, London: Paul Chapman.

Observer (2007) 'A Little Divine Intervention', A. Purvis A. in 'Enterprising Solutions' Special Report, *The Observer* (21 Oct.).

OECD (1970) *Innovation in Higher Education: Three German Universities*, Paris: OECD.

OECD (1998) *Fostering Entrepreneurship: The OECD Jobs Strategy*, Paris: OECD.

OECD (1999) *Business Incubation: International Case Studies*, OECD - LEED Programme.

OECD (2000) 'Enhancing the Competitiveness of SMEs in the Global Economy: Strategies and Policies', Workshop 2, Local Partnership, Clusters and SME Globalisation, Conference for Ministers responsible for SMEs and Industry Ministers, Bologna, Italy, 14–15 June.

OECD (2003a) *Entrepreneurship and Local Economic Development: Programme and Policy Recommendations*, Paris: OECD.

OECD (2003b) *South-East Europe Region: Enterprise Policy Performance Assessment.*

OECD (2004) *Entrepreneurship: A Catalyst for Urban Regeneration*, Paris: OECD.

OECD (2010) *SMEs, Entrepreneurship and Innovation*, OECD Studies on SMEs and Entrepreneurship, Paris: OECD.

O'Farrell, P. N. and P. N. W. Hitchens (1988) 'Alternative Theories of Small Firm Growth: A Critical Review', *Environment and Planning* 20(10), 365–83.

Ohmae, K. (1990) *The Borderless World: Power and Strategy in the Global Marketplace*, London: Collins.

Ohmae, K. (1995) *The End of Nation States: The Rise of Regional Economies*, London: HarperCollins.

ONS (2009) 'Economic and Labour Market Review', *Office for National Statistics* 3(5): 43.

OST (1998) *The Dynamics of S&T Activities in EU Regions*, report prepared by Barry, F. Laville and M. Zitt) Paris: OST.

Oviatt, B. and P. P. McDougal (1994) 'Toward a Theory of International New Ventures', *Journal of International Business Studies*, 25(1): 45–64.

Oviatt, B. and P. P. McDougal (1997) 'Challenges for Internationalization Process Theory', *Management International Review* 37(2), 85–99.

Parker, S., D. J. Storey and A. van Witteloostuijn (2005) *What Happens to Gazelles? The Importance of Dynamic Management Strategy*, Durham: Durham Business School.

Patel, P. and M. Vega (1999) 'Patterns of Internationalisation and Corporate Technology: Location versus Home Country Advantages', *Research Policy* 28: 145–55.

Pearn, M., C. Roderick and C. Mulrooney (1995) *Learning Organisations in Practice*, London: McGraw-Hill.

Pedler, M., J. Burgoyne and T. Boydell (1991) *The Learning Company: A Strategy for Sustainable Development*, Maidenhead: McGraw-Hill.

Penrose, E. T. (1980) *The Growth of the Firm*, Oxford: Blackwell.

Penrose, E. T. (1959) *The Theory and Growth of the Firm*, New York: Oxford University Press.

Performance and Innovation Unit (PIU) (2002) 'Social Capital: A Discussion Paper', Performance and Innovation Unit, London.

Phan, P. H., D. S. Siegel and M. Wright (2005) 'Science Parks and Incubators: Observations, Synthesis and Future Research', *Journal of Business Venturing* 20: 165–82.

Phillips, R. (2005) 'Challenging the Primacy of Lectures: The Dissonance between Theory and Practice in University Teaching', *Journal of University Teaching and Learning Practice* 2(1): 2005 1–12.

Phipps, L. (2002) 'Are You Reasonably Adjusted?' *Educational Developments* 3(4): 6.

Pike, A. (2007) 'Whither Regional Studies?' *Regional Studies* 41: 1143–8.

Piore, M. and C. Sabel (1984) *The Second Industrial Divide: Possibilities for Prosperity*, New York: Basic Books.

Plummer, L. A. and Z. J. Acs (2004) 'Penetrating the "Knowledge Filter" in Regional Economies', discussion paper on Entrepreneurship, Growth and Public Policy, Max Planck Institute for Research in Economic Systems, Jena, Germany.

Polanyi, M. (1962) *Personal Knowledge: Towards a Post-Critical Philosophy*, London: Routledge.

Polanyi, M. (1967) *The Tacit Dimension*, New York: Doubleday.

Politis, D. (2008) 'Does Prior Start-Up Experience Matter for Entrepreneurs' Learning? A Comparison between Novice and Habitual Entrepreneurs', *Journal of Small Business and Enterprise Development* 15(3): 472–89.

Porter, L. W. and L. E. McKibbin (1988) *Management Education and Development: Drift or Thrust into the 21st Century?* New York: McGraw-Hill.

Porter, M. (1979) 'The Structure within Industries and Companies' Performance', *Review of Economics and Statistics* 61: 214–77.

Porter, M. (1990) *The Competitive Advantage of Nations*, London and Basingstoke: Macmillan Press.

Porter, M. (1994) 'The Role of Location in Competition', *Journal of the Economics of Business* 1(1): 35–9.

Porter, M. (1998) 'Clusters and Competitiveness', *Harvard Business Review*, 76: 77–90.

Porter, M. (2001) 'Strategy and the Internet', *Harvard Business Review* 79(3): 62–78.

Porter, M., E. C. Ketels and M. Delgado (2007) 'The Microeconomic Foundations of Prosperity: Findings for the Business Competitiveness Index, Chapter 1–2. From the Global Competitiveness Report, 2007–8, World Economic Forum.

Porter, M. and S. S. Stern (1999) *The New Challenge to America's Prosperity: Findings from the Innovation Index*, Washington, DC: Council on Competitiveness.

Porter, M. E. (1980) *Competitive Strategy: Techniques for Analysing Industries and Competitors*. New York: Free Press.

Porter, M. E. and K. Schwab (2008) *The Global Competitiveness Report, 2008–9*, Geneva: World Economic Forum.

Potter, J. (ed.) (1998) *Entrepreneurship and Higher Education*, Paris: OECD.

Powell, W. W., K. W. Koput and L. Smith-Doerr (1996) 'Interorganisational Collaboration and the Locus of Innovation: Networks of Learning in Biotechnology', *Administrative Science Quarterly* 41: 116–45.

Prahalad, C. K. (1997) 'The Role of Core Competencies in the Corporation', in M. Tushman and P. Anderson (eds), *Managing Strategic Innovation and Change: A Collection of Readings*, Oxford: Oxford University Press, pp. 172–81.

Prahalad, C. K. (2005) *The Fortune at the Bottom of the Pyramid: Eradicating Poverty through Profits* (Indian subcontinent edn), Singapore: Pearson.

Prahalad, C. K. and M. S. Krishnan (2008) *The New Age of Innovation: Driving C-Created Value through Global Networks*, New York: McGraw-Hill.

Prebisch, R. (1959) 'Commercial Policy in the Underdeveloped Countries', *American Economic Review* 49(2): 251–73.

Probst, G. and P. Buchel (1997) *Organisation Learning*, London: Prentice-Hall.

Putnam, R. D. (1993) 'The Prosperous Community: Social Capital and Public Life', *American Prospect* 13: 35–42.

Raposo, M. (2009) 'Support Policies to Entrepreneurship', in J. Leitao and R. Baptista (eds), *Public Policies for Fostering Entrepreneurship: A European Perspective*, International Studies in Entrepreneurship 22, New York: Springer.

Ravallion, M. (2008) 'Evaluation in the Practice of Development', Policy Research Working Paper 4547, Washington, DC: World Bank draft.

RBS (2010) RBS SE100 Data Report: Charting the Growth and Impact of UK's Top Social Businesses.

Reber, A. S. (1993) *Implicit Learning and Tacit Knowledge: An Essay on the Cognitive Unconscious*, Oxford: Oxford University Press.

Reynolds, P. (1999) 'Creative Destruction: Source of Symptom of Economic Growth', in Z. J. Acs, B. Carlsson and C. Karlsson (eds), *Entrepreneurship, Small and Medium-Sized Enterprises, and the Macroeconomy*, Cambridge: Cambridge University Press.

Reynolds, P. D., B. Miller and W. R. Maki (1995) 'Explaining Regional Variation in Business Births and Deaths U.S. 1976–1988', *Small Business Economics* 7: 389–407.

Rickne, A. and S. Jacobsson (1999) 'New Technology-Based Firms in Sweden: A Study of their Direct Impact on Industrial Renewal', *Economics of Innovation and New Technology* 8: 197–223.

Ripsas, S. (1998) 'Towards an Interdisciplinary Theory of Entrepreneurship', *Small Business Economics* 10: 103–15.

Robbins, R. (2008) *Global Problems and the Culture of Capitalism*, 4th edn, Boston: Pearson.

Robock, S. H. and K. Simmonds (1989) *International Business and Multinational Enterprises*, Boston: Irwin.

Rodrick, D., A. Subramanian and F. Trebbi (2002) 'Institutions Rule: The Primacy of Institutions over Geography and Integration in Economic Development', NBER Working Paper no. 9305, Cambridge, MA.

Rogers, M. (2004) 'Networks, Firm Size and Innovation', *Small Business Economics* 22: 141–53.

Roman, Z. (2005) 'An Audit of Entrepreneurship Education in Hungary', background paper, OECD Conference on 'Fostering Entrepreneurship: The Role of Higher Education', Trento, 23–24.

Romer, P. (1986) 'Increasing Returns and Economic Growth', *American Economic Review* 94: 1002–37.

Romer, P. (1990) 'Endogenous Technological Change', *Journal of Political Economy* 98(5): 71–102.

Romme, Georges and Ron Dillen (1997) 'Mapping the Landscape of Organizational Learning', *European Management Journal* 15(1): 68–78.

Ronstadt, R. (1988) 'The Corridor Principle', *Journal of Business Venturing* 1(3), 31–40.

Roper, S. (1997) 'Product Innovation and Small Business Growth: A Comparison of the Strategies of German, UK and Irish Companies', *Small Business Economics* 9: 1–17.

Rosenberg, N. (1963) 'Changing Technological Leadership and Economic Growth', *Economic Journal* 73(289): 13–31.

Rosenberg, N. (1982) *Inside the Black Box: Technology and Economics*, Cambridge: Cambridge University Press.

Rosenberg, N. (2000) 'American Universities as Endogenous Institutions', ch. 3 in *Schumpeter and the Endogeneity of Technology: Some American Perspectives*, London: Routledge.

Rosenfield, S. A. (1997) 'Bringing Business Clusters into the Mainstream of Economic Development', *European Planning Studies* 3(1): 13–17.

Rostow, W. W. (1960) *The Stages of Economic Growth*, Cambridge: Cambridge University Press.

Rothwell, R. (1989) 'Small Firms, Innovation and Industrial Change', *Small Business Economics* 1(1): 51–64.

Rothwell, R. and M. Dodgson (1994) 'Innovation and Size of the Firm', in M. Dodgson and R. Rothwell (eds), *Handbook of Industrial Innovation*, Aldershot: Edward Elgar.

Ruggles, R. (1998) 'The State of the Notion: Knowledge Management in Practice', *California Management Review* 40(3): 80–9.

Rutten, R., F. Boekama and E. Kuijpers (2003) *Economic Geography of Higher Education: Knowledge Infrastructure and Learning Regions*, London: Routledge.

Sachs, J. (2010) 'Millennium Development Goals at 10', *Scientific American* (June), 11.

Saemundsson, R. (2003) 'Entrepreneurship, Technology, and the Growth Process: A Study of Young, Medium-Sized Technology-Based Firms', dissertation, Chalmers University of Technology, Department of Industrial Dynamics.

Salomon, G. (ed.) (1993) *Distributed Cognition: Psychological and educational considerations*, Cambridge: Cambridge University Press, pp. xxi, 275.

Sanchez, R. and A. Heene (eds) (1997) *Strategic Learning and Knowledge Management*, Chichester: John Wiley.

Sandberg, W. R. and C. W. Hofer (1987) 'Improving New Venture Performance: The Role of Strategy, Industry Structure, and the Entrepreneur', *Journal of Business Venturing* 2: 5–28.

Sanderson, M. (1972) *The Universities and British Industry, 1850–1970*, London: Routledge & Kegan Paul.

Sarasvathy, S. (2001) 'Causation and Effectuation: Towards a Theoretical Shift from Economic Inevitability to Entrepreneurial Contingency', *Academy of Management Review* 26(2): 243–88.

Sassen, S. (2002) 'Locating Cities on Global Circuits', in S. Sassen (ed.), *Global Networks, Linked Cities*, London: Routledge.

Sassen, S. (2007) *A Sociology of Globalisation*, New York: W. W. Norton.

Sawhney, M. and E. Prandelli (2004) 'Communities of Creation: Managing Distributed Innovation in Turbulent Times', in K. Starkey, S. Tempest and A. McKinlay (eds), *How Organisations Learn: Managing the Search for Knowledge*, London: Thompson Learning.

Saxenian, A. (1990) 'Regional Networks and the Resurgence of Silicon Valley', *California Management Review* 33(1): 89–113.

Saxenian, A. (1996) *Regional Advantage: Culture and Competition in Silicon Valley and Route 128*, 2nd edn, Cambridge, MA: Harvard University Press.

Saxenian, A. (1999) *Silicon Valley's New Immigrant Entrepreneurs*, San Francisco: Public Policy Institute of California.

Saxenian, A. (2002) *Local and Global Networks of Immigrant Professionals in Silicon Valley*, San Francisco: Public Policy Institute of California.

Saxenian, A. (2006) *The New Argonauts: Regional Advantage in a Global Economy*, Cambridge, MA: Harvard University Press.

Scarborough, H., J. Swan and J. Preston (1999) *Knowledge Management: A Literature Review*. London: Institute of Personal and Development.

Scherer, F. M. (1965) 'Firm Size, Market Structure, Opportunity and the Output of Patented Inventions', *American Economic Review* 55: 1097–125.

Scherer, F. M. (1984) 'Using Linked Patent and R&D Data to Measure Interindustry Technology Flows', in Zvi Griliches (ed.), *R&D, Patents, and Productivity*, Chicago: University of Chicago Press, pp. 417–61.

Scherer, F. M. (1991) 'Changing Perspectives on the Firm Size Problem', in Z. J. Acs and D. B. Audretsch (eds), *Innovation and Technological Change: An International Comparison*, Ann Arbor: University of Michigan Press, pp. 24–38.

Schön, D. (1983) *The Reflective Practitioner: How Professionals Think in Action*, London: Temple Smith.

Schön, D. (1987) *Educating the Reflective Practitioner*, San Francisco: Jossey-Bass.

Schon, D. A. (1999) *The Reflective Practitioner: How Professionals Think in Action*, Aldershot: Ashgate.

Schoonhoven, K. and E. Romanelli (eds) (2001) *The Entrepreneurship Dynamic: Origins of Entrepreneurship and the Evolution of Industries*, Stanford: Stanford University Press.

Schrader, R., B. Oviatt and P. McDougall (2000) 'How New Ventures Exploit Trade-Offs among International Risk Factors: Lessons for Accelerated Internationalisation of the 21st Century', *Academy of Management Journal* 43(6): 1227–47.

Schramm, C. J. (2006) *The Entrepreneurial Imperative: How America's Economic Miracle Will Reshape the World (and Change your Life)*, New York: Collins.

Schultz, T. W. (1961) 'Investment in Human Capital', *American Economic Review* 51(1): 1–17.

Schuman, S. P. (1995) 'Valuing and Using Data in Group Decision Making: An Examination of Decision Conferences and the Effect of Decision Makers' Perceptions of Data and Empirical Process on Outcomes', Ph.D. dissertation, Rockefeller College of Public Affairs and Policy, University at Albany, State University of New York, Albany.

Schumpeter, J. (1934 [1911]) *The Theory of Economic Development: An Inquiry into Profits, Capital, Credit, Interest and the Business Cycle*, Cambridge, MA: Harvard University Press.

Schumpeter, J. A. (1939) *Business Cycles: A Theoretical, Historical and Statistical Analysis of the Capitalist Process*, New York: McGraw Hill.

Schumpeter, J. A. (1942) *Capitalism, Socialism and Democracy*, New York: Harper & Row.

Schumpeter, J. A. (1950; 3rd edn 1994) *Capitalism, Socialism and Democracy*, New York: Harper & Row.

Schumpeter, J. A. (1934; 1996) *The Theory of Economic Development*, London: Transaction Publishers.

Scott, A. (1998) *Regions and the World Economy: The Coming Shape of World Production, Competition, and Political Order*, Oxford: Oxford University Press.

Scott, A. J. (2001) *Global City-Regions*, Oxford: Oxford University Press.

Scott, A. J. (2006) *Geography and Economy*, Oxford: Clarendon Press.

Segal Quince Wicksteed (1985) *The Cambridge Phenomenon: The Growth of High Technology Industry in a University Town*, Cambridge: Segal Quince.

Sen, A. (1984) 'Well Being, Agency and Freedom: The Dewey Lectures, 1984', *Journal of Philosophy* 82(4): 169–221.

Sen, A. (1993) 'Capability and Well Being', in M. C. Nussabaum and A. K. Sen (eds), *The Quality of Life*, Oxford: Oxford University Press, pp. 32–53.

Sen, A. (1999) *Development as Freedom*, Oxford: Oxford University Press.

Senge, P. M. (1990) *The Fifth Discipline*, New York: Doubleday.

Senge, P. M., A. Kleiner, C. Roberts, R. Ross and B. Smith (1994) *The Fifth Discipline Fieldbook*, New York: Currency, Doubleday.

Senor, D. and S. Singer (2009) *Start-Up Nation: The Story of Israel's Economic Miracle*, New York: Twelve, Hatchett Book Group.

Shackle, G. L. S. (1972) *Epistemics and Economics*, Cambridge: Cambridge University Press.

Shane, S. (2004) *Academic Spin-Offs: University Spin-Offs and Wealth Creation*, Cheltenham: Edward Elgar.

Shane, S. and S. Venkataraman (2000) 'The Promise of Entrepreneurship as a Field of Research', *Academy of Management Review* 25(1): 217–26.

Shane, S. and T. Stuart (2002) 'Organisational Endowments and the Performance of University Start-Ups', *Management Science* 48(1): 154–71.

Shaw, E. (1997) 'The Real Networks of Small Firms', in D. Deakins *et al.* (eds), *Small Firms: Entrepreneurship in the 1990s*, London: Paul Chapman.

Shinn, T. (1998) 'The Impact of Research and Education on Industry: A Comparative Analysis of the Relationship of Education and Research Systems to Industrial Progress in Six Countries', *Industry and Higher Education Journal* (Oct.), 270–89.

Simon, H. (2009) *Hidden Champions of the 21st Century: Success Strategies of Unknown World Market Leaders*, New York: Springer.

Simon, H. A. (1959) *Administrative Behaviour*, 2nd edn, New York: Macmillan.

Simon, H. A. (1976) 'From Substantive to Procedural Rationality', in S. J. Latsis (ed.), *Method and Appraisal in Economics*, Cambridge: Cambridge University Press.

Simon, H. A. (1979) 'Rational Decision Making in Business Organisations', *American Economic Review* 69: 493–513.

Sinha, K. (2008) *China's Creative Imperative: How Creativity is Transforming Society and Business and China*, Singapore: John Wiley.

Smith, K. (2004) 'Interview: Sleepless in Singapore', *Financial Times* (24 Feb.).

Smith, Mark K. (1999, 2006) 'Informal Learning: The Encyclopaedia of Informal Education', www.infed.org/biblio/inf-lrn.htm.

Snow, C., Miles, R. and Coleman, H. 'Managing 21st century organizations', *Organizational Dynamics*, Winter, 5–15.

Social Enterprise Coalition (2009) *State of Social Enterprise Survey 2009*, London: Social Enterprise Coalition.

Soetanto, D. P. and M. V. Geenhuizen (2005) 'University-Linked Incubators as a Model of the "Modern" Triple Helix'. Fifth Triple Helix Conference, 'The Capitalization of Knowledge', Turin, Italy, May.

Solomon, G. (2005) 'The 2004–2005 National Survey of Entrepreneurship Education in the United States', background paper, OECD Conference on 'Fostering Entrepreneurship: The Role of Higher Education', Trento, 23–24.

Solow, R. M. (1956) 'A Contribution to the Theory of Economic Growth', *Quarterly Journal of Economics* 70: 65–94.

Sontag, S. (1994) 'The Aesthetics of Silence', in *Styles of Radical Will*, London: Vintage Books.

Specht, P. H. (1993) 'Munificence and Carrying Capacity of the Environment and Organisation Formation', *Entrepreneurship Theory and Practice* 17(2): 77–86.

Starkey, K. (ed.) (1996) *How Organizations Learn*, London: Thompson Business Press.

Starr, J. and W. D. Bygrave (1992) 'The Second Time Around: Assets and Liabilities of Prior Start-Up Experience', in S. Birley, I. C. MacMillan and S. Subramony (eds), *International Perspectives on Entrepreneurship Research*, New York: Elsevier Science, pp. 340–63.

Stenstrom, M.-L. and P. Tynjala (2009) 'Towards Integration of Work and Learning: Strategies for Connectivity and Transformation', Springer, UK; cited in *SMEs, Entrepreneurship and Innovation: OECD Innovation Strategy, OECD Studies on SMEs and Entrepreneurship*, Paris: OECD.

Sterman, J. D. (1989) 'Modeling Mangerial Behaviour: Misperceptions of Feedback in a Dynamic Decision Making Experiment', *Management Science* 35(3): 321–39.

Stern, N. (2009) *A Blueprint for a Safer Planet: How to Manage Climate Change and Create a New Era of Progress and Prosperity*, London: Bodley Head.

Stevens, C. E. (2004) 'Do Business Incubators Work? Perspectives on Incubator Success. Cleveland, Ohio', Case/Weatherhead School of Management.

Stevenson, H. H., M. J. Roberts and H. I. Grousback (1985) *New Business Ventures and the Entrepreneur*, Homewood, IL: Irwin.

Stevenson, L. and A. Lundstrom (2002) *Beyond the Rhetoric: Defining Entrepreneurship Policy and its Best Practice Components*, Stockholm: Swedish Foundation for Small Business Research.

Stinchcombe, A. (1965) 'Social Structure and Organisations', in J. G. March (ed.), *Handbook of Organisations*, Chicago: Rand McNally, pp. 142–93.

Storey, D. (1991) 'The Birth of New Firms – Does Unemployment Matter? A Review of the Evidence', *Small Business Economics* 3(3): 167–78.

Storey, D. (1994) *Understanding Small Business*, London: Routledge.

Storey, D. (2003) 'Entrepreneurship, Small and Medium Sized Enterprises and Public Policies', in Z. J. Acs and D. B. Audrestsch (eds), *Handbook of Entrepreneurship Research*, Boston: Kluwer, pp. 473–511.

Storey, D. J. (1992) 'Should We Abandon the Support to Small Businesses?' CSME Working Paper no. 11, Centre for Small and Medium Sized Enterprises, Warwick Business School.

Storey, D. J. (1994) *Understanding Small Firms*. London: Routledge.

Storper, M. (1995) 'The Resurgence of Regional Economies, Ten Years Later: The Region As a Nexus of Untraded Interdependencies', *European Urban and Regional Studies* 2: 191–221.

Storr, V. (2002) 'All We have Learnt: Colonial Teachings and Caribbean Underdevelopment', *Journal des Economistes et des Etudes Humaines* 12(4).

Sunley, P. (2008) 'Relational Economic Geography: A Partial Understanding or a New Paradigm?' *Economic Geography* 84: 1–26.

Sutton, J. (1997) 'Gibrat's Legacy', *Journal of Economic Literature* 35: 40–59.

Swann, P. (1989) *Academic Scientists and the Pharmaceutical Industry: Co-operative Research in Twentieth-Century America*, Baltimore: Johns Hopkins University Press.

Swedberg, R. (2000) 'The Social Science View of Entrepreneurship: Introduction and Practical Applications', in R. Swedberg (ed.), *Entrepreneurship: The Social Science View*, Oxford: Oxford University Press.

Teece, D. (1992) 'Competition, Cooperation and Innovation: Organisational Arrangements for Regimes of Rapid Technological Progress', *Journal of Economic Behaviour and Organisation.*

Tennant, M. (1997) *Psychology and Adult Learning*, 2nd edn, London: Routledge.

Tennant, M. (1999) 'Is Learning Transferable?', in D. Boud and J. Garrick (eds), *Understanding Learning at Work*, London: Routledge.

Thareja, P. (1998) 'Communal Spread: The Growth Paradigm for Small Scale Industry', in J. S. Saini and S. K. Dhumeja (eds), *Entrepreneurship and Small Business*, Jaipur: Rawat Publications.

Thompson, R. and C. Mabey (1994) *Developing Human Resources*, Oxford: Butterworth-Heinemann.

Thurik, R. and S. Wennekers (2004) 'Entrepreneurship, Small Business and Economic Growth', *Journal of Small Business and Enterprise Development* 11(1): 140–9.

Tidd, J. and J. Bessant (2009) *Managing Innovation: Integrating Technological, Market and Organisational Change*, 4th edn, Chichester: John Wiley.

Time (2009) 'Hip Berlin', by P. Gumbel, in *Time* (16 Nov.).

Time (2010) 'Corporate Conscience: Answering the Call', by Tim Padgett (with reporting by Jessica Desvarieux), *Time* (9 Aug.).

Tuomi, I. (2006) *Networks of Innovation: Change and Meaning in the Age of the Internet*, Oxford: Oxford University Press.

Tushman, M., L. P. C. Anderson and C. O'Reilly (1997) 'Technology Cycles, Innovation Streams and Ambidextrous Organizations: Organizational Renewal through Innovation Streams and Strategic Change', in M. Tushman and P. Anderson (eds), *Managing Strategic Innovation and Change: A Collection of Readings*, Oxford: Oxford University Press, pp. 3–23.

UKBI (2004) National Business Incubation Framework: Summary Report. UKBI.

UK Trade and Investment (2007) *Information Sheet: Science Parks and Business Incubators in the UK*, London: UKTI.

United Nations Conference on Trade and Development (1993) *Small and Medium Sized Transnational Corporations: Role, Impact and Policy Implications*, New York: United Nations.

United Nations Economic and Social Commission for Asia and the Pacific (ESCAP) (2008) 'What is Good Governance?' http://www.unescap.org/pdd/prs/projectactivities/ongoing/gg/governance.asp

United Nations Environment Programme (UNEP) (2008) *Green Jobs: Towards Decent Work in a Sustainable, Low-Carbon World*, Washington, DC: Worldwatch Institute.

Utterback, J. M. and W. J. Abernathy (1975) 'A Dynamic Model of Process and Product Innovation', *Omega* 3: 639–56.

Van Praag, M. (2003) 'Business Survival and Success of Young Small Business Owners', *Small Business Economics* 21: 1–17.

Van Schaik, T. (2002) 'Social Capital in the European Values Study Surveys', Country Paper prepared for the OECD-ONS International Conference on Social Capital Measurement, London, 25–27 Sept.

Van Stel, A. J. and D. Storey (2004) 'The Link between Firm Births and Job Creation: Is There a Upas Tree Effect?' *Regional Studies* 38: 893–909.

Van Stel, A. J., M. Caree and R. Thurik (2005) 'The Effect of Entrepreneurial Activity on National Economic Growth', *Small Business Economics* 24(3): 311–21.

Varblane, U., T. Mets and P. Formica (2005) 'Report about the Current Developments in the Teaching of Entrepreneurship in the European Transition Economies', background paper, OECD Conference on 'Fostering Entrepreneurship: The Role of Higher Education', Trento, 23–24 June.

Varga, A. (1999) 'Time–Space Patterns of US Innovation: Stability or Change? A Detailed Analysis Based on Patent Data', in M. Fisher, L. Suarez-Villa and M. Steiner (eds), *Innovation, Networks and Localities*, Berlin: Springer, pp. 215–34.

Varga, A., L. Anselin and Z. J. Acs (2003) 'Regional Innovation in the US over Space and Time', discussion paper on Entrepreneurship, Growth and Public Policy, Group Entrepreneurship, Growth and Public Policy, Max Planck Institute for Research into Economic Systems, Jena.

Veblen, T. (1929; 1970) *The Theory of the Leisure Class*; repr. London: Unwin.

Venkatraman, S. (1997) 'The Distinctive Domain of Entrepreneurship Research', *Advances in Entrepreneurship, Firm Emergence and Growth* 3: 119–38.

Vesper, K. (1979) 'Strategic Management and Organisation Types: Commentary', in D. E. Schendell and C. W. Hofer (eds), *Strategic Management*, Englewood Cliffs, NJ: Prentice Hall.

Waverman, L., M. Meschi and M. Fuss (2005) 'The Impact of Telecoms on Economic Growth in Developing Countries', LEGC, London.

Webb, B. (1883) 'My Apprenticeship'; extracts quoted in F. R. Leavis (1950), 'Introduction', in *Mill on Bentham and Coleridge*, London: Chatto & Windus, pp. 18–29; referred to in R. Bronck (2009), *The Romantic Economist: Imagination in Economics*, Cambridge: Cambridge University Press.

Weber, M. (1930) *The Protestant Ethic and the Spirit of Capitalism*, London: George Allen & Unwin.

Weber, M. (1947) *The Theory of Social and Economic Organisations*, New York: Oxford University Press.

Weick, K. E. and K. H. Roberts (1993) 'Collective Mind in Organization: Heedful Interrelating on Flight Decks', *Administrative Science Quarterly* 38: 357–81.

Wei-Skillern, J. C., J. E. Austin, H. B. Leonard and H. H. Stevenson (2007) *Entrepreneurship in the Social Sector*, Los Angeles: Sage.

Wenger, E. (2004) *Communities of Practice: Learning, Meaning and Identity*, Cambridge: Cambridge University Press.

Wennekers, A. R. M., N. G. Noorderhaven, G. Hofstede and A. R. Thurik (2001) 'Cultural and Economic Determinants of Business Ownership Across Countries', paper presented at Babson College–Kauffman Foundation Entrepreneurship Research Conference, Jönköping, 13–16 June.

Wernerfelt, B. (1984) 'A Resource-Based View of the Firm', *Strategic Management Journal* 5: 171–80.

Westhead, P. (1990) 'A Typology of New Manufacturing Firms in Wales: Performance Measures and Public Policy Implications', *Journal of Business Venturing* 5: 103–22.

Westhead, P. and D. J. Storey (1994) *An Assessment of Firms Located on and off Science Parks in the United Kingdom: Executive Summary*. London: HMSO.

Westhead, P., M. Wright and D. Ucbasaran (1998) 'The Internationalisation of New and Small Firms', *Frontiers of Entrepreneurship Research* 464.

Westland, J. C. (2008) *Global Innovation Management: A strategic Approach*, Basingstoke, Palgrave.

Williams, C. (2006) *The Hidden Enterprise Culture: Entrepreneurship in the Underground Economy*, Cheltenham: Edward Elgar.

Williams, R. (1963) *Culture and Society, 1780–1950*, Harmondsworth: Penguin.

Winter, S. G. (1984) 'Schumpeterian Competition in Alternative Technological Regimes', *Journal of Economic Behaviour and Organisation* 5: 287–320.

Wong, P. H., Y. P. Ho and E. Autio (2005) 'Entrepreneurship, Innovation and Economic Growth: Evidence from GEM Data', *Small Business Economics* 24: 335–50.

Wouters, P., J. Annerstedt and L. Leydesdorff (1999) *The European Guide to Science, Technology, and Innovation Studies*, Brussels: European Commission, DG XII.

World Bank (2009) *World Development Report 2009: Reshaping Economic Geography*, Washington, DC: World Bank.

Yang, C. (2010) 'Strategic Coupling of Regional Development in Global Production Networks: Redistribution of Taiwanese Personal Computer Investment from the Pearl River Delta to the Yangtze River Delta, China', in H. W.-C. Yeung (ed.), *Globalizing Regional Development in East Asia: Production Networks, Clusters and Entrepreneurship*. Abingdon: Routledge.

Yeung, Henry W.-C. (2005) 'Rethinking Relational Economic Geography', *Transactions of the Institute of British Geographers* 30(1): 37–51.

Yeung, H. W.-C. (2010) 'Globalizing Regional Development in East Asia: Production Networks, Clusters and Entrepreneurship', in H. W.-C. Yeung (ed.), *Globalizing Regional Development in East Asia: Production Networks, Clusters and Entrepreneurship*. Abingdon: Routledge.

Yli-Renko, H., E. Autio and H. J. Sapienza (2001) 'Social Capital, Knowledge Acquisition and Knowledge Exploitation in Young Technology-Based Firms', *Strategic Management Journal* 22: 587–613.

Zacharakis, A. (1997) 'Entrepreneurial Entry into Foreign Markets: A Transaction Cost Perspective', *Entrepreneurship Theory and Practice* 21(3): 23–39.

Zahra, S. A. (2005) 'Entrepreneurship Education and Economic Development in Central, East and Southeast Europe: The Role of Higher Education', background paper, OECD Conference on 'Fostering Entrepreneurship: The Role of Higher Education', Trento, 23–24 June.

Zahra, S. A., R. D. Ireland and M. A. Hitt (2000) 'International Expansion by New Venture Firms: International Diversity, Mode of Market Entry, Technological Learning and Performance', *Academy of Management Journal* 43(5): 925–50.

Zapalska, A. M. and W. Edwards (2001) 'Chinese Entrepreneurship in a Cultural and Economic Perspective', *Journal of Small Business Management* 39(3): 286–92.

Zucker, L., M. Darby and M. Brewer (1998) 'Intellectual Capital and the Birth of U.S. Biotechnology Enterprises', *American Economic Review* 88: 290–306.

Index

Taylor & Francis

eBooks

FOR LIBRARIES

ORDER YOUR FREE 30 DAY INSTITUTIONAL TRIAL TODAY!

Over 23,000 eBook titles in the Humanities, Social Sciences, STM and Law from some of the world's leading imprints.

Choose from a range of subject packages or create your own!

Benefits for **you**

▶ Free MARC records

▶ COUNTER-compliant usage statistics

▶ Flexible purchase and pricing options

Benefits for your **user**

▶ Off-site, anytime access via Athens or referring URL

▶ Print or copy pages or chapters

▶ Full content search

▶ Bookmark, highlight and annotate text

▶ Access to thousands of pages of quality research at the click of a button

For more information, pricing enquiries or to order a free trial, contact your local online sales team.

UK and Rest of World: **online.sales@tandf.co.uk**

US, Canada and Latin America:
e-reference@taylorandfrancis.com

www.ebooksubscriptions.com

ALPSP Award for BEST eBOOK PUBLISHER 2009 Finalist

Taylor & Francis **eBooks**
Taylor & Francis Group

A flexible and dynamic resource for teaching, learning and research.